MANAGEMENT FOR THE FUTURE

Edited by
LEWIS BENTON
Professor of Management
School of Business
Hofstra University

McGraw-Hill Book Company
New York St. Louis San Francisco Auckland Bogotá Düsseldorf Johannesburg London Madrid Mexico Montreal New Delhi Panama Paris São Paulo Singapore Sydney Tokyo Toronto

Library of Congress Cataloging in Publication Data

Main entry under title:

Management for the future.

Includes index.
1. Management—Addresses, essays, lectures.
2. Economic forecasting—Addresses, essays, lectures. I. Benton, Lewis R.
HD38.M3186 658.4 77-22862
ISBN 0-07-004818-5

1234567890 KPKP 7654321098

The editors for this book were William H. Mogan and Esther Gelatt, the designer was Elliot Epstein, and the production supervisor was Teresa F. Leaden. It was set in Caledonia by University Graphics, Inc.

Printed and bound by The Kingsport Press.

For Valerie, Roger, Craig, Karen, Bret, and their peers, many of whom will be our managers for the future, with the earnest hope that they will do a better job for mankind than we have done.

CONTENTS

FOREWORD

We may not be able to solve the world's major problems, but efforts in that direction are decidedly warranted. The contributions of the well-known participants in this book—the Secretary General of the United Nations; some of our most distinguished executives in federal, state, and local government; highly respected chief executives of major corporations; management scholars and university administrators—should serve to stimulate discussion that could bring us closer to the solutions we seek.

What do these administrators consider our major problems? Overpopulation, famine, exhaustion of our limited natural resources, atomic war, pollution of our planet's fragile environment, worldwide inflation and unemployment. Obviously, some suggest global approaches to the prevention and solution of these problems.

With what are the authors concerned? The move from an age of abundance to an age of scarcity (with reductions in standard of living and quality of life), fiscal difficulties for governmental and educational institutions, and nationalization discouraging investment in the countries most in need of capital.

Ross Goble asks who will feed the 200,000 people added to the world's population every single day, the predicted 7 billion population by the year 2000, and the 14 billion only 50 years later. Thomas Malthus taught us that people at a feast can be hospitable to an occasional beggar but that there is no feast when they attempt to feed too many beggars. Dr. Goble fears that adverse climatic changes may lead to shorter growing seasons and that the monsoons required for crop production in much of Asia will, as in recent years, fail to occur.

Organizational theorist Dr. William Newman is concerned with inadequate design and inept use of managerial controls. Unfortunately, these controls are not oriented to the future and often have an inappropriate influence on behavior. Dr. William Ronan suggests that failure to energize bureaucracy is a worldwide phenomenon occurring in both socialist and capitalist countries. Management's creativity is often buried under an avalanche of operational detail, adds Dean H. J. Zoffer.

What do authors predict? Dr. Keith Davis is optimistic. He predicts that during the next two or three decades we shall continue to move toward a more humanistic, socially concerned society. This encourages government intervention and control, with all the advantages and disadvantages thereof. Dr. Davis traces the American transition from an *agrarian* to an *industrial* to the first *service* economy. As a result, he predicts a shortage of managers, since service work tends to have a smaller span of supervision than industry or agriculture. A service economy does not require people to crowd into large cities. They can opt for easier life-styles in suburban and rural areas. Davis goes on to predict that the United States is about to become the first *knowledge society*, one in which employees use intelligence and information more than strength. This requires lifelong learning in our constant race against occupational obsolescence. The *biprofessionals*, for example, those who combine law and accounting, are often quite useful to their organizations and have great occupational mobility. Just as many of you are now biprofessionals, some will become *multiprofessionals.*

In the future, managers in both the public and private sectors will shift from excessive reliance on intuition for solving problems to a more behavioral and management-science approach, predicts Dean Edward Mazze. He anticipates less adaptation to change and more planning of it. Sophisticated buyers, for example, will have higher expectations about quality and performance. Dr. Mazze expects greater acceptance for the three- and four-day workweek. (University faculty have had these schedules for years.) He also predicts that large numbers of foreign executives will be trained in American business schools, thus continuing the transfer of management technology. This is now causing a commercial revolution that will later spark an industrial revolution in developing nations.

Sigmund Ginsburg predicts continued swings in the pendulum from people-oriented to task-oriented organizational climates and greater emphasis on decentralization with use of guidelines for purposes of control. He forecasts greater use of job enrichment, project management, and sabbaticals for training to improve performance and to help implement the policy of promotion from within. As vice president for administration of a major university, Ginsburg predicts that declining birthrates in the United States will decrease elementary, high school, and college enrollments and, therefore, the need for teachers (and, we might add, administrators) on all levels.

Managers attempt to satisfy many publics. Two long-neglected publics may become more demanding in the future, predicts David Reynolds. They are blue-collar youth, who often have dull jobs, and retired people, who often have dull lives. Reynolds gives examples of the turmoil facing most organizations because of the ever-increasing rate of change. In such a dynamic environment, the past—in which work may have been central to a person's existence—is of little help to managers who attempt to predict the future. Similarly, decisions based on short-run considerations become obsolete almost immediately.

What do authors recommend? That we reduce our expectations in order to avoid exhausting our supply of energy. John deButts recommends more systematic management of the processes of discovery, and Dr. Richard Weeks prescribes both conservation and massive infusions of capital for the development of alternative sources of energy.

Within organizations, Sigmund Ginsburg sees the need for restudying reward systems, compensation, and fringe benefits in the light of greater concern for productivity. As a university administrator, he calls for improved continuing education along with effective systems and procedures for delivering it.

Drs. Kenneth Black and Robert Wilson recommend *humanistic capitalism* that first develops and then employs multiple measures of social, not just economic, costs and benefits. Humanistic capitalism offers employees information and opportunities to participate in the decision-making process. They obtain intrinsic job satisfactions in addition to such extrinsic rewards as pay and fringe benefits. Corporations, say Black and Wilson, should be designed to fit people, not vice versa, and should distribute profits to a far wider group of owners than they do today.

What are some of the authors' conclusions? Harry Ekblom believes that managing the future consists of managing change and that there is direct correlation between our success in this endeavor and the progress of our civilization. It is possible that *if we fail to manage our future, we may not have one.* Since the world is running out of energy, food, and other resources, population must be limited. We need to reach consensus on priorities based on research findings. For example, is reducing unemployment more important than reducing inflation? How are they related?

Some contributors to this book write about the year 2000. Perhaps by then we shall have changed the significance of the phrase "more is better." By more, we now mean more gadgets. We hope that more gadgets will give us more leisure, more art, more independence, more beauty, and more time for meaningful human interaction.

It is our wish that you, the reader, after digesting the thoughts of our distinguished contributors, may also be stimulated to provide recommendations for the creation of a better society for us all. Please read on.

DEAN HAROLD LAZARUS
Director of the
Hofstra University
Management Series

PREFACE

Issues and problems of great complexity and gravity confront mankind today, and the quality of management that we bring to bear in coping with them will play a highly significant role in their solution. It will also profoundly affect the course of society throughout the world. "Quality of management" embraces not only business management, but also management of the economy, government, labor, society, and academia. In a very real sense these areas are interdependent. The quality of management in any one area almost always has a "rub-off" effect on the others. For this reason, Dean Lazarus, Director of the Hofstra University Management Series, and I invited outstanding people from the fields of business, government, labor, and academia to give us the benefit of their thoughts on management for the future—to help solve the serious problems facing us. And thus was born this book.

According to the Club of Rome, an international private group of businesspeople who are concerned with the future of mankind, only change in the world's social and political institutions, as well as its growth patterns, can avert catastrophe. This group considers prompt action essential to solving global problems in a democratic fashion. Professor Heli Jaguaribe, a Brazilian political scientist, summarizing a conference held in Philadelphia, stated that without corrective measures democratic and humanistic institutions would be destroyed long before mankind perished from lack of food or raw materias. Aurelio Peccei, founder of the Club of Rome and former managing director of Olivetti, considers it necessary to puncture the myth of national competence.

The call for a new international economic order was made at the sixth and seventh special sessions of the United Nations General Assembly. This new order has generally been interpreted as one that would better serve the interests of developing countries, particularly their poor masses. The Nobel Laureate, Professor Jan Tinbergen of the Netherlands, in a study commissioned by the Club of Rome, urges international economic planning as a substitute for the uncontrolled play of market forces. We have been "flying by the seat of our pants" far too long. For the future, careful global planning by our best minds is imperative.

Indicative of global anarchy is the painful fact that while the world's food supply has been growing almost twice as fast as the world's population since 1950, at least 500 million people throughout the world live on the edge of starvation, according to the Secretary General of the United Nations, Kurt Waldheim. Equally pathetic is the statistic of 650 million people with incomes of less than $50 a year, according to the World Bank. This distressing evidence of world governments' ability to make the worst of things illustrates all too well the gross lack or ineptitude of international planning.

Many of the writers included in this book have dealt with the serious problems of our domestic area—the ecology, labor-management relations, inflation, unemployment, provision for the health and safety of our labor force, care of our aging population, sound government management on all levels—problems embracing all facets of our society.

It is my wish that this book will serve to stimulate thought, comment, and action by our foremost executives in business, labor, government, and academia toward the global goals of eliminating international and domestic difficulties, eliminating unemployment and hunger, increasing our concern about sickness and old age, ameliorating or resolving other problems facing us. Planning for the future on a scientific basis has been too long ignored. Consequently, problems often become major crises for which we are not adequately prepared and necessitate emergency measures that result in duplication or waste of resources.

As we continue to increase the rate and scale of our scientific and technological advance, it becomes vital that we learn to look ahead in a planned, systematic way with the maximum cooperation of every major knowledgeable segment of our society; the alternative may well be that business and society as a whole will be unable to survive as they are today. Portents indicate that we are moving into an era of tremendous potential for accomplishment. We surely possess the knowledge and the wealth and the power to remake the world into an almost limitless utopia. If we are able to marshal the judgment and cooperative spirit required to achieve this, we shall succeed in one of the greatest ventures in the history of mankind.

For highly competent and accurate typing of the voluminous international correspondence entailed in this project, my sincere thanks to Stella Sinicki, supervisor of Hofstra University's Secretarial Services, and her staff, in particular Dorothy Trombecky, always so efficient, courteous, and cheerful.

I am especially grateful to Dean Harold Lazarus for his encouragement and cooperation.

LEWIS BENTON, Editor
Professor of Management
School of Business
Hofstra University

1

THE CONSTRUCTIVE ORCHESTRATION OF CHAOS

JAMES G. AFFLECK
Chairman, American Cyanamid Company

The future of management is "nonmanagement." It will be the development and utilization of people organized to employ all of their individual creative talents to the maximum, within an environment of continuous and dynamic change. The rigid and highly structured organizational framework of the past will be replaced by a cohesive interdependence of thought and action, perhaps without conscious direction or apparent leadership as we have understood it. Management's main job will be to exercise sensitivity and an educated intuition to draw the maximum from a highly skilled and intellectually sophisticated force of managers and workers.

It is axiomatic that any organization, whether business or government, exists to perform a specific function or it should not exist at all. What we often fail to realize, however, is that the organization's function is not static in today's society. Pressures from competitors, government, consumerists, and others often take businesses abruptly into new areas. Research and marketing developments prompt major changes. No organizational charter can be immutable; rather, the organization must seek to adapt itself continuously to the outside environment to remain productive and useful to society. The alternative is to cease to exist.

This modern dynamism has major implications for the structure of organizations and how they should develop and evaluate the human resources which are their basic asset. Our past methods of reaching short- and long-term objectives by methodical step-by-step progress, usually with various specialties and functions separated until drawn together by the master puppeteer labeled "chief executive," will be replaced by a new, much less structured way of life. All aspects of management's job ahead will be more subjective, more complex, more shades of gray on any problem. It will be, in many ways, the constructive orchestration of chaos, and to the initiate will probably seem both inconsistent and paradoxical, without the logic of neat pyramids of organizational boxes and the territorial imperatives which have grown up around so many corporate functions.

Up to now, organizational structures have served to treat people as surrogate machines, or to replace them with machines wherever possible in the name of efficiency. In the future, we as managers will have to develop new attitudes and practices if we are to lead the men and women of the last quarter of the twentieth century and give them the kind of rewarding and fulfilling work experience they are being conditioned to expect. We are going to have to employ people as people, taking into account all the interests, habits, attitudes, and learned skills which when properly exercised lead the human being to new heights of individual and collective achievement. We are going to have to employ 100 percent of the individual, not the 20 or 50 percent which may fit the current job description.

For too long we have been inspired by the military chain of command which from the time of the Caesars has been designed to carry decisions from the top to the bottom, and which has shaped the organization to carry out those decisions in the most efficient way we could devise with clear-cut assignments of authority and responsibility. The individual employee of the future, however, will be as different from Rome's legionnaire as the space vehicle is from the chariot. Perhaps the biggest circumstance facing management today and in the future is the rise in educational levels of the people who compose the organization. Throughout the Western world and in much of the East, people are being educated well beyond the narrow limits of professional specialties and the scope of specific job assignments. Even in developing countries, multinational corporations are finding today that increased literacy—combined with progress in nutrition, sanitation, and health—is unalterably changing traditional modes of personal behavior and individual aspirations.

People are being taught, or more accurately are teaching themselves, to become eclectic, catholic, and diverse, and are seeking a wider sphere of individual personal accomplishment in the search for a wholly satisfying and productive life. This exposure to many disciplines and outlets for self-expression has a major portent for the organization and the role it assigns each of its members. More and more, individuals are bringing to their jobs the interests and attitudes they have developed earlier, or which relate to their "private lives" outside the factory or office. It is becoming less and less possible to drop a curtain separating the corporate person from the private person, offering one set of incentives and rewards to each half while keeping them unrelated. Furthermore, within the organization the old-style divisions of assigned responsibility are constantly being crossed, often without formal or official recognition, by individuals whose inquiring minds, ambition, or dedication simply will not permit them to be limited by lines on a chart. This broaching of boundaries is a positive, promising, and irresistible development because it will bring into the organization the maximum application of the abilities and talents its people have to offer. Just as we have found the lines dividing the physical sciences becoming less definable as we learn more about the nature of matter and energy, so we will find that the previously accepted allocation of functions within the organization will blur as we discover more about the capabilities of human achievement.

This is not, as it may appear, a recipe for anarchy or a denegation of the need for highly specialized and sophisticated functions, and the people trained to do them, in the organization of the future. Indeed, organization with its rules will always be with us, as will the need for leadership, judgment, and decision making. But they will take new forms and will be shared by more participants. For example, we will have to recognize that no chief executive or management team can or should attempt to manage the activities of thousands, or hundreds of thousands, of individuals under their nominal control eight hours a day. That cannot be done any more than their thoughts can be managed. Actually, we will achieve a quantum leap ahead in management effectiveness when we recognize this as a fact and turn our attention as managers to where our ship is sailing instead of how the trained crew is performing. Our job is to redefine the objectives of our organization in terms that will challenge the employee to reach deeper into himself or herself for the motivation and the satisfaction in stretching to accomplish the maximum. The ultimate success or failure of the organization will depend largely on how well management contributes to the ability of each individual employee to understand and pursue the productive work that the employee knows needs to be done.

Picture, for example, the almost instantaneous mobilization of 150 million Americans on December 8, 1941. Then picture our country years later, wracked by strikes, divisions, and pent-up hostilities. In the forties the youth of the country were drained into the armed forces; our resources were exploited as never before; inexperienced leadership abounded in government, industry, and the military; women were not oriented to what we call the work experience—yet, from a standing start, this nation rapidly became the arsenal of the democracies, pushed back its enemies in the Pacific and the Atlantic, and still ended the conflict with enough industrial might to rebuild its former enemies as well as its allies.

In spite of the hundreds of boards, commissions, and other "management" bodies thrown together in the early forties, no one really managed the war effort. It really happened as a vast unstoppable expression of the will of the people. It was nonlogical in the sense that no one could possibly have masterminded the outpouring of creative ingenuity and dedication, much less every formal plan or activity which sprang up in the process. Individuals everywhere sensed what needed to be done and what they themselves could contribute to the final objective, and they applied themselves willingly. Thus, the national goal was formulated by all of us together, and we all shared in the ultimate victory. The essence of America has always included this form of basic participation by the people in the development of the goals of society, and we have always succeeded when that was understood by the leadership. Sometimes, as in our Civil War, the struggle was extremely costly, yet the national consensus was achieved.

This intuitive and amorphous development of national goals, often crystallized as in wartime to specific objectives, can be likened to a similar process within organizations. Organizations and their leadership fail when the process of management denies the dynamic turbulence which of necessity must work to bring creativity, innovation, and achievement to the surface. Organizations, however, once they are rigidly structured, are inherently dictatorial in nature, with commands from the top imposed upon and interfering with the job at the operating level as those at that level see the job necessary to be done. Too often, events are commanded to happen, organized to happen, made to happen, and in the process never happen at all.

In contrast to World War II, two events in our recent history that were supposed to be made to happen were victory in Vietnam and defeat of poverty by the Great Society. The Vietnam war was the most organized, planned, and detailed campaign in human history. The war on poverty was implemented by the best financed and organized attack by social scientists, educators, and psychologists our government could mount. But both failed. Vietnam failed because we could not enlist the participation and resourcefulness of the American or Vietnamese peoples. The Great Society failed because it tried to impose responsibilities and attitudes on the poor and the nonpoor alike that they were neither able nor willing to accept. Neither effort grasped the essential quality of the collective will of the people, a factor which exists in every society and organization and which ultimately determines where and how the organization will actually move regardless of orders issued from the the top.

It is essential for management to identify this collective will, influence it as possible, and adjust to its boundaries and limitations, even as those boundaries are changing. The general who finds out which way the army is going before he gets in front to lead is not making a mockery of leadership; if he is a good general, he will have shaped the will of the troops beforehand to march toward his own objectives. Woe to the leader who takes the organization to the place it should not be on the strength of his rank alone and then finds himself isolated and unsupported, as was the late President Johnson.

In dealing with people and with the organization of the future, management must address the task of creating the structure and the environment which will best challenge each individual's innate yearning to achieve. This means that the very definition of bureaucracy as an inflexible and unbending procedural system must give way to a structure aimed at reaching well-articulated and thoroughly understood objectives through a collective synergism within the organization.

As organizations have become more complex and more specialized, we have tried up to now to relate to a proliferation of information and the need for specialized skills by compartmentalization. Information is made available on a "need to know" basis under the assumption that management knows, in fact, what employees really need to know to do their jobs effectively. Likewise a whole syndrome of jargon, professional literature, and mystical rite has grown up around dozens of corporate functions that used to be relatively simple. What has become lost in the process is a perception by the individual of the totality of the organization—where it is and where it is heading—and of his or her own potential for contributing to its progress. Obviously, unless employees clearly understand the job and the expectations of the supervisor, they cannot perform satisfactorily. But unless employees also understand the goals and direction of the organization as a whole, its relative position with respect to its industry or other references, and its place in society as a whole, they cannot be expected to contribute up to their potential to the final attainment of the organization's identified goals.

Management by Objectives has taught us the need for employee participation in setting work goals and the necessity for the employee to identify those that seem to be reasonable and attainable and to join with management in evaluating the progress made toward them. In a larger perspective, the same psychology must apply to the entire organization; it must be structured to permit and encourage individuals to see beyond the narrow limits of the job description and to contribute however their talents permit. We must come to recognize that jobs, like institutions, do not stand still in a changing world. If a job is routine or unchallenging, employees of the new breed will seek to enlarge it to suit their own creative ambitions. Failing that, they will look for satisfaction in outside pursuits or with another employer. If the job itself cannot be changed to grow with the growing individual, the alternative is to regard monotonous and humdrum work as transitory, fitting only a certain period in one's lifetime, much as the fast food restaurants of today concentrate on employing teen-agers, knowing that the practice suits both their needs and their employees of the moment. The two- and three-career history, already noted with retired civil servants and military, will become even more commonplace in the future.

Another increasing need of future management will be to assure that all elements of the organization have the specific information they need to do their jobs properly. Though this may seem elementary, all too often relevant information is gathered by one unit and sent upward through channels only to repose in the files of an executive, and is not transmitted further to the people who really could make use of it. Indeed, the problem is that potential users usually do not know it exists. Our difficulty today is not so much with gathering useful and pertinent information or in storing it and releasing it on demand, but in using judgment to extract key information from masses of fact and in assuring its being brought to the attention of the people who actually need it.

All of this might appear quite alien to the manager who believes a day's pay is sufficient for a day's work, and employees should unquestioningly carry out their assigned jobs. But that manager will never be able to lead the work force of the future—never be able to draw from the individual a willing and full commitment to make the organization succeed and flourish. Instead, that manager's people will be turned off from the challenges of their jobs and will seek personal satisfaction elsewhere.

What I am really discussing here are perceptions of the reality of work today as seen by different levels of management and by employees throughout the organization. Because of our traditional, parochial organizational patterns, we often find that reality is defined according to one's field of vision. A sales manager, controller, corporate planner, or chief of research, for example, understandably concentrates almost exclusively on his or her function, and sees success or failure of the entire enterprise hanging on his or her unit's performance. Each pursues individual goals confident that senior management will draw together all the threads and will resolve conflicts over budgets, development funds, personnel, and the many other areas in which the organization must apportion its resources. No wonder then that typical employees of any given department will have a stronger allegiance to their department's function than to the entire organization, since the organization is too remote from their daily jobs to be concerned about.

We have to step outside ourselves as managers and view the organization from the vantage point of an interested coach and guide, rather than look down from the top of a pyramid. As a coach, the executive of the future will be a diagnostician who will analyze the working of the corporate team and the contribution of each of its players, perhaps allowing now one, now another, to carry most of the load at any given time. This executive will encourage the team to perfect itself, not by concentrating on the perfection of each component part, but by making sure that all parts come together into one entity of productive energy. As the coach and guide, the executive will plan future strategy, assure the resources, and encourage the employees to perfect their most effective winning style. The executive will observe the organization from a clear vantage point on the sidelines, instead of presiding over it from an apex with vision obscured by his or her own shadow.

If we fail to alter our traditional views of management, especially in dealing with people, several trends already in motion will accelerate and force change on us. Some trends would hand over management prerogatives to the uninformed and unequipped—government officials, workers' councils such as we already have in Europe, or others demanding a share in corporate decision making because of inability to have their views and identities acknowledged by management.

One especially disturbing phenomenon in recent times is the growth of white-collar and professional unionism. Doctors, nurses, public employees, engineers, and even midmanagement employees have been attracted to trade unionism out of sheer frustration caused by working in what they perceive to be an atmosphere insensitive to their individual needs and aspirations. The demand for identity, pride, and recognition among these groups is as real as their demand for a better standard of living, and sometimes it is even stronger. Consider what has happened to our public services, for example, with the advent of unionism among professional and administrative public employees. The demands of good administration are often subordinated to the dynamics of union collective bargaining, with the system sometimes unrealistically perverted to serve the needs of the public employees first, rather than those of the citizens. Certainly the dismal picture of New York City's financial ills has been painted in large strokes by the political power of the unions, many composed of professional and skilled workers. This trend to collective representation for "management-type" employees may be an inevitable reaction to the complexity of modern times; yet the management which understands its underlying motivation can work to mitigate the conditions which bring the trend about.

The circumstances and factors which I have described suggest that we will witness a rather fundamental change in the nature of attitudes toward work in the coming quarter century, and in the way organizations will have to be managed to be effective. These changes will probably be evolutionary and will first affect large corporations and government bureaucracies which are public or quasi-public in nature and must be responsive to outside political and social pressures. Such pressures certainly will intensify in the future, as the inner workings of all large organizations are exposed to public scrutiny to an even greater degree. Further, advances in science and technology will exacerbate the problem of machines displacing people in more occupational specialties.

While the full dimensions of these developments cannot be seen now, it would be realistic and prudent to begin assessing our organizations and prepare to absorb and adapt to these changes, rather than resisting them. In addition, we must begin now to instill in potential senior executives an understanding of the broad social, economic, and political issues which will shape our future environment.

We should periodically redefine and reevaluate our current mission, and try to assure that everyone affected within and without the organization has a clear understanding of what we do, why we do it, and what factors determine success or failure. This means that we must share more information with employees, customers, stockholders, governmental agencies, and the press, and seek a real dialog rather than one-way communication with our "key publics."

Next, we must appreciate and adapt to the needs of the employee of the future. This will mean changes in our traditional views of job and career development, mobility, training, cross-disciplinary experience, performance evaluation, and many other aspects of the employee-employer relationship. Perhaps we will be turning more in the future to minicareers which last 10 or 15 years, after which a potential for regeneration can be offered. Meantime, the educational process will extend further into the adult years, and people who have achieved a degree of accomplishment in one speciality may be training for a second at the same time and using the new knowledge on the job.

Organizations will slowly become more fluid and less dimensional at all levels, with growing participation by subordinates in key decisions affecting them and even the enterprise as a whole. The lines between divisions and departments will become less definite. Inevitably, both jobs and relationships will become more complex and demanding. This will necessitate effective outlets to relieve tensions and permit feedback to management from articulate and sophisticated employees.

Executives will have to intensify their awareness of personal relationships and their readiness to step aside from the chair of the commander to that of the guide and coach, concentrating even more on broad strategy and future planning after building the best operational management team possible. These people and planning problems will take increasingly more time and attention, and their solution will be essential. We know today that insulated, isolated chief executives lose touch with reality. In the years ahead, our nerve endings will have to be increasingly sensitized and we will become even more astute at identifying potential problems and working out solutions with the participation of the people directly involved.

Whether we are in private business or government, maximum productivity and optimum use of human, financial, and physical resources will be required of tomorrow's management. That is one demand that is unchanging. How well we respond to it, and to the new tests that arise when applying this standard to a fluid and often disordered environment, may determine our ultimate survival.

2

THE ENVIRONMENT OF MANAGEMENT IN THE FUTURE

KENNETH BLACK, JR.
Dean,
School of Business Administration,
Georgia State University,
and Regents Professor of Insurance

ROBERT O. WILSON
Assistant Dean,
School of Business Administration,
Georgia State University

The United States is in the midst of one of the great transformations of Western civilization. What is happening is that the old ideas and assumptions which once made our great institutions legitimate, authoritative and confident are fast eroding. They are slipping away in the face of a changing reality and are being replaced by different ideas and different assumptions which are as yet ill-formed, contradictory and shocking. This transition is neither good or bad. There is the possibility of plenty of both. The point is simply that it is taking place.

Professor George Cabot Lodge
Harvard University Graduate
School of Business Administration

Those institutions and systems which have shaped Western industrial society include the nuclear family; Judeo-Christian religions and institutions; compulsory mass education; lifelong career patterns; the work ethic; bureaucratic political processes; multilevel, elaborate judicial systems; internal combustion engines for transportation; electronic and sound frequencies for instantaneous communications; and fossil fuel energy sources. The institutions and systems are in the process of being transformed toward the end of the twentieth century. We are witnessing a "clash of culture," as major confrontations occur between existing institutions and moralities and their emerging alternatives. Management in the future will be management in an Age of Changing Values.[1]

The Impact of Science on Culture

Science is a powerful producer of knowledge, and knowledge changes people's beliefs. It is, in fact, the scientific revolution that is changing people's beliefs about what is valuable. People's values, what they believe to be valuable, are central to their culture. When a culture is challenged by change, the group's population is checked and the culture is fragmented or a new culture is developed. Social change, as the anthropologist sees it, is inherent in the basic fabric of civilization. There are special situations, however, known as "culture crises." Our present culture crisis is associated with the breakdown of the existing industrial world view in the face of new knowledge. The term "culture" was coined by anthropologists in the nineteenth century as they began to study the artificial extensions of human beings which help them to survive within their physical environment. It was recognized that not only people's tools, but also their beliefs, poems, songs, religions—all the things and devices people use to enhance, protect, or express themselves—are designed to help groups survive. With changing conditions, however, people's culture must change.

Peter Drucker has pointed out that we get our view of the world from René Descartes, the French philosopher and mathematician. Descartes gave us the axiom upon which much of our thought is based. This axiom states that the whole is merely the result of its parts. This is the way we generally think about reality; it is "common sense" for us. The dominant world view has prevailed for 300 years and involves (1) development and application of the scientific method; (2) wedding of scientific and technological advance; (3) intense application of the division of labor; (4) increasing scientific and educational specialization; (5) the positivistic theory of knowledge—only that is true which is operationally useful; and (6) the dominance in social policy of economic considerations, in private life of acquisitive materialism and in the work ethic of Puritanism.[2]

This world view of the past 300 years has been remarkably successful, but the beginning of its disintegration can be seen in the paradox that its successes have created many of our major problems. Its logic is beginning to encounter the paradoxes of extreme positions. For example: (1) Affluence and the accumulation of goods lead to environmental decay, mounting pollution, materials and energy shortages, and a widening gap between rich and poor countries; (2) technological advances in "defense" lead to the threat of worldwide destruction; (3) rising standards of living lead to world overpopulation; (4) advances in communication and transportation lead to greater urbanization and increasing risk of societal breakdown from action by very small groups; (5) industrial engineering efficiency leads to the dehumanization of work; and so on.

This cleft between the dominant industrial world view and the new knowledge is dramatically displayed in many ways. One of the most obvious symptoms is the sharp drop of people's confidence in our major institutions, be they medicine, government, press, clergy, or business. As Leo Cherne pointed out, we expect an institution to moderate the rate of change and somehow or other control the forces which play on us.[3] We have, in many cases, lost faith in the ability of institutions to moderate the extraordinary quantity of change to which we have been subjected. The clash of values, rooted in the crisis of culture, which results from these opposing views of the world has made such situations inevitable. We must recognize the need for revised perceptions as to what is valuable and a consequent redefinition of concepts and systems which provide the foundation for management decision making.

Capitalism Redefined

As a case in point, capitalism is in the process of redefinition. Unfortunately, few theoretical economists have recognized this development, since it involves the "invasion" of economics by other subject matter. By and large, economists have tended to ignore those social and economic realities that do not fit their theoretical models.[4]

Our society is experiencing a change in its view of the world caused by the powerful scientific revolution which is providing new knowledge of the universe, the earth and its functioning, and mankind's place in nature. Humankind is now seen as a part of nature, inseparable in its fate from the fate of nature itself, and subject to the ongoing relatedness of events. The result is to redefine capitalism and to question the old culture of a consumptionist society of acquisition materialism, as people now strive to adapt to a research-based economy of environmental balance that offers long-term prospects of sustaining civilization. This concern for the environment, the quality of life, and the culture and its need to change does not mean the end of economic growth. Rather, it means the recognition of new knowledge and a service-based wealth of the future. The source of our wealth that offers the most promise of growth is not in the proliferation of consumer goods but in the growth of knowledge and service to others.

Carl Madden suggests that the future might see[5]

> **Corporations dedicated to what might be called "humanistic capitalism" pursuing limited but well-defined social and economic purposes, developing measures of social and economic costs and benefits, and making profits distributed to a very wide group of owners, far wider than today, with a much more responsive process for the exercises of management trusteeship.**

"The alternative," he conjectures, "is the increasing regulation of the corporation and a far larger role even yet for government."

These shifts in values, stemming from new knowledge and perception, are challenging our concepts of rationality. Since corporate management of economic resources derives its political and social legitimacy from the presumably rational allocation of resources, disputes over the nature of rationality itself are bound to affect corporate strategies, management, markets, and products. Regardless of the uncertainty of future directions, management must prepare itself to deal positively with this crisis in culture and the concomitant changing values and value systems.

Industrial Society Questioned

It is apparent that industrial society itself is being questioned in an unprecedented way. Madden supplies a partial list of questions now being asked about American society:

- Is our industrial civilization favorable or threatening to human survival?
- Are we now living in a "golden age" better than what has gone before or is to come in the next century or so?
- Are we going to have an environmental crisis by 1985?
- Will continued material growth in our economy be a threat to human survival?
- Do we understand what wealth is and how to create it?
- Are our major economic policies to maximize output any longer tenable?[6]

It should be noted that these questions are not mainly ideological. They apply to the economics of our present industrial civilization, whether capitalist, socialist, or communist. It should be obvious to business leaders that these and similar questions are aimed at the foundation of beliefs that business, up to now, has taken for granted. There is no doubt that the life and work of the business manager has been impacted by this cultural transformation.

Egalitarianism[7]

One of the changing values impinging on management is a drive for equality that cuts across the nation's entire social and economic fabric and is becoming a significant factor in U.S. life today. Many see the pursuit for equality as part and parcel of the American Dream. Others see it as an oncoming nightmare of bureaucratic rule, deepening torpor, and—in time—national insolvency. On July 21, 1975, Casper W. Weinberger, retiring Secretary of Health, Education, and Welfare, warned against "egalitarian tyranny" in these words:

> **If social programs continue growing for the next two decades at the same pace they have in the past two, we will spend more than half of our whole gross national product for domestic social programs alone by the year 2000. Should that day ever come, half of the American people will be working to support the other half. . . .**

The real social agenda of America, still unfinished, is to discover and reward excellence wherever we find it. . . . If we fail to see this as our real agenda, we risk delivering our destinies over to the cold and lifeless grip of a distant egalitarian government whose sole purpose is to ensure equally mediocre existence for everyone, achieved at the cost of personal liberty.[8]

Equality itself is not a totally new issue in this country, or elsewhere. The nineteenth-century French scholar Alexis de Tocqueville described equality as a driving force in Western civilization, gathering momentum with the Reformation, the voyages of exploration, and the rise of the democratic ideal in the Western world. As he predicted, it is in the United States that the struggle for equality is moving toward a climax.

The first century and a half of our country's existence brought a succession of equalizing changes—universal education, an end to the property test for voters, a Civil War that freed slaves, a graduated income tax, and the voting right for women nationwide. For most free Americans before this century, the principle "all men are created equal" was considered to mean equality before God and parity in law. Opportunity for a livelihood and advancement was taken for granted in a young nation where frontiers constantly offered new lands and an expanding economy offered jobs to all willing workers.

To the extent that the current drive for egalitarianism means better education and more public services for the underprivileged, the U.S. system can accommodate it—at a price. When the principle is extended to mean equal pay for unequal work and advancement without regard to qualifications, egalitarianism comes into conflict with individual achievement and the basic principles of sound business management, which rely on differentials in rewards to provide an environment within which employees will be motivated to perform.

In an economy based primarily on private enterprise, governmental efforts to promote equality represent a deliberate interference with the results generated by the marketplace, and they are rarely costless.[9] The push for equality of results, the theory that every person should share equally in economic rewards without regard to effort or ability, puts an increasing strain on the split-level institutional structure of U.S. society, which combines democratic government with a capitalist economic system.[10] Financial rewards (in the form of wages and profits) are a basic motivator in the U.S. economic system. Wage differentials move workers from the less productive industries to the more productive. Profit differentials move capital from decaying industries to growing areas. Middle and upper incomes are the primary source of capital for expansion. The steady growth in the redistribution of income in the United States eventually must seriously impair the effectiveness of the economy.

Even the socialist and communist systems have found that pay incentives play a major role in improving production. The Soviets who began with the Marxian doctrine of total equality, have developed a wider differential in real income between the bottom and top than exists in most United States corporations.[11] The continuation of this move from equality of *opportunity* to equality of *results* will be a major factor affecting the ability of management to provide the balanced productivity essential to stable, viable economic growth.

The Search for Identity

As has been pointed out, the scientific revolution has helped to complicate our society. It becomes more difficult with each passing year for the individual to identify with the society and to achieve a sense of self-fulfillment. The individual who does not perceive an appreciation for his or her presence or efforts and cannot identify a route to self-fulfillment does not perform as a productive member of a group.

In other vertebrate societies, the young mature with the assurance that in their natural society they will find a place uniquely their own. Robert Ardrey suggests that the human youth has no such assurance.[12] He points out that specialization limits the individual's chance of achieving identity by taking much of the meaning from work, that a worker will be denied the right of excellence by the union where longevity and oneness rule, and that as an organization person, one will be required to give up identification with the products of his or her creative talent.

Within the limits and directions of an individual's genetic endowment, a state of satisfaction is sought which will inform the person as to why he or she was born. We have no true choice. It is identity—what Abraham Maslow would call self-actualization—that presents the most incisive challenge to the habituated human mind. Who am I? Where am I? Have I actualized myself, singularized myself as my genetic potential proposes?

There is general agreement that people are most human at the point of choice or when they are engaged in decision making. It is this ability to make conscious choices based on understanding of past events and prediction of future consequences which distinguishes humans most markedly from other animals. The human animal is vastly superior to others in its capacity to visualize the long-range consequences of alternative courses of action. It is the ability and the right and the freedom to make decisions and choices and to influence outcomes that permit men and women to maintain their individual identity, to develop a self-image based upon a matrix of values—an individual value system—all their own. Individual reaction to varying degrees of uncertainty which influence one's choice and decisions again provides individualistic identity.

The freedom to make a decision based upon individual values is the final and finest criterion of self-determination. Freedom of choice also is the essence of personal identity in a situation in which individual value systems are pressured and molded by the interactions of a human being with his or her environment and other individuals. The individual who has not been successful in identifying his or her value system or determining who he or she is will not perform well as a rational decision maker. Kenneth Boulding has stated that "the forces which determine a person's image of his own identity are important in determining his behavior, whether the image corresponds to objective reality or not."[13] Individuals with confused or negative self-images are unlikely to perform in a responsible manner.

IMPACT ON MANAGEMENT AND THE CORPORATION

The changes in values that are inherent in the transformation of the American culture are the catalysts of a broad environment of change which is apparent to individual and organizational members of society. As a result, today's business leader or manager is experiencing a series of shocks. As has been pointed out, because of the scientific revolution through which we are living, today's executives are being required to alter markedly the way they perceive business enterprise and the society in which it exists.

It is widely accepted that the corporation is under attack. To many, the corporation is seen as a means to systematize greed and is often perceived as unable "to relate and to help" with society's problems. David Rockefeller stated that many corporations are energetically working to prevent urban decay, to train and place the hard-core jobless, and to minimize pollution. But he asks whether these activities are regarded by the business leader as "costly extras" or, as the community itself sees business, as an absolute obligation for which corporate ownership and leadership should be held strictly accountable. His conclusion is that "businessmen have no choice but to respond by becoming reformers themselves, making a conscious effort to adapt the market system to our changing social, political and technological environment."[14] Rockefeller notes that today's attack on the corporation is broadly based; it is "the individual against business—all business," in contrast to earlier eras of criticism against particular businesses such as railroads, banks, or Wall Street. He interprets this present criticism as demands for a revision of the social contract and believes that business must coordinate its efforts with other reformers. To do otherwise will result in an unwise adoption of extreme or emotional remedies by the other reformers.

One proposed remedy, viewed by many as extreme, has recently surfaced in the form of a bill introduced by Senator Humphrey and Representative Hawkins in March 1976, known as The Full Employment and Balanced Growth Act. Under this act, a Full Employment and Balanced Growth Plan is to be prepared with the assistance of the Council of Economic Advisors and in consultation with the Office of Management and Budget. It shall

> **propose priority policies and programs that comprise a full employment program that provides non-wasteful jobs and that reorder national priorities and employ the jobless in the production of goods and services which add to the strength of the economy, the wealth of the Nation, and the well-being of the people.**

Further, under this act "the appropriate committees of the Congress shall review and revise, to the extent deemed desirable, the economic goals, priorities, policies, and programs proposed." And "the Congress shall initiate or develop such legislation as it deems necessary to implement these proposals and objectives, after such modifications in such proposals as it deems desirable."

It has been pointed out by skeptics that the process of centralized planning will force the government to consider long-run implications and that it will establish a framework for the rational consideration of goals. The question then becomes, what about the consistency of goals?

Three years ago, the Club of Rome, working in the rarefied atmosphere of pure analytical thinking, arrived at the conclusion that the world needed zero growth to escape disaster. Now its members have decided that they were wrong and that, after all, economic growth does have merit. Consider on a national level the fickleness with which our goals are determined. We have seen major commitments to the Fair Deal, the New Frontier, the Great Society, the New Federalism, the grandiose housing program of the sixties, and many other goals that sprang to life and faded away with the change of the political constellation. Is it not reasonable to ask, "Why should a governmental planning organization do better?"

Senator Humphrey argues that the planning system would be voluntary, except with regard to the federal government's own activities, and would not impose any restraints upon the private sector.[15] Other supporters of the legislation, however, seem less sure of that point. The Initiative Committee for National Economic Planning, an organization of prominent economists and politicians, has stated that the economic planning board should have, among other things, responsibility to specify the labor, resources, financing, and other economic measures needed to realize these programs and plans. The committee added that it should be clear that the Planning Office would not set specific goals for General Motors, General Electric, General Foods, or any other individual firm; but it would indicate the number of cars, the number of generators, and the quantity of frozen foods we are likely to require in, say, five years, and it would try to induce the relevant industries to act accordingly.[16]

The drive for centralized economic planning may be viewed as one more step toward greater dependence on government, and greater governmental intervention in the free market economy. It has also been argued that America was founded, and has grown great, on the theory of equality of opportunity. There is a growing concern that it may now founder on the theory of equality of results and the loss of the discipline of the marketplace. It is important to remember that an increasing proportion of the working population is employed in the governmental sector. Given our political system and bias toward short-run considerations, there is justification for such concern.

HUMAN RESOURCES

An area of increasing concern is the ever-widening chasm between the rationalization of productive activity and human satisfaction. This is not a new concept. Max Weber predicted that we would pay a high price in human satisfaction with every step we took toward perfecting the process of rationalization.[17] He also noted that one consequence of increasing efficiency would be to strip life of all mystery and charm. Above all, he feared that the process would extend beyond regulation of economic and political activities to stifle the individual's private and personal life.

More recently it has been pointed out that in the post-World War II culture of the United States, the process of rationalization has reached deeply into our social structure.[18] In the past few years, a questioning of the values of efficiency has begun to reach beyond the confines of the counterculture. Many of today's best-educated youths see the emphasis on efficiency, quantitative methods, and cost-effectiveness as expressions of minds blinded by dogma, if not by evil incarnate. Even though people are annoyed when the television receiver does not work or their garage mechanic does not correct their automobile problems, they more and more are becoming suspect of the merits of values centering on efficiency, planning, and the organization of time.

Daniel Katz and Basil S. Georgopoulous listed four major changes which have occurred in our society that challenge both the production and social subsystems of organization:

1. A break with traditional authority and the growth of democratic ideology
2. Economic growth and affluence
3. Resultant changes in needs and motive patterns
4. Accelerated rate of change[19]

These changes are significant for organizations since, as open systems, they are continually interacting with their environment, with respect to both production inputs of materials resources and social inputs from the culture and the larger social structure.

Some of the formerly dependable maintenance processes of organizations have eroded with the break from the older pattern of authority. In the past, it was morally wrong to reject in word or deed the traditions of cherished institutions. It was wrong to seek change other than through established channels. Those who deviated generally felt guilty, and if they did not, they usually were considered to be psychopaths. Organizations had the advantage of a degree of built-in conformity to their norms and, in some cases, to their values because of the general socialization in the society about agreed-on standards. Today we are finding that member compliance with organizational norms and values no longer can be sustained on the basis of authority.[20]

This decline in traditional authority and the economic growth and affluence, which have been so apparent over the last several decades, are related to a shift in motive patterns in our society. David C. McClelland called the American society the achieving society and, indeed, a review of earlier years provides sufficient justification for the title.[21] A pronounced decline in emphasis on achievement has occurred, however, during more recent periods. This decline in the older motive patterns has had one direct consequence for all organizations. The extrinsic rewards of pay, job security, fringe benefits, and conditions of work are no longer the major attractions. The intrinsic job satisfactions are being demanded with greater frequency.

It is becoming continually more apparent that not only are we witnessing significant shifts in the economic and value patterns of society, but they are occurring at an ever-increasing rate. As a result, history is becoming less relevant for predicting the future. All organizations face a period of trouble and turmoil because of this rapid change. Many of the traditional values of the social system, such as the concept of private property, conventional morality, work and economic achievement, and the good life as the conventional enjoyment of the products of mass culture, are under fire. The Protestant ethic, as discussed by Max Weber, is no longer pervasive and paramount in American society.[22]

RESTRUCTURING THE WORK SYSTEMS

It has been predicted that organizations will necessarily undergo significant structural changes in the future in order to remain in existence.[23] Warren Bennis stated that, in view of the rate of change, organizations will necessarily become more adaptive by depending mainly on rapidly changing, temporary systems that deal with different problems as they arise.[24] The need for increased knowledge sharing, as well as the changing goals and expectations of employees, has undergirded a movement toward the use of project task forces and the restructuring of work systems. During the 1960s, a limited number of companies launched experimental work systems which were designed primarily to counter the problems of worker alienation generally expressed by passive withdrawal, but sometimes exhibited in violent disruption of work routines. These innovative systems strove to achieve a total, "systemic" restructuring of the way work was done. In recognition of the changing employee expectations regarding work and the inadequacy of piecemeal reforms which were felt to be underlying factors contributing to the alienation, these companies redesigned the way tasks were packaged into jobs. This redesign of work systems was expanded to cover the way workers relate to each other, the way performance is measured, the way rewards are made available, the way positions of authority and status symbols are structured, and the way career paths are conceived. Specifically, tasks were grouped to de-emphasize one man–one job in favor of self-managing work teams. Tasks were made "whole" by incorporating functions that previously were performed by other service or control units. Finally, flexibility in work assignments was built in.[25] Although not all of the involved companies have realized fully their objectives in this experiment, some notable successes have been achieved.

Continued experimentation and research will be necessary if organizations are to meet the challenges brought on by our cultural transformation.

The structures and processes of organization are being questioned as to adequacy and responsiveness. By developing a greater understanding of the changes taking place in value systems, the manager will increase his or her ability to define and make the changes in organizations and work systems which must be forthcoming to accommodate our changing value systems.

REVISED CONTROL SYSTEMS

Changes in organizational planning, structure, and processes are necessarily followed by revisions of organizational control systems. This is essential to organizational success in meeting goals and objectives if the control systems are to accommodate new approaches to planning as well as structural and process changes.

An area of major current concern must be the control associated with those plans and processes involving natural resources and pollution. The exploitation of natural resources and the creation of pollution have been two areas in which considerable criticism has been lodged against industrial organizations. The magnitude of concern is apparent from the unprecedented systematic, comprehensive, and regular measurement of the quality of the world environment. The launching in 1972 of a globe-circling satellite demonstrated that technology exists, ready for large-scale testing, to inexpensively monitor the earth's resource patterns.

As pointed out earlier, managers and business organizations are perceived all too often as socially irresponsible. Comparisons between current organizational goals, activities, and products and the emerging values of the new culture have resulted in this perception. Regardless of the managers' understanding of the standards of the new culture or the plans they develop to accommodate change, they must have adequate systematic feedback to monitor their efforts intelligently. Improved and innovative use of information technology will be an essential factor in future management.

IMPLICATIONS FOR FUTURE MANAGEMENT

Management of a vibrant, productive organization has never been an easy task. The manager has been and will continue to be buffeted by multiple forces which necessitate decisions and positive action. The management process, however, has become more complicated over time. In years past many resources were taken for granted; today many of the same resources are much less plentiful. And as noted earlier, preservation of both resources and our physical environment is another concern which further complicates the life of the manager. Expanding technology and knowledge have introduced changes in almost every aspect of our lives, intellectual and physical. The future manager will have to function in an environment of chronic change, and he or she must learn to accommodate it as a normal state.

Managing Chronic Change

Today's managers are faced with chronic changes stimulated by advanced technology in an environment permeated with changing values and perceptions. In discussing the question of the ability of current managers to adapt themselves to managing chronic change, George Kozmetsky suggested a series of inquiries regarding today's managers:

1. Do they have the time to spare from the current short-run problems and pressures generated by their institutions?
2. Do the operational rules of their institutions permit them to concentrate on anything but the short run?
3. Do they have the motivation necessary to tackle problems whose time frame extends beyond their tenure of office or position?
4. Do they have the current means of distribution of resources (especially capital) to provide sufficient resources to meet the demands?
5. Do the current problem solvers have the appropriate conceptual apparatus to perceive the wider problems facing society?
6. Do they have the techniques (including hardware, software, and communication) to structure solution models and procedures?
7. Do they have the information technology required to gather the data for problem formulation, problem solution, and monitoring of results in a timely and effective fashion?
8. Do they have the appropriate organization structure and mechanisms to solve the problem?[26]

If the answers to these questions are not all negative, or if factors for stimulating the institutional adaptability have been identified from an examination of the premises underlying the responses, it is probable that an "evolutionary revolution" will occur. This term describes the predominant form of social, political, cultural, economic, and technological change experienced in the United States since 1776. For example, this country made what is *conceptually* a revolutionary change by moving from a rural agrarian society to an urban industrial society; but it did so in an evolutionary manner. Similarly, business institutions went through a *conceptually* disruptive change by moving from a craft-mercantile economy into an industrial business economy; again, the process was evolutionary. In higher education, a *conceptually* disparate change from selective private institutions to mass public higher education was made in an evolutionary manner. Such changes are revolutionary when viewed on a conceptual basis, but the societal *process* of achieving this revolution is evolutionary.

Kozmetsky submits that the problem today is to be able to perceive and formulate revolutionary concepts and then to link them to mechanisms and triggers that bring about evolutionary changes in a *desired time,* while preserving the stability of society. Desired time is the critical factor. No longer can we use time as an evolutionary filter to smooth disruptions and deficiencies at a micro or macro level. We must have the ability to cope with multiple changes taking place simultaneously in a large number of institutions. Thus, we are denied a stable institutional base from which to evolve changes; rather, we must work from a base that is itself evolving.

Role of Information Technology

Since technology is the cause of this rapid pace of change, we must look to technology, particularly information technology, for the means to manage this change. We must use information technology as a substitute for time in smoothing out changes. Having identified the time constraint as a critical factor, Kozmetsky suggests also that we can identify the critical need for managers with the ability to:

1. Perceive and formulate those problems facing society and its institutions
2. Relate the formulated problems into a unified conceptual model that starts with the current structure and identifies the desired structure of society and its institutions
3. Translate these problem formulations into understandable opportunities for execution and implementation by the policymakers of society's institutions
4. Provide a means for the problem solvers to validate the acceptability and efficiency of their solutions, including their ability to make the deficiencies of the formulations, conceptual models, and solutions known to the problem formulators[27]

Today, too often, problem formulators are working on predicting problems of the future without reference to present realities of available resources to actualize their predictions. Similarly, problem solvers are frequently working on current problems without considering adequately the consequences of their actions in the future. It is clear that we are in an era of critical social experimentation. It is tempting to assume that we will find "the best way," but, as Kozmetsky points out, there probably is no best way at all, only better ways for a while, for different groups, different areas, and so on. But we are well advised to monitor closely what we are about and what results from what we do.

The management of change is, in essence, the management of the creation and application of knowledge. The problem for managers involved in the policymaking process becomes one of assessing and selecting those elements of information technology that will enable their institutions to achieve their goals within a wider context of social objectives.

The Emerging Manager

The emerging manager is likely to be viewed as an information processor. If information technology can provide him or her with a dynamic picture of the firm's activities, institutions will be seen as something that can be designed to fit people, rather than vice versa. The new manager will also have a broader measure of performance for his or her firm; the concept of profitability will extend from profits to include other benefits that might accrue to the firm or society, including protection of the integrity of the individual. This does not mean the new manager will abandon his or her responsibility to the shareholders. Rather, the manager will realize that the new information technology will provide multiple measures of performance that will permit one to perceive alternatives to enhance profits in the traditional sense while advancing to achieve other benefits for the firm. In sum, decision making for the new manager will be based more on participation and superior information than on authority. The new manager will operate from a conceptual basis. In addition to experience, the new manager will depend on narrative conceptual models in his or her decision making—models which give a flexible base for evaluating the past and for meeting novel situations. Since these conceptual models usually have a verbal foundation, the new manager is better able to communicate his or her decision premises. Thus, discussion can take place on the assumptions and framework underlying decisions; and once agreement is reached on the premises, agreement on the actual decision should be easier.

In contrast, the traditional manager has been viewed as a people manipulator or, in terms of the political and economic radicals, as an exploiter of people. The traditional manager perceives institutional frameworks as rigid structures into which people must fit (or be made to fit), and he or she defines managerial problems in terms of deviations from the static framework. Such deviations precipitate a "managerial crisis" for the traditional manager and require suspension of the normal process of business (as he or she defines it) until the crisis is resolved. Solutions to such crises tend to be in the form of organizational overreactions and to become institutionalized as part of the rigid structure of doing business. A good example of this can be observed in the management reorganization that occurs in response to declining profit margins or market shares. The traditional manager also can be characterized as an instinctual or experiential manager, whose training has come through experience, and he or she makes decisions by relying on judgment based on that experience. In many cases the manager's effectiveness is limited by his or her ability to generalize from past occurrences in meeting new problems of radically different nature from those in the past, and the traditional manager is often left feeling impotent and frustrated. Failing to communicate the basis for their decisions and thus gain acceptance (or understanding), traditional managers often fall back on vested authority to impose their decisions.

One way to clarify the suggested profile is to contrast the management styles by noting their perceptions of several issues. For example: (1) Traditional managers see *changing markets* as a source of uncertainty and a departure from established patterns. The new manager sees changing markets as a natural part of dynamic society and a source of opportunity to expand current business and establish new business. (2) *Labor unions* are viewed by traditional managers as competitors for authority as well as economic and political opponents. Conceptual managers view the labor union as a means of redistributing wealth and, as such, a potential source of future capital, and as a way of managing and educating workers. (3) With regard to *education*, the traditional manager acknowledges the importance of education but views it as a one-shot deal, for example, a graduate degree, but no substitute for experience. The new manager sees education as a replacement for some experience and views it as a process to be engaged in throughout life.

Thus, management in the future will require managers capable of functioning in an environment of chronic change with their decision making based more on participation and better information than on authority. The individual manager will require a confident self-image based on a clearly defined hierarchy of values and a continuously updated knowledge base as his or her frame of reference.

Emphasis on Human Resources

Within the United States, and in many other parts of the world for that matter, the emphasis of economic activity has evolved from land, through capital, and finally to human resources. A review of the literature of management thought reveals that the value of the human resources of the organization was receiving attention at least as far back as shortly after the turn of the century. Frederick W. Taylor, commonly called the "father of scientific management" in the early 1900s, voiced an appreciation for the value of the human assets of the organization and stressed the importance of developing this resource.

Even today, however, many organizations show much more concern for the technology of work than for their social inputs and human resources. The provision of a safe and attractive physical work environment has received much more attention than the creation and maintenance of an attractive social and psychological work climate. With the emphasis on technical and economic efficiency, primary attention has been directed to recruiting and selecting members with the "proper" training and aptitude for filling inflexibly defined jobs rather than to problems of member attitudes, needs, and values. The approach has been to fit the individual to the job, and organizational redefinition has been largely disregarded as a problem-solving mechanism. Organizational restructuring to improve the adaptability of the system has been regularly resisted. Most organizations have avoided social innovation and renovation and have sought technological innovation as the answer to all their problems.

Most of the opportunities the manager of the future will have to develop his or her organization's human resources are not new. The element which is new involves expectations. As the standard of living has improved and communication technology has expanded, the expectations of people have changed. Individuals probably have always yearned for the chance to perform and for recognition and feedback as to the level of their performance. In the past, however, they suffered quietly when these desires were not fulfilled. Productivity was not what it could have been, but worker dissatisfaction was not a significant problem. Today, the quality of life has taken on major significance, and motivation and productivity hinge on the employee's finding meaning in his or her work. The cultural transformation and changing values are mandating a new, more flexible and empathetic manager.

The Manager as a Model

The manager must provide a sound role model if he or she is to be successful in meeting this challenge. Not only must he or she be perceived as a personally responsible individual, but the organization must be viewed as responsible. The concept of "social responsibility" involves the need for the corporate firm or organization to adapt itself to the change in values that the cultural revolution has created. To be responsible, the corporation, as part of the social and economic process, must adapt itself to the new cultural milieu. The critical element in the adaptive process is a change in perception by top corporate leaders from the fixed values of the past to the values of the newly emerging society.

The issues frequently raised by critics include present perceptions and the content of basic economic concepts—wealth, income, productivity, and cost. Thus, they include the prevailing philosophy of "bigger and better." Attention is directed, however, to the concrete ends of today's corporate process—what is produced; what is distributed; what is sold; how it is sold; what the productive process is said to produce; what it is said to mean to the people, the nation, the human race; what is prescribed as work is said to mean; how the work is organized; and what are said to be the objectives of the work. Critics of corporate social responsibility are critics of top management's perception of what it is doing and what it believes it is doing.

Future Role of Business

Thus, it is clear that the time has come to recognize that the future role of business must be social as well as economic. The task is for business itself to organize its effort to achieve social goals. Business, until recently, was lauded for its performance, but now that same performance earns responsibility for pollution, abandoned cities, growing trash heaps, and ugly landscapes; the public's demands have changed.

As has been pointed out, the concept of a corporate life cycle is as valid as that of the human life cycle. The phenomena of decline and decay and even mortality are as grimly present among business enterprises as they are among people. If an organization is to continue in existence in the future, the manager must serve as both strategist and entrepreneur.[28] He or she must provide entrepreneurial leadership. As the manager, he or she will be responsible for managing the business in which the company is engaged in a way that optimizes its profit results *and* social contribution. In the entrepreneurial role, the manager bears the responsibility for ensuring the long-term vitality of the company by shaping its strategic direction, moving it into new businesses, and adapting it skillfully to changing external forces.

It is not uncommon that the role of manager is performed reasonably well in most large, well-established business organizations. The role of entrepreneur, however, is often performed poorly, if at all. As a result, managements of many businesses conceive of their job as that of "keeping things going," serving as the caretaker of the organization to ensure that it functions smoothly. In this context, most managers are oriented far more toward maintaining effective operations—getting the job done, turning out the work, handling problems, and keeping things on an even keel—than they are toward changing and upgrading operations or moving in new directions in light of changing conditions.

What is needed, today more than ever, is the form of entrepreneurial leadership that will give the members of an organization a clear sense of direction and an almost consuming sense of urgency. This is true because of the accelerating rate of technological change, the intellectual revolution, and the shortening of product life cycles. The ever-increasing rate of change makes it increasingly difficult for the manager to maintain productivity levels, let alone enhance them. Yet, with the increased demands for the allocation of more of the country's goods and services to improve the lot of the disadvantaged, the need for improved productivity becomes evermore pressing. Managers with integrity and a sense of personal responsibility providing empathetic leadership to workers who find real meaning in their work are the sine qua non of a bright future for American society.

REFERENCES

1. See Carl H. Madden, *Clash of Culture: Management in an Age of Changing Values,* report no. 133 (Washington, D.C.: National Planning Association, 1972).
2. See Peter F. Drucker, *Landmarks of Tomorrow* (New York: Harper & Row, 1959), chap. 1.
3. Leo Cherne, *1975 CLU Forum Report* (Bryn Mawr, Pa.: American Society of Chartered Life Underwriters, 1975), p. 76.
4. See Carl H. Madden, "The Greening of Economics," Annual Meeting of the Institute of Life Insurance, Washington, D.C., Nov. 27, 1973.
5. Ibid.
6. Carl H. Madden, *Clash of Culture.*
7. See "Equality: American Dream—or Nightmare?" *U.S. News and World Report,* special report, Aug. 4, 1975, pp. 26–31.
8. Casper W. Weinberger, "On Losing Our Freedom," *Newsweek,* Aug. 18, 1975, p. 11.
9. For a detailed statement of this position, see Arthur Okun, *Equality and Efficiency* (Washington, D.C.: The Brookings Institution, 1975).
10. For a discussion of the theory of equality of results, see Daniel Bell, "The Revolution of Rising Entitlements," *Fortune,* April 1975, p. 98.

11. John Cobbs, "Egalitarianism: The Corporation as Villain," *Business Week*, Dec. 15, 1975, p. 87. See also Michael C. Jensen and William H. Meckling, *Can the Corporation Survive?*, Public Policy Working Paper Series, University of Rochester, April 1976.

12. Robert Ardrey, *The Social Contract* (New York: Dell, Co. 1970), pp. 172–173.

13. Kenneth E. Boulding, "The Future of Personal Responsibility," *American Behavioral Scientist*, vol. 15, no. 3, January-February 1972, p. 331.

14. David Rockefeller, "The Role of Business in an Era of Growing Accountability," address delivered at the Advertising Council Dinner, New York, Dec. 13, 1971; published in *Looking Ahead*, vol. 20, no. 3, April 1972.

15. Hubert H. Humphrey, "National Economic Planning: Pro and Con," the New York *Times*, Dec. 21, 1975, p. 12-F.

16. For additional discussion of the functions of a centralized planning agency, see interview with Daniel Bell, "Big Challenge: Creation of a Genuine National Society," *U.S. News and World Report*, July 5, 1976, p. 57.

17. Max Weber, *The Theory of Social and Economic Organization*, trans. A. M. Henderson and T. Parsons (New York: Oxford University Press, 1947), pp. 228–250.

18. Daniel Yankelovich, "The Meaning of Work," in Jerome M. Rosow (ed.), *The Worker and the Job* (Englewood Cliffs, N. J.: Prentice-Hall, 1974), pp. 36–45.

19. Daniel Katz and Basil S. Georgopoulous, "Organization in a Changing World," *Journal of Applied Behavioral Sciences*, vol. 7, no. 3, 1971.

20. See Amitai Etzioni, *Modern Organizations* (Englewood Cliffs, N.J.: Prentice-Hall, 1964).

21. David C. McClelland, *The Achieving Society* (New York: Van Nostrand, 1961), chap. 3.

22. Max Weber, *The Protestant Ethic and the Spirit of Capitalism*, trans. T. Parsons (New York: Scribner, 1952), chap. 5.

23. Bernard M. Bass and Edward C. Ryterband, "Work and Organizational Life in 2001," in Marvin D. Dunnette (ed.), *Work and Nonwork in the Year 2001* (Monterey, Calif.: Brooks/Cole, 1973), pp. 142–146.

24. Warren Bennis, "Organizational Developments and the Fate of Bureaucracy," *Industrial Management Review*, 1966–67, pp. 41–55.

25. For more information, see Richard E. Walton, "Innovative Restructuring of Work," in Jerome M. Rosow (ed.), *The Worker and the Job* (Englewood Cliffs, N.J.: Prentice-Hall, 1974).

26. George Kozmetsky, "Future of Management: Managing the Future," Franklin Foundation Lecture delivered at Georgia State University, Atlanta, Apr. 12, 1972.

27. Ibid.

28. Richard F. Neuschel, "The Challenges Facing Top Management in the 1970's," keynote address given before the Insurance Industry Seminar in Tokyo, Japan, July 27, 1970.

3

EFFECTIVE MANAGEMENT IN THE FUTURE

CORNELIUS BREVOORD
Dean, Graduate School of Management, Delft, The Netherlands

There is every indication that management—at least in Holland—is in a crisis situation. Management is beset by the labor factor (demands to increase wages and establish a profit-sharing system); by the government (price-control regulations, antipollution measures, and the legal requirement to discuss important decisions with the works council); and by society at large (questions regarding the legitimacy of the company's existence and its manufactured products). And all that is occurring in a period of economic depression and profit squeezing. In the light of these developments, it is understandable that recently the chairmen of the nine biggest Dutch companies sent an alarming letter to the Dutch government in which they pleaded for more elbowroom, more freedom to maneuver to improve the profitability of their companies.

This was a noteworthy step by our chiefs of industry. Never before has such unanimous and penetrative action been undertaken to direct the attention of the government and the Dutch community to the problems with which business is confronted and—according to those nine chairmen—to the consequences these developments might have for the welfare and well-being of our society. After a few weeks, the discussion about the "letter of the nine" was closed, the general feeling being that the underlying slogan "what is good for business, is good for the country" is outmoded and has not earned a renewed consideration. We have to tackle our present and future problems with new creative and imaginative concepts.

Management needs a new orientation. Formerly, management had mainly a technical-economic viewpoint; nowadays environmental and value issues are at stake and have to be incorporated in management thinking. The environment—including its prevailing value systems—has been relatively stable in the past, with occasional periods of turbulence; nowadays it is constantly in turbulence, is causing many uncertainties, and needs to be explored. In that respect, the past is not a reliable indicator for the future. A forward-looking analysis, exploring the future environment (including value systems), is necessary to ascertain the kind of climate in which the organization will have to live and flourish. What role has management to play in future? How can it help to create effective organizations which are doing the "right things" in turbulent and uncertain circumstances? And how can we measure the effectiveness of organizations? In short, how effective can management be in creating effective organizations in the turbulent decades to come?

DESCRIPTION OF THE ENVIRONMENT AND VALUES SYSTEMS

During the past eight years we have gone from an alluring environment to a threatening one. From about 1950 to 1970 the Western world went through a period of relative political and social stability, expansion of profit-oriented organizations, national economic growth, and an increase in welfare. In business, profits increased, and diversification and integration proved to be successful. There was practically no scarcity of raw materials, environmental issues could be ignored, and we could afford expanding systems of health care and education. One might say that everyone in the Western world seemed happy.

Nowadays the situation is dramatically different. As the French president Giscard d'Estaing remarked, "*Le monde est malheureux.*" ("The world is unhappy.") And, stated in another way; "I am concerned about a society that has demonstrably lost confidence in its institutions—in the government, in the press, in the church, in the military—as well as in business."

The enormous increase in economic welfare in Western countries has promoted a rise in attention to other than economic factors and, as a consequence, has induced resistance to the domination of economic principles in our society and in the behavior of organizations. We are in a period of transition and uncertainty. To mention a few of these uncertainties: Relative political stability is gone; we have lots of large and small action groups beating and besetting the present societal system—minority groups, antipollution groups, antinoise groups, and anti-Concorde groups. Instead of harmony, there is conflict. Any action in society—a new highway, shopping center, or production plant—conjures up a reaction, and we have not yet found the ways and means to solve these current differences creatively and effectively. The political system is not working satisfactorily: there are, outside parliament, other competing power centers, and the parliamentary system cannot cope effectively with long-term issues. There is a preference for short-term issues and successes.

There is a shift in morale and in the spiritual sphere. Formerly, people were highly motivated by money, career, and status. Today there is a tendency to abstain from salary increases and to devote more time to leisure; a recent survey in Holland revealed that about 50 percent of our working population had no objection to a three- to five-year freeze of income. In Holland, the rate of divorce is increasing rapidly, the rate of absenteeism due to illness has doubled in a few years' time, and the membership of churches is declining rapidly. There is a search for new values such as general well-being, social justice, equality, participation, rights of minorities, and concern for underdeveloped countries. There is a tendency to plead the cause for the underdog in our society, meaning that property and property rights are becoming less important and are being replaced by membership and membership rights (social security).

The rate of economic expansion—in Western Europe—has recently slowed down. During the early seventies a recession spread over the world, causing production and trade to decline. In Holland, this recession has structural aspects: parts of our Western production process are shifted to underdeveloped countries and there are no sufficient replacement opportunities for the work force concerned. Also, the inflation is generally high; some raw materials, such as energy, are getting scarce; and in general prices of raw materials have increased substantially. There are indications that in some markets the old market mechanism is not working satisfactorily anymore, due to lack of competition, government regulations, or international political pressure.

The increase in welfare in Western Europe has to be stopped or slowed down, mainly because it will become unpayable; we can hardly afford the present system of health care, education, and social security. Participation in increasing welfare is pleasant and readily acceptable; sharing the burden of decreasing welfare is annoying and almost unacceptable.

Our national societal problems are becoming increasingly complex and interrelated. One cannot consider a societal problem detached from its consequences on other societal issues. In Holland, for example, the problem of unemployment cannot be tackled without considering how it affects the growth of welfare, level and direction of investments, control of the physical environment, and international trade and balance of payments.

There is a situation of international economic-structural imbalance and international political instability. The basic raw materials, predominantly used by the developed countries, are often abundantly available in the less-developed countries; the biggest food-producing countries are not generally the biggest consuming ones; and the standard of living in the developed countries is growing faster than in the less-developed countries. To bridge these gaps, there is a need for leadership, vision, and a new and creative approach to the problems ahead. Instead, we observe a sophistication in destructive weapons such as atomic bombs of all kinds and sizes, nearly no progress in the disarmament negotiations, and in Western Europe almost a complete standstill in the unification process.

Environmental disturbances include poisoned rivers, polluted beaches, growing scarcity of clean water and fresh air, spreading cities, and chaotic traffic, all of which require governmental attention and legislation. Furthermore, the work population is growing at a rapid rate and a serious problem of food supply may result. As a Dutch poet described it: "Thine eyes see the chaos in the street. The murdering pace, the fugitiveness, the touching along plastic and concrete, the search for a starving nature. With the insipid imitation taste of food that may not nourish in their mouths. Thy smells, O Lord, the steams and the stenches, an incense with no song. Thine ears hear the noise of days and nights. Are these, O Lord, Thine creatures? Is that Thine creation, starving time and time again?"

And last but not least, there is a proliferation of new knowledge and technologies and their applications in organizations; in general, an increased rate of technological change in all aspects of our society with sweeping—often unforeseen—consequences on the structures and processes of organizations.

If the period 1950–70 can be characterized by relative stability, expansion of profit-oriented organizations, national economic growth, and increase of welfare, the coming period must be labeled one of relative instability (politically, economically, and socially), selective expansion of profit-oriented organizations, zero national economic growth, stabilization of welfare, and increase of government influence.

What are the main basic changes in our value system which can be observed in the foregoing description of symptoms and trends in our society? These changes are discussed below and summarized in Table I.

1. *Changes in Human Values:*

- From the idea that all human beings are alike to the notion that all human beings are different. This implies that we are interested in the particular abilities and characteristics of each human being. Therefore we try to find work for each individual based on his or her particular capabilities, instead of structuring the workload first and then trying to find someone who can do it.

- From individualism to participation. The emphasis on individual values such as success, income, and status is in general shifting to the opinion that results can only be achieved by teamwork, that is, a participative approach, especially in situations of nonroutine work.

- From an economic production orientation of life to a total well-being orientation of life. The emphasis is shifting from work to living, from strenuous labor to the quality of life, from a need for performance to self-realization.

Table I
CHANGES IN VALUE SYSTEMS AND ORGANIZATIONAL CONSEQUENCES

From	*To*
Changes in human values:	
All people are alike	All people are different
Individualism	Participation
Need for performance	Self-realization
Ignorance	Lifelong education
Changes in social values:	
Property	Membership
Product orientation	Community orientation
Limited government	Overruling government
Changes in organizational philosophy:	
Functional specialization	Interdisciplinary approaches
Authoritarian decision making	Democratic decision making
Negative control system	Positive control system
One task per worker	Teamwork
Vertical information systems	Functional information systems

- From ignorance to lifelong education. We live nowadays in a learning society. The general level of education—especially in Western Europe—has improved considerably and will increase further if the notion of continuing education is accepted. As a result, expectations about job content, income, and status have risen; such expectations can lead to discontent if the job content does not offer opportunity for personal development. Better-educated people tend to pay more attention to professional values and the professional content of their work than to loyalty to the organization which employs them. That means an increased degree of mobility.

2. *Changes in Social Values:*

- From property to membership. Formerly, individual rights were best guaranteed by property rights. Nowadays individual rights are far more loosely connected to property. In the present legislation every individual has lots of rights: education, health care, pension, social securities, housing, and civil rights. A shift to a membership society is evolving in which it makes no difference whether one owns property or enjoys property.

- From product orientation to orientation on consumer needs. That is, competition is diminishing in several branches, partly because it is considered wasteful of the scarce resources of mankind. Organizations are more responsive to the needs of the community at large and interested consumer groups, thus earning an image of responsibility in a responsible society (legitimacy of business).

- From a limited role of government in society to an overruling one. Compared to the days of Adam Smith in which governmental activities were only required in cases where the market mechanism failed or was nonexistent, we can observe nowadays an ever-increasing range of activities of governmental agencies. As a result of the failure of market mechanisms (prices of agricultural products), scarcities of raw materials and such natural commodities as fresh air, clean water, and green fields; the increased extent of public education, health care, and defense; compounded by the consequences of the interrelations between all these problems (not in the least because of the need to set priorities); the role of government is now preponderant in our society. One might question whether the governments in Western Europe are working on an ad hoc basis or along precisely and consciously defined, interdisciplinary constructed policy lines.

3. *Changes in Organizational Philosophy:*

- From scientific functional specialization to an interdisciplinary approach. We have discovered that most problems are of an interdisciplinary nature (systems) and consequently can only be tackled by integrating different disciplinary approaches. Therefore a breakthrough of the disciplinary boundaries and specializations is necessary and a coordination of an integral approach is required.

- As a result of the changes in value systems, there is a shift from an authoritarian to a democratic style of leadership; from a negative control system (punishment in case of errors) to a positive control system (with acknowledgments and appreciation for provided performances); from specialization in routine work to teamwork; from a vertical information system (top-down) to a functional system, in which attention is focused on the process of decision making rather than on the process of reporting.

On the basis of these observations and conclusions it is possible to make a rough profile of the coming era. It is reasonable to expect that the well being of society at large and that of individuals will get the highest priority. This means there will be a shift from individual values to communitarian values and the relative importance of work, performance, status, income, and career of the individual (economic factors) will diminish. Quality of life, self-realization, and continuing education will become the goals of individuals. There will be an urge for equality and democratic decision making.

With the growing influence of the individual and interested groups on the different decision processes in all types of organizations, there may be on the one side a tendency to grant more independence to units within an organization ("small is beautiful"), and on the other side an increasing conflictual pattern of behavior. That leads to a diminishing degree of predictability about the outcome of these decision processes and to a general feeling of uncertainty, which will decrease the willingness of the parties concerned to make long-term agreements. To ensure to a certain extent a stabilized development of society and the well-being of its population, the power of government will increase and some degree of centralized planning seems unavoidable. A serious discussion about the role of government in public life, the extent of its interference for the sake of public and private interest, and the priorities which have to be set is at hand.

As a result of all these developments, both profit-oriented and nonprofit-oriented organizations will be the battleground where these environmental forces meet. In the future, organizations will have to cope with an increasing degree of governmental intervention and regulation; a suspicious community asking nasty questions about the legitimacy, purposes, and products of the organizations; and a better educated and organized work force, which has its own vision on the quality of life and its own role in the decision-making processes within the organizations. The environment will become meddlesome with regard to all activities of organizations. The result will be an active interaction between organizations and their particular environment, more discussion in the political sense (questions regarding the need for investments, expansion, and new products), and an increasing influence of the work force in the behavior of organizations. The separation between technical-economic management and humanization of work will vanish. Management will be involved in a much broader setting of problems than formerly, and therefore must possess the scientific and political means to cope satisfactorily with these new challenges. This will lead inevitably to a greater variety and a greater degree of conflict. These conflicts will no longer be restricted to capital and labor, but will arise between a large number of interested groups, all with their own value system. This has serious implications on the managerial decision-making process.

The French Revolution was for freedom; between 1950 and 1965 there was a revolution for welfare. What we are now experiencing in Western Europe might be called a revolution for well-being.

THE NEW FUNCTION OF MANAGEMENT

Formerly, the main function of management in profit-oriented business was to plead the cause for shareholders. Today, management is primarily involved in the continuity of the organization and monitoring its level of employment. But the emphasis is mainly on the technical and economic aspects of the organizational process. Although there is much discussion about the humanization of work, the incorporation of behavior concepts in management thinking is shaky. Until recently management emphasized the tension between technical-economic and behavior concepts rather than their interrelation, their separation and antithesis rather than their synthesis. The same applies to the meddlesomeness of the environment; management appraises it more as a constraint than as a valuable contribution to a new and better well-being–oriented policy.

In any case the function of management is at stake. The reaction of "the nine chairmen" mentioned earlier indicates a hesitation on the part of management to accept the realities of life; there seems to be a stronger tendency to rely on values and structures of the past than to design new concepts to conquer the challenges ahead. One might in fact question the function of an organization. Is it mainly a source of income for shareholders; is it providing employment and income for laborers; or is there any relation to societal goals, purposes lying outside the organization? A new goal definition for organizations seems to be required.

Such a renewed concept might run as follows: The purpose of an organization is the creation of wealth in a socially and scientifically responsible manner. It consists of economic wealth (income for employees, government, and sometimes shareholders), humanitarian wealth (joy of life for employees working under socially acceptable conditions), and societal wealth (improvement of the quality of life for individuals and the community at large). In this way of thinking, the necessity of survival of individual organizations is not the ultimate purpose; an organization becomes a means to reach communitarian goals, and from that viewpoint such an equation as "social concern + profits = survival" must be rejected.

Accepting such a goal setting (sometimes called theory Z), the new function of management might become the structuring and running of organizations which produce wealth in a socially and scientifically responsible manner. Such a system can be symbolized as shown in Figure 1. In this view an organization is a system with four elements: goals, people, technology, and structure embedded in an environment. The new function of management is

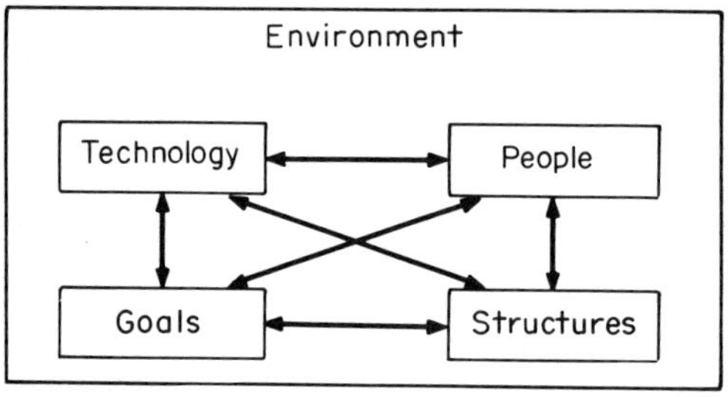

Figure 1 **The organization as a system.**

the search for combinations of these elements under changing environmental conditions. An effective organization is one that does the "right things": responds easily and timely to changes in the environment (the societal value system), in the attitude and behavior of people (the human value system), and in technology. In such an organization, controlled by an effective management, there is a constant drive to lessen or remove the tension between the elements of the system or its environment, or both. In principle, there is no antagonism between the goals of the organization and the aims of employees, consumers, and community, no matter how conflicting their interests might seem to be sometimes. The underlying idea is that by means of intensive, and often strenuous, discussions between all groups concerned, creative solutions, or perhaps compromises, for competing views would be found.

These creative solutions are conditio sine qua non for our society. If management—as the group most committed to achieve a goal and entitled to lead the bargaining process—cannot find them, organizations are left to the mercy of centrifugal forces: the striving by management for an economically acceptable result (defined in terms of profit or market share), the urge by employees for more industrial democracy ("every employee an executive and every executive a worker"), and their interest in well-being, the intervention and regulation by government, and the meddlesomeness of the environment. Management knows what has to be done to survive.

My views are rather consonant with the ideas expressed in a recent Harvard Business Review (HBR) survey. The results obtained are worthy of recall. Of about 1800 HBR readers:

- 71 percent adhere at present to an individualistic ideology.
- 62 percent think that an individualistic ideology is prevailing nowadays.
- 73 percent think that a communitarian ideology will be prevailing in 1985.

No one can assert that he or she will be caught by the developments in our society. All signs point in one direction. It is wiser to anticipate than to demean.

EFFECTIVENESS OF ORGANIZATIONS

After this exploration of the general trends in the environment of organizations, the concept of effectiveness has to be explored. "Doing the right things" can be a preliminary approach; from a scientific viewpoint it is an unsatisfactory definition. It is subjective (who judges what is right?), it presumes that organizations have one total systems goal (a multiple goal seeking seems more appropriate), it supposes a consensus of value systems between the interested groups involved (which is seldom the case), and moreover effectiveness becomes unmeasurable. Of course, this article is not the appropriate place to review all literature regarding effectiveness; so a rather pragmatic approach is required. How can effectiveness be operationalized?

A first approach to effectiveness can be considered in relation to the activities of the individual organization operating as one total system. This approach to system evaluation for profit-oriented organizations suggests that a system is effective only if it is profitable, growing, or successfully coping with competitive organizations for its market share. A proponent of this view, suggests that infinite growth seems to be possible for social organizations. The assumption is that the growth rate is a measure indicating how well the organization is adapting to its environment. Other proponents of this view suggest that the effectiveness of a division (a subsystem of the total organizational system) can be readily measured if it is competing for its share of the market. This conception makes use of one or two isolated (economic) effectiveness criteria to indicate the degree of effectiveness of an organization. This opinion can be questioned. If a large number of variables is capable of influencing effectiveness and effectiveness is also considered as an indication of the degree of organizational responsiveness to changing environmental conditions, there is little reason to believe that effectiveness can be measured by a few isolated, economic criteria. So it might be expected that even in this conception of effectiveness a broad set of criteria is required for its measurement. In a study R. M. Steers indicates that in 17 models for measuring effectiveness 15 criteria were used (Table II).[1]

This information proves that in effectiveness measurement there is more at stake than only growth or market share. P. E. Mott also refers to this

Table II
FREQUENCY OF OCCURRENCE OF EVALUATION CRITERIA IN 17 MODELS OF ORGANIZATIONAL EFFECTIVENESS

Evaluation criteria	*No. of times mentioned* (N = 17)
Adaptability-flexibility	10
Productivity	6
Satisfaction	5
Profitability	3
Resource acquisition	3
Absence of strain	2
Control over environment	2
Development	2
Efficiency	2
Employee retention	2
Growth	2
Integration	2
Open communications	2
Survival	2
All other criteria	1

complexity in his book about organizational effectiveness.[2] He defines effectiveness as the ability of an organization to mobilize its centers of power for action, production, and adaptation. This concept of effectiveness belongs clearly to the aforementioned first approach of effectiveness, because of its focus on a self-generated organizational goal.

A second approach of effectiveness can be found in the stakeholders view. In this view the organization is not considered as a total system with one goal, but as a set of multiple subsystems with multiple goals. In this approach there is no such thing as "the effectiveness of an organization," but the different groups involved have their own concepts of effectiveness: for owners' profitability; employees' income, employment opportunity, and job satisfaction; and consumers' usefulness of products. In this concept, effectiveness is measured by using a different set of criteria for every group involved. Here, measurement of effectiveness is replaced by the indication of an effectiveness profile. This means an extension and broadening of the effectiveness concept. Every organization has its own effectiveness criteria and profile: a different set of effectiveness criteria for every type of organization.

A third approach to effectiveness might come from the societal level. In this concept society at large is considered to be a direct stakeholder and the societal requirements have to be included in the effectiveness orientation of the organization. In this approach the goal of an organization is not only restricted to the liberation and mobilization of human energies but there is no particular emphasis on human performance, which is both goal and test. Above all, there is a constant search for an equilibrium—or a reduction of strain—between the interests of all the groups which are interacting with an organization. This means that new effectiveness criteria have to be added to the aforementioned, such as the degree of noise and nuisance, air and water pollution, and energy usage. In this situation, there is a need for a set of effectiveness criteria adjusted to the goals and functions of each particular organization and related to its societal role.

General conclusions that can be drawn from these approaches to effectiveness of organizations are: There is no single definition of effectiveness. The content differs according to the preferred viewpoint: different sets of criteria for every type of organization, depending on the prevailing circumstances. Many definitions are possible, the broadest perhaps being that the highest level of organizational effectiveness is reached when the organizations maximize their bargaining position and optimize their resource procurement.

What might be a suitable set of criteria for one type of organization might be useless for another type. Profitability and market shares are some of the relevant criteria for profit-oriented business; carefulness and accuracy are more relevant for governmental organizations. The relation of the effectiveness criteria to the goals of the organization prevails, and the existence of one effectiveness model for all types of organizations might be an illusion.

In general, there is a contradiction between the effectiveness criteria. The advantage of a multivariate concept (an effectiveness profile) is that the desired plural approach is realized. On the other hand, one has to accept the contradiction between the criteria, for example, profitability-carefulness versus satisfaction, profitability-carefulness versus flexibility, and profitability-carefulness versus absence of strain.

One must never forget that the content of the notion of effectiveness is ever-changing. The environment is constantly on the move, value systems are continuously changing, and the requirements from relevant stakeholders groups are dynamic. It is therefore impossible to ascertain once and for all the purposes of an organization, just as it is impossible to settle for a long-lasting future the effectiveness criteria as a static instrument to measure the effectiveness of an organization. There exists no stability in the weight of the effectiveness criteria. Sometimes profitability and liquidity are considered more important (in recession periods), sometimes the emphasis is on behavioral aspects (in periods of growth).

In all the situations mentioned previously there is a possible distinction between effectiveness in the short turn, middle run, and long run. What might be effective in the short run (for example, a cut in the expenses for research and development) is generally not effective in the long run. An effectiveness model which comprises short- and long-run considerations does not exist.

It seems logical therefore that it is more important to follow the intrarelations and developments in the factors which influence effectiveness and how they affect the effectiveness criteria than to measure the degree of effectiveness only. Maximization of one of the effectiveness criteria cannot be the ultimate purpose of an organization; the emphasis must be on an optimalization of all the criteria involved, which means a constant search for an equilibrium as responsive as possible to the relevant effectiveness criteria. And those effectiveness criteria must be chosen in relation to the goals of the organization. Effectiveness, according to Amitai Etzioni, has to be described in terms of goal attainment, that is, the capacity of an organization to use its resources successfully toward specific ends.

For the purpose of this article I will define effectiveness as the degree of responsiveness to the needs and requirements of the relevant stakeholders of an organization. This definition is chosen for two considerations. First, I reject the idea that an organization can be considered without its interactions with its own environment. Second, using the concept of stakeholders in the broad sense, it is possible to give concrete form to the needs and requirements of the environment of an organization.

THE EFFECTIVE ORGANIZATION

What is in this perspective of effectiveness of an effective organization? It is possible to differentiate between two levels of activities:

1. The process of defining the goals of an organization attuned to the needs and requirements of the relevant groups of stakeholders
2. The process of structuring and running an organization to achieve those goals

The first process has to do with goal setting (strategy) and the second with goal attainment (operation). By setting criteria to goal attainment (effectiveness criteria) in relation to the ascertained needs and requirements from the relevant stakeholders, it is possible to establish the degree of effectiveness of an organization. This whole process can be described by the following set of questions: What is a good company? What is human in work, needs, and rights? How do we measure progress?

What steps have to be taken to ascertain these effectiveness criteria for an organization? The first is an environmental forecast of the future to make explicit assumptions on which all the organizational plans for marketing, production, finance, and social behavior can be based. An appropriate way to get such an overall environmental analysis is to produce separate views on environmental aspects relevant to the particular organization, which might be called tunnel visions, each dealing with probable developments in distinct spheres. Examples might be studies of international political developments in countries where the organization is operating or will be operating; studies of legal and economic developments in all countries relevant to the organization; studies concerned with environmental issues; studies concerned with basic societal values (such as the degree of respect for rights of others, the emerging opinions about the role of competition, and the developing conceptions about equality in opportunities, rewards, or possessions). In these studies special attention must be given to expected developments within the groups of probable stakeholders, to potential discontinuities, and to consequent effects on strategy and operation of the organization. So the major questions are: which groups will be stakeholders in future, what is their aim and what criteria are they using or proposing, what might be their impact on the organizational activities? Segmented views of the future have to be blended together and can lead to alternative environmental scenarios of different groups of (external) stakeholders.

The second step is a social analysis of the future mainly meant to discover the social trends regarding internal stakeholders groups. What is going on socially, which value systems can be expected in future within the different groups of stakeholders (for example, management, labor unions, clerical employees, production workers), what criteria for job content and job context (degree of participation, leadership style) will be emphasized, and what might be the effects on the internal structures and decision processes of the organization?

The third step is a technological analysis of the future. Technological developments might have a big impact on organizational activities. New types of raw material can have a devastating effect on markets which the organization is serving; new technologies can open novel opportunities; technological innovations can change the whole operational process, in production as well as in the case of clerical labor (computers). Technology also requires scenarios of the future.

The fourth step is an analysis of alternative organizational goals and strategies to achieve them. The advantage of approaching the organizational goals from such a rich variety of alternative scenarios of environmental, social, and technological developments is that the future organizational problems are considered as a system of interrelated issues and pressures. All problems can be stated in integrated terms; they can be considered in their complexities, interrelations, and relative contradictions, which are very important for profit and nonprofit organizations. There is no piecemeal approach to the organizational problems, no confrontation with one problem at a time; on the contrary, everything is considered in a well-organized and integrated way with emphasis on the stakeholders issues. Before a decision is made about future goals and strategies, it is advisable to evaluate the present strategy. It is not inconceivable that the factual strategy has been different from the one laid down on paper and that in practice another, rather than the intended, goal has been achieved. This can occur for all sorts of reasons: the promotion campaign had more effect on another type of customer than originally intended, the distribution channels were different from the ones proposed. As a result, it might be that another strategy was followed rather than the one intended; that the relation between the goal to be achieved, the intended strategy, and obtained results is less evident than management is inclined to think; and that the factual strengths and weaknesses of the organization deviate from the intended and supposed ones. This can have radical effects on the new goal and strategy formulation, and therefore an analysis of the factual strategy followed in the preceding period is desirable. The result of this fourth step is a formulation of new goals and strategies for the future.

The fifth step is to design an organizational structure to achieve those goals by way of the proposed strategies. In this new structure attention is given to the consequences of the new goal setting and strategies, the influence of new technologies, the desired communication patterns with the stakeholders groups in the environment, and changes in value systems inside and outside the organization. In general, the organizational structure and process is adapted to the challenges that lie ahead, taking into account all the factors which influence effectiveness (technological as well as human). This may cause changes in the style of leadership, the degree of worker participation, the structure of the decision-making process, the construction of job tasks, and so on. Here we touch on problems of management development, a process which will demand increasing attention in future as a result of the accelerating rate of change in society and within organizations.

The sixth step is the identification of the criteria which will be used for effectiveness measurement. It is logical to use for this purpose the stakeholders approach again and to ascertain: (1) which criteria for achievement are used by the different stakeholders groups involved, and (2) which criteria are acceptable for the organization and to what degree they are attainable (and payable). This approach provides the organization with all the relevant effectiveness criteria for the next phase of its existence. It can be reproduced as shown in Figure 2.

Because every organization has its own set of effectiveness criteria, it is impossible to arrange a complete list. Moreover, the problem of effective-

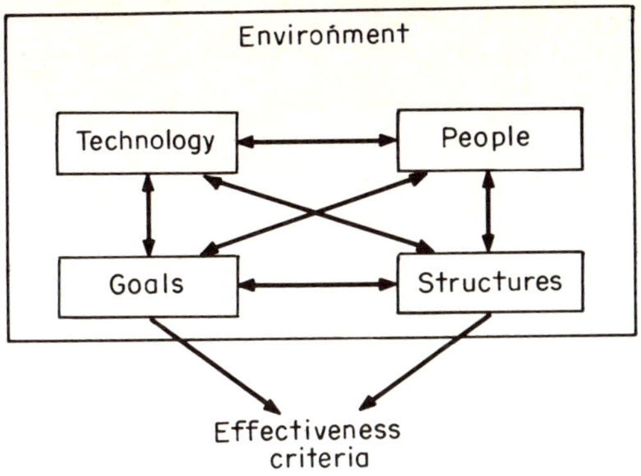

Figure 2 Organization effectiveness criteria.

ness measurement has not yet received enough attention; a lot of thinking and research about measurable criteria has still to be done. Therefore, only a preliminary list of general effectiveness criteria can be made, including a few criteria that are relevant for all types of organizations:

1. *Consumers:*

- Degree of public acceptance of the organization (legitimacy)
- Degree of public acceptance of products or services
- Public opinion about quality of products or services

2. *Government:*

- Degree of compatibility with national goals
- Degree of compatibility with governmental regulations

3. *Activist Groups in the Environment:*

- Degree of pollution
- Degree of noise
- Degree of discrimination
- Opinion about resource usage

4. *Labor Unions:*

- Image of organization (a good place to work)
- Degree of progressiveness
- Contribution to problems of minority workers
- Contribution to problems of disabled workers

5. *Employees:*

- Opinions about job environment
- Opinions about labor conditions
- Opinions about job content
- Opinions about reward system
- Opinions about possibilities for self-realization
- Opinions about promotion system
- Opinions about absence of strain

6. *Management:*

- Level of general organizational results
- Opinion about the prospects of the organization
- Information about level of efficiency
- Information about number of errors (quality control)
- Information about overtime
- Information about number of workers
- Amount of absenteeism
- Amount of turnover of employees
- Degree of adaptability (ability to anticipate problems)
- Degree of flexibility (ability to cope with unpredictable temporary problems)

7. *Shareholders:*

- Profit margins
- Future profitability

Many of these criteria are well known and are relatively easy to measure; some, such as the degree of adaptability or flexibility, are rather difficult to measure; others require appropriate measuring techniques such as workers' opinions about their work, based on a diagnostic survey. In this article no further attention will be given to the virtual measurement techniques of the different effectiveness criteria. From a review of the available literature it appears that much research has still to be done.

Nevertheless, I think this approach opens the way for effectiveness measurement, especially in cases in which a number of comparable organizations are in a competitive situation with each other. An effectiveness profile does not deliver one absolute figure for organizational effectiveness; it delivers relative figures for every criterion, the full meaning of which can be assessed only in those cases in which effectiveness profiles can be compared. The comparison of effectiveness profiles is still a problem in itself; which organization has a higher level of effectiveness: one with a higher customer acceptance compared to one with a higher degree of employee satisfaction? For the time being, I think the results of effectiveness surveys have to be considered with utmost caution. In fact, the (static) relative effectiveness figures are not very important; far more important is their (dynamic) movement: is the degree of effectiveness per criterion improving in the course of time or not?

This indicates that effectiveness surveys have to be done regularly, that is, at least once a year. It seems reasonable to expect that effectiveness measurement requires many learning experiments. Such a measurement system can be set up step by step. One could start with the preliminary definition of criteria for one group of stakeholders, for example, the employee group (a social audit), and try to perfect these criteria and their measurement in the course of time, in view of the encountered particular characteristics of the organization and its employee group. Thereafter the criteria for a second group of stakeholders can be tackled, then a third group, and so on. This may be a long learning process, but it is a rewarding one.

One of the advantages of such a regular effectiveness survey is that it reveals indications about the relevancy of the established goal setting and strategy. A diminishing effectiveness on criteria such as consumer acceptance, governmental appraisal, or labor-union relations is a strong indication that a renewal of the organizational goals is required.

EFFECTIVE MANAGEMENT

In this context of effective organizations, what is an effective management? The answer is: a management building an effective organization in terms of goals, structures, and operations. This requires a management philosophy that is both acceptable and accepted by all groups involved in the organizational process. Which elements have to be included in such a management philosophy? The first element is the creation by management of an organizational climate in which people are motivated to contribute to the formulation and execution of organizational goals. This climate has to be in accordance with the existing and evolving value systems (regarding the degree of participation in decision making, style of leadership, internal promotion policy, conditions of employment), as well as with the technical, economic, and environmental constraints in force. Such a climate is not built up over a short period of time; it requires a long and lasting learning process of all people involved and needs constant full support and attention from management.

The second element is a constant search by management to improve organizational effectiveness. It is the function of management—in charge of goal definition—to integrate various views in a set of goals acceptable to all parties concerned. This synthesizing process consists of a number of components:

- Synthesis of the still soft behavior aspects with hard technical and economic aspects
- Synthesis of work (specialization, rules, procedures, conditions) with well-being (job enrichment, satisfaction, self-realization, absence of strain)
- Synthesis of the intended degree of progressiveness of the organization regarding the humanization of labor with its potential to bear such costs
- Synthesis of the sometimes required autonomy of (top) management with the evolving desire of the work force to participate in the decision-making processes
- Synthesis of the requirement from groups in the environment of the organization with the interests of the different groups working within the organization
- Synthesis of the accelerating degree of risk and uncertainty regarding future developments with the requirements of a sound and reliable planning system
- Synthesis of the notions of (long-run) adaptability and (short-run) flexibility with the formal control system of hierarchy, procedures, and rules in the organization
- Synthesis of the need for centralized integral problem definition and problem solution with the advantages of a decentralized execution of the designed policies
- Synthesis of new scientific developments with the potentials and learning processes of management and employees

In general, one might say that management has to determine continuously the constraints and degrees of freedom for an organization and synthesize them creatively in new strategies and plans. In view of the accelerated degree of uncertainty it seems a wise management policy to indicate regularly only the rough course of actions (broad goals and policies) and to adjust them from time to time in an adaptive or flexible way.

The third element is the regular test of organizational effectiveness. This means two things: testing the effectiveness of the goal setting and testing the effectiveness of the execution. No practical solution of this problem is available yet. The management audit and the social audits are parts of it, but both are still in their infancy, in part because of the lack of effectiveness criteria.

The fourth and last element is the development of an action program for management to tackle the problems of organizational effectiveness, emphasizing the priorities in the effectiveness approach. Much depends on the individual circumstances of each organization. In general, a few guidelines can be mentioned on the basis of the foregoing analysis. For almost every organization a rough time lies ahead: this means a selective course of growth; more emphasis on cost reduction, cost-effectiveness, and cost efficiency; development of organizational scenarios of the future; focus on more decision-oriented communication patterns; attention to political issues. It is not unthinkable that organizations need new structural forms (flexible structures) to cope satisfactorily with their own particular problems. Just as each organization requires its own set of effectiveness criteria, so also it needs its own structure.

CONCLUSIONS

In the past the net result (effectiveness) of an organization was measured with mostly economic criteria. Today and more so in the foreseeable future—within the context of a more human society—the result of an organization will also be measured in terms of social criteria (its contribution to the level of employment), the dialog with its stakeholders groups, and the well-being of society at large. This broadening of the effectiveness-measurement concept has far-reaching consequences. New criteria have to be ascertained and defined (for different types of organizations and different sets of circumstances) and methods for criteria evaluation have to be developed. Up to now we have not been very successful in the shift from economic to social and societal criteria. Although there is no reason yet for despair, organizational effectiveness is indeed a complex and complicated topic.

This new evaluation process of organizational effectiveness has implications on the role of management in all types of organizations. Two opposing trends can be observed: the economic-technical development requires a centralization of decision making to become or to remain effective, whereas the social development requires a decentralization process to realize the urge for participation. These two trends can be synthesized only if management in profit and nonprofit organizations (including government) restricts its activities to the formulation of broad policy lines and grants the maximum degree of freedom for amplification to the operational levels. In my opinion, the central governments in Western Europe in particular are eagerly setting up very detailed, short-run regulations instead of developing broad, long-run policy lines.

The reaction of management to the new challenges can be that of apathy, defense, and offense. Only an offensive reaction, in the form of a creative and imaginative dialog with the different stakeholders groups, can lead to a socially acceptable situation. This may include a discussion about the legitimacy of management: its role in the goal definition of an organization and in the desired participative decision-making structure inside the organization.

In the near future, in which economic growth will not be the predominant factor, the emphasis will shift to the quality of life. That is, good management now (market-oriented) does not necessarily mean good management in the future (societal-oriented). But this improvement of the quality of life will be realized only if we can creatively control the evolving conflict situations: conflicts between East and West and South and North, conflicts between nations, conflicts between stakeholders groups about organizations, and conflicts between people within organizations. Are all parties involved prepared and willing to settle conflicts by negotiations? Do we have and can we manage the necessary techniques for conflict handling? Can people remain healthy under the pressures to come, or will we as a group gradually become (at least in the so-called developed countries) nations of physically and mentally ill people? Can we enjoy the qualities of life and at the same time work to the best of our abilities? Well-being is not a possession; it must be earned anew every day.

These are really big questions. And if we cannot tackle them and do not work strenuously and effectively to earn our well-being, there will be no quality of life to enjoy whatsoever.

REFERENCES

1. R. M. Steers, "Problems in the Measurement of Organizational Effectiveness," *Administrative Science Quarterly*, December 1975, p. 54.

2. See P. E. Mott, *The Characteristics of Effective Organizations* (New York: Harper & Row, 1972).

4

MANAGING THE UNMANAGEABLE

RALPH G. CASO
County Executive,
Nassau County, New York

In the year 1720, a visitor to Florence wrote to a friend that "the people in this city are very heavily taxed. There is an imposition on everything they either wear or eat." The tourist's observation demonstrates that the problems of local government have not changed very much in two and a half centuries, nor, indeed, in as many millennia, since similar laments about the exactions of the tax collector can be read in Latin, Greek, and Egyptian—and they all have a contemporary ring.

What have changed are the size, complexity, and scope of society's problems and society's perception of government's responsibility in solving them. Governments in earlier times levied heavy taxes to maintain armies for defense or conquest and to keep the royal house living in the style to which it had grown accustomed. But government did not concern itself with the average citizen who was poor or sick or hungry. People were on their own, unless they got restive, at which point government might resort to proletarian anodynes like the bread and circuses used by officials in Rome to mollify its masses of urban poor, but rarely to social programs to remedy the causes of urban poverty.

Taxes have been one of mankind's inescapable burdens since the first faint dawn of civilization, and they are as ineluctable a part of civilization as the concept of government itself. Government evolved because society needed it, because when people first began living together in cities instead of living in isolation on farms they needed a social framework, an organization, a structure within which their mutual interests could be safeguarded and their basic institutions forged. People did not consciously determine to create civilization. A committee did not meet one day and decide, "Let's begin civilization." Civilization started slowly, uncertainly, and there were as many aborted civilizations as there were ultimately successful ones. Civilization, by definition, means urban life; and urban life, even in its inchoate and most primitive stages, was infinitely more complex than rural life. Urban life required an agricultural surplus rather than subsistence agriculture, and it required a system for distributing the surplus and commodities crafted by artisans for which the surplus could be bartered. Egyptian civilization could never have been born without taming the Nile, and taming the Nile—as well as food distribution—meant social organization and political administration.

According to A. V. Toynbee, each civilization that has prospered down through the ages owes its prosperity to its success in surmounting the challenges confronting it. How each people faced its challenge—choosing Athenian democracy or Spartan militarism, for example—was a function of its own peculiar genius. And whether the civilization flourished and survived or atrophied and perished was the result of the choices it made.

As society has grown more sophisticated, complicated, and humane, government's role in society has expanded and governmental services have multiplied, along with the taxes to pay for them. Earlier in this century, people were perceived as essentially rational, responsible, and independent. And their rationality, responsibility, and independence dictated that government should be severely limited. It should do no more than was absolutely necessary to preserve the social and economic structure. The laws of economics were laws of iron incised in steel. The economy had an immutable life of its own and moved in acceptable albeit dimly understood cycles. If one of its cycles produced mass unemployment and widespread suffering, it was simply adjusting to market imperatives for which the next cycle would compensate. Government could—and should—do nothing about it.

This hard doctrine assumed that every person was, or ought to be, a rugged individualist. It expressed itself in classic laissez-faire economics. It expressed itself also in a laissez-faire social consciousness which equated poverty with sin, failure with heredity, and felt no moral compulsion to intervene in the economic or social order even to mitigate human suffering. But that view of people—and of government—began yielding in the 1930s to a new view of people as essentially dependent, as helpless products of their environment, a view which led to the New Deal, Fair Deal, and Great Society philosophy of massive intervention with massive amounts of money to solve every social problem. The old laissez-faire ethic, which abandoned individuals to their own devices, lost out to the new interventionist ethic, which believed that human behavior can be modified by curing the social ills that are the "root causes" of antisocial conduct. This view holds that it is not the individual who deserves blame for misconduct or even criminality but society; and since society is at fault, society must and can be changed.

In earlier days, for example, crime was punished—sometimes mildly, often savagely, but always certainly. But the credo that crime was caused by environmental factors rather than by character defects meant that it could no longer be punished, or even deterred by the prospect of punishment. Instead, it has to be treated, much as one might treat measles. The result was all the current institutional and semantic impedimenta of the criminal justice system—correctional institutions instead of jails, psychotherapeutic treatment, job training, halfway houses, probation. Yet, crime continues to grow, and now the pendulum is starting to swing back toward the view that the way to treat criminals is to lock them up and throw away the keys.

The pendulum is also swinging back in other areas. The interventionist ethic led to a proliferation of well-intentioned social programs, at enormous cost, and the public perception is that few of them worked. The dual legacy of the Great Society, of the interventionist ethic, is a nearly confiscatory tax burden borne by local taxpayers to pay for programs imposed on them by higher levels of government, and the mounting frustration of local government officials in trying to manage the unmanageable.

MANAGEABILITY

A few years ago, it was chic to say that New York City was ungovernable. Its asphalt agonies, its teeming poor, its gargantuan problems, its ferociously competing social and economic interests made it the urban maelstrom of the nation. The extent of the city's ultimate unmanageability under the traditional political process is indicated by the fact that it is now being managed by the state and a state-appointed emergency financial control board. Although the facade of home rule has been maintained, executive authority, for all intents and purposes, has passed to the State House and to a group of unelected business persons and bankers who, by law, have superseded the elected city administration.

The passage of power to the state, however, really means that the city is no longer being managed by its municipal labor unions. The relationship of the unions to the city, at least in labor's view, was summed up in a remarkably candid statement by the leader of one of the city's major public employee unions. Discussing the growing political clout of the unions, he said, "We have the power, in a sense, to elect our own boss."

A report by the Temporary Commission on City Finances, issued in June 1976, portrayed how that power had been wielded. The commission said that the aggregate cost of health and welfare benefits for New York City public employees had soared 3369 percent in the past 15 years, rising from \$8.4 million in 1961 to \$291.4 million in 1976. Along with other benefits—paid vacations and leaves, uniform allowances, sabbaticals, and other nonsalary contributions—the city spends approximately two dollars on benefits for every three dollars it spends on base salaries.

The average city worker's base pay is \$16,091 but the total dollars-and-cents cost to the city, when all fringe and leave benefits and pension payments are added in, is $26,707. A teacher has a base pay of $20,350 but costs the city a total of $30,288. A senior clerk has a base pay of $11,150 but costs the city a total of $18,952. A sanitation worker has a base pay of $15,731 but costs the city a total of $28,033. The total labor cost for a police officer is $35,915; for a fire fighter, $35,288; for a social worker, $31,009; for a professor, $45,591; for a police captain, $66,476; for a tree climber and pruner, $27,351.

New York City has paid dearly for its capitulation to labor unions. For years, city administrations regularly rolled over expenses to create the illusion of balanced budgets. Since 1965, they have buried an estimated $2.5 billion in operating expenses in the capital budget at an added interest cost of $250 million. Under the Stabilization Reserve Corporation—established by the state to help the city recover from its debts—the city actually began borrowing money to repay money. On June 30, 1965, the city's short-term debt was $526 million. By February 1975, it had soared to $5.7 billion.

Of course, other factors contributed to New York City's desperate fiscal condition. Two out of every eight city residents are getting some kind of welfare assistance, and the total costs consume 25 percent of the city's $12.5 billion budget, more than the city spends on elementary and secondary education. But a major impetus behind the drive to default was unquestionably runaway union settlements. The result of these settlements was the condition that prompted one congressman, when asked if he would vote to assist New York City, to say that he would not, because a New York City sanitation worker gets paid more than the congressman was paid when he was mayor of Salt Lake City.

Municipal bargaining also led to a staggering growth in the variety and expense of pension programs. Between 1960 and 1970, the State Legislature passed 54 city pension bills. The consequences, as described by the State's Scott Commission, were that retirement and social security contributions cost the city $260.3 million in 1961; $739.9 million in 1972; and $1.3 billion in 1975. An example of the system is that a New York City bus driver or subway worker can retire at age 50, after 20 years on the job, at half his or her pay for the previous 12 months. An employee who gets a lot of overtime during the year before retirement, and most of them do, can retire on as much as $20,000 a year.

It is instructive that the media played a not insignificant role in helping New York City build its fiscal house of cards. While the seeds were being sown that would lead New York City to reap the whirlwind, the media—either through ignorance or complicity—remained silent or, worse yet, abetted and cheered, in the name of social progress, every fiscal gimmick that postponed the inevitable day of reckoning. It was not an unusual role for the media, which enjoy the luxury of indulging in melioristic rhetoric without having to exercise responsibility. Indeed, the media had a field day editorializing in support of newer, more ambitious, and more expensive social experiments while ignoring their current and ultimate costs. The few lonely prophets of disaster were scorned and ridiculed.

If New York City finally fell under a series of trip hammer blows from its unions, it was bludgeoned into the ground by the federal and state mandates under which it must operate, mandates that affect every local government in New York State more acutely than local governments anywhere else in the nation. It remains to be seen whether New York City's efforts, undertaken at the prompting of the federal and state governments, can save it. In the final analysis, its sheer size and the magnitude of its problems are its biggest impediments to effective management.

While size is the trademark of New York City, crazy-quilt diversity is the hallmark of the suburbs. Suburban legend is replete with stories about next-door neighbors who live in separate fire districts, garbage districts, and water districts; who have different telephone exchanges; who have their mail delivered by separate post offices; and whose children go to different school districts. The political boundaries of Suffolk and Nassau Counties—and of the towns, villages, cities, and districts within them—are lines on a map, and it would take a surveyor to figure out where each one runs down the center of some suburban street. The same is true of most of the Eastern seaboard where governmental jurisdictions were created to meet the specific needs of the new communities that seemed to spring up overnight during the post-World War II suburban population explosion only to find themselves soon bumping up against neighboring communities that were growing and spreading out just as fast.

Whereas New York City has absorbed and consolidated powers into a single, albeit unwieldy, political macrostructure, the suburbs have dissipated powers into an almost infinite number and variety of jerry-built microstructures which sometimes overlap and frequently compete. Nassau County, for example, contains 398 separate jurisdictions—including the county itself, 2 cities, 3 towns, 57 school districts, and 64 villages, as well as assorted fire districts, water districts, sewage collection districts, sewage disposal districts, and even one escalator district. All of them were created when the suburbs were being built literally from the ground up and, at the time of its creation, each microstructure met a specific need. But needs change. The need today is for efficiency and economy, for lean governmental structures set up to exercise discrete responsibilities within precisely and specifically delineated parameters.

THE CHALLENGE

Nationwide, there are some 78,000 separate and distinct units of government. New York State has 2362 separate taxing jurisdictions—57 counties, 62 cities, 557 villages, 755 school districts, and 931 towns. Many of these jurisdictions, in turn, contain various authorities and districts. The tristate metropolitan New York region alone has 775 units of government.

During the past 25 years, while total U.S. employment was rising by 44 percent, total state and local government employment rose by 193 percent, nearly tripling in size from 4.1 million workers to 12 million. Total state and local government payrolls rose from $915 million to more than $8.8 billion, an increase of 862 percent. The money to pay for these vast increases in government payroll costs came from taxes. Between 1950 and 1974, total property tax collections went up 550 percent, sales and gross receipts taxes rose 749 percent, and personal income taxes soared 2373 percent.

The rise in federal government civilian employment paralleled the growth in overall U.S. employment, rising from 1.9 million workers in 1950 to 2.7 million in 1975, a growth of only 42 percent. At first glance, the data suggest that the federal government is far more conservative in its employment practices. But the data are misleading.

A complex, heavily urban society such as that of the United States obviously needs a sizable number of public employees to service its needs. But the federal government provides few direct services to its citizens. It does not pick up the garbage, clean the streets, put out fires, police our neighborhoods, or teach our children. Yet, these are the most basic municipal services. Without them, civilized society would be impossible. The federal government provides for national defense. It also legislates a wide variety of social programs which it only partially funds. It requires the states to implement the programs and to share in the funding. And the states, in turn, to a greater or lesser degree, pass on the fiscal burdens to the polities within them.

Many local government departments and agencies exist to satisfy federal and state requirements. Many of the employees on state and local government payrolls are there because federal and state regulations stipulate the staffing ratios for federal and state programs. As a result, a significant part of a local government's operating budget, and the taxes it must levy, is predetermined by federal and state laws. In some counties in New York State, for example, as much as 60 percent of the local budget is being spent on welfare under formulas determined by Washington and Albany. In such circumstances, the capacity of local government executives to manage is severely constricted. Federal and state mandates leave them little latitude for decision making. Worse yet, both higher echelons sometimes cut back their level of support for mandated services, leaving the local government no option but to dig deeper into property and sales tax revenues to make up the difference.

Excluding its community college, part-time and seasonal workers, and people on the county payroll under federal job programs, Nassau County in June 1976 had a total of 16,837 employees. During political campaigns, some candidates have charged that we have more employees than 15 of the states. But we also have a bigger population than 15 of the states. And if we were Nassau City instead of Nassau County, we would be the sixth-ranking American city in population—smaller only than New York, Chicago, Los Angeles, Philadelphia, and Detroit.

In 1975, to curb rising costs and to avoid, if possible, laying people off, I ordered a job freeze. The result has been a steady shrinkage, month by month through attrition, from the 17,439 employees that we had in December 1974 to 16,837 in 1976. Personnel working in the criminal justice system—police department, probation department, district attorney's office, county jail, and courts—account for 36 percent of all county government employees. Another 27 percent work in the county hospital, in the parks system, or on maintaining our extensive road network. Thirteen percent work in our social services department where the ratio of social workers to clients is fixed by state law and where having fewer claims checkers, for example, would result in increased welfare costs.

We have entered what is popularly known as the era of lowered expectations. The fiscal crunch that all local governments are experiencing is forcing us to look more closely at what government does and what it should and should not do. It is obvious that there are essential services that cannot be eliminated. A school without teachers cannot teach. A city without fire fighters will burn down. A community without police will turn into a jungle. Yet, costs must be curtailed. One way of reducing the costs of local government is by attrition and job freeze. We are doing that and it works. Another way is productivity improvement. We tried that, too, and it did not work.

This is not to say that it is impossible, or even difficult, to design more efficient ways to carry out certain functions. Indeed, Nassau County's productivity program, which was unique in the extent to which it involved labor and management cooperation in setting goals and techniques, did succeed in streamlining operations in several departments. But productivity improvement in the sense of doing something faster and with fewer steps has no fiscal impact without a measurable dollar saving. Productivity is not quantifiable as an abstraction. It is quantifiable only in terms of getting more work out of fewer people.

New York City's state-appointed financial control board recognized the myth of unquantifiable productivity when it questioned a labor pact between New York City's Transit Authority and its union. The pact called for a pay increase to be financed out of increased productivity. The board demanded to know how productivity would generate the additional funds. The answer was that it would not, and that it could not, unless people were fired. That may sound hardhearted, and I am not advocating wholesale layoffs to balance local governments' books. I am insisting only, if we are going to talk about productivity improvement, that we should make sure that we are talking about something real. The challenge facing government today is a management problem. It is the problem of reducing costs while maintaining essential services, of allocating available resources most efficiently so that they will do the most good.

PRIORITIES

Few events have so radically shaken the national psyche as the energy crisis of 1974. For the first time, Americans, conditioned to think of their country as a land of boundless plenty, came face to face with the harsh reality that our resources are finite and nonrenewable. Although Americans in general are now behaving as if the crisis had never happened, there is still a lingering residuum of self-doubt. The energy crisis, coupled with political and economic crises, made us turn inward to examine our national goals and assess our ability to reach them.

The practical consequence of this self-examination has been a gradually spreading public debate about priorities. It is not an empty debate, nor is it a new one. In essence, every dispute over how to allocate available resources is a dispute over priorities—whether in the home, business, or government. The housewife makes a judgment on priorities when she decides to buy one item and forgo another. The business person chooses priorities when he or she decides whether to dispense profits as dividends or plow them back into expansion. And the issue of priorities is really the fundamental question on the table when union and government negotiators sit down to begin bargaining.

Nassau County has set up a formal organization to assess its programs and priorities. Its basic purpose is to permit us to anticipate change and plan for it, instead of reacting to it. Our Commission on Priorities was appointed in January 1975 to review and analyze the demographic data contained in a population study and projection prepared by Nassau County Planning Commission.

The population study made clear that the assumptions underlying our allocation of available resources to meet public needs over the past decade are becoming increasingly invalid for the next decade. It made clear that the patterns of the past are no longer an adequate blueprint for the future and that the solutions evolved for yesterday's problems may not work for tomorrow's. The study confirmed that the Nassau County population boom. which had made us the most populous suburban county in the nation, was over. The population that grew 112 percent between 1950 and 1970 had grown by less than one-quarter of 1 percent between 1970 and 1975, and will have grown by less than 1 percent from 1970 to 1985.

But while the size of Nassau's population is stabilizing, its composition and demographic distribution are changing and will continue to change dramatically. Between 1970 and 1975, for example, the size of our school age population had declined by nearly 14 percent. By 1980 it will have dropped another 25 percent. In 1985 there will be 46 percent fewer school age children in Nassau County than there were in 1970. On the other hand, the number of young adults between the ages 20 and 24, those entering the job market for the first time and looking for homes of their own, had grown an astonishing 58 percent since 1970. The 15-year projected growth for this age group is nearly 48 percent.

At the other end of the age spectrum, the number of people over 64 had increased by 15 percent since 1970, will jump another 20 percent by 1980, and by 1985 will have grown 68 percent higher than in 1970. This is a development that has the most serious human and fiscal implications for the county's senior citizen programs, particularly Medicaid, which in 1975 was costing us an estimated $85 million. Finally, and most significantly, the so-called prime taxpayer group, the people who pay all the bills, had grown by only 2 percent between 1970 and 1975. Its projected 15-year growth is 16 percent.

All these drastic changes in the makeup of the county have revenue and funding implications—and all of them are underscored by the fact that Nassau's assessed valuation, its tax base, is unlikely to expand significantly because the county is already 97 percent developed. These data showed that Nassau County was entering the last quarter of this century as a mature, settled suburban municipality, facing realities far different from those that it faced during the burgeoning, bustling fifties and sixties. The problem of the last two decades was to create and pay for the services needed to meet the constantly increasing requirements of a rapidly expanding population. The problem of the next decade is to adjust those services to match new realities. The mandate of the Commission on Priorities is to tell us how to meet the needs of the future out of the finite resources of the future.

The seven-member commission planned a course of action. It set up four subcommittees to inventory existing service delivery systems and facilities for youth and the aging, to study the fiscal impact of county programs on taxpayers, and to analyze the county's economic base. A member of the commission chaired each subcommittee. Each subcommittee included departmental commissioners and agency directors whose departments or agencies had responsibilities for the constituency under study. The subcommittee on the economy consisted of government administrators and representatives from labor, private business, and industry.

Industry's analysis of Nassau County's economy won plaudits as one of the most comprehensive reports ever made on a single county. Although it concluded that Nassau's economy was basically healthy, it stressed our regional interdependence and warned that taxes would continue to rise inexorably over the next decade unless a major reordering of government priorities occurred. Of course, when you are dealing with priorities, you are not dealing with sterile academic theories. You are dealing with people, and human nature inevitably asserts itself.

The report that sparked the most controversy was an inventory of county services. Prepared by the Planning Commission for the subcommittee on taxpayer services, the inventory defined and cataloged more than 2000 services delivered by 40 agencies. As displayed on a chart, the inventory suggested apparent duplication and even triplication of services. The second phase of the subcommittee's task is to determine whether the duplication is real or apparent, a process that is well under way.

The reaction of many people to the services inventory was to protect their own turf, deny that any duplication existed, and take refuge—in many cases, quite legitimately—in state and federal laws. This is not to suggest that government administrators are any more apt to behave that way than anybody else. But most agencies, once created, tend to acquire a life of their own. Each one works within the web of federal and state laws and administrative rules and regulations that affects it. The laws and regulations are often so different from those that affect other agencies that they have little in common. They do not even speak the same language, so there is little or no communication, even when their service constituencies begin to impinge on one another.

One of the very first discoveries made by the Commission on Priorities was that it was impossible to collect comparative data because many agencies had no common data base. Pursuant to whatever rules govern them, some gather statistics by census tracts, some by towns and villages, some by ZIP codes, and some by variously defined catchment areas. The police department does it by precincts. So one of the first executive orders that flowed from the initial deliberations of the Commission on Priorities was a directive that I issued to all agencies and departments to begin reporting data by census tracts so that the commission would have a basis for comparison. It was ironic that one of the commission's first steps actually required duplication, but there was no way to avoid it. The agencies still had to report to their respective federal and state overseers in the prescribed manner, and then had to translate their data into census tracts for the commission's purposes.

One of the major and most immediate obstacles to effectively reordering priorities is that every government service does meet a legitimate need, however circumscribed, and each one has a dual constituency, both of which will resist and oppose change. First, there is the client constituency, those who receive the service, which will vociferously battle any diminution in services even if the need has demonstrably declined. Second, there is the delivery constituency, which is apt to be even more vociferous.

The United States has 12 million people on welfare, for example, and 2 million welfare workers—or one worker for every six recipients. For these welfare workers, continuation and expansion of social services programs mean continued employment, and cutbacks or curtailments of services mean loss of employment. So they will vigorously protest the inhumanity of reducing services, or even of consolidating them to make them more efficient. This is not to suggest that the welfare workers, or other government employees with similar clientele, are insincere. On the contrary, they are quite sincere in their belief that what they do is essential, just as all of us are. But the lesson in this is that any political leader who really means business, who is really determined to challenge the status quo, is immediately going to find himself or herself the target of organized obloquy from self-serving public employee unions and organizations for whom perpetuation of the system means perpetuation of their jobs.

One of the most difficult parts of attempting to restructure government is reasserting managerial authority and responsibility. Management organization spans the spectrum from the very formal to the very informal. The military is perhaps the best example of the very formal. Its members wear their ranks on their arms or on their shoulders and the lines of authority are very clear and very clean. Government is perhaps the best example of the very informal. The federal and state laws that govern the operations of local departments create departmental satrapies, subject to minute federal and state regulations but often, in practice, beyond the effective control of the local chief executive. Authority flows laterally, when it should flow downward from a central administrative locus, with responsibility linked to real authority and its exercise.

THE MICRO PROBLEM

A particularly egregious example of the impediments to effective local management is Medicaid. This is a valid and legitimate program, serving a genuine need and fulfilling valid and legitimate federal and state social policies. But the costs of this federal and state program fall disproportionately on local governments which lack the tax base to support it.

In 1975 I asked our county Health Department to prepare an analysis of county personal health expenditures from 1950 through 1974. The results were shocking. Nassau County's gross costs for delivering health services, or paying to have them delivered by other agencies, rose from $3 million in 1950 to $168 million in 1974—a 24-year increase of more than 5000 percent. Net costs to county taxpayers—costs that have to be paid out of property tax revenues—went up nearly 3000 percent. Obviously, one explanation for this remarkable spurt in health costs was the rapidly increasing county population and the development and expansion of medical and health services necessary to meet its needs. But the other cause was Medicaid.

Between 1950 and 1960, the county's population increased by 94 percent, growing from 673,000 to 1.3 million, while gross health service costs jumped by 266 percent, rising from $3 million to $11 million. Between 1960 and 1966, expenditures nearly doubled, rising from $11 million to $20 million, while the population grew another 7.4 percent. Most of the increase during this period was generated by the expansion of health department clinics and by state-mandated contractual arrangements for delivering mental health services. But the introduction of Medicaid in 1967 nearly doubled our gross costs in a single year—from $20 million to $39 million. Since the state's adoption of Medicaid, the county's gross medical services expenditures have more than quadrupled, rising from $39 million in 1967 to $168 million in 1974 during a period when our population was stabilizing and experiencing only minimal growth.

The sharpest increases in costs came in the welfare area where medical assistance costs rose from $16 million in 1967 to $98 million in 1974, and to $110 million in 1975. In 1975 medical assistance accounted for 57 percent of our total social services department expenditures, with costs running at $9 million a month for medical assistance to the county's poor. Fifty-one percent of our total 1975 medical care budget was spent on nursing homes and health-related facilities caring for 4500 county residents at state-approved rates ranging from $950 a month to $2200 a month per individual. In other words, slightly more than half of all the money we spend on medical assistance was spent on services for only 7 percent of all the people eligible for it—and these people constitute considerably less than 1 percent of the county's total population.

The costs of welfare, which rose 258 percent from 1971 to 1976, follow a similar pattern. Welfare accounts for 33.6 percent of our total county budget. As a spokesman for Nassau County as well as for the New York State County Executives Association and the National Association of Counties, I have long advocated federal takeover of all the costs of welfare. That is not passing the buck but trying to put the buck back where it belongs. The present welfare system, which is such a drain on the resources of local governments, is rife with inequities. It makes about as much sense as would making Alaskans pay a heavier share of the nation's defense budget simply because Alaska is closer to the Soviet Union, or making Floridians pay higher social security taxes than the rest of us simply because so many of the elderly happen to like their climate. Such a rationale would be patently ludicrous if applied to national defense or social security. But that is precisely the rationale that we accept for welfare.

In the years following World War II, there was a massive shift in the national welfare population, a shift that accelerated during the past decade as thousands of indigent people, primarily from the South and Puerto Rico, flocked to urban centers in general and to New York City and its suburbs in particular. Today, New York City, with 3 percent of the nation's overall population, has 10 percent of its welfare population. Nine out of ten heads of welfare households in Mississippi, for example, were born in Mississippi, while two out of every three heads of welfare households in New York State were born somewhere else. Mississippi gets federal reimbursement for 80 percent of its welfare costs and pays each welfare family of four $47.74 a month. New York State pays each welfare family of four $336.67 a month but gets only 50 percent federal reimbursement.

Welfare payments in all the urban states, to which the poor have immigrated, are much higher than in the South, from which the poor have fled. The 1975 average monthly family payment in New York, California, Illinois, Pennsylvania, New Jersey, Rhode Island, Massachusetts, Michigan, and Minnesota was $246. The 1975 average in Alabama, Florida, Georgia, Louisiana, South Carolina, Texas, Mississippi, and Puerto Rico was $91. In New York, the state compounds the problems of local governments. New York is one of only 14 states that require their local governments to pay any part of the nonfederal share of welfare and Medicaid. Among the other 13, only four exact the same 50–50 split that New York does. The other nine require a local contribution ranging from 1 or 2 percent to 40 percent. In the other 36 states, local governments pay nothing.

These numbers give some idea of the staggering dimensions of the management problem faced by local government officials. So much of their available funds are precommitted, by law, to covering federal and state mandated programs that they have little executive discretion in planning their budgets to address local priorities. The federal and state governments tell them what they must spend, and then leave it to them to explain to their taxpayers why taxes are going up.

THE MACRO PROBLEM

In the late 1950s, airline pilots flying the Florida-to-New York route at night began reporting a new phenomenon. They could remember flying the same route in earlier years and seeing a city's lights twinkling beneath them—and then, before the next city—flying over vast stretches of unsettled countryside with the darkness below broken only here and there by the tiny lights from an isolated rural village or farmhouse. But by the late fifties and early sixties, the lights had begun spreading out in all directions, merging into each other and blanketing the empty spaces. Long before the professional statisticians caught up with them, the pilots were reporting that the entire Atlantic seaboard was turning into one gigantic metropolis that sprawled 1000 miles from Florida to New York.

Some theorists seized on the phenomenon, christened it megalopolis, and advocated doing away with all local governments, replacing them with regional supergovernments that would be more efficient and less parochial. It is true that few problems respect political boundaries. Most of them are at least regional in scope—transportation, air and water pollution, and crime are four examples. But dismantling local governments, which are the closest and most responsive to the people, is not the answer.

Regionalism is a valid, indeed critical, approach to solving subnational problems. But it must be done on a voluntary basis, on a cooperative basis, with local units of government pooling their talents and planning capabilities to produce results that will benefit all of them. Regional cooperation is already a reality in the New York metropolitan area where some 500 units of local government from New York State, New Jersey, and Connecticut are participating members of the Metropolitan Regional Council. We are not a regional government. But we do talk to each other, compare problems and solutions, and hold regular closed-circuit TV conferences that enable us to consult on a wide variety of regional issues.

One significant outgrowth of this dialog, in the New York region and elsewhere, is that cities and suburbs no longer see each other as antagonists. They still have different goals which sometimes clash, but they have come to recognize that they have more in common than in conflict. The nation's cities and the mature suburbs that surround them really constitute a new urban metropolity that can gain more for both components by cooperating than either could gain for itself by competing. The congressional and state legislative power shift, reflecting population changes, gives them a political power that they can exploit most effectively by working together—or that they can dissipate by opposing each other.

The director of the U.S. Bureau of Labor Statistics has described New York State as a disaster area for workers. The metropolitan New York City region—including the city itself and Nassau County—has a vital stake in regenerating the region's economy. But there is serious doubt that even the most intensive cooperation among the three states that comprise the region can really cure the region's economic malaise. The entire northeastern part of the United States is suffering the same economic decline as New York because jobs and industry from the Northeast are flowing to the so-called Sunbelt. The lure of the Sunbelt is not only climatological. Its economic attractiveness to business and industry is lower taxes, lower salaries, and right-to-work laws that weaken unions.

The economy is the cornerstone for everything else, including the ability of local governments to pay for essential services. If the economy of the

Northeast collapses, as it shows every sign of doing, governments will collapse too. New York City cannot stanch this drain on its economic resources all alone, nor can Nassau County, nor can both of us together, nor can the more than 700 local governments in the metropolitan region, because it is bigger than all of us. It has to be tackled on a massive scale. It has to be faced by the entire Northeast acting in concert.

A regional effort of such geographic breadth and economic scope is unprecedented in American history, and it will take some hard answers to some hard questions. It will mean developing a new political and economic mind set. It will mean thinking macro instead of micro, thinking ecumenically instead of parochially. It will mean fitting the needs and assets of each political component of the Northeast ecumene into a regional plan encompassing at least nine states.

To launch such an effort, we must all begin by conceding that the Northeast economy, which is the key to giving each local government within it the resources to manage its own problems, cannot be rebuilt county by county, city by city, or even state by state. It has to be done by people willing to make sacrifices, willing to work together, and capable of transcending local biases and prejudices to achieve a long-term goal.

SOLUTIONS

Nassau County is well into its priorities assessment. Now what? We have compiled statistics and written reports that indicate an imperative need for fundamental change. But can we initiate change? Is local government, even with the best intentions, really able to progress beyond describing the problems to doing something about them? Is it able to overcome bureaucratic inertia?

Reordering priorities means not only reorganizing the infrastructure of county government, but triggering similar reorganization in subcounty governments. Each one of the 398 discrete jurisdictions in Nassau County taxes the same people. It will not help the taxpayer to survive if county taxes, for example, go down but school district or town taxes go up. The taxpayer is paying a total tax bill and, when it comes, is often too irate to figure out which municipality or district is charging how much.

County and subcounty governments must begin to allocate responsibilities for specific functions in order to end duplication. Although such a division of labor will require sound planning, and ultimately state legislative sanction, it basically means sitting down at a table and saying, "We'll do this, and you'll do that." Such a procedure will require belt tightening, not only as a rhetorical phrase but as a reality, and not only in finances but in aspirations. It cannot be done unless everybody concerned is ruthlessly and determinedly realistic.

One tool for achieving reductions in local government expenditures is zero-base budgeting or its cousin, the sunset law. Zero-base budgeting was implemented in Nassau County for the first time in planning the 1977 budget. A sunset law is being seriously discussed in Congress and, proving that it is an idea whose time has come, is attracting both conservative and liberal support. Simply put, a sunset law would prescribe the life span of any governmental program, either existing or contemplated. At the end of a stipulated period of time, the program would be reviewed. If it cannot be justified, if it cannot be shown that it meets a genuine need, its sun would set. Zero-base budgeting is essentially the same idea. It means that departments cannot use last year's budget appropriation as a jumping-off point for next year's budget request. Instead, the department has to justify its existence and the existence of every program it administers, as if the department and the programs were being proposed this year for the very first time. That sounds like so obvious an idea that one wonders why it has not always been done. In fact, budget directors normally question department heads very sharply on their budget requests and challenge items they do not consider justified. But zero-base budgeting formalizes the procedure and applies it to every dollar in the budget. The budget director and the department head know what is expected of them.

Local government has two basic problems. One is that taxpayers do not always see what they are paying for and, when they do, sometimes fail to make the connection. When we go into a store to make a purchase, we put down cash and walk out with a commodity. But the connection between May's tax bill and December's snowplow is not always so obvious. The other problem is that the property tax, though basically a fair tax, is carrying a burden it was never intended to carry. It was intended to pay for local municipal services. But now it is also paying for a host of federal and state social programs it simply cannot support. Poverty, for example, is not a local or even a regional or state problem. It is a national problem, and its alleviation should be a national responsibility, not a local one.

Local governments can go only so far in reordering their priorities and redesigning their management structures to achieve greater efficiency. Then they run into the stonewall of federal and state mandates. To achieve maximum efficiency, we have to work toward reordering the interrelationship among the units of our three-tiered federal system, reordering it so it more closely resembles the design originally given it by our Founding Fathers. Federalism means that each level of government has a role to play and responsibilities to meet. But federalism is not working properly when national responsibilities—most notably welfare and health care—and state responsibilities—most notable education—are thrust on local governments and local taxpayers.

PHILOSOPHY OF GOVERNMENT

The most ancient and most basic question of political philosophy is what should government be doing and what should it not be doing. Does government have an obligation to provide recreation facilities and tax-supported higher education? And do the people want these things at the price it will cost? These are fundamental questions of public policy and I do not think the people know the answers. It can be argued that government leaders are elected to lead, and that they should give the answers and act accordingly. But in a democracy leaders cannot lead where the people will not follow.

I am convinced that Americans' perception of the role of government at all levels is undergoing a transformation. The average American citizen, scrabbling to make ends meet, may have little time and even less inclination to study statistical tables and fiscal reports. But the average American is quite capable of reviewing what government has done during his or her lifetime and of drawing up a mental balance sheet; of recognizing that many exorbitantly expensive programs of the past, programs launched with such glowing promises that they would effect miraculous changes, have changed nothing. The average American does not object to helping the poor, but wants the money spent on poverty to go to the poor, not to the poverty "apparat"; wants government reduced in size and ambition; wants government better managed; wants tax dollars to be well spent, not wasted. The American people have always been characterized by their sense of compassion and their passion for efficiency. They want both in government, and they want them balanced.

I do not know how long it will take for America's changing view of itself and its government to come into sharp focus. But out of our current national introspection, the people will eventually decide whether less is better, or whether less is simply less.

5

SOME FUNDAMENTAL TRENDS AFFECTING MANAGEMENT IN THE FUTURE

KEITH DAVIS
Professor of Management, Arizona State University

All of us are well aware of the many potential problems facing business and our other institutions during the next decades. A variety of difficulties have appeared on the horizon, and more are sure to come. We are struggling with such problems as consumerism, ecology and environment, business and public ethics, varieties of oppressive controls, protest groups, and assorted other developments. One way to deal with these problems is the fire fighting approach: wait until a problem occurs and then try to do something about it. We may be able to muddle through by fighting fires, but a better approach is to cut through all the details and try to understand the fundamental issues that cause many of these developments. We need to see the big picture to come up with the right answers.

In the following discussion I will focus on certain fundamental developments that are at the root of many of the changes which are taking place. The effects of these developments fan out through the whole society like waves from a large rock thrown into a lake. We need to understand these developments to deal intelligently with the changes they are causing and will cause in the future. As the saying goes, "You cannot solve a problem until you can find it." The best plans that our managers and leaders can make are of no useful value if they attack the wrong problems. Before we can influence our future, we first must understand where we are and what is happening.

There are four fundamental trends that we cannot ignore. Each is important by itself; together they serve as predictors of many substantial, forthcoming changes. There are likely to be significant changes in the ways that business and our other institutions operate, in the activities of our society, in the ways that people live, and in the quality of life. These fundamental trends are identified not with the proposal that this is the way society *ought to go,* but merely that this is the way it appears that society *is going.* It should be understood that we are talking about the future, and the future is often seen darkly. Nevertheless, these long-run trends appear quite evident.

A SERVICE ECONOMY

The first fundamental development is the move toward a service economy. In the 1960s the United States became the world's first service economy. This is not a vague concept, but one with a specific meaning. It means that the majority of labor hours in the economic system became employed in service industries such as retailing, banking, insurance, education, and communication rather than in direct production of material goods such as manufacturing, farming, and construction. Most of our labor is used to provide services rather than goods. The reason is quite simple. Factories, farms, and construction have become so efficient that they no longer require the majority of the labor force to meet our needs. The changes occurred *because* of our success in providing material needs, not because of our failures in this area. Accordingly, labor was released to meet our service needs, which are entirely different types of needs requiring different kinds of work and different ways of life.

Significant Change

At first glance the change to a service economy may not sound important, but it is. Most of the population of the world today still lives in an agrarian economy, meaning that most nations are compelled to use most of their labor force in food production for their people. A moderate number of more advanced nations have an industrial economy in which more labor is invested in material goods industries such as manufacturing and construction. Each type of economy creates a different way of life for its people. For example, it is evident that American society changed dramatically when it moved from an agrarian to an industrial economy in the late 1800s and early 1900s. Factories with large labor forces developed. Other factories developed around them to provide related activities. As a result, jobs tended to concentrate in specific places, and workers deserted the farms for jobs in the large cities that grew around the factories. Cities led to new needs for government services and controls, labor gained power, and a host of other changes developed. Because of the expanded waves from one fundamental development, the way of life of a whole society was substantially altered. The same changed way of life is likely to occur from moving to a service economy.

One fact that makes this change so significant is that, as far as we know, no other nation in history has ever become a service economy. We are the first one. We are moving into uncharted waters. We have no real guidelines learned from the experiences of others, so we must be careful how we handle the situation. Dislocations from a service economy are magnified because the pace of change toward it is moving fast. One analyst states that service workers in the 1970s compose about 60 percent of the labor force, and by 1980 about 70 percent will be in the service area.[1] Very quickly seven workers out of every ten will have moved into service work.

The magnitude of the changes that are happening perhaps can best be understood in terms of the following statement: Most nations have remained agrarian for many centuries, but in one century the United States has moved from an *agrarian* to an *industrial* to a *service* economy. This rapid shift reflects the remarkable capacity of our society to adapt to the needs of its people. Although we cannot predict exactly what will happen in a service economy, the following developments are likely to occur.

Declining Rate of Productivity Growth

One result of the service economy is that the rate of productivity growth is likely to be slower. Productivity could even become stagnant or decline. Productivity growth is not the same as economic growth. Economic growth refers to a net increase in total economic output, and for a number of reasons, primarily environmental, a number of persons want a stable, no-growth economy. However, productivity is a measure of *output* in relation to *input*. It is a measure of how effectively any society uses its resources, regardless of that society's level of economic output. Quite simply, lack of productivity is a measure of how badly a society wastes its existing resources, so practically no one favors less productivity.

There are many reasons for the slower productivity growth of a service economy, but the main one is that service work is labor intensive and difficult to mechanize. The result is that service work generally has low productivity compared with other types of work. For example, though services employed about 60 percent of the labor force in 1975, their output was only 38 percent of the gross national product.[2] Obviously service work was not as productive as other parts of the economy, and because of its labor-intensive nature it is unlikely to be so. As a greater proportion of our labor force enters service work, the evident result will be slower growth in productivity.

As the United States grows more slowly, other nations that are in an agrarian or an industrial economy will have a chance to catch up with the United States in productivity, because productivity growth in these types of economies is easier to accomplish. This means that the gap between the rich and the less rich nations could narrow, though there are many other complex factors involved in this relationship.

More Managers and Supervisors

One requirement of a service economy is more managers and supervisors, particularly at the lower levels. Statistics consistently show that for a number of reasons, particularly its labor-intensive nature, service work has a smaller span of management than industry or agriculture. In effect, this means that more managers are required for each 100 workers in the labor force. This development forecasts a continuing shortage of capable management talent. If the proportion of managers and supervisors increases by just one percentage point during the next decade, such as from 10 to 11 percent of the labor force, close to 1 million more managers and supervisors will be required. These are *new requirements* in addition to all the managers and supervisors required to replace the tens of thousands who retire, die, or leave management. In addition, it is predicted that the labor force will be larger in the next decade, with increases in the neighborhood of 10 million persons. The increases result particularly because of a population bulge of job-eligible persons and the entry of more women into the labor force. Applying current management/labor ratios, this increase in the labor force may require another million managers and supervisors.

When all of the foregoing influences are added together, the result is likely to be a massive shortage of capable management talent for operating the society. Unless we put much more effort into supervisory and management development than we have in the past, it is unlikely that we can prepare needed competent managers in the time we have. As management shortages intensify, existing managers will be overloaded and there will be raiding by other employers. There will be more competition for managers and more mobility among them. To offset these developments, organizations will need to recruit capable managerial talent more widely from minorities, women, community college graduates, and younger persons.

More White-collar Workers

Another requirement of the service economy is more white-collar workers who are more technically and professionally prepared, rather than blue-collar ones. Most service work tends to be white-collar work, compared with blue-collar work in factories and on farms. A substantial proportion of service work also tends to require technical and professional preparation such as accounting, investment counseling, nursing, teaching, and computer programming. The result is a different kind of labor force working under different conditions. These developments require adjustments on the part of employers if they are to maintain a motivated and stable work force.

An example of employer adjustment is the growing use of variable work schedules that allow white-collar employees the flexibility in work hours that fits their needs. This kind of scheduling is easier to apply in white-collar work than in the traditional factory, such as on an assembly line where all must be present at the same time for the operation to be efficient. Another practice, used mostly for professional and managerial workers, is variable benefit plans which allow compensation packages to fit needs of individual employees. Variable benefit plans are sometimes called cafeteria pay plans, because they allow employees to use an agreed-upon total compensation to select their own individual array of benefits, as they would select food in a cafeteria.

More Decentralized Operations

Service industries tend to be smaller and more decentralized than manufacturing, which typically requires large numbers of people to work on a physical product in one place. Service work tends to decentralize to where the need for service is, such as an accounting office, a legal office, medical office, restaurant, or tennis club. Even though the firm that provides a service may be a large national one such as a short-order restaurant chain or a national firm of accountants, the actual work operation tends to be decentralized to render the service. These smaller operating units provide different working conditions that generally improve employee satisfactions. It is easier to get to know people, establish friendships, and develop satisfying teamwork in smaller operations. Studies comparing large and small operating units doing similar work consistently report higher job satisfaction in the smaller units.[3]

A contributing factor to decentralization is that much service work deals with ideas and information. Breakthroughs in electronic communication have made it easy and economical to transmit information, so operations that work with information such as branch banks can more easily be decentralized to areas where the service is needed.

Increasing Suburban and Rural Living

Decentralization makes possible further moves into suburbs and smaller towns. From an economic and technical point of view, there is no longer much need for the large cities and giant factories that led to increased crowding of people into small pieces of expensive urban real estate. People and their employers may opt for an easier life-style in less crowded areas. A large number of central cities are likely to face problems as people desert them to follow decentralized service jobs that allow an easier life-style. Urban real estate will become less desirable, and its real value could decline in many areas. Employees will have more of an open option regarding the type of life-style they want. In any case, the service economy will lead to a changing character for cities.

There will be other effects of the service economy. The items mentioned provide only a sample of key influences. When all of these are added together, it can be seen that the developing service economy will be a root cause of significant changes throughout the society of the United States.

A KNOWLEDGE SOCIETY

A second key development is that the United States is becoming a knowledge society. A knowledge society is one in which the majority of the labor force performs work based on knowledge rather than on manual skill. People primarily use their intellect rather than their physical strength and skill. Examples are educators, journalists, and accountants. Even the surgeon, who must have a delicate manual skill, is working primarily from a knowledge or intellectual base.[4]

As a capstone to the growing use of knowledge around the world, it is estimated that in the 1970s the United States became the world's first knowledge society. As is the situation with the service economy, no other nation in history has ever become a knowledge society. Again we are without guidelines, but we can be sure that its effects will be felt throughout the whole society. There will be changes in the life-styles of people, their motivation, education, and employer-education interface.

Educated Work Force

In a knowledge society, knowledge rather than manual skill becomes the principal means of serving human needs. To serve these needs, the knowledge society *requires* a large proportion of knowledge-oriented citizens. No longer can it afford the luxury of a small and isolated intellectual elite such as exists in many nations of the world. Knowledge must be widespread because it is the foundation of most of the society's occupations. In economic terms, knowledge becomes the chief human factor in production; however, it is important to realize that a knowledge society is much more than a narrow economic concept. It applies to the whole social system. The change to primary use of the human intellect, rather than physical strength and skill, is one of the most significant developments in the history of civilization.

In a knowledge society colleges and universities are required to expand their facilities because increasing proportions of citizens must attend them to assume a useful role in society. No longer are colleges educating a self-motivated elite comprising 5 or 10 percent of young persons who have natural intellectual interests. Now the colleges have the upper 50 percent, many of whom are less motivated and less prepared for intellectual work. Many of these less-motivated students feel imprisoned in an educational cycle of 14, 16, or more years before they are ready to enter full-time productive work. They biologically mature before they occupationally mature, so they do not have a feeling of social usefulness and accomplishment at the time they mature. (This condition compares with 50 years ago when young people had perhaps 10 years of schooling, allowing them to enter the world of work at about the time they matured.)

The result of these developments is a high degree of psychological dissonance on the part of many students. When they cannot resolve it, there is increasing unrest, frustration, and alienation from the system. Some withdraw from society into their own little circle of alienated friends, while others simply criticize the system, often without constructive proposals. A number of approaches have been helpful in reducing this alienation. One is for students to get some work experience before pursuing advanced education. Another is for students to work part-time while finishing their education, thereby maintaining a feeling of occupational usefulness. Another approach is to develop more career-oriented educational programs, particularly in community colleges. Community colleges have been especially useful in providing more flexible programs fitting individual student needs and providing technical and professional education in a more occupationally oriented environment. A further improvement in both community colleges and universities is to develop instructional systems that are more participative, experiential, and self-motivating.

Interface between Employers and Higher Education

The need for more educated workers in a knowledge society also requires a more active and close interface between employers and higher education. Employers need intellectually prepared workers, and educational institutions need to educate people who can fill useful occupational roles in life. Twenty-five years ago (I was there) educators kept close to their ivory towers and had little interaction with the world of work. Employers kept close to their own practical world and had little to do with educators in their ivory towers. Today there is a much closer interface with mutual attendance at professional meetings, reading the same types of literature, interchanging of people, consulting with each other, and so on.

Essentially, because employers need large numbers of knowledge workers, they have become more dependent on educational institutions. There is also a need for employers to work more closely with university faculties for research projects, consulting, and continuing education of employees. This employer-education relationship is distinctly new.

New Directions in Employee Motivation

Another effect of the knowledge society is to place additional responsibilities on employers for improvement of employee motivation. Intellectual work requires different kinds of motivation than manual work. Normally a person can be persuaded to dig a ditch by the use of authority. The threat of penalty is usually enough to get results. However, it takes more sophisticated motivation to lead a person to do research or write creative advertising copy. Intellectual workers require internal motivation and a more positive motivational environment that appeals to their complex, higher-order needs. If employers of knowledge workers fail to provide this type of environment, their employees will work less effectively. Both the employer and employee will be losers in this ineffective relationship. Society also will lose, because less of its needs will be provided.

A SOCIALLY CONCERNED, HUMANISTIC SOCIETY

A third major development is that the United States and much of the rest of the world are becoming a more socially concerned, humanistic society. Values are being reexamined and many of them are changing. People are becoming more concerned with the broad and complex quality of life, instead of primarily material gain. Managers who are not aware of these developments need to take a crash course to understand what is happening, because it affects all that they do. For example, it affects employee relations, customer relations, public relations, and just about everything else an organization does.

One important reason for emphasis on the quality of life is that economic affluence has provided a minimum satisfaction of material needs, so people are more free to pursue social, ethical, and humanistic needs. This point of view can be explained in terms of the familiar Maslow need hierarchy used in motivation theory. Abraham Maslow proposed that human needs exist in some order of priority so that as basic needs are minimally satisfied, higher-order social needs move in to dominate human expectations. Thus employees become concerned with autonomy and participation at work, and they seek a better quality of life away from work. Similarly, consumers insist on better treatment, and citizens become concerned with the environment. Assuming that lower-order needs are minimally satisfied in many parts of the world, the Maslow thesis suggests that the changes in public expectations are fundamental, far-reaching, and significant. Although the Maslow thesis does not predict exactly what the new public expectations will be, it does predict the direction in which they are moving. That direction is toward a more socially concerned, humanistic society. Some effects of these trends are as follows.

Changes in the Work Ethic

The work ethic is an attitude of mind that makes useful work a central life interest in persons. They derive internal satisfactions from work, and they work willingly because of the satisfactions that work brings. The work ethic has its origins in both religious and secular values. From the religious point of view the work ethic was supported by the Protestant Reformation and by the Puritan way of life in the United States. The religious view of the work ethic holds that talents have been given to people by their Maker for the purpose of use to serve others, so hard work and lack of waste become moral obligations. Individuals become better persons by the act of working, and they also help build a better society to help fulfill God's plan. Secular origins of the work ethic are thought to have arisen from the hard necessities of pioneer life. People had to work hard to stay alive, so they found reasons to glorify work. It was a central fact of their environment, so it naturally became a central life interest for the psychological person. It also was the only possible path toward improvement in the standard of living, so it was seen as a desired ideal by which each generation could contribute something to the generations that followed.

Since most people in the United States now have the basic necessities of life, it might be expected that interest in work would decline as it competes with other activities. In any case, studies of the work ethic show that it has been declining gradually for the last two or more decades. Although work remains a strong interest with people, it is now shared with social, environmental, and humanistic interests. The result is different kinds of motivational problems for managers. Since workers are less internally motivated at work, managers need to build more motivation into jobs. Ideas such as participation, organizational design, teamwork, job enrichment, performance feedback, and Management by Objectives are helping restore a motivational environment to jobs. In this situation, though money continues to be an important reward for work, it tends to play a *relatively* lesser role as more attention is given to human and social values.

Variety in Life-Styles

Another result of the humanistic society is more variety and independence in life-styles as employees and others "try to do their own thing." With regard to employees, loyalty to the organization is harder to build, and turnover tends to increase. Many employees are less interested in their job than they are in their general life-style. When the job conflicts with life-style, the job tends to be sacrificed rather than making a change in life-style. People leave for seemingly insignificant reasons, such as not being allowed an extra day for a weekend vacation at a ski lodge.

Social Accountability

A major result of all this concern with quality of life and humanistic values is a strong emphasis on social accountability for all organizations, public and private. People seem as disillusioned with their public institutions as their private ones. In both they expect a higher standard of ethics, more response to needs of the people, and more concern about how an institution affects quality of life. For example, business was formerly viewed as an independent system that could pursue its own interests as long as it obeyed the law. Now business is considered as a system within a larger social system that it is obligated to serve. Business must be concerned with its *social outputs* as well as its economic outputs.

One area of social accountability, for example, is ecology. Environmental issues have created especially difficult and costly adjustments for all institutions, particularly business. Formerly, air and water were considered free public goods that anyone could use. Almost any amount could be consumed and polluted in the quest for economic efficiency. The result was that costs of pollution were externalized by business, that is, passed on to the community. Now that the quality of life is more important, critics are insisting that business internalize its ecological costs, that is, bear those costs as part of its basic cost structure. Expensive equipment to control pollution is required, thereby adding to costs that are passed on to consumers and adding fuel to inflationary fires. Quality of life such as ecological improvement is economically very costly. Citizens probably do not yet realize how costly these efforts have become, so there may be some easing of pressures when costs are calculated. Nevertheless, long-run attitudes have changed to give more emphasis to the quality of life. Essentially economic efficiency as an end in itself tends to be downgraded when it comes into conflict with the quality of life.

More Governmental Intervention

A particularly difficult result of the socially concerned, humanistic society is more governmental intervention in the lives of organizations and individuals. The situation is loaded with conflicting crosscurrents. Theoretically, a humanistic society is supposed to be much concerned with individual needs and freedoms; but in their haste to achieve its objectives, its proponents have openly welcomed governmental intervention. As a result, freedoms also have been lost. For example, small businesses such as foundries or mines have been forced out of business by governmental intervention in the name of ecology. As a result, owners lost investments and people lost jobs. Consumers find the cost of their automobiles increased by environmental and safety devices. At an individual level, motocycle riders may be required to wear helmets, or an older person who has looked to seniority as a means of security now finds it threatened by equal employment opportunity regulations. In each instance the government has intervened to accomplish social purposes, but in the process some persons have lost long-cherished freedoms.

When people see a problem, it is perhaps a natural attitude to want government to solve it. In many cases, however, there is further erosion of organizational and personal freedoms when this happens. The rapid attitude changes of the humanistic society especially have encouraged governmental intervention. The formerly well-defined public policy of economic efficiency is being replaced by a vague policy of social justice that is imposed before it is adequately defined or has the common support of citizens of the nation. Further, since definitions are rather vague, many interventions are easily subject to the whims and personal prejudices of politicians and government bureaucrats. An immense amount of governmental administrative controls has developed that may be counterproductive and could lead to a public backlash. Nevertheless, for the next two or three decades the humanistic society seems certain to increase governmental intervention and control.

A FAST-CHANGING, UNSTABLE SOCIAL SYSTEM

A fourth major development that in a way overlays all the others is a fast-changing, unstable social system. This kind of social system is one in which a large amount of change is taking place so frequently that most people are able to make only short-term links with their environment. So many changes are happening so fast that many people feel without roots, disoriented, and unable to cope with the situation. The result is that people are placed under considerable stress as they face instability in family life, community life, jobs, and almost everything else. This is truly the Age of Discontinuity that Peter Drucker called it.[5] It is also the source of "future shock" as seen by Alvin Toffler.[6] It is major social revolution in which established ways of doing things and cherished traditions are crumbling so fast that people have inadequate time to develop new traditions to replace the old ones. For example, one study showed that about 40 million persons in the United States change their residences every year. This group amounts to about one-fifth of the total population. Many of them also change their jobs, the schools that their children attend, and the cities where they live. The changes are not just geographical. They are also technological, educational, organizational, and so on. With this large amount of change, the social system is bound to develop difficulties.

Learning Curve for Change

Social science research shows that social systems, whether large or small, operate in various states of harmony among their interacting parts. When there is substantial harmony, the system is in equilibrium. When there is considerable lack of harmony, the system is in disequilibrium. Change introduces tendencies toward disequilibrium. The normal pattern for change is (1) equilibrium before a change, (2) introduction of change, (3) a period of disequilibrium following the change, and (4) a new equilibrium as the system adjusts to new conditions. This typical sequence with change may be called the learning curve for change, because it reflects the substantial problems that change causes in an ongoing social system. There are so many dislocations connected with a change that immediately following its introduction the situation tends to become *worse* rather than better. This condition tends to exist even when a change is considered desirable by those involved in it.

Essentially, the learning curve for change predicts that things are likely to become worse before they get better. Even if the long-run results are likely to be better, the short-run results are unlikely to be so. Change tends to have unfavorable consequences in its early stages, regardless of its favorable consequences eventually.

Increasing Pressures on Management

Since a large amount of change is expected during the next two or three decades, the learning curve for change predicts a large amount of problems in the social system. Managers will be working in a system that places increasing pressures on them as they try to deal with change. Since future conditions cannot be easily predicted, planning will be difficult. Most plans will need to be made with a series of variations built into them so alternative courses of action can be taken as surprise developments occur. Product life cycles may be reduced as new developments, technological and otherwise, quickly outmode a successful product. Dissatisfactions with the organization may be aggravated by dissatisfactions that employees develop from the unstable social system. The foregoing items are merely examples of a multitude of difficulties that organizations are likely to face in an unstable society. Managers could, and should, make this type of list to develop plans for dealing with potential change.

Since change will introduce more instability into the organizational system, the manager who wants to have a successful organization will need to develop various organizational arrangements to respond quickly to change. There will be more use of temporary teams and more transfers across organizational lines. Project management and matrix organizations will be created to respond to new situations the organization is not used to handling. Organizational development, which is a behaviorally oriented program to improve response to change, is likely to become more common rather than less so. Organizational designs will be streamlined to encourage teamwork and allow quicker response at lower levels to whatever changes occur. In sum, management will need to introduce many new practices into its "kit of tools" for dealing with change.

Emphasis on Boundary Mediation Activities

A related development is more emphasis on the boundary mediation activities of managers. A manager's ability to interface with other groups will become primary evidence of managerial competence. People with different values, both inside and outside the organization, will make conflicting demands that must somehow be mediated successfully. For example, environmentalists and economic efficiency advocates cannot both have their way. Some middle ground will be required. Mediation also will be necessary with consumers, minorities, social activists, government bureaucrats, and others. In a similar manner, internal mediation must be achieved between skilled and unskilled workers, engineers and production specialists, and various other groups.

To deal effectively with these complex system relationships, managers will need to extend their outlook beyond their own organization into the world about them. They must be more sophisticated in terms of system understanding and more aware of the role social values play in the operation of systems.

Requirement for Lifelong Learning

Another effect of the unstable society will be requirement for lifelong learning, both for management and employees. The quick pace of change will keep employees in a constant race with job obsolescence. Just as accountants have had to learn computers and lathe operators have had to learn numerically controlled machines, future workers will need to learn new technical knowledge and new occupations. They actually may have two or three occupations during their working life. In this environment of change, continuing education will become the rule rather than the exception. Most persons will be going back to school frequently, either in their employer's training program or in an educational institution. Universities will maintain both credit and noncredit programs as they try to serve the new needs of their employed adult clients. Lifelong learning will be a necessity.

Many professionals will train to become biprofessionals or multiprofessionals. That is, they will prepare themselves in two or more occupations so that they can be more useful in their present jobs and more flexible to move into new jobs as the environment changes. Examples are accounting and law, or engineering and management. Employers will want to encourage part-time education of this type because they never know when it will be needed among their employees.

CONCLUSION

In the next two or three decades four fundamental developments will have a great influence on the social system and, consequently, on the business system and management practice. These developments are:

1. A service economy
2. A knowledge society
3. A socially concerned, humanistic society
4. A fast-changing, unstable social system

No organization will escape the effects of these fundamental developments. Organizations that hope to operate successfully during the next decades will require managers who are better prepared than ever. The managers will need more behavioral, social, political, and system understanding. They, as well as their employees, will face lifelong learning as they attempt to deal constructively with all the changes taking place.

Although some managerial stress and disorientation will occur, managers will have an exciting, challenging job. They will work not for perfection (because that is impossible in an uncertain environment), but for a high batting average. The best of their intellectual abilities will be required to achieve results that meet human expectations. There will be disappointments, but hopefully with capable management there will be more successes. *The future is an opportunity, not a problem.*

REFERENCES

1. Donald E. Law and Cesar L. Pereira, "Word Processing: How to Cut Administrative Costs," *Management Review*, March 1976, p. 28.
2. Law and Pereira, loc. cit.

3. Keith Davis, *Human Behavior at Work,* 5th ed. (New York: McGraw-Hill, 1977) pp. 207–209.

4. Additional comments about a knowledge society may be found in Keith Davis and Robert L. Blomstrom, *Business and Society,* 3d ed. (New York: McGraw-Hill, 1975), pp. 391–395.

5. Peter F. Drucker, *The Age of Discontinuity: Guidelines to Our Changing Society* (New York: Harper & Row, 1968).

6. Alvin Toffler, *Future Shock* (New York: Random House, 1970).

6

THE MANAGEMENT OF COMPLEXITY

JOHN D. DEBUTTS
Chairman and Chief Executive Officer, AT&T

It has become fashionable in recent years to lament that humankind is fast losing control of both institutions and technology and that, like the sorcerer's apprentice, is becoming the slave instead of the master of human inventions. Again and again we are told that the sheer scale and complexity of contemporary institutions give them an irreversible momentum we are powerless to manage.

Can people manage complexity? My own experience with one quite sizable and highly technical enterprise convinces me that the answer is an unqualified "yes." In my observation, three elements have enabled the management of the Bell System to give direction and purpose to an organization that is controlled in scope but which at the same time must match its operations to the unique needs of each community—indeed, each individual—it serves. These elements are organization, technology, and management philosophy.

THINKING IN SYSTEMS

A few years ago—when there were already intimations that the government was once again readying a move to dismember the Bell System—the White House convened a conference on "Business in the 1990s." It was persuasively argued by one of the more farseeing participants that it was time the

United States faced up to the inadequacies of an economy for the most part organized—or, more accurately, fragmented—along product lines and therefore lacking command of a sufficient range of resources to mount the fundamental research and systematic application of its results that would be required for successful delivery of some of society's basic needs in the years ahead. He cited housing, transportation, health care, and a number of other social services as candidates for the kind of structural innovation he recommended. And, agreeably, as a model for his futuristic vision, he cited an organization then a century old, the Bell System.

What attributes of the Bell System's structure commend it as a model for the organization of complex undertakings? First of all, it should be recognized that for all its size the Bell System is no monolith. It is, instead, a unique experiment in decentralization and shared responsibilities. AT&T is the head of an association of regional operating telephone companies, each with its own president and board of directors. And while AT&T owns all of the stock in most of them, the companies themselves decide how best to serve their customers. It is this concept of a nationwide association of companies, each separately managed but all joined in common purpose and sharing common operating procedures, that permits the Bell System to achieve coordination on a national scale at the same time that it remains responsive to the unique needs of each community it serves.

This basic structure—*Fortune* called it "a venture in federalism"—has existed essentially unchanged though by no means unchangeable for the better part of a century. That it has not needed to be greatly modified is to my mind attributable to the creative genius of one man, Theodore N. Vail.

Although not widely known, Theodore N. Vail must nonetheless rank among the half-dozen or so preeminent architects of American enterprise. Vail had two careers with us—the first from 1878 to 1887, when he undertook to organize the infant telephone industry on behalf of its proprietors; the second from 1907, when he was urgently called back to restore a troubled business to financial stability and the regard of its customers, to 1919, when—a year before his death—he relinquished command. In those dozen years, he completed in all of its essentials, and most of its particulars, the model of the enterprise that is today's Bell System. He transformed what had been a loose association of companies into a nationwide system, employing common practices throughout its territories and pursuing common aims. He took the lead in articulating the concept of public regulation under which those companies operate today. And he made it unequivocally clear that service was the standard to which the business had committed itself and for which he expected it to be held publicly accountable.

In short, Vail was an inventor—one of the greatest in the history of a business renowned for invention. And yet no patents bear his name. Nor does legend credit him with any notable talent in technology. Rather did his inventiveness lie in the realm of organization. He invented the Bell System.

By setting service as its goal, Mr. Vail did more for our business than helping to assure its responsiveness to its customers' expectations. Surely he would have set us on a quite different course—and shaped a quite different organization than the one we know today—had he declared our aim to be simply selling telephones. It is because he did not and because he had the vision to define our business' function in terms of it societal purpose—providing communications services—rather than in terms of the hardware it takes to produce it that the Bell System is today in fact a system. Service to us is a managed process spanning the entire spectrum of functions necessary to provide it: from scientific research to product development to hardware manufacture to operation of a nationwide network that will provide—upon demand of any of its users—any one of the 10 million billion possible connections it takes to link any one of the nation's 150 million telephones with any other. Each of these functions—research, manufacture, operations—enhances the performance of the others and all are subordinate to the single aim that all together serve.

Many will recognize what I have just described as the "systems concept," the organizing principle underlying the massive production achievements of World War II. Since then, it has taken us to the moon and back. But long before the phrase was invented, the systems concept was a way of life in our business. The systems concept, or systems engineering, is essentially a method by which one looks at a problem in its totality—objectives and alternatives, inputs and outputs, costs, benefits, sequences, and schedules—and tries to think through early in a project, before serious mistakes and big commitments are made, which approach will work best. Pioneered by the Bell System, it enables us to accomplish five things:

First, to identify needs, opportunities, and limitations so overall goals can be stated and priorities assigned. Second, to appraise alternative solutions and develop measures of their relative costs. Third, to distinguish between what is known and what still needs to be learned. Fourth, on the basis of the foregoing, to select and develop the most promising avenues for action. Fifth, to constantly review or monitor the whole process by which innovations are introduced to the public so the needs of users will be met as fully and promptly as possible. Thus, the systems approach binds our operations together and helps assure that the various units of our business are marching together toward the social goal of providing ever-improving service at reasonable cost.

My purpose here is not to recite the accomplishments of the telephone industry or to praise its famous men. I seek rather to convey my own urgent sense that our obligations to the future cry out for new Vails, for innovations in the structuring of our society's undertakings—in business, government, education, delivery of social services—which reflect the basic social purposes that give rise to them.

Reawakened by our great country's two-hundredth birthday, all of us charged with a measure of leadership responsibility have some thinking through to do in light of the prospect that we may confront—or, as some people say, may already have passed—a turning point in our country's history, a Great Divide in the American condition.

From their first beginnings on the rim of this enormous continent, Americans have continuously—and almost heedlessly—spent their resources as if there were no limit to their supply and no tomorrow to hold us to account for their spending. One does not have to subscribe to the initial projections of the Club of Rome to recognize the clear signals on every side that we are moving from an age of abundance to an age of increasing scarity of material we had hitherto considered in almost limitless supply, from an age that set Growth Unlimited as its goal to an age that may not be altogether without its blessings because it will force us to examine—virtually for the first time—the quality of that growth. The first lesson of this new age is one that we have heard before and never really believed: you can't have everything. It will take some hard thinking—and painful choices—to decide what it is we really want.

I would not presume to prescribe what reshaping of our institutional arrangements this new age will require. Already, however, the energy shortage has served notice on us that it may be an age in which, increasingly, we shall need to scale our ambitions to the limits of available resources. We are also on notice that to extend those limits—not only in the supply of energy and materials but in the larger future our supply of food as well—will call for organization of the processes of discovery on a much more comprehensive scale than has been necessary up to now. And we are on notice that our environment is fragile and its preservation will demand that we scrupulously balance the risks of exploiting it against the purported benefits of doing so. In the face of such prospects, the future calls for people and organizations trained to think in systems—that was Vail's chief heritage to our own industry.

TECHNOLOGY OF MANAGEMENT

The nationwide telephone network is a machine of formidable intricacy. The number of connections it must provide grows geometrically with each additional terminal. It is made up of literally trillions of parts. We think of it, however, as a single mechanism—in effect a very large data processing machine—operable on demand from any one of the more than 150 million input-output terminals, any of which is capable at any moment of selecting one of the 10 million billion possible connections it takes to reach any other.

Given that degree of complexity, it is perhaps small wonder that a few years ago when, for the first time in generations, we began to experience severe service difficulties in a few major metropolitan centers, a number of journalists—more imaginative than informed—were quick to see our troubles as the first signs of an irreversible disorder that, as our operations grew more and more complex, would eventually overwhelm us.

We haven't seen much "fine writing" of this sort in a long time. This can be attributed to our recognition that to manage the complexities technology creates calls for not less technology but more. In particular, we saw in the computer—or computer-based information systems—the means to manage the complexity of our own technology.

Today we use computers for scores of applications. (1) To help us size and locate our switching offices, to optimize the timing of additions to our facilities, and to "write" the specifications for them. (2) To help administer the flow of long-distance communications. A system introduced last year automatically reroutes calls when equipment malfunctions or extra heavy calling threatens congestion. (3) To provide centralized remote maintenance of our electronic switching offices. (4) To monitor pressurization on our cable routes, for inventory control, and for automatic diagnoses of troubles on the trunks connecting central offices. From all of this, it should not be construed that we have abdicated the management of the Bell System to machines—nor could we if we wanted to.

A quarter century ago, it was freely predicted that the computer would represent an enormous force for centralization, that it would remove not only the need but the occasion for decision making from the grass-roots manager and reserve it to a headquarters elite who would be constantly apprised—in real time—of every significant aspect of the business requiring their intervention. That has not happened in my business nor in any business that I know of. I have not observed that thinking machines have reduced the need for human cerebration. Somehow with each passing day we need not less but more of that painful practice.

If the predictions of a quarter century ago had been realized, my job would long since have been transformed and I would be spending my days seated at a console in a dimly lit room lined with displays of data that capture minute by minute the throbbing flow of the Bell System's transactions from coast to coast—the status of our trunks, the traffic offered to each of our central offices, the number of phones we connect and disconnect in every district, and the incidence of absenteeism among our 1 million employees. Furthermore, it would take no more than the push of a button for me to undertake whatever interventions, not previously programmed for self-corrective action, may have been reserved to provide some sense of residual authority.

But for better or worse, life is not like that at all. Instead, I occupy today the same office that Theodore N. Vail occupied 60 years ago. Only my telephone is different and only my Picturephone is new. But the desk is the same and the paneled walls are the same. And much the same, I imagine, is the way I spend my days—conferring, corresponding, pondering, and somehow trying to cope with the maddeningly diverse interests and concerns of that defiantly unprogrammable species, people.

Clearly—at least from the perspective I have outlined—neither the dire consequences nor the utopian promise of the computer's applications have come to pass. What happened to the "revolution" so confidently predicted 25 years ago? The answer is the revolution has already taken place—quietly and utterly without catastrophic disruptions many prophets thought would accompany it—and most people go about their lives and work as if today's world were the same world they grew up in—a little more complicated perhaps and a little faster-paced, but in all of its essentials the same. The fact of the matter is that the computer arts *have* changed our world—for the most part benignly. They have given us the means to manage a degree of complexity that might otherwise have overwhelmed us.

The Bell System's main aim in seeking to apply the computer to our operations is not efficiency; it is freedom. That has been the guiding principle governing all the projects that taken together we call—admittedly with some lack of imagination—BIS, for Business Information System. BIS is actually a "system of systems" that, beginning with the customer's initial request for service, encompasses a spectrum of subsystems, each compatible with all the others, for all the major activities that the customer's requests puts in train—the customer premise facilities it calls for, the assignment of cable pairs, the directory changes, the billing information, and so on.

BIS has been under development since 1967, and on completion a few years from now will represent the largest single application of computer technology outside of government. The brightest promise BIS offers is the freedom of managers to manage, of engineers to engineer, and—the greatest freedom of all—the freedom of people to deal *with* people *as* people. The Bell System has long recognized that, while it numbers its customers in the millions and millions, it serves them one at a time. It is to customer need that the entire BIS program is addressed. Far from dehumanizing our operations, its aim is to scale them to the unique requirements of each individual we serve.

It will be some years yet before our BIS programs are completely deployed across the Bell System. But our experience of them thus far and our sense of their benefits to come provide a sufficient basis for my conviction that far from depersonalizing our society, the computer can exert an enormously civilizing influence on the management of our affairs, the opportunity to personalize our society and its institutions in ways hitherto beyond our scope.

BEYOND TECHNOLOGY

It is uncertainty rather than complexity that challenges the capabilities of business management these days. The Bell System is no more immune to the social ferment of our times than any other institution of what some people choose to call the Establishment. Civil rights, consumerism, environmentalism—all these issues converge on business and converge with special intensity on ours, the nation's largest.

Moreover, in the telephone's centennial year we confronted a serious question as to whether the policies that gave our business purpose and direction over its first 100 years would provide a sufficient guide to its second century. That question came to the fore as a consequence of a series of regulatory decisions that opened more and more of the field of telecommunications to "competitors," who are free to serve selected segments of the market but do not at the same time share the regulated common carriers' obligation to serve the entire public.

This is not the place to debate this issue. However, its emergence confronts telephone management with a degree of uncertainty with respect to the public policies governing our industry matching the uncertainty of its earliest days. Not surprisingly, then, this is for us a time of decision—decisions that for better or worse may prove quite as crucial to the future course of our business as Vail's were between his time and ours.

It is in the nature of decisions, if they are in fact decisions, that the requirement to make them always precludes the availability of sufficient information to assure that among alternatives we choose the right one. In short, decisions are choices made under conditions of uncertainty. It is this uncertainty that gives management its zest—and I would not welcome the day when a triumphant technology might limit our choice to one trajectory. Indeed, I am confident that day will never come.

Nonetheless, not only in our business these days but in a great many others, the risks of being wrong are sufficiently high that no prudent management can neglect to apply as precisely disciplined an approach to the decision-making process as the current state of the management sciences permits. In short, where the zone of uncertainty can be narrowed, it is simply unintelligent to neglect any means of doing so.

It was with this thought in mind that a few years ago I sought the assistance of our own management scientists to help us find ways to extend our corporate planning horizon, thereby giving us greater lead time for decision making. What I hoped they might do—and what they have since done—is to provide a means for tracking the complex interactions of policy and organization with the realities of supply and demand for our services, the cost and availability of capital, and all the other major factors bearing on our future.

As interesting as what they have done is the way they did it. They did *not* return to their cubicles to develop a model that, however elegant it might be, could in the final analysis do no more than extend old trends and impose the patterns of history on a trackless future. Instead, they designed a *participative* process that joined the power of the most advanced management technology to the expertise and insights of their colleagues in general management. In the process they took as much account of the value judgments that affect the future as the presumed inexorabilities of established trends. In effect, what they sought to do was join their science to our art.

While this effort is a relatively new one, already we feel ourselves better equipped than ever before to appraise the integrated economic effects of a wide range of management options, all of them presented to us in language to which we are accustomed and in forms appropriate to our decision style. In short, when we ask "What if . . . ?" we may now look for an answer that takes account not only of immediate consequences but of second-, third-, and fourth-order effects as well.

This planning effort has produced a side benefit that may be as important as the effort itself. It has breached the barriers that have hitherto divided the art of management and the science of management in our business. The wariness of the computer's "black arts" that some in general management may have entertained in the past and the matching wariness with which some management scientists view business persons have altogether dissolved in the course of joining our separate but mutually dependent skills in a common effort. We are merely at the beginning of this new road—far enough along, however, for me to commend it with enthusiasm.

But expertise in the management sciences and experience in the realm of practice, however happily conjoined, can carry us only so far and no farther. Inevitably there comes a time when, the experts having picked up their priorities and departed, management will have to ponder the imponderables, to weigh uncertain consequences against unforeseeable costs, to balance the interests of opposed constituencies and conflicting responsibilities, and finally—through a process nobody has yet managed to quantify—to decide.

I must now consider the most important element of the Bell System's response to the complexities and uncertainties of our times. Yet it is the most difficult to describe. It may, for example, be more mystifying than helpful to report that over recent years we have been steadily moving toward a style of management which is both more participative and more directive. It has been our ability to pursue these apparently contradictory trends that has been the key to our ability to cope with the dilemmas with which the current controversy over national telecommunications policy confront us.

That our style of management has become more directive does not mean we have abandoned the decentralization of authority established by Vail. No less than in his day the Bell telephone companies are autonomous on matters pertaining to their own territories alone. What has changed, however, is that no longer are there many such matters. What in Vail's day was a nation of neighborhoods has become in effect one neighborhood, and there is hardly a significant matter affecting any one of our associated companies that does not have the potential for affecting all of them. As a consequence of this and of the need for consistency of responses to the range of complex policy issues confronting our industry, more and more we must act, not as a confederation of autonomous entities but as one system.

As we have come to recognize the necessity of acting as one system, we have quite deliberately set out to broaden participation in the process of deciding *how* we shall act as a unitary system. To the extent we can, we seek to engage our entire management in discussion of the policy issues confronting us. The key to the success of this venture, is uninhibited, candid communications up, down, and sidewise throughout the organization. Only thus can we develop the common understanding that breeds common conviction and concerted action.

Obviously there are some decisions affecting the business as a whole that can only be made by people with responsibility for the business as a whole. But even on matters of systemwide significance—perhaps I should say *especially* on such matters—AT&T's management is pledged to make no decision, embark on no new course that might affect our associated companies without providing their presidents the opportunity to have their say in the matter.

That opportunity is provided by the frequent meetings of AT&T's officers with the presidents of all Bell companies, twice a year for a full week and, in the interims, almost monthly for a day or so. The spirit of these conferences is difficult to convey. Certainly self-congratulation does not figure very prominently in their agendas. Instead, we view these meetings as occasions for rigorous corporate introspection. Together we look at the organization's shortfalls and consider how they might be amended. In our discussions, no policy is held to be so sacred as to be immune from reexamination and no heresy, assuming it is based on sound information, is so outrageous that it is denied an opportunity to be heard. Not infrequently our first address to a problem finds us of many minds with respect to its solution. Usually—not always but nearly always—when we have talked the matter out, we are of one mind.

In like spirit, the presidents of the Bell companies conduct their own meetings with their own subordinates, and they in turn with theirs. Being human, not all our managers are equally successful. Nor, in all candor, are all of them equally committed to a process that is admittedly not without its elements of risk. Nonetheless we are trying. I am not yet ready to claim unqualified success for this approach to corporate decision making and goal setting. And yet I do sense a gathering commitment to common goals on the part of Bell System management that I can only attribute to the common understanding this process has helped develop. In short, I have no reason, so far, to regret that we ventured on this course. My experience of it confirms my conviction that the key to managing change and complexity lies in establishing a format for decision making that provides both adequate context of continuity and order and sufficient scope for those restless spirits—essential in any really vital organization—whose views, heresies perhaps today, might well become tomorrow's doctrines.

In the foregoing I have sought to convey how one company copes with the mounting technological, social, and political complexities of our times. Certainly I do not propose the Bell System as a model for managing change. However, I do feel that the essential elements of our response to the times may have some application to society at large.

The experience of recent years has taught us that our society urgently needs better ways of proportioning means to ends. What jeopardizes the proportion is the disposition of each segment of society to seek gratification of its aims without regarding its impact on all the others. Surely these are times that call for: (1) a heightened sense of the "interconnectedness of things" and the shaping and reshaping of institutions so we may cope with that interconnectedness rationally, systematically; (2) instead of an unreasoning rejection of technology a recognition that technology itself supplies the means to control the complexities it creates; and (3) a renewal of our confidence in each other. Amidst today's uncertainties, no one person, no one party, no one position commands a range of vision and experience sufficient to prescribe right answers to the diverse and interrelated issues confronting our country and the world. It is not only faith but in some measure experience that tells me the quest for right answers is more likely to be successful to the extent that it is broadly shared. I believe—despite the prophets who say that only a new authoritarianism will see us through the complexities of our times—that our best hope lies in more rather than less individuality and greater rather than less trust in freedom.

Finally, these are times that demand not a dramatic leadership but a reasoning one, a leadership disciplined by experience in matching aims to the resources necessary to achieve them, a leadership unafraid of complexity and confident that complexity can be managed.

7

MANAGING THE FUTURE IS MANAGING IDEAS AND CHANGE

H. E. EKBLOM
Chairman and Chief Executive Officer,
European-American Bank

We are living at a time when one age is dying and the new age is not yet born. . . . To live with sensitivity in this age of limbo indeed requires courage.
***Rollo May*[1]**
The Courage to Create

I would disagree with Rollo May in only one way: the new age has already been born. The problem is growing pains, not birth pains. As a result, there is constant change, conflict, and a struggle to find new human harmony. The only real limit to this new harmony is in the creative mind—in the ability to recognize that accelerating change is the key that must be understood and managed. *This* is management for the future. Before we can understand it, however, we must try to understand, as much as possible, where we are and how we got here.

Economically, there have been two great turning points in human history—two periods of sudden and explosive growth. The first happened about 8000 B.C. in the Middle East, when tribal people first stopped migrating and learned to till the land. Gradually this "agrarian revolution" spread around the world, creating a new concept of land ownership that drastically changed the quality of life and laid a foundation for great civilizations as well as great wars. Arable land became the finite, crucial economic commodity.

From then on, real gross world production per capita practically stood still until 1776. That year, which marks the publication of Adam Smith's *Wealth of Nations*, also traditionally marks the birth of the "industrial revolution" in Holland and England. This second economic revolution produced—is producing—equally dramatic changes but at a far faster, ever-accelerating pace.

Changes that constantly affect and make necessary adjustments in every part of human life.

. . . 200 years ago almost everywhere human beings were comparatively few, poor and at the mercy of the forces of nature, and 200 years from now, we expect, almost everywhere they will be numerous, rich and in control of the forces of nature.[2]

I think the distinguished author Herman Kahn, a forceful optimist, is probably right. Much of the evidence supports his view. No doubt many unexpected problems are waiting, as in the past century, any of which could change the whole picture. Nor will progress be straightforward and smooth, but rather result from the constant ebb and flow of countervailing forces. Nevertheless, we are heading forward. I also believe, based on surrounding evidence, that growing interdependence is part of the future and that it benefits mankind to move prudently this way. Nowhere is this more clearly seen than in banking.

Finally, I submit that our progress will depend even more on the interworking efforts of government, science, and business, that same maligned trio which, despite numerous fumblings, has nevertheless, in the last 200 years, led us to a level of freedom, safety, affluence, and social responsibility unprecedented in human history. The businessperson has been and will remain an unrecognized advance scout, testing the waters, pointing the way. As global interdependence grows, so will the range and scope of knowledge he or she must command at an ever-quickening pace. No easy mandate. I agree with Louis Banks of Harvard when he writes that the "responsive" corporate manager of the future is going to be very busy.[3] But what a fulfilling, dynamic time in which to live.

In *Civilisation*, when explaining the historical background that produced Holland's early seventeenth-century period of great art and, ultimately, the genius of Rembrandt, Kenneth Clark writes, " . . . it goes back to a revolutionary change in thought—the revolution that replaced Divine Authority by experience, experiment and observation. . . . Holland—economically and intellectually—was the first country to profit from the change. When one begins to ask the question 'does it work?' or even, 'does it pay?,' instead of, 'is it God's will?' one gets a new set of answers. . . ."[4] Which is to say, the good, devout burghers of Holland were beginning to seek knowledge of God's will on earth through a very practical, nonarbitrary test: does it work? Based on experience, experiment, and observation, does it pass the test of time?

A free, tolerant society works because it challenges, because it stimulates creativity—not just problem solving, but constant opportunity exploration. Profit works because it enforces an impartial discipline, echoing the voice of no single individual but of the entire marketplace. A society based on free enterprise works because it spreads the greatest benefit of every kind to the greatest number.

This is the "revolutionary change in thought"—what works best *is* best—carried to America throughout the seventeenth and eighteenth centuries by

Dutch and British colonists, all seeking opportunity exploration of a very down-to-earth kind. Early adventurers may have come to stake out greater glory and fortune for a European monarch, the missionaries may have been motivated by dedication to a higher Being, but the colonists—those who settled and built the cities and farms—were above all dedicated to their own individual free enterprise.

It is important to understand this historic base to see clearly the role of business in America, past and future—"business" not in the narrow sense of smokestacks and balance sheets but in its fullest sense, which means risk, enterprise, and, according to the dictionary, "maximum effort" for tangible reward. It's important, too, to understand that while the revolutionary change in thought may have originated in Europe, it sank its deepest roots when protected by the Atlantic Ocean. Here, in a virgin land, there were no long-entrenched, counteracting, medieval-based traditions to overcome and, equally significant, no obvious need to surrender individual freedoms for the sake of mutual defense against neighboring armies.

"The business of America is business." Though his wording appeared rather cold-blooded and his timing proved most unfortunate, Calvin Coolidge was fundamentally correct.[5] From the beginning, America has been an economically motivated society. Human dignity has been equated not with class structure but with the right to work, to prosper by effort. As Alexis de Tocqueville, the visiting French sociologist, noted in 1835, "The love of wealth is therefore to be traced, as either a principal or accessory motive, to the bottom of all that the Americans do; this gives to all their passions a sort of family likeness . . . love of prosperity and spirit of enterprise . . . seem to be the distinctive characteristics of the race."[6]

Most of our great moments in history have been economically inspired, including our first, the Revolutionary War, one of the largest "communication gaps" on record. King George III could not understand why his colonists would rebel against being used to fill England's military coffers; after all, what were colonies established for? His colonists, on the other hand, could not understand why their hard-won prosperity should be handed over to the divine right of a distant king. Clearly, such a proposition did not meet their basic criteria—it did not work—it brought no benefits large enough to outweigh the price. And Americans have been measuring their leadership against the same logic ever since.

This perhaps has been the nation's secret strength. When one keeps asking, "does it work the greatest good for the greatest number?" sooner or later, one must get to the heart of matters. Moreover, such a measuring rod, by its very nature, brings changing answers as the social environment changes. And it demands a democratic form of government for, with all of democracy's admitted imperfections and inefficiencies, no other governmental form yet devised is flexible enough to accommodate the chronic need for change.

There is a continuing cycle. Free enterprise stimulates new technological and economic developments that, in turn, change the social environment in which they evolved. Government must then provide whatever new rules are necessary to protect freedom within the new environment so that free enterprise can go on. This is never an easy process. Many understandably fight to retain their cherished old environment. Few can see its inevitable obsolescence except in retrospect. And the doomsayers are chronically in evidence. But such an ongoing struggle is, in fact, the mark of a healthy living state. Again to quote Tocqueville, " . . . they [the Americans] all consider society as a body in a state of improvement, humanity as a changing scene, in which nothing is, or ought to be, permanent; and they admit that what appears to them today to be good, may be superseded by something better tomorrow."[7]

Once rugged individualism was called for to survive under wilderness conditions, but the same standards used to herald achievement and excellence on a frontier do not necessarily apply when the time has come to build communities. Although full laissez-faire may be the ultimate expression of free enterprise, once commercial interdependence enters the picture, laissez-faire sets the stage for exploitation of the weak—the voiceless—threatening all who could by circumstance become voiceless. It debilitates and impoverishes those who otherwise could contribute much more to the economy, both as producers and consumers. It does not work. For over 100 years a spirit of proud and independent isolationism served America well. But by the second quarter of the twentieth century, two world wars and a great international Depression finally proved that technology had so shrunk the globe, no ocean could any longer hold at bay the concerns of other nations.

Again in *Civilisation*, Kenneth Clark writes, "I believe in genius. . . . Nevertheless, one can't help feeling that the supremely great figures in history—Dante, Michelangelo, Shakespeare, Newton, Goethe—must be to some extent a kind of summation of their times. They are too large, too all-embracing, to have developed in isolation."[8]

So it is, too, I believe, with the genius of a visionary new idea that is "suddenly" put into action at a crucial time by supreme cooperative thought and effort. Such was the case in the late forties when American statesmen enlisted academic and business expertise in launching the European Recovery Program, or "Marshall Plan," under then Secretary of State George C. Marshall—ironically, a career army officer and former chief of staff who won the 1953 Nobel Peace Prize for his brilliant leadership in both integrating and advancing this economic program. Marshall's $15 billion "giveaway," its detractors called it—$15 billion that rebuilt shattered cities in Europe and Asia, halted famine and disease among many desperate peoples, eliminated the possibility of the postwar depression then widely predicted, and launched a period of dynamic economic growth more far-reaching than any ever before known.

"A brilliant job of resuscitation . . . now taken for granted," writes Leonard Silk of *The New York Times*. "In effect, the United States was acting like the big winner in a poker game who knows that unless the poker chips are redistributed, the game is over. . . . The concept of an interdependent world economy was no mere intellectual abstraction, but the basis for shared prosperity and growth."[9]

The Marshall Plan worked. It worked because, within the changed environment, government had once again established a secure launching pad for the entrepreneurial spirit. This time on a global basis. It worked, too, because it unleashed an invading horde. Not plunderers. Persons conditioned instead for over 175 years to think in terms not so much of redividing the existing pie but of finding, building, or devising a bigger, better pie.

American business persons were quick to head overseas in the wake of the Marshall Plan. They traveled on new planes reducing their Atlantic crossing from 4 days to 12 hours. They not only introduced products and sought a widening array of imports, but also established subsidiaries, built plants, and expanded production facilities, all of which pumped more capital into Europe's economy—energizing its productivity, creating jobs, and enlarging U.S. corporate profits simultaneously.

As cold war tensions lessened and the threat of nuclear holocaust became more obviously an unthinkable option by worldwide consensus, early tentative explorations swelled to a tide of U.S. overseas investments. By 1950, direct foreign investment by U.S. firms amounted to $11.8 billion. But from then until 1974, the figure swelled to over $119 billion, a growth rate of 10 percent annually.

Meanwhile, Western European nations were gaining know-how as well. They began adopting the most appropriate of American methods in technology, systems, marketing, and administration. They met the "American challenge" of economic invasion by also moving out beyond their own borders. And they did so in part with the direct encouragement of the United States. Throughout the fifties and sixties, America was a leading proponent of the "open-door" trade and investment policy among all nations. For the most part, the United States found a receptive audience. Recovering nations all too well remembered the bitter lesson of the early thirties, when fierce nationalism brought a domino chain of retaliation policies—competitive devaluations, export subsidies, restricted trade, and capital movements—that virtually destroyed international commerce, plunging everyone far deeper into the worldwide Depression.

By the early sixties, a general lowering of government barriers on trade, travel, payments, and capital flow among the advanced countries—plus improvements in communications and transportation—were producing decided results. Goods, money, people, and ideas streamed back and forth across international borders in accelerating volume. Free world exports, for example, exploded from $77 billion in 1951 to $790 billion by 1975, an average growth rate of 10 percent annually. Since export prices rose at an annual average of only about 3.5 percent, the jump in sheer volume was obviously tremendous.

In 1958 the European Economic Community (Common Market) was born. Six Western European nations agreed to try to wipe out trade, labor, and capital barriers against one another, to gradually equalize their various restrictions on trade with the rest of the world, and to establish a common antitrust policy, thereby eliminating ancient holds on competition. It would mean that Roman shoppers, for example, could bring home quantities of German housewares, French clothing, Dutch dairy products, and Belgian linens at reasonable prices. Above all, it would mean that, through the medium of open exchange, each area would be freed to specialize in what it does best, to use its total resources most efficiently, so that more would be produced and consumed by all.

From the beginning, this massive new free-trade area, as large in population as the United States, was a success overall. Its real GNP (gross national product) has grown over 5 percent annually. Its living standard has soared. In 1958 the nine member nations of today's Common Market had $34 billion in exports. Seventeen years later, they were supplying over one-third of the world's total exports, about $300 billion, almost three times that of the United States. Seldom has there been a more eloquent dramatization of the benefits that can result from an idea that makes sense.

Concurrently, in all developed nations, there evolved what Peter F. Drucker has termed "perhaps the most fruitful social innovation of the century,"[10] the multinational corporation (MNC). A few large global firms had been on the scene for many decades, but before 1940 relatively slow travel at high cost made it difficult for any parent organization to establish a well-integrated, ongoing strategy among far-flung divisions. In addition, trade repression by the various governments was usually reflective of and aided by equally restrictive tactics on the part of business against any foreign competition.

V-E Day signaled the start of a new ball game. Not hundreds but many thousands of firms gradually realized that the scope of their potential "territory" had opened up. American companies especially, as indicated earlier, were building European branch offices almost before the rubble had been cleared. In the beginning, most American businesses considered these offices just that—branches; a nice "colorful" touch for the annual report, no doubt, and valuable, but not a part of the critical main trunk or organizational body. Domestic policy considerations dominated the corporate mind and dictated fundamental management decisions.

Then, by the late fifties, as foreign volume and profits grew, the game rules began changing again. Within 10 more years, MNC no longer stood for a corporation with overseas branches. It meant an organization whose total commitment of resources, brainpower, objectives, strategy, and control worked within a global framework. Geographic distinctions blurred in a jet-age search for additional sources of raw materials, reliable labor, fresh capital, executive talent, and market outlets. The does-it-work measuring rod had begun crisscrossing the world. Through practice, business was developing an entirely new economic philosophy, and economic textbooks were hard pressed to keep up.

By 1970, U.S.-based MNCs, which clearly dominated the world total, were producing almost half of all U.S. exports and sending out 62 percent of the manufactured export products, largely to their own affiliates overseas. One result was an increasing nervousness among European nationalists at the threat of American economic dominance, and at the mushrooming inflation which a continuing dollar inflow was helping to stimulate. Nevertheless, little overt action was taken against American expansion. First, of course, it brought growth and employment. Second, in less than 20 years, the entire Atlantic community had become a far more synergetic unit. Its cohesion went beyond anything within the powers of government to dictate. What were once rival factions had been knit together in large part by private enterprise—by a free exchange of workaday cultures and a commonality of workaday goals.

To paint a picture of total harmony would be ridiculous. Nevertheless, relations among the Western European nations and North America were in marked contrast to those of the twenties and thirties. Robert McNamara, then U.S. Secretary of Defense, commented on the fundamentals involved in his 1966 Montreal address before the American Society of Newspaper Editors. Security is not military hardware—though it may include it. Security is not military force—though it may involve it. . . . Security is development. . . . Military force can help provide law and order—but only to the degree that a basis for law and order already exists in the developing society: A basic willingness on the part of the people to cooperate. The law and order is a shield, behind which the central fact of security—development—can be achieved.[11] International banking, as a result, was undergoing an evolution of its own. Prior to the sixties, few domestic banks competed for loans and deposits on foreign soil. Clients were served abroad primarily through a wide international network of correspondent banks. American bankers shattered this pattern by following their expanding corporate clients overseas. Again, the early trickle became a tide. Short-term claims (mostly loans) on foreigners by U.S. banks swelled from $968 million in 1951 to almost $50 billion by the end of 1975. Also, there was a qualitative shift. International banking no longer meant simply the arm's-length financing of trade; gradually it was coming to mean major investment projects, fuel and mineral explorations. By 1974, about 135 large U.S. banks had more than 700 branches around the world, with assets of over $155 billion. At the same time, American international finance, once the exclusive domain of New York City banks, had spread its U.S. "center" to include such cities as Boston, Chicago, Los Angeles, Philadelphia, and San Francisco. In 1972 Robert Ball wrote in *Fortune:*

> The chief cause of the change in international banking was a quantum leap in the financial requirements and the geographic spread of the great multinational companies. The few hundred giants of world business are outgrowing the banking system that has helped them become what they are. Not only do they now expect the instant mobilization of huge sums in a great variety of currencies; they also expect "one-stop" service for all their banking needs, from loans and issues to foreign exchange and liquidity management, from comprehensive cash plans to advice on mergers and acquisitions.[12]

One inevitable result, begun in Europe, was a growing trend toward consortium banking—groups or teams of large banks, each from a different nation, working together, not merely on a deal-by-deal basis but in every area of international finance and with no one national focus. The only historical parallel that might be drawn is the economic alliance of several independent European nations into a single Common Market. Indeed, each economic phenomenon was interrelated. No one bank, however large or strong, could deliver the combination of geographic spread, mixed currency deposits, and universal financial skills coming into demand.

American banks were interested particularly in consortia for medium-term lending, mostly in Eurodollars, which gave them a chance to join investment (or "merchant") banking activities off limits at home. They led in the development of leasing techniques abroad. They developed sophisticated intelligence systems for supplying customers with economic, financial, and credit information from any part of the world. But their main method of answering the challenge of both MNCs and the burgeoning Eurodollar market was a boom in foreign branch openings. Transnational branching, like consortium banking, meant bankers could move loans and deposits around the continent—or the world—to wherever the need was greatest. And Eurodollars (or Eurocurrency) was becoming a popular form of capital distribution.

Those U.S. trade or investment dollars that stayed on deposit in Europe — "good as gold" at $35 per ounce, according to the 1944 Bretton Woods agreement—began circulating there after the late fifties, when exchange controls were largely removed. The term Eurodollars was coined about 1960 or so, then gradually expanded into another new term, Eurocurrency, meaning any currency on deposit in another country's bank. Both corporate and government treasurers increasingly turned to this unique money market for funding, while it grew at a furious pace, freed of national banking restrictions and fed by inflation as well as by further dollar investments from America. Between 1968 and 1975, the Eurocurrency market ballooned at an average rate of about 30 percent annually; at the end of 1975, over $200 billion (three-fourths of it dollars) was circulating within the system.

During a brief 20 years, we had come full cycle once again: Through such creative inventions as the Marshall Plan and the Common Market, government had built an excellent shelter for the vitality of postwar private enterprise and, consequently, prosperity. Private enterprise, in turn, had stimulated developments in technology and human organizational systems, such as the multinational corporation, international banking structures, and the Eurocurrency market. All these, in turn, were revolutionizing our total environment, strengthening universal interdependence, challenging governments to keep pace by creating the new safeguards that changing circumstances demanded.

In one area, the international monetary system, the challenge has been particularly difficult, particularly critical, nor is it over. But recent events show me what people can accomplish when the chips are down—when a person asks "does it work?", then listens carefully to the answer and keeps listening.

In 1947 the International Monetary Fund (IMF; now over 100 nations strong) was set up as a result of Bretton Woods to promote monetary cooperation, exchange stability, and trade expansion. Each member country contributed according to its economic strength, at least 25 percent in gold or U.S. dollars, the rest in national currency. Each agreed to consult the Fund on all major external monetary problems and not to devalue its currency by more than 1 percent without official sanction. Fund monies were to be used primarily as emergency insurance, to help members adjust their temporary deficits and maintain exchange rate stability without resorting to any measures possibly destructive of international prosperity.

IMF has been an active tool. It helped generate even closer cooperation by the leading central banks, which now share major responsibility for IMF operations. It moved time and again to restore confidence in the face of speculative currency runs on pounds, francs, or dollars. It finally installed a "two-tier" gold system to help defeat private speculators. But in gold itself lay a chronic dilemma.

While IMF founding fathers were agreed that the economic horror of 1931 must never happen again through readoption of an inflexible gold standard, they could not imagine totally abandoning gold or fixed rates of exchange for each currency tied to gold through the dollar. For example, at Bretton Woods, America agreed to back its currency with one ounce of gold for every $35; that is, it would pay out gold accordingly to foreign claimants. Without such an exchange standard, they felt, how could world trade go on? How could nations maintain a balance of trade? Theoretically, if imports increase significantly over exports, gold payments must flow out and, once that happens, a nation's money supply must constrict, forcing a reduction in imports and, conceptually at least, restoration of balance. But this theory, as well as the International Gold Reserve Standard established after World War II, revolved primarily around exports and imports. Both failed to foresee either the coming importance of major capital movements among nations, which would affect payment balances nearly as much as trade, or the rapid accumulation of U.S. dollars in international monetary reserves.

Since 1945, the entire drama of international growth and prosperity had been platformed on a tremendous outflow of U.S. dollars—plus the soundness of those dollars. In the beginning, as we have seen, there was no other way. America knowingly created deficits in its balance of payments through government loans and foreign aid programs, military spending, and the spread of U.S. private investments overseas. In turn, of course, U.S. investors accumulated a huge volume of assets abroad—factories, oil refineries, assembly plants. Plowed-back earnings represented a big part of total new foreign investments each year—about three-fourths by 1970. There was yet another stimulant: at the fixed exchange rate, dollars remained chronically overvalued in relation to gold and other currencies. This made imports, foreign travel, and overseas investments a beautiful bargain for Americans, year after year.

Traditionally, payment deficits should reflect falling exports and rising imports. But the tradition was being broken. Although America's annual export surplus remained sizable, its payments deficit kept growing. Private long-term investments and government spending, not a deteriorating export position, tipped the scales. Obviously, trouble lay ahead. No currency, economists believed, could stay strong indefinitely when its expanding obligations were backed by slowly dissolving gold reserves.

There were repeated attempts to stop the outflow: the interest-equalization tax of 1964, the voluntary credit restraints of 1965, and the foreign investing program of 1968. But when nothing took hold in the way needed, international alarm deepened. America carried the major burden of defense spending for Western nations and of economic aid to the less-developed countries, which all agreed were vital, but America's weakening dollar stood as a planetary sun around which the free world's stability and prosperity revolved. Finally, on August 15, 1971, the unthinkable happened. The United States closed its gold window. No longer could foreign claimants even theoretically turn in their surplus dollars for bullion. Now, officially as well as implicitly, only American economic strength stood behind the soundness of the dollar. Subsequent events had to follow.

On December 18, 1971, at the Smithsonian Institution in Washington, D.C., IMF member nations agreed that the international dollar price of gold should increase to $38.50 per ounce, which in effect devalued the dollar by 8.5 percent. Also, the Bretton Woods fluctuation band of 1 percent was raised to 2.25 percent; in other words, all currencies could fluctuate by that much, plus or minus, from their established exchange rate, according to market demand. This was an attempt to install what is sometimes called the "sliding peg" standard—a form of compromise between the gold reserve standard and freely fluctuating exchange rates. This, too, did not work as planned. America's overheated domestic economy absorbed more and more goods, cutting into the real expansion of U.S. exports.

In March 1973 there was a second formal devaluation, this time at 10 percent, and the United States also announced it would no longer defend a fixed dollar parity. This action triggered a stampede of dollars into West Germany for exchange. At first, German monetary officials paid out marks to all who came knocking, trying to defend their exchange rate, but the effort soon looked like a quick route to inflation. Finally, Germany let the mark float upward. The dollar floated down. The marketplace took over, and the fixed rate system was no more.

Today's international monetary system functions under the standard of fluctuating exchange rates or, more strictly speaking, a "dirty" (or controlled) float. That is, by agreement among major central banks and the IMF, exchange rates can float freely until there appears a serious jeopardy to international stability. Although the picture is still far from clear, "fixed forward pricing" in trade has deflated many fears that floating rates could cripple international commerce by leaving merchants up in the air about future currency values. Meanwhile, the IMF is proceeding with programs to fine-tune the system and demonetize gold. And the dominance of the dollar is being replaced by a more balanced relationship among all Western currencies, a realistic marketplace buoyed by the combined strength of all.

In the short term, world monetary stability stands or falls on monetary confidence. A worldwide confidence crisis—fueled by unexpected crop failures, major cyclical adjustments, a run on commodities, the oil embargo, and unwarranted fear of petrodollar takeovers—produced in large part the unprecedented combination of inflation-recession that gradually engulfed all free nations during 1970–75. Two hard lessons have come out of this experience. Old economic theories no longer always apply; fresh, new ground rules are the order of the day. And where once it was said that an earthquake in Italy could rattle dishes in London, now tremors in the Middle East clearly could rattle them in Ridgewood, New Jersey, and Tokyo as well. Economically, we have all very much become our brother's keeper.

Modern behavioral science teaches that creativity in problem solving is the ability to shift thinking from one obstacle to another rather than finding various ways of overcoming the same obstacle. Near-success can be a fatal trap; persistency quickly turns into obstinacy when one is partially successful or falls just short of the goal. Malaria was not conquered until scientists finally gave up semisuccessful attempts to treat the disease itself and began tracking its source. Unfortunately, through conditioning, and especially in time of crisis, many individuals fall back repeatedly on the same old techniques, pitted against the same established obstacles, no matter how many times both have produced negative results.

Now it can be seen that this was the case in our futile struggle to prop up an enshrined fixed rate system, long after several major changes in the socioeconomic environment had sounded its death knell. Now, we realize, not only exchange rates but monetary management, monetary thinking, must "float"—that is, be flexible rather than fixed or rigid—to function effectively in a world of accelerating change. Nor is our international monetary system the only area in which this lesson has been driven home recently. In domestic economics, too, the management of change represents an ongoing challenge that sometimes stimulates the best in creative thinking and sometimes sends people retreating into false comforts—instinctive but outmoded defenses. For example, despite 25 years of mounting evidence that cooperative interdependence is the keystone to peace and fulfillment in an industrial age, we still find those who, almost out of reflexive action, reach for jingoism and more restrictive controls when trouble, real or imagined, unexpectedly looms near. Such has been the case in many nations—including America—during the past few years.

After World War II, of necessity, Japanese, European, and Latin American companies had concentrated on growth at home—building up a strong capital base, depth of management, and organizational sophistication. But by the late sixties, they were established enough to begin looking eagerly across an ocean at the large, stable American market. After 20 years, suddenly the tables were turning. Entrepreneurial traffic began heading the other way. Although there had always been foreign investments in the United States, some behind long-familiar household names—Good Humor, Kool, Lipton, Nescafe, Pepsodent, and Shell—most foreign money traditionally went into portfolio investment as opposed to direct investment, which implies some degree of control over the business.

During the seventies, however, two things happened to accelerate foreign direct investment: the pull of dollar devaluation and a depressed stock market, which put much of U.S. industry within buying reach for the first time, plus the push of restrictive economic measures that were sweeping many other nations in the aftermath of worldwide recession. There were other attractions, too: avoidance of trade restrictions, relatively plentiful energy and raw materials, high labor productivity, narrowing cost differentials, subsiding inflation, political stability, and a secure place for private capital.

By the end of 1974, direct foreign investment in the United States totaled roughly $26.5 billion—a figure that paled beside the $119 billion in direct U.S. overseas investment. Nevertheless, some Americans were becoming uneasy. The tempo had shifted. Foreign direct investment here was now rising faster than U.S. investment abroad. And foreign banks were following their customers across U.S. borders, even as their American colleagues had done roughly 10 years before. A mid-1975 tally showed 175 foreign banking institutions on U.S. soil, with $57 billion in assets. Their loans alone, the activity of fastest growth, more than doubled in amount from $14 billion at the end of 1972 to $29 billion in June 1975. But, again, these figures looked relatively insignificant beside those for U.S. banking activity overseas.

Nearly half of the foreign companies coming in chose acquisition, even though they usually introduced their own product advantages. Many acquisitions made headlines: Bantam Books, Gimbel Brothers, Baskin Robbins, General Cable, Travelodge, Certain-teed Products, Magnavox, Indian Head. But an equally significant number of corporate "immigrants" built entirely new plants: Cadbury-Schweppes in Pennsylvania, Michelin in South Carolina, BASF Wyandotte in Louisiana, Bic Pen in Connecticut, Baekart in Georgia, Bayer in Texas, Kikkoman soy sauce in Wisconsin, Sony in Alabama as well as California. In general, the response of U.S. business and labor to these new arrivals was a welcoming one, and for good reason. With every new job created, on the average, four more jobs would result among company suppliers and those businesses serving employee families. Also, these foreign-owned plants obviously were not speculative ventures but carefully considered, long-term investments in the strength of the American economy.

Nevertheless, in some areas, old instincts were rising. By 1975, nearly three dozen bills had been introduced in Congress to curb the "threat" of foreign investments. A surprise tender offer by Imetal, the huge French metals combine under Baron Guy de Rothschild, to acquire Copperweld Corporation in Pittsburgh, set off strong repercussions that included "Frenchie Go Home" street demonstrations by American workers, fearful their jobs would be exported, and a court battle which drew nationwide press coverage. Imetal won its battle and, in the process, aroused considerable sympathy, not only from the American press but from their former opponents—the employees and management of Copperweld, who now reportedly are quite happy to share technical knowledge and expanded markets with the Rothschild parent organization.

Gradually the furor subsided before an accumulation of powerful evidence that OPEC (Organization of Petroleum Exporting Countries) nations were not bent on a takeover of American industry and that foreign direct investment brings multiple benefits to the United States—many of the same benefits, in fact, American businesses brought to Europe following World War II. Besides being increased, U.S. jobs have actually been saved on several occasions through acquisition by a foreign multinational that gave the employer-company new competitive strength. Besides adding fresh capital to the economy at a time when it is in increasing demand, foreign research and engineering skills have introduced the U.S. consumer to a growing number of modern products—radial tires, stainless steel razor blades, swing-needle sewing machines, compact cars, contact lenses, jet aircraft engines, Valium, and Librium, to name a few familiar examples. Further, there is clearly no possibility or intent of economic dominance—total foreign investment at the end of 1975 was *less* than 3 percent of total capital investment in this nation.

There is another side to the coin, too. After three decades of intensively promoting—and taking advantage of—an open-door policy for U.S. investment abroad, this nation could not possibly justify closing its door to equal opportunity for foreign investors now. Even putting aside all moral questions of national integrity, any serious attempt to restrict foreign investment on American soil could easily lead to reciprocal action against U.S. investments overseas. This, in turn, would jeopardize U.S. balance of payments and production at home because approximately one-third of all our exports go to the foreign branches or subsidiaries of American companies. In fact, it could be said, the major lesson of the twentieth century is that enlightened self-interest dictates wider, not narrower, open doors everywhere.

This leaves a clear directive for managers of the future. Whether or not they ever cross a U.S. border, they are now entering a worldwide arena. Every year, the chances will increase that each element of their overall responsibility—financing, purchasing, production, distribution, marketing, organizational structure, recruitment, employee relations, management development, public and government relations—all will be affected by global considerations and have global meaning. There will be few standard answers and few areas of standardized conditions. Simultaneously, on a shrinking planet, there can be no safe shrugging off of the human needs and rising expectations that previously have been considered outside the profit responsibility.

We can, then, project a fundamental picture of what the future holds from what our past and present have taught. That picture focuses on two words: accelerating change. There is no choice in this. The first 200 years of the industrial age brought a constant acceleration in change; the next 200 will bring more. We do, however, face one fundamental choice: whether we manage change or let change manage us—whether we cultivate an environment where change is a positive force, at our command, or whether we keep struggling to adapt after the fact.

Fortunately, I see evidence that many are beginning to understand this. Many also are realizing to a greater degree the crucial checks and balances that must exist among government, industry, and science to both energize and harmonize human progress. Greater understanding and interaction *is* happening among leaders in these three critical areas. Greater numbers of managers are assuming individual responsibility for working within the total picture—for keeping an eye not only on the obvious but on that which creates the obvious. In recent years, business has entered more wisely into the ongoing cycle that causes change, which in turn causes progress, if managed correctly.

That's the important point—if managed correctly. To undermanage the reality of change will lose us both our freedom and the hope of a better level of life for all mankind. Imagination, ideas, and hope are still the road map for the future. Nothing can replace them. Peter F. Drucker put it so well when he said:

A little reflection will show that the rate of capital formation, to which economists give so much attention, is a secondary factor. Someone must plan and design the equipment—a conceptual, theoretical, and analytical task—before it can be installed and used. The basic factor in an economy's development must be the rate of brain formation, the rate at which a country produces people with imagination and vision, education, and theoretical and analytical skills.[13]

Managing the future is managing ideas and change. There will be a direct correlation between our success in this and the quality of progress mankind achieves.

REFERENCES

1. Rollo May, *The Courage to Create* (New York: Norton, 1975), p. 1.
2. Herman Kahn, William Brown, and Leon Martel, *The Next 200 Years* (New York: Morrow, 1976), p. 1.
3. Louis Banks, "The Mission of Our Business Society," *Harvard Business Review*, May–June 1975, p. 65.
4. Kenneth Clark, *Civilisation* (New York and Evanston: Harper & Row, 1970), pp. 193, 195.
5. President Calvin Coolidge, speech before the American Society of Newspaper Editors, Jan. 17, 1925.
6. Alexis de Tocqueville, *Democracy in America* (New York: Oxford University Press, 1947), pt. 2, third book, chap. 17.
7. Alexis de Tocqueville, Ibid., pt. 1, chap. 18.
8. Kenneth Clark, op. cit., pp. 201, 203.
9. Leonard Silk, "How the World Economy Got into This Mess," *The New York Times Magazine*, July 28, 1974, pp. 11, 13.
10. Peter F. Drucker, as quoted by Carl Madden, *The Clash of Culture* (Washington: National Planning Association, 1972), p. 51.
11. Robert McNamara, address before the American Society of Newspaper Editors, Montreal, Canada, May 19, 1966.
12. Robert Ball, "International Banking Gets the Team Spirit," *Fortune*, June 1972, pp. 100, 101.
13. Peter F. Drucker, *The Age of Discontinuity* (New York and Evanston: Harper & Row, 1969).

8

TWO DEVELOPMENTS WHICH CHALLENGE MANAGEMENT FOR THE FUTURE

HENRY FORD II
Chairman of the Board,
Ford Motor Company

In free societies, most challenges to the role and legitimacy of business are effectively answered by goods, materials, services, jobs, and economic benefits. This places responsibility for public sanction and endorsement of the enterprise squarely on the performance of its management. But the task has become increasingly complicated by two significant and fairly recent developments affecting the nature, conduct, and objectives of business. The first is the increasing internationalization of business and production. The second is the widening intervention of nonmarket forces and nonbusiness constituencies in business planning, decision making, and operations. These developments are growing concurrently. Both have implications for management at almost every level.

INTERNATIONALIZATION OF BUSINESS

Making business plans on a multinational scale, as many enterprises do today, is acknowledgment not only of unfilled human needs around the world but also of the promising profit and production opportunities that exist outside the United States. The effort to enter or hold foreign markets has resulted in a tenfold increase in direct U.S. investment during the past quarter of a century. Today, this represents more than half of the total estimated stock of all foreign investment in the world, most of which is owned by multinationals. In 1975 U.S. business received over $6.5 billion more in remitted earnings than it sent overseas in direct investment, mostly through multinational companies.

EXPERIENCE OF FORD

The internationalization of business is not new to most large American corporations, including Ford Motor Company. In 1904, only one year after Ford was incorporated in the United States, a subsidiary was established in Canada. Since then, Ford has expanded worldwide with the increased use of motor vehicles and tractors outside North America. As our overseas business grew and the economic climate changed, Ford companies were progressively formed into four regional groupings: Europe, Latin America, the Asia-Pacific area, and most recently the Middle East and Africa. These geographic groups have enabled local Ford affiliates in each region to coordinate their activities, unify their product lines, and pool resources and know-how to reduce costs, meet competition, and benefit from economies of scale. Today, Ford manufactures or assembles its products in 20 countries and sells them in about 185 countries and territories. Of every 100 cars we manufacture, 68 are sold in North America, 22 in Europe, and 10 in the rest of the world.

For Ford, as for other companies, "going overseas" has meant new opportunities and new problems. The new problems represented by the internationalization of business are compounded both by excessive expectations and unfounded suspicions of multinational enterprises. Many expect the multinational to solve problems of massive hunger, poverty, and unfulfillment that are actually greater today, in absolute terms, than they were 25 years ago. In a world which has seen the United Nations add 106 member nations to the original 38 with which it began after World War II, many expect the multinational to be the social instrument for bringing nations with marginal economies and few marketable resources or skills into the twentieth century. In more developed nations, extreme economic nationalism has driven governments to impose unrealistic obstacles in the way of open competition and profit.

Multinational managers can expect to encounter continuing outside pressures and restrictions on their operations that will add unrecoverable costs, upset business plans, and make it difficult to anticipate future markets. Today, for example, they must cope with cost drains that go beyond labor, materials, plant, equipment, or taxes. Five major nonmarket trends that seem likely to dominate the horizon for the foreseeable future are: national legislation, suspicion of multinationals, the codetermination movement, governmental control of business, and the unstable currency exchange.

NATIONAL LEGISLATION

The first nonmarket trend is national legislation. In almost every country, managers find it necessary to conform with new laws and regulations intended to improve the quality of life. As a result, they must meet new legal specifications governing the performance, composition, and use of products; the work environment; and business operations. Frequently such measures are enacted for such laudable public objectives as reducing atmospheric pollution, saving jobs, or strengthening the national economy. But for the individual manager, their immediate impact is more apt to be a test of his or her ability, ingenuity, and cost-consciousness in meeting and maintaining these requirements.

The auto industry offers a striking example of the high cost of some of these nonmarket forces. Ford economists have estimated that federally mandated safety, emission, and damageability standards for cars have cost American car buyers about $25 billion in the past 10 years. There is no doubt that some positive benefits have resulted from these legal requirements. But we cannot ignore the magnitude of such costs or the fact that our customers are our only source of revenue for meeting them. As a result, the process of complying with such standards as efficiently and economically as possible imposes a continuing challenge to the managerial initiative and judgment of every automobile company of every nationality operating in the U.S. market.

SUSPICION OF MULTINATIONALS

Widespread suspicion of the power of multinational corporations underlies a wave of studies by at least eight international bodies and constitutes the second nonmarket force affecting business. Almost uniformly, these proposals hope to regulate the conduct of business management and to control the accountability of the enterprise. Much of the public criticism of multinationals underlying such proposals is based on erroneous generalizations; some of the resulting legal constraints are predicated on less-than-certain public benefits. Both criticisms and constraints are frequently founded on misunderstanding of the legitimate place of business competition and often on the role, record, and objectives of specific companies. Although well-publicized instances of questionable corporate conduct have monopolized recent public attention, too few people realize that these deplorable lapses actually represent a small handful of exceptions compared to the literally millions of legal but unspectacular business transactions conducted daily around the world in mutual trust and to mutual advantage of the participants.

Certainly, some of these proposed nonmarket restraints and guides for business behavior are motivated by legitimate concern. But there is equally no doubt that continuing attention to the negative actions of a relatively few enterprises could translate into additional antibusiness bias and deterrents to business confidence, efficiency, and profit. To maintain a broad sense of business morality and accountability first requires that the managements of the world's business enterprises police themselves by voluntarily setting high standards and examples for their employees to follow and their competitors to emulate.

As a result of other misconceptions, the large, profit-motivated enterprise is at times viewed either as a vehicle primarily for social pioneering at home or for the extension of national policy abroad. Pressure to put either distorted view into practice wastes money and diverts the business from its natural function in the marketplace.

CODETERMINATION MOVEMENT

A third and vital nonmarket trend affecting our business, particularly in Europe, stems from pressures that simply reflect the genuine and deep-seated desire of working men and women to better themselves, to have more leisure, more money, more security, better working conditions, and a greater voice in business decisions affecting their lives. But they also stem from a deep-seated antipathy to private ownership and the profit motive on the part of many workers, politicians, and academicians. As a result of a combination of mistrust and misunderstanding, profits are criticized per se, independent of the investments required to produce them.

One result of these pressures has been growing support for laws requiring equal representation of employees on corporate supervisory boards. In addition, business enterprises are facing proposals for compulsory profit sharing, compulsory transfer of stock ownership to workers and unions, work restructuring, and a steady expansion in the scope of collective bargaining. While most of these proposals have been identified with socialist parties, public support for them stems from a far-broader organized labor constituency. How much more of a role organized European labor will demand in the codetermination of private business policies is still uncertain. But it is clear the issue will remain in the forefront for some time to come.

GOVERNMENTAL CONTROL OF BUSINESS

A fourth nonmarket concern for business is the increased control by national governments of major companies in key industries. A good example is the European automobile industry. The consideration of governmental points of view as part of the corporate planning and programming of many of Ford's European competitors reflects the fact that almost all of these companies are now either state owned or state influenced to a remarkable degree.

Ford manufacturing companies outside the United States are privately owned, essentially autonomous, and usually locally managed. We have always been confident of our ability to operate more efficiently than any business that is not subject to the stringent discipline of the profit motive. But efficiency does not necessarily guarantee success if inefficiency is subsidized by national governments to preserve jobs and generate export income.

UNSTABLE CURRENCY EXCHANGE

The fifth and final nonmarket force on this admittedly incomplete list is the economic uncertainty caused by unstable exchange rates, differing monetary policies, and varying degrees of inflation. Inflation, which has been called "the most politically regressive force at work in the world today," is equally the arch enemy of business planning, rational investment, and profitability.

Perhaps worst of all, inflation erodes consumer confidence and business morale.

Until and unless there is a cohesive attempt to reestablish an international climate of confidence through responsible economic policies, long-term investment will suffer in all but a few countries. The ever-present danger is that political considerations could move monetary authorities toward overly expansionary measures. While such a course might bring short-term recovery, the longer-term consequence would lead to an acceleration of inflation and possibly even another global recession.

There is no doubt that both the internationalization of business and the impact of nonmarket forces pose substantial challenges to large enterprises such as Ford. These challenges involve four aspects of our corporate operations: planning, decision making, organization, and the operating environment.

PLANNING

Planning has always been especially critical in the automobile industry because of the long-lead times and huge investments needed to design and coordinate the production of modern cars and trucks with their tens of thousands of components. These plans must be based in part on assumptions about future conditions, and any element likely to change these assumptions is a challenge to management.

The essence of good planning is minimization of uncertainties. In the past, uncertainty about the direction of the market and technological advances were the two main concerns for those in industry. Today, reflecting the global stresses of nationalism, race, environmental degradation, poverty, ignorance, and inequity, social uncertainty has joined those two traditional management concerns. Needless to say, it has further complicated the task of accurately projecting and planning the business future.

DECISION MAKING

Businessmen and businesswomen cannot afford to forget that almost any decision they make may send ripples into the lives and fortunes of others. Corporate decision makers must consider the social, political, economic, and environmental impacts of their actions and remember that labor unions and governments stand ready to claim a voice in the formulation of their decisions. While many of the concerns expressed by critics are legitimate, few of them—from atmospheric pollution to racial injustice—represent ills that can be either blamed on or cured by the business community alone.

ORGANIZATION

The organization of the multinational company gives it a unique perspective from which to consider resources on a worldwide basis and to make recommendations to all parts of the total enterprise for maximum productivity and profit. This liaison enables individual companies within the multinational organization to respond efficiently to market opportunities. It represents a principal reason for the success and survival of multinational business organizations in an increasingly competitive world market.

Because the multinational is interested in productive results and profits, it can objectively assess natural resources as well as human capabilities and needs in specific geographic areas. On occasion, it is able to develop complementary programs to enable nations with limited domestic resources and low technological skills to make and contribute parts to a common regional product. But even the best organizations and worthwhile programs require continuing cooperation and mutual responsibility from each of the host countries involved.

OPERATING ENVIRONMENT

The modern business enterprise is highly susceptible to abrupt changes in its operating environment, and consequently it is the task of responsible management to anticipate such developments and try to mitigate their adverse effects. The current list of such undesirable possibilities is long and familiar: work stoppages, material shortages, trade restrictions, inflation, boycotts, unfair competition, expropriation, and so on.

The first and most desirable requirement for a hospitable business climate is a state of peace. Not only does this mean the absence of war, it also includes the continuing assurance of civil stability and normal economic activity. Other desirable conditions for business include freedom of choice for consumers, freedom from harassment by government, and broad understanding of the role of business competition and profit in motivating human beings and organizations. By actively promoting and working for these conditions, members of management fulfill not only a valuable social service but a legitimate business interest as well.

From the catalog of business changes and challenges I have outlined, it is evident that enterprises of every size and nationality are entering a new era. Their conduct, loyalties, organization, and decision-making processes—even their traditional freedom to operate at maximum efficiency—are all undergoing public scrutiny and questioning. About the only certainty in their future is that they will continue to face more, if different, problems. Many of these changes and challenges originate in sectors far from the world of business and remote from the site of the factory or showroom they ultimately affect. Unrecognized and unanswered, those that represent abrupt changes in the business environment could become critical problems, particularly for complex, highly structured, interdependent companies.

MODERATING THE THREATS TO EFFICIENCY

How can we best moderate these threats to the efficiency of the multinational concept and the existence of the individual enterprises within it? I can think of at least five ways. First, we must recognize that the world expects more of business than ever before. Because it is unique in organization, resources, and potential, business has no option but to respond. But we must plan our actions thoughtfully and assume no greater burden than we can reasonably carry out.

Second, the private business firm is the best and virtually only medium presently available for doing the job without massive regimentation and loss of freedom of choice. Consequently, we must guard against ill-conceived proposals that could set into motion irreversible processes that, in turn, could seriously impair or destroy business' ability to do the job.

Third, we must counter misinformation and unrealistic expectations about multinationals. We must put the so-called global power and influence of even the largest multinational into proper perspective. The fact remains that although multinationals can do much, they cannot do everything. Nor can they try simultaneously to answer the demands of all their constituencies. Moreover, they can do nothing without at least tacit government approval and public support, no matter where they operate.

Fourth, business should not be afraid of criticism. While it may be too much to expect that it be always objective and factual, even nonobjective criticism may sometimes be helpful in revealing deep-seated attitudes and causes of unhappiness regarding business. Criticism performs a valuable function in refining and setting our self-imposed standards. It gives perspective beyond the immediate moment or the bottom line on the balance sheet. Criticism, in the form of open debate, has given American democracy health and resiliency by ventilating its flaws publicly and making it accountable to those it serves. Even more, criticism forces us to identify possible alternatives and through research and debate to determine their relative advantages and costs.

Fifth, managers at every level must assume the responsibility to demonstrate the validity of the free market system. If the managers of the future can follow these five guidelines—while continuing to produce the goods and services which are the primary objective of their businesses—the years ahead can be filled with great promise. Not only will great strides be made toward meeting the needs of the world's growing population, but the multinational enterprise can also prove itself as an instrument for serving the cause of peace among nations.

9

MANAGEMENT FOR THE FUTURE: A Prognosis and Prescription with Specific Concern for University and Governmental Management

SIGMUND G. GINSBURG
Vice President for Administration and Planning, and Treasurer, Adelphi University

I should like to discuss my views as to management in general and university and governmental management in particular. My time frame is for the period of a decade or a decade and a half. My assumption is of a period without massive wars (and of relatively few, if any, small military actions), natural disasters, deep economic depression, or inflation. Clearly, if any of the basic assumptions are wrong, the time frame prognosis and prescription would be changed and the content could be radically altered.

In regard to general management, I shall comment very briefly in a stream-of-consciousness fashion on questions of: management philosophy, leadership, and style; productivity and performance; technological and scientific advances; social forces and changes; governmental and competitive forces. I shall analyze in greater depth university and governmental management. In essence, there is throughout this article a mingling of prognosis and prescription.

MANAGEMENT PHILOSOPHY, LEADERSHIP, AND STYLE

I foresee a continuing tension between people-oriented and production-oriented management philosophies and styles, with swings of the pendulum at different times for different industries and organizations. The "group executive" concept will be more widespread, with more emphasis on decentralization in general, with guidelines, monitoring, and control by central staff.

Compensation, fringe benefits, recognition, and reward systems for all levels of employees will have to be restudied in light of social forces and concern for productivity and performance. Planning and control will receive increased attention and organizations will tend to be more flexible in regard to organization principles as the use of project managers and coordinators and the blurring of line and staff accelerate. Training, motivation, and assessment evaluation will be key concepts in practice as well as in theory. There will be more emphasis on training our own rather than bringing in outside talent. Emphasis will be increasingly put on executives who demonstrate skills, capabilities, and potential in regard to what I have called the "I-Test": intelligence, individual confidence and self-knowledge, intestinal fortitude, interpersonal relations, innovation, intensity, implementation, identification, influence-inspire.

Given these demands on executives, compensation and reward systems will have to be reviewed to include sabbaticals for training and reenergizing. Management by Objectives, or a modified title for basically the same concept, will become the standard approach with titles, reputations and positions, and stock prices, depending upon the outcome.

Ethics of management will be of increasing concern as an aftereffect of Watergate and the business payoffs of the early and mid-seventies. Investigative reporters will find nongovernmental organizations a juicy target for scrutiny, and the leaks of confidential information so common in government may happen in business and industry, particularly in regard to environmental safety, bribery, and entertainment or executive perquisites issues. Top executives will have to wrestle with issues of the six- or seven-figure bribe, commission or finder's fee, or the $8.98 bottle of liquor at Christmas.

Leadership will have to be concerned with setting a tone, style, and reward system which emphasizes full effort at work and dedication to quality and quantity of effort. Too often we have been satisfied with significantly less than full effort (and have attributed poor results to union pressures, laziness of people, and legislation). We can no longer afford to be satisfied with managers whose brain cells are operating at 50 percent capacity most of the time. This will involve issues of recruitment, selection, training, mobility, and job classifications, standards, and enrichment. Further, because of the various forces at work, management, labor, and government will have to be concerned about featherbedding, laws and regulations which add to costs, procedures and practices that in effect restrict effort and increase costs. From time to time, firms and unions will have to engage in do-or-die battles if either or both sides prove adamant.

Productivity and Performance

Under the various competitive pressures and governmental regulations there will be increased concern for productivity and performance. Analytical tools and techniques will be improved and become standard operating procedure.

A major concern will be for cost-effective ways of performing every work activity, and much of the traditional wisdom concerning division of work, motivation, organization, assembly lines, and work-place layout will be reviewed and replaced. We will have to deal with social forces and their impact on all levels within organizations. This stress on productivity and performance will bring about better ways of measuring and evaluating, training and motivation, assessing performance and potential, with increased concern for job enrichment and retraining and reenergizing the staff.

I note here that the strains on leadership and performance will lead to increased problems of executive "burn out," and means and methods to deal with such problems as taking truly nonworking vacations of different types and frequencies at different times and places; developing hobbies, outside interests, or community and organizational involvements that do not create added or similar tensions or always call for the same kind of activities; and changing the pace and type of work. Lateness, absenteeism, sick leave, and quality and consistency of effort will be more tightly monitored, and better incentive programs will be adopted with union cooperation.

Technological and Scientific Advances

Since my time frame is basically limited to under 15 years, I do not forcsee revolutionary technological advances. However, I would expect the following to be characteristic of management technology of large organizations:

1. Heavy reliance on computerized information systems using program languages readily learned in a few days. The computer, through terminals, is less a giant accounting machine and more an information, planning, data analysis, and data storage facility. The manager will have ready personal access via terminals to computer files on a real-time, on-line basis at work, at home, and, when necessary, while traveling.
2. More sophisticated control and monitoring devices and reports tied in to computer data banks.
3. More use of telephones for computer tie-ins, transmission of copies, and viewing as well as talking. In addition, users will be able to dial special instructions into the system in regard to screening calls, forwarding calls, ringing patterns, asking computers to check on credit cards, and so forth.
4. Improvement and mergence of typewriter and computer, to some degree, for much faster typing and printing. I believe it will also be possible to develop a voice-activated typewriter tied in to dictating equipment, thus eliminating a considerable amount of secretarial help.

Beyond these advances, more time and money will have to be spent by both government and industry in regard to basic and applied research to upgrade and revolutionize technology and scientific processes.

Social Forces and Changes

The next decade and a half will see increased attention to the emerging social forces at work today. In regard to concern for both productivity and people, the following will require greater attention:

- Increased recruitment and opportunities for women, minority groups, and the physically and mentally handicapped
- Migration away from the old central cities to suburban areas and the Sunbelt of America
- Current attitudes about the work ethic
- A somewhat more conservative tone to American politics
- Increased concern for a good, less-pressurized life; recreation; comfort; and leisure
- Increased consumer advocacy in all areas, in regard both to products and services
- A somewhat aging population coupled with a steady-state birthrate, with impact therefore on such matters as health care, mandatory retirement age, social security, and the tax base

Governmental and Competitive Forces

The scope, depth, and consistency of governmental concern, regulation, interference, and encouragement will depend upon the economic outlook, business practices, and political philosophy of the party in power. Governmental action in regard to consumerism, environmental issues, safety, affirmative action, antitrust tariff legislation, and price supports will vary with changing times and needs, but I believe it will not be radically different from the present, except in cases of wide abuse, scandal, or threat to the nation. At a given time and under a particular party, there may be more or less regulation, encouragement, or interference. The one general area of increased governmental action, in my view, will be in the general area of health care, facilities, and research. As for competitive forces, one can anticipate increased competition both within the United States and worldwide, with greater emphasis on survival of the fittest. I foresee a trend toward mergers and conglomerates—in short, the big getting bigger.

UNIVERSITY MANAGEMENT

Universities will be facing a real management crisis during the next decade. Given a decline in the birthrate, we know that the traditional college population will be smaller than in the past. Thus, there will be excess capacity at universities. Furthermore, a significant portion of the undergraduate and graduate students were in college to become elementary and high school teachers or to gain graduate credits and degrees toward promotion in the educational hierarchy or qualification for salary increases. However, there will be fewer elementary and high school students, thus less need for teachers. This will certainly have a decided effect on teacher education programs. Moreover, there will be a decreased number of college and university teaching positions available. The demographics, economy, doing away with the draft, different life-styles, and questioning of the relevance of a college education for life or for a job, all combine to indicate that the strain on universities for student enrollments will be great. Private universities must be concerned both about maintaining or increasing enrollment—the primary source of income for almost all private universities—and about attempting to increase gifts and support from foundations, alumni, parents, and friends. They will also have to be concerned with maintaining federal and state funding for scholarships and institutional aid. In fact, in a time of pressure on state and federal funds, private education will have to ask for more support. At the same time, public universities will increasingly feel the crunch of cutbacks. Thus, the relatively quiet fight between public and private universities for increasingly scarce public resources will become more open. The funding source—federal or state—will become more concerned about evaluating the results of its funding efforts in terms of the economy, efficiency, and effectiveness in the use of its funds. Thus the duplication, proliferation, and waste in various programs at competing public and private institutions will become of more concern.

The financial squeeze of a steady-state enrollment or of only slight increases if one has been highly successful as an entrepreneur, or significant decreases if not, will reach the crisis stage. Up to now universities have not been successful at managing in a fiscal economy crisis atmosphere. They expect or hope for some type of bail out, but as the financial problem hits more and more universities at approximately the same time, such expectations may not be fulfilled. Universities react too slowly to changing times and needs. They find it extremely difficult, if not impossible, to cut programs, staff, salaries, fringe benefits, and various expenditure categories.

Like governmental units, universities appear unable to make cuts and changes in an incremental or evaluationary fashion when danger looms quite clearly ahead. The use of a scalpel over two or three years would solve the problem. However, because of the need of an absolute crisis, for example, the fiscal situation of New York City, one has to wait until disaster has struck before making changes; then, instead of a scalpel, one must use a hatchet. This problem involves questions of confidence, credibility, different reality perceptions, the politics of the situation, the problem of crying "wolf," and openness of communication. Like governmental units, universities believe it can't happen here.

In short, the growth in university costs has outpaced income despite significant tuition increases. This is due to now apparent overbuilding in the sixties; increase in the number of faculty, tenured faculty, and various administrative and support staff; catching up with previously low salaries and fringe benefits and unionization of faculty; long overdue plant maintenance; and escalation in fuel, utilities, and other costs. It should be noted that university salaries have increased appreciably over the past decade. At the same time, some fringe benefits given many years ago in lieu of salary have been kept; but since salaries are now generally adequate, these fringe benefits seem open to question—for example, many institutions give sabbatical leaves every eighth year, with perhaps honorary leaves, and practically iron-clad, lifetime job security with tenure, normally granted after six years of teaching at a university.

Thus, an individual might begin teaching at a university or college at age 25, 26, or 27 and six years later at 31, 32, or 33 have an almost iron-clad guarantee of work until 65, 68, or 70. Finally, in possibly 40 years of work, he or she may receive sabbatical leaves (generally one year at half pay or one semester at full pay) on five occasions plus one honorary leave, thus not working three years at full pay. It should be noted that most faculty put in a long workweek because of teaching, counseling students, committee work, research, or public service activities. However, the system allows an individual to do a minimum of work, perhaps 20 hours or even less a week, if he or she merely comes in to teach classes over a period in which the university is in formal session (classes being taught), approximately 30–32 weeks a year. The above practices and traditions in regard to tenure and sabbaticals can be strongly defended on academic grounds; however, in times of austerity they merit discussion for possible revision.

Futher, universities have not been particularly noted for being well managed. In the next decade and a half, a variety of public and private organizations—boards of trustees, funding sources, legislatures, policymaking groups, and accrediting bodies—will be increasingly concerned with how higher education institutions are being managed. Of interest to outside groups as well as for self-examination purposes are such matters as the organizational and decision-making structure: who has authority to do what among the various decision makers (president, faculty senates, trustees, chief academic officers, or various committees) and how various functions are organized; how responsive the institution is to change—what new programs, majors, courses, student services, and marketing techniques have been initiated, and what has been dropped? How has the institution reached out to new groups of students and established new ways of teaching? How has it fared in regard to faculty collective bargaining? What kind of budget planning and control systems does it have; what are the results and how are resources allocated? How effective, efficient, and economical are the various systems and procedures in all administrative and academic areas? What is the nature of the interaction with the neighboring community? What sense of identity does the institution have and how is it able to get various constituencies to identify with it? What is the institution all about—what are its strengths—what services and programs does it offer and to whom? How well is the institution doing in regard to governmental relations, including such matters as funding for research, scholarships, and institutional aid, and how is it able to comply with the wide range of governmental regulations and reporting requirements? Finally, the question of management style—how does management lead, inspire, communicate, consult, and coordinate? For too long, management or administration has been something of a dirty word in the academic atmosphere. However, if it remains so, it will be the very rare and very lucky university that survives.

Certainly, university administrators will have to understand and respect academic life and traditions. However, they will also have to be more skilled, experienced, and trained in regard to basic management skills and functions such as planning, control, budgeting, and resource allocation directing. In fact, a higher premium will have to be placed on their abilities in regard to the I-Test and managerial skills than experience as a professor.

Of major concern to universities will be the role of the federal government. In recent years, the federal government has issued rules governing institutions to grant equal admissions to minority groups and women; opened confidential files to students; amended tax laws that affect the public's willingness to make charitable contributions to universities; cut certain programs and increased support of others, thus influencing university priorities and imposing requirements which affect faculty hiring and promotion. All of these and other actions have led to a mass of regulation and paperwork and thus increased costs to universities forced to comply. These are due to needs for new staff, the time of many officials, and the subtle cost of increased bureaucratization of educational institutions, as well as the increased time spent on these regulatory matters by faculty, thus reducing time available for teaching, research, and contact with students. Colleges and universities, in associations and individually, will have to be more aggressive in seeking to work with Congress and executive agencies in regard to various federal requirements. Too often, government has considered universities comparable to industrial organizations and simply applied the same laws in the same frequently unsuitable ways. Thus, with regard to existing and new regulations universities must seek to inform and influence the agencies of government as to their particular needs and concerns. Overshadowing all of this will be the role and the power of the federal (and state) government in influencing and controlling the content and administration of education.

The result of the factors described, in my view, is that some universities will certainly fail, others will merge or become state controlled or subsidized (assuming the state has the funds to take over the institution, a rather optimistic assumption). Except for the very few highly prestigious universities with large endowments, survival of the fittest will prevail among universities. Competition, at times cut-throat or cut-price, will also become pronounced. There will be much more emphasis on marketing and advertising, on being creative and innovative, of concern for new markets and new approaches in regard to: *Students*—mature adults, senior citizens, women in general and housewives with grown children returning to the labor market or with small children (with provision made for child care centers), the very bright high school junior or senior, armed forces personnel, prisoners, and public servants such as court, police, fire, and health services employees; *Time and Place of Teaching*—evenings, weekends, early morning, away from a set campus, on trains, at vacation resorts, and in hospitals, libraries, prisons, and places of employment; *Programs and Method of Education*—credit for life experience and accomplishment rather than solely on the basis of courses taken, credit for qualifying examinations and noncollege courses or training, less reliance on the classroom lecture and more on the laboratory, independent study, "universities without walls," work at home, linkages to TV programs and lectures that can be seen at home or on campus, cassettes and records, and film strips. All of these can emphasize work done at home or at one's place of employment rather than on the campus. There will be more stress on internships, cooperative education, and independent study.

There will be more combined undergraduate and graduate programs, thus bringing about greater interdisciplinary cooperation and integration of fields of knowlege, while saving students a year or more of study. Further, there will be combined graduate programs, saving time and integrating knowledge in regard to business and public administration and law, engineering and business and law, various specific health fields and management, and other combinations. In undergraduate education there will also be greater use of interdisciplinary approaches. In both graduate and undergraduate education in all fields, there will be increased emphasis on the general knowledge of quantitative skills and techniques and the computer sciences. In the field of management, students will be better trained in management as a general field with applicability to specific fields such as business management, governmental management, nonprofit organizations' management. There will also be concern for short, intensive courses and for certificate-type and perhaps credit-type programs for the person with a B.A. in liberal arts who has difficulty finding a job, for example, lawyer's assistant, development specialist, administrative assistant. Last, in all professional fields and perhaps many others, there will be increased pressure for refresher courses and continuing education, and thus universities will respond to these skills and in so doing develop better courses and administrative procedures for all students.

Sharing of Resources—among two or more universities—teaching staff, space, laboratories, computer facilities, administrative staff and facilities, technological equipment, and consortium approaches. *Financing Higher Education*—a concern for financial aid based on achievement as well as on financial need; various loan programs extending years beyond graduation; pressure on governmental funding by institutions as well as directly on students so that universities will have to offer attractive programs and other features that appeal to students.

There will have to be better, tighter, and more creative management in terms of expenditures; productivity of faculty and staff; reduction in the number of courses, sections, and programs offered; management of resources space, people, endowments and cash, compensation, and policies. Finally, colleges and universities will have to face squarely decisions about: vocational versus professional versus liberal arts training and education; the amount and nature of services to students; a consumerism approach by students; a delineation of teaching versus research, with many universities and colleges recognizing the paramount priority of teaching both in terms of service to students and in determining faculty promotions and tenure; how universal higher education should be; how tough or rigid standards for admission and graduation should be; the university's degree of obligation to supply students with specific skills and knowledge; and the university's difficulty in maintaining collegiality in the context of collective bargaining.

GOVERNMENTAL MANAGEMENT

Government at all levels will have to wrestle with the issue of how involved it should get in various issues and what the level of involvement should be in areas of funding, controls, and research. The pendulum swings back and forth between government being perceived as doing too much (normally, when there is a fiscal crunch or poor results) or doing too little (normally, when there are horror stories as to existing conditions). The question of the role of the federal government vis-a-vis the other jurisdictions will continue to be a troublesome one, with swings from very tight centralization in the federal government to the federal government's either acting as a conduit for funds or keeping out of an area. All too often clichés are heard—the "feds" are too remote, don't understand local conditions, or are hamstringing us; the "locals" are corrupt, too political, or not too bright.

Fundamentally, assuming limited fiscal and manpower resources, it will become a question of priorities—defense versus social welfare, foreign versus domestic, health versus transportation. If we must cut on the local level, do we economize on hospitals, police, welfare services, or transportation? Even within a school district budget, do we cut out buses or teachers, sports or guidance counselors, science or languages? The present New York City and New York State fiscal crises have been helpful in the long run in focusing attention on the limits of governmental action, the interrelationship between the private and public sectors, and the question as to management and fiscal practices and policies. My concern here is basically the nonfederal sector of government, particularly large metropolitan areas, though some of the points will apply to all governmental jurisdiction.

One of the problems for the future is the extent and validity of governmental planning. Clearly, we need better short-range and long-range planning, but the crisis of the moment often precludes the thoroughness needed. Too often ideas are tacked together to meet an immediate need. It also is not too helpful for the administrator that plans are frequently expressed in legislation which takes little or no account of the administrative burdens or practicalities involved. And frequently good concepts, plans, or ideas just do not work as well as expected. For example, it is certainly expected that competitive bidding procedures should increase competition and lower the price for the governmental agency buying goods or services.

However, in New York City, because of the very slow payment process for work performed and the layers of red tape, competitive bidding frequently led to only one or two bidders who built in extra costs to take into account the fact that the vendor might have to borrow money while awaiting late payment. In fact, New York City at times forced small businesses into bankruptcy because of very slow payment. Thus the practice resulted in less competition at higher costs. Another example, the new Employee Retirement Income Security Act, while an excellent idea, forced a number of companies to discontinue their pension systems.

We shall have to look at new ways of organizing and approaching governmental problems. Perhaps we need new types of public authorities rather than traditional governmental departments (keeping in mind that often we turn to public authorities to gain the so-called efficiency of business and the public concern of government and in fact turn out to have public authorities with the so-called efficiency of government and the public concern of business). We certainly need to look at contracting out certain public functions such as garbage collection or school crossing guards, and substituting less highly trained (and less costly) civilians for police officers serving as clerks or as traffic directors. We shall also have to work out better ways of dealing with national problems that have the greatest impact on large cities or counties and that are beyond the resources of the city, county, or state to deal with. I refer here to the need for federal takeover of all welfare costs.

We need to have management audits rather than merely financial audits of government agencies. We must ascertain their objectives and the effectiveness, efficiency, and economy of their performance. Thus, we may need independent bodies with sufficient political and public impact to coordinate and evaluate all activities performed; to discover what agencies, jobs, or functions have been created as political plums and payoffs (this applies to legislative bodies and committees as well as executive agencies); and to learn whether sound decisions are being avoided or negated because of "higher" political consideration, which military and civilian installations are not really necessary, what functions are duplicated and should if necessary be eliminated such as New York State *and* New York City Veterans' Affairs offices and Consumer Affairs offices, what we are getting for our money in terms of service, problem solving, and productivity (when I talk about productivity I not only mean the $6000 clerk, I also refer to the $35,000 judge).

We shall have to deal with issues of privacy, secrecy, and the public's right to know, and questions of national security and civil disorder as related to illegal activities by the CIA, FBI, and other agencies. Of major concern will be attracting and keeping the highest quality individuals on all levels of federal, state, county, and city government. Government is too important to be left to the mediocre, the dilettante, or the individual who comes in for a year or two in order to make important contacts for his or her future career.

The next 10 to 15 years will see increasing concern about the proliferation of separate school districts in suburban areas and the maintenance of small police forces by villages, towns, and boroughs. Due to reasons of history, pride, control, prestige, and patronage, they are much greater in number than economy, efficiency, and effectiveness might demand. The same may be said for other special districts such as water districts, sewer districts, or sanitation districts. Eventually, there will be a merger or confederation of such districts and forces, thereby reducing their number and saving considerable sums in salaries, equipment, supplies, busing, and other costs, while providing equal or better services and economies of scale.

Another area for rethinking is the need for compulsory arbitration rather than the right to strike for employees in vital public services. Although this concept is traditionally opposed by practically all labor unions, it will turn out to be a necessity for those public employees in vital services such as police, fire, and some health services occupations. And to introduce greater realism into public service collective bargaining, consideration might be given to the arbitrator choosing either of the last offers of the union and the governmental units rather than some compromise position. Thus, each side would be forced to be more realistic and in fact they might therefore be able to reach agreement without presenting the issue to an arbitrator.

The agenda for governmental emphasis and reform is indeed a full one, constrained by the monetary and manpower costs involved. What shall the priorities be—foreign or domestic, or both? And within domestic concerns, which particular areas? Modern management tools of PPBS (Planned Program and Budget Systems), computer simulation, PERT-CPM (Program Evaluation and Review Technique–Critical Path Method), and cost benefit analyses do not answer the fundamental questions of what must be addressed as the highest priority items. However, in the domestic area, as one man's agenda, I would indicate very high priority in regard to major changes concerning the philosophy, policies, organization, and administration of: our criminal justice *nonsystem* involving police, district attorneys, courts, corrections, probation, and parole; our health care system; our human services system; our general management and civil service systems.

We shall have to pay increasing concern and devotion to the concept of this integrity and morality in government. In all branches and at all levels we should be concerned with no-show or part-show jobs and functions; influence favors, bribes, corruption, and profiteering; those in power helping themselves and their friends; featherbedding and junkets; barely competent or incompetent individuals appointed to judicial and executive positions and serving in the legislature. Beyond this we must be concerned with truth and openness, with not overglorifying what we are attempting to do. We must be more concerned with substance rather than overemphasizing style or the immediate press headline. We must be concerned with the why, what, and how of governmental plans, policies, and practices, and then with their implementation. We need a better sense of understanding of divergent views, of empathy, of civility. There must be more emphasis on what one knows and less on whom one knows. We can be pragmatic and realistic while at the same time developing and implementing programs and policies that are right and just, that seek very simply to correct wrongs, right inequities, advance human progress and fulfillment, leave the country and the world at least a little better than they were.

Government in general is weak on sound program development and implementation. We suffer from a murky sense of accountability and a frequent inability to assign authority commensurate with responsibility. We have not yet been able to mesh the private and public sectors in identifying and meeting problems, nor have we been successful at intragovernmental or intergovernmental jurisdictional planning, cooperation, and joint problem solving. We lack a service orientation to citizens or a crusading spirit to right wrongs, injustices, and plain incompetence. We are losing our sense of indignation and a feeling of healthy dissatisfaction with the status quo.

We shall have to understand and come to terms with the tensions between a political system and a public service system. These two are not mutually contradictory and it is recognized that the democratic process is not necessarily effective or efficient. But one must calculate the costs of political hacks, influence peddling, vested interests, and decisions based on political expediency, gain, and advancement.

The nonfederal government executive, aside from the traits indicated in the I-Test, will have to have a fuller understanding of government forces which may delay, dilute, and destroy change—the "GRUBSNIGS."

G represents the various groups in urban society—the pressure, good government, ethnic, and professional groups. We normally have a confrontation of conflicting demands. The administrator must take account of these group pressures and consult, cajole, and strive for acceptance of—or at least only minor opposition to—his or her recommendations.

R stands for reelection—cost benefit analysis, wise administrative practice, the greatest good for the greatest number, all have to be tempered with a realistic appraisal of whether this will advance the reelection chances of the chief executive or his or her aspirations for higher office, or whether this will help the executive to make his or her mark in history or choose a successor. Critical to one's reelection opportunities is the role of the media and thus there is a real art to dealing with it. The urban administrator needs the news media (and vice versa) and often uses and misuses them (and vice versa). There is a dynamic tension between the reporter's fight for the public's right to know and the bureaucrat's fight for the public to know what is right about the government.

U represents the civil service unions. The public sector is the growth area of unionization, and the unions not only have major impact on the fiscal health and service levels of the government, but they may also play an important role in the political life of the governmental jurisdiction. Further, a few unions, by striking, can cripple a city. Thus, labor relations will play a critical role in the life of a city, county, or state.

B represents budget and bureaucracy. Cities are generally unable to keep up with relatively increasing expenses and decreasing revenues. Costs of operating and salary, pension, and fringe benefits increases have outdistanced the ability to raise revenues by a variety of taxes. Further, in the older cities, particularly in the North, the middle and upper-middle classes have tended to move to the suburbs or the Sunbelt, and have largely been replaced by poorer people who need more in services and contribute less in taxes. In the face of about 15 percent yearly increases in expenses and 5 percent increases in income, the urban decision maker is faced with some enormously difficult decisions as to where to cut. Are schools more important than police, fire more important than sanitation? Clearly, the issue is what services, in what quality, quantity, and ease of access, can be delivered to the citizen up to the point of risking bankruptcy.

A big part of the budgetary cost is the bureaucracy. As cities have had to provide more services, often started with federal help that diminishes or is cut off, there has been a very significant increase in the number of employees. Their salaries and fringe benefits and the pension payment to retirees represent the largest portion of any city budget. Further, through union power or because they and their families and friends may constitute an important segment of the electorate, they have considerable influence in the election and reelection of political leaders. But in most cases our public personnel systems are inadequate and not responsive to the present day. We have to recruit and select good people and so motivate and reward them that they achieve high productivity and levels of service. Performance and productivity have not kept pace with the pay, pension, and practically iron-clad lifetime security of position. The New York City crisis has demonstrated that we can freeze salaries, reduce the numbers of staff, and eliminate functions that are no longer necessary or duplicate others.

In summary, the public personnel system, particularly in urban areas, should be reformed in the following ways:

1. Positions should be based on performance and potential assessment rather than examinations.
2. Salary increases should be a function of performance, not the result of longevity or across-the-board applications.
3. We should cease overcredentializing and narrowly specifying positions—there should be broad categories of positions.
4. Written examinations should be employed only when their validity can be demonstrated.
5. More upper-level positions should be filled at the discretion of management rather than through written examinations.
6. The system should stop discriminating against "outsiders." Both those within and outside the system should be able to compete for positions,

with those best qualified selected. Of course, one consideration would be experience in the governmental system.

7. Performance appraisals must be used not only for rewards and promotions but also for determining fitness to continue in the position.

8. The relationship between career public servants and transient political appointees must be analyzed and delineated. At the least, we must try to recruit the best political appointees and give them appropriate orientation and training in regard to the governmental system and their particular responsibilities. We need to require screening panels for the most important governmental positions.

9. We should consider a Public Administration Service Corps as a career for the most talented public managers. They might serve in one or more places and levels of government during their careers.

10. College and graduate students and professionals in other fields should be considered for government internships or short periods of service.

11. Pension systems should be reformed to tie in with social security and to ensure that one does not earn more than 100 percent of the final year's base salary after retiring at age 62 or 65. Further, there should be radical changes in the bonus-type, lump sum payments, in addition to regular annual pension, whereby some individuals receive one week's pay for each year of service, payment for unused sick leave, payment for unused vacation—all of which can add up to as much as $20,000 to $75,000, depending on one's salary. Overtime pay should not be a factor in calculating pay; cost of living factors should be strictly limited or eliminated in improving upon pensions; and instead of calculating one's lifetime pension on the last year of employment, it should be calculated on one's average base salary over the last three or perhaps five years. (It is interesting to note a report issued by the mayor of New York City's special pension study panel in April 1976.[1] The report indicated that New York City spends about 40 percent of its payroll on pension costs, while in private industry the figure is 13 to 18 percent. Further, in comparing New York City employees retiring at age 55 after 31 years of service to employees of seven major private firms, the New York City employee retires on 88 percent of final salary, while the private sector employee paid the same salary retires on from 44 to 70 percent of final salary.)

12. Sick leave systems should be reformed and controls tightened to reduce excessive use and abuse of sick leave.

13. Productivity goals and measures for each government department and its various subunits should be established and performance should then be evaluated. Thus salaries, promotions, continuance of service, special merit awards, and demotions should be based upon performance.

14. Training opportunities should be greatly increased to improve the motivation and performance of employees. Job counseling and career planning should be emphasized as well as mobility in assignments, tuition refund plans, evening courses, and released time programs. Job responsibilities should be enriched and enlarged.

The people side of government is critical, both in terms of the quality and dedication of those who serve as public employees as well as the respect, goodwill, and appreciation of those who are served. The public service is too vital and costly to be left to those who cannot do well elsewhere or are only concerned with security. We may in fact have to pay more than we presently do to the most capable and productive because at the highest levels, the scope of responsibility is equal to or higher than those in the private sector who earn from 25 to 750 percent more than comparable public servants. We may have to see more of the city manager type of government. But in any event, we must fight constantly against static bureaucracy.

S is for societal problems. Our cities, counties, and states must pull and pool together to meet problems that are largely beyond the scope of any one jurisdiction. But even then, dealing with poverty, air pollution, health, transportation, crime, employment, and many other problem areas requires the full involvement of the federal government and the private sector.

N represents neighborhoods and the need to build a sense of identity and cooperation. Government must become more responsive to citizen needs in the local areas and communities. The sense of neighborhood and involvement includes not only legal geographical units or districts but also community, civic, religious, and business groups.

I is for investment. We need far more funding in scientific and technological research into better ways of doing things, in dealing with such matters as air and noise pollution, disposal of solid wastes, and transportation systems. But this requires a long-term commitment of resources and, by and large, this has not been done.

G is for government structure. Frequently, the organization of government defies logic and represents political expediency, bowing to pressure groups or maintaining the status quo. In New York City in the sixties, there were well-baby clinics that were underutilized, and sick-baby clinics that were overutilized. But one could not send the staff from the underutilized to the overutilized area or sick babies to the well-baby clinics, because two different departments were involved. Also, pot hole repairs were done by three different departments depending on whether the pothole was in a city street, bridge, or parkway.

S represents state and federal relations. Too often the state and federal governments are isolated from knowledge and concern about the real problems of the urban areas. Thus the urban administrator must be concerned about creating greater interaction and understanding programs that are related to needs, as well as allowing maximum flexibility and minimizing red tape.

The foregoing discussion might lead to the conclusion that Alexander Pope was absolutely correct in stating: "For forms of government let fools contest: Whate'er is best administer'd is best."[2] I should like to suggest, however, that in the future the United States and Western democratic governments will have to reevaluate the reasons for their commitment to a certain form of government. The philosophy of government will be in question as well as the practice of government.

Whether we shall win out in our struggle with other ideologies is not so much a question of keeping our powder dry and our technology in gear. It is more a question of instituting conditions for the greater and fuller development of the individual. This is not an easy thing to do for it involves great tension. In all of us there is the tension of being hard-minded realists or idealists, of being bound by traditions or living by dreams of the future, of being Burkeans or Benthamites, of being loyal to our heritage or having aspirations for the future, of stressing the human being's immanence or transcendence. The paramount question is whether we are flexible enough to remain loyal to those elements of the Western tradition that are meaningful and relevant for a changing world while daring to change and modify, to refurbish and create.

Though recognizing the dangers and hardships involved in bringing together traditions and idealistic goals, I submit that the future growth and even the survival of Western civilization will be determined by its capacity to reevaluate, refurbish, innovate, and create those institutions in Western and uncommitted nations, which provide the greatest opportunity for the recognition and development of the worth and value of the individual.

For those in management over the next decade and a half it will be a most stimulating and difficult time. We must question everything we are doing and why and how we are doing it, and try to arrive at better insights and approaches. Despite increasing problems and pressures, the management executive must "dare to dream things that never were, and say, why not?" Perhaps the best way to sum up the credo and the epitaph of the manager for the future is Theodore Roosevelt's statement, "To the man in the Arena . . ."

It is not the critic that counts nor the man who points out how the strong man stumbled or where the doer of deeds could have done them better. The credit belongs to the man who is actually in the arena; whose face is marred by dust and sweat and blood; who strives valiantly . . . ; who knows the great enthusiasms, the great devotions, and spends himself in a worthy cause; who, at his best, knows the triumph of high achievement; and who, at his worst, if he fails, at least fails while daring greatly, so that his place shall never be with those cold and timid souls who know neither victory nor defeat.[3]

REFERENCES

1. The *New York Post*, Apr. 13, 1976; the New York *Times*, Apr. 14, 1976.

2. Alexander Pope, "An Essay on Man," epistle III, no. 1, line 303, 1704.

3. *The Works of Theodore Roosevelt*, Herman Hagedorn (ed.), national edition, 20 vols. (New York: Scribner, 1926), vol. 13, p. 510.

10

LEADERSHIP FOR A SOCIETY IN TRANSITION

ROSS LAWRENCE GOBLE
Dean, School of Management,
Clarkson College

Washington, D.C.—it is late September 2000. Another subfreezing morning, the U.S. Secretary of Food Policy notes as he boards an Ottawa-bound flight with his subordinates, the Secretary of Agriculture and the Secretary of State. In Ottawa they are met by their Canadian counterparts; within the hour they have set about their grim annual task of allocating the food produced by their nations to the balance of a hungry world. Surely nothing short of worldwide famine could lead the United States to create a new cabinet level post—The Secretary of Food Policy—to whom both the Secretary of Agriculture and the Secretary of State are subordinates.

A prediction from science fiction? No, indeed. It was published in the conservative and much respected *Wall Street Journal* and is based on scientific evidence of future world weather conditions, anticipated world population growth, and the inability of the world of the future to feed itself.[1] Is it an unrealistic illustration? Perhaps not. At least, it is far more realistic than it would have seemed a decade ago. Consider, for example, the fact that over 80 percent of all the world's export grain is now being produced by the United States and Canada, and some experts predict that by the year 2000 they may be the only countries in the world able to produce more than they consume.

Thoughtful individuals, whether or not they accept the inevitability of the above prediction concerning future world food supplies and weather conditions, will surely speculate about what kind of leaders we will need to make future decisions of such magnitude. And that will be the central topic of this paper—who will train tomorrow's leaders and what will they be like? But we will not attempt to answer these questions until we first examine our current social fabric, look back 30 years to gain an understanding of how we got where we are today, and *then* look forward to what our leaders of the future should be.

TODAY: THE AGE OF AMBIGUITY

In a recent lecture at New York University, George Shultz tagged our current American society the "Age of Ambiguity." Shultz believes that each economy, each society is " . . . held together and operates on a sort of consensus about basic things, and agreement on points that are generally taken to be so." Traditionally, these basic values, or factors of consensus, have changed slowly; thus value transitions over a comparatively long period of time were not generally upsetting to the society involved. In recent years, though, a great many social values have undergone sudden and sweeping change. The result has been a profound sense of unease or uncertainty—creating an Age of Ambiguity.[2]

Although our major concern here is with the United States, a few significant world issues that have contributed heavily to a worldwide sense of unease must be mentioned. First, *detente*—probably the most overused, misused, and least understood word of the last decade. And little wonder. In all but the French-speaking nations this is a borrowed word with the vaguest of definitions. How different from the "cold war" period. Then we had our enemy and we knew what to do with him. But detente? The clearest explanation by the average person is characterized by contradiction. For example, we must keep our defenses as strong, or stronger, than the Soviet Union's; but we must provide grain to the Soviets when their harvests are inadequate, even though this inadequacy may be due to the inordinate amount of money and resources they use to increase their military power. To the observers of the world scene, this new condition is ambiguous and has contributed heavily to the present worldwide sense of tension and unease.

The distribution of the world's wealth has undergone sudden and dramatic change, largely precipitated by a Middle Eastern oil cartel (OPEC). The impact of this phenomenon on most nations of the world, including those who reaped the most benefits, has been unsettling. But the two most critical world issues are and promise to remain accelerating population growth and an increasing shortage of food.

World Population and Food Shortage

"Today—during this one day—the world's population will increase by some 200,000 people, the size of a Des Moines, or a Salt Lake City, or a Grand Rapids. Tomorrow there will be a similar increase, and the next day, and the next—for many years to come."[3]

Even more startling is the fact that these figures, released by demographers of the United Nations, far exceed the predictions of less than a decade ago. In fact, only 10 years ago it was predicted in a *Wall Street Journal* article that by the year 2000 the world's population, now 4 billion, would not exceed 6.5 billion. The same experts now predict the world's population for 2000 at 7 billion or more, fully one-half billion more than predicted a scant 10 years ago. To look even further ahead, the world's population will have doubled to 14 billion by the year 2050, at the *current* rate of growth. Who will feed them?[4]

Predictions of mankind's future have always included an impending global food shortage. The best known of such predictions is that of Thomas Malthus who stated (simply) that the world's population growth would be geometric while the earth's ability to feed its people would grow at an arithmetic rate. Rapidly advancing technology in the period since World War II and the increased food production that resulted temporarily buried the fears of worldwide starvation, but the specter is rising again. This time the authority behind the fears is commanding more respect. Two major forces are responsible. One is the energy crisis; the other is the weather. As an example of the energy crisis: in the United States, corn yields were increased by 240 percent between 1946 and 1970—but this increase was accompanied by a 310 percent increase in the amount of energy (added fertilizer, mechanization) used to produce the corn.

In a special report, released by the National Science Foundation in 1975, it was pointed out that at some point food production could no longer be increased, regardless of the increased application of fertilizer or improved mechanization. "Modern agriculture . . . is an energy consumer of a magnitude that raises profound doubts as to its ability . . . to prevent wholesale starvation."[5]

To further compound the problem, world weather conditions have taken a decided turn for the worse (1976–77 is a good example), and more and more countries are importing more and more food. A consensus exists among meteorologists that the world will not again experience a prolonged period of bountiful weather such as that of the sixties, and, at worst, the food-growing centers of the world (with the exception of the United States and parts of Canada) may have already entered a long-run period of cooler temperatures and shorter growing seasons. Some experts also predict that the monsoon seasons, required for crop production throughout much of Asia, will fail to occur. So far, two failed to occur in the seventies.[6]

From a *national standpoint* what has contributed to this Age of Ambiguity? *Urban decline and accelerated crime rates* cannot go unmentioned. Over the past 30 years our older cities have been vacated by families and commerce alike in an unparalleled migration to the suburbs, leaving behind a population consisting primarily of a few very wealthy and many very poor. This population migration contributed to the well-known and highly publicized inner-city decay, with the accompanying problems of permanent second- and third-generation welfare recipients and unprecedented increases in many forms of crime. Hence, there is an atmosphere of unease within the cities—an unease shared by those who visit them.

Inflation could have been cited as a world problem as easily as a national one, but it is mentioned here because its impact on most Americans was so unexpected and so great that it could be considered as being atypical of the American scene; therefore, it is singularly important in this discussion of the current state of our society. To all persons living on a fixed income, the contribution of inflation toward a sense of insecurity can hardly be exaggerated. In addition, high unemployment rates during the past few years have promoted feelings among the people of this country that range from deep resignation over a seemingly hopeless situation to rage against the system which permits such conditions to exist.

Again, the *energy shortage* must be mentioned because of its relationship to conditions peculiar to the United States. Over the past 30 years Americans have become voracious consumers of energy. Second (vacation) homes, multiple cars, recreational vehicles, and a variety of household appliances have become an integral part of the lives of many Americans. We have been encouraged in our accumulation of energy-consuming products by every giveaway device imaginable as well as cheaper electric rates for more electricity used.

Long accustomed to the world's cheapest energy, with no end in sight to the supply, is it any wonder that the American people are now bewildered by large and continuous increases in the cost of oil, electricity, natural gas, and fertilizer? Not to mention the threatened shortage? The energy problem is puzzling and frightening to our people not only because it signals the end of an era but because it has contributed enormously to the national problem of inflation, and because they see no obvious solution; in fact, our leaders have yet to develop a meaningful plan for lessening the problem. Even recognizing that the problem exists no longer seems fashionable.

THE AGE OF PAINFUL TRANSITION (1946–1976–2000)

Not only have the past 30 years been an age of painful transition, but these years also represent the most rapidly accelerated period of *change* the world has ever known. It is true, of course, that readers less than 30 years old have known no other world, but even to this group the effects of these changes have made an indelible impact on their lives.

If we have correctly identified some of the major factors that now contribute to our present sense of national unease, how did we get this way? Clearly, *technological progress* has been a major contributor since through advanced technology the world has shrunk at an alarming rate. Men can walk on the moon and we can watch them—or we can explore Mars by way of a computerized machine—but this same electronic age has contributed heavily to dehumanizing society. We have become numbers fed into a computer; we are bombarded with the crises of the world through TV satellites, causing us to feel that the world is vastly more evil and corrupt than at any other time in history. At the same time, millions of people have developed unrealistic expectations and become dissatisfied with their lot in life because of the "ideal" portrayed in TV life. Even in our affluent society, the desire for material goods has outstripped the ability of many to obtain them, creating unrest.

Despite the inability of all persons to secure everything they want, the past 30 years have been a time of almost unbridled *affluence* in American society. So much has been written about this topic and its influence on our social structure that it is unnecessary to repeat it here; however, conventional wisdom suggests that this period of long-term affluence has made significant negative contributions to our social fiber. These allegations usually support the view of a "soft society"—illustrative perhaps of the last days of Rome—a society of too much for too little effort for too many people. The younger generation in particular is usually singled out as being lazy, dirty, and lacking in respect for material goods and property that are too easy to get.

Whatever one's views may be on this issue, few disagree that America has become a society in which a general disrespect for the property of others is a hallmark. Two illustrations may suffice. Litter, mountains of it, now defaces our landscape. Cans, bottles, and plastics of every description decorate the American scene. Perhaps the most telling of all is a recent advertisement in *Fortune* magazine picturing a highly successful executive, immaculately dressed, sitting in his corporate helicopter with his feet (shoes and all) propped up on the seat across the aisle.

Interlocked with this period of general affluence has been a period of *social upheaval* probably unparalleled in human history. It too has occurred in a microcosm of our history—roughly 30 years. One need only mention a few of the most obvious events to support this point: enormous changes in the area of racial relations; widespread factory worker discontent and the general movement toward worker participatory governance; the female liberation movement; and the unprecedented change in social and sexual mores. These fomenting social issues have kept large segments of the population off balance, feeling inadequate to cope with such rapid change.

By combining the factors just discussed and adding one more—the high mobility of our present society—a portrait emerges of a social structure in which many individuals feel unable to contend successfully with a frightening array of major problems. Is it any wonder that increasingly large numbers of persons have sought some way to "drop out" of organized society?

Dropping out has been achieved in a variety of ways, from establishing communes in pursuit of a simple, self-sufficient life to seeking insulation from society's problems through a hedonistic life-style. Whatever the method employed to avoid social responsibility, it is apparent that more people in our society feel *alienated* by the seemingly endless array of intractable problems and social unrest—cast adrift from their former moorings and drifting aimlessly without strong leadership. Recorded history is replete with other periods equally as troublesome as today's, albeit in a different sense, but in all such previous periods the times themselves seemed to have given rise to great leadership. Our bicentennial year reminded us that the American Revolution was a period of unrivaled trauma, but it was also a period that provided us with many outstanding leaders.

Where are such leaders today? Would anyone suggest that the Vietnam war, the horrors of the Nixon administration, the devaluation of the dollar (twice), and the congressional scandals have produced comparably great leaders? Why has this particular period in America's history been so different?

INSTITUTIONAL FAILURES

If outstanding—even competent—leaders are not emergng on the national scene, has there been an institutional failure to train such persons? Maybe a brief look at some of our major institutions will shed some light on this question.

The *home* is a basic unit of most societies and most people agree on the importance of the early childhood training it provides. There is general agreement too that this training profoundly affects a child's personality throughout its lifetime. Exactly what this training ought to be is a subject of strong disagreement. Among the most important elements of a child's life is the overall environment the home provides and, specifically, the value system of the family. If forced to use a single word to label the American home environment since the end of World War II, "permissive" would seem most appropriate.

Prior to World War II, and especially during the Great Depression, the home and family served as an integrated economic unit of survival. During this period, the need and the right for every person to work seemed as American as apple pie and baseball. Not all people did work and the Depression left an indelible mark on all those who lived through it, a mark so profound that many of them dedicated themselves to the idea that their children would never suffer the same trauma.

And indeed they have not. Since the end of World War II American home life has been stamped not only with a general aura of permissiveness but also with a steady erosion of the "work ethic" as a basic philosophy of life. But society still demands that most of its members be productive. As a result of these conflicting situations, many young people today have difficulty in adjusting to the change from a protective, permissive, and nondemanding home environment to the "real world" expectation that individuals be self-sustaining. If our current American home life has been depicted reasonably accurately, a logical question might be—what positive contribution is the home making to the development of our future leaders?

It is also irresistibly tempting to mention the drastic changes in curricula and the total environment of our *elementary* and *secondary schools* in recent years. Middle-aged readers would scarcely recognize today's schools as the same institutions they once attended unless, of course, the buildings and grounds are the same. Very little else is. We seem to have fulfilled the small child's dream of 30 years ago. Gone are the tedious tasks of diagramming sentences, memorizing the multiplication tables, working hour on hour with flash cards to learn addition and subtraction, practicing handwriting, and long hours of homework. Also gone, forever it seems, are those relatively high SAT scores for incoming college freshmen. These scores, determined on a national basis, are used to produce scales for predicting the probability of successfully completing college-level work. For over a decade SAT scores have steadily declined.

And what about our *colleges?* Surely they must represent the only untarnished institution left. It must be pointed out that of the institutions criticized thus far none has stated that its *single objective* is to train the leaders of tomorrow. One might ask then, if institutions do not, who will? Most of the nation's colleges and universities *do* state the training of tomorrow's leaders as one of their major objectives; the other objective is usually said to be, "providing a well-rounded education."

Such a statement is sure to be followed by myriad questions. One would surely be, "what is an educated person?" A number of years ago the Royal Bank of Canada, in its monthly newsletter, attempted to answer this perplexing question. "The aim of an educational institution is to give students a living fund of knowledge from which they may generate ideas. When you can bring relevant background to bear on a problem, assemble pertinent data, grasp relationships, appraise the values involved, and make a judgment, when you can do that, you are an educated person."[7]

Perhaps. Certainly there are many educators who believe this verbatim. But if indeed this is the portrait of an educated person, we may seek in vain among the educated for tomorrow's leaders. For, at the very least, an educated person must also be able to communicate his or her ideas to others. In fact, in the article just mentioned, the author at a later point says, "There is not much prospect for advancement . . . unless you can express your thoughts confidently. You cannot buy or sell, give instructions to subordinates, make a report, win friends or influence people unless you can say clearly and appealingly what it is in your mind to say."[8]

Anyone who agrees with these statements and has had the opportunity to read what most of our current college graduates write and has listened to them express their views or feelings, must feel that institutions of higher education are failing in their efforts to graduate well-educated individuals. Unfortunately, even if every college and university in America produced only graduates with these desirable attributes, we would still not be assured of having the supply of leaders we will need for tomorrow. We will come back to this.

Are there *other institutions* responsible for the training of leaders in the past that are failing us now? Yes. Great leaders have emerged from broken homes (or no homes), have graduated from the poorest of schools or dropped out of school, or have backgrounds that include a combination of other negative influences. In the instances where leaders have arisen from an unorthodox pathway, though, other institutions have helped in the molding of their character; for example, institutions such as the church, which, until recently anyway, preached the work ethic (those who worked hard enough would succeed). At one time this reflected the attitude of society as a whole, which is itself an institution.

Although it may be unwarranted to characterize an entire society as a social institution, for the sake of illustration it serves a purpose to do so here. Our present leadership vacuum supports the idea that American society as a macro institution has failed to mold untrained but eligible candidates for leadership. If all the aforementioned institutions have failed to train the leaders needed today, again we must ask, who will train the leaders for tomorrow? After looking at logical changes to expect in the future, we will attempt to answer this complex question.

THE YEAR 2000

Perennially, humans have been fascinated with predicting their own future, and understandably so. It's fun; and if the predictions are made far enough into the future, one need have little concern about being proved wrong. The "world of tomorrow," predicted 30 years ago for the seventies, was exemplified by futuristic cities. This has not come to pass. In fact, if those futurists are around to see for themselves, they must be surprised to note how few differences there are between the cities of today and those of 1940. Even less change may occur between now and the year 2000.

Still, the predictions of extreme future technological change go on, partly because most of us believe that anything is possible. The next 22 years may prove such predictions to be wrong. Technological changes will certainly occur, but the rate will be slower. A prediction from the sixties can be used as an example. At that time the "green revolution" prediction stated that the world had an endless capacity for producing more and more food through intensified technology. Today this prediction is unacceptable.

This article opened with the frightening statement that the world of 2000 will be unable to feed large segments of its geometrically growing population. The evidence to support this prediction grows daily, and technological advancement in this area is expected to slow down dramatically within a decade or so. The future management of these two interlocked problems has deep-rooted and disturbing implications. Many observers feel that American leaders will be infinitely involved with the selective allocation of foodstuffs on a country-by-country basis—with all the political ramifications this situation implies.

Underlying it all is the *energy problem.* Futurists of 10 years ago predicted more, bigger, and better transportation systems for the year 2000; now it appears they may have been wrong on all three counts. Because of the recent focus on accelerating energy costs and because energy is almost certain to be far more costly in A.D. 2000, predictions regarding future transportation are relatively easy. The continuing trend will be toward smaller, lighter, less-fuel-consuming automobiles, and fewer families will own two or more cars.

Auto industry predictions do not now call for radical changes in technology or any revolutionary breakthroughs in the next 22 years, and the computer-controlled highways predicted for the mid-seventies will still not be a reality by the year 2000, not because the technology will be unavailable—it is now—but because the cost will simply be prohibitive. Cars that are now referred to as "mid-size" will be considered "highway cruisers" by the turn of the century and small three-wheel electrically driven shopper cars will be appearing in the suburbs. By then, the airlines may have been nationalized and the SST will probably be a thing of the past, survived by second-generation smaller but still wide-bodied jets. The major factors guiding the development of transportation in the future will be fuel and environmental conservation, and the outward appearance of such transportation will not be radically different from today's.[9]

As a final illustration of a constraint on technological change and growth, let's look at what may be expected to happen to the nation's wealth. The best estimate of the population in the United States by the year 2000 is now 262 million. Unlike estimates for the rest of the world, this is down sharply from the 340 million projected a scant decade ago. Since the wealth of the nation is inseparably linked to its population, this new projection has a profound effect on the projection of the national wealth for the future. National wealth is computed as gross national product (GNP), a measure of the estimated sum of all products and services for a given year; therefore, the sharp downward revision of the population for the year 2000 results in a hypothetical "loss" of 78 million people and $177 billion in the GNP for the year 2000 (at 1960 constant dollars).

In 1966 forecasters of the National Planning Association predicted a GNP for 2000 of $2280 billion (1960 dollars), and the most conservative estimate by the U.S. Department of Commerce was $2103 billion. Even this figure may now prove to be too high. In 1975 the GNP was about $815 billion (1960 dollars), so the $180 billion reduction in earlier estimates amounts to nearly one-fifth of all the goods and services produced by Americans in 1975.[10] The 1966 projection of 340 million Americans by the year 2000 was based on each American woman's bearing 3.1 children. Today's estimates are for 2.1 children or less. Many factors have contributed to this declining birthrate: widespread use of contraceptives, legalized abortions, inflation and unemployment, and the desire of an increasing number of women for a career outside the home.

Other factors that are difficult to measure and even more difficult to forecast may also affect the GNP of the year 2000. For example, all forecasts are based on the assumption of an average, per worker increase in the production of goods and services (productivity) of 3 percent per annum, but this may not be possible even though this has been about the rate of increase since the close of World War II. Factors that might inhibit the sustained rate of growth would be inflation and a continued high level of unemployment, higher than the assumed 4 percent. Inflation would inhibit growth because investors tend to avoid long-term commitments that will be repaid in cheaper dollars, while unemployment at any rate above the assumed 4 percent (1976 rate was above 7 percent) infers a lowered productivity rate with an attendant increase in social costs.

If these changes are all that occur, will our society in the year 2000 be substantially different from today? The answer seems to be "yes" and "no." No, it probably will not differ radically from today in a technological sense or in physical appearance. Yes, our society will change as the period of value transition continues, and the changes, while difficult to predict accurately, will be of great importance to us. For our discussion it will be helpful to consider the 30 years before 1976 as a downhill slide into the present Age of Ambiguity, and the time between now and the year 2000 as a period of uphill progress out of this age of unrest.

The indications for this prognosis seem abundant. First, if we were to select a single thought that threads its way throughout the previous discussion, it would be the idea that American society is undergoing a collective value change of substantial magnitude without strong leadership or a unifying purpose. Thus the 1970s, which we have called the low point in this period of change, has been referred to by one writer as " . . . an era when a things-first, people-second culture reasserted itself as a people-first, things-second culture."[11] Nineteen seventy-seven, then, might very well have been the turning point in American society. From this time forward to the turn of the century the national sense of ambiguity may gradually be replaced by a general feeling of national purpose. But this purpose must first be defined at an institutional level.

In most societies the quickest and surest way to unify national effort behind a common purpose is to identify a common enemy. Traditionally, autocratic societies achieve this by promoting fear of military conquest. Such a strategy would be doomed to early failure in this country, challenged by our growing numbers of educated and informed citizens. In the United States, the "common enemy" may be the declining quality of life. The ability to recognize this and to articulate clearly the ever-growing but not unified demands of the people will characterize tomorrow's effective leaders.

Interestingly, the very factors that have contributed most heavily to the present feeling of national unrest may also be responsible for its elimination by the year 2000. As an example, the steadily increasing energy and food shortage throughout the world will force our nation to reassess its national goals and priorities. The task will not be an easy one, but national survival may depend on it. And internally, the value transition will continue toward a "people" rather than a "things" society, with the period of "use up or throw away" coming to an end—both through necessity and by choice of the people.

There are many independent activities we can point to already making substantial contributions toward this transition, but they have yet to be woven into a single pattern of goals or values. An emphasis in recent years on an improved quality of life has resulted in increasing challenges to "big business," "big government," policies involving the United States and other nations and the basic thought that the United States must serve as the leader of the free world, the traditional relationships between men and women, and the general acceptance of economic growth at any price.

The die is cast and the trend for the future seems irreversible. Past policies in the areas mentioned above have demanded a cost that many are no longer willing to pay, and to expect the movements favoring such values as consumers' rights, environmentalism, and minority rights to disappear or be reversed is unrealistic. We could not turn back the clock now even if we wanted to. So the value transitions will continue with a growing emphasis on the human side of life, making the year 2000 different—much different—from today. Social responsibility may then *literally* identify an American culture that has finally matured, become stable, and is united in a common cause.

TRAINING AND CHARACTER OF TOMORROW'S LEADERS

This article opened with the questions: who will train tomorrow's leaders and what will they be like? To avoid the temptation of providing an early simplistic answer, we attempted to illustrate the complexity of the problem, in a gestalt sense, by first sketching a picture of American society as it now is, identifying some of the major elements that have contributed to today's sense of unease, and then attempting to predict some of the changes that may occur by the year 2000. Earlier on we labeled this period from 1946 to the year 2000 as the Age of Painful Transition and implicit in this description has been the need for a new kind of leadership. In view of our extensive discussion, we should now be able to propose a speculative answer to our first question, who will train tomorrow's leaders?

The obvious answer would seem to be—all the institutions already discussed even though they have failed to train leaders for today. This is partially correct since they will continue to have an influence on our young people. Only one of these institutions, however, seems preeminently qualified to lead the way as an *agent of change*—our post-secondary educational system. The reasons are twofold: first, a large number of tomorrow's leaders are already in our universities or colleges; second, the needed intellectual leadership is also there. But that is not enough. For many years we have had both bright students and able professors, yet together they have not produced the capable leaders needed for our unique times. Just as this part of our educational system has failed in its social obligation to train today's leaders, so will it fail to train leaders for tomorrow unless a basic change in philosophy is adopted.

Today many of our universities and colleges appear to be obsessed with the development of technological skills for "entry level" positions in industry or government. Judging by the popularity of professional and semiprofessional areas of study, students seem to share this obsession. If an overemphasis on technological skills is an error and misses the basic point of a student's education, so does the counter side of this view—a view that advocates a "pure liberal arts" education and believes that teaching even the rudiments of technology approaches "vocationalism."

The basic point is that whatever a student's undergraduate pursuit may be, we must unite our professorial talents and our students behind a common goal that provides graduates who are alert to what the problems of the future will be in a transitional society. The challenge seems clear. Not so clear is whether or not our universities and colleges can rise to the occasion. If they do, they will have overcome a number of formidable obstacles.

For example, our universities and colleges must put their own houses in order, to accomplish the desired results. Far too many of our schools have become too large, too bureaucratic, and too activity-oriented to accomplish any major and significant goal. This has led George Odiorne to comment that the "activity trap" characterizes *most* of our universities and colleges. Odiorne defines an activity trap as the situation institutions find themselves in when they start out for what was once an important and clearly defined objective, only to find themselves so involved in getting there that they forgot where they were going. As an example, Odiorne cites the initial granting of grades to signify the satisfactory completion of course work as a meaningful objective. But over the years the number of courses taught and grades given began to multiply. Thus, persons were hired to record and store the grades, statisticians to interpret their meaning, security personnel to protect them, and appeal boards were formed to defend them. As the clerical functions began to proliferate, office managers were obviously needed, until quite naturally they became vice presidents. The reorganizational structure, now feeding upon itself, increased as the need for other activities, with a rising level of tiers, was built one upon the other, " . . . all removed farther from reality and purpose than the one below."[12]

If our post-secondary schools are to train tomorrow's leaders, they must rally the support of the American people behind this mission; untangle themselves from the activity trap by reorganization, decentralization, and the establishment of techniques designed to measure the results achieved in reaching their objectives; and demonstrate their understanding and ability to lead a society involved in a period of profound value transition. Only then will they have accepted the challenge of training tomorrow's leaders.

In summary, our universities and colleges will not only need to *state* but must *accept* the training of our future leaders as their primary goal, and to do this they must adopt an effective mechanism for achieving and measuring the results of their efforts. What will tomorrow's leaders be like? They will not be characterized by a list of "personality traits" or by some specific "leadership style"; they will emerge from among those who best understand and are able to lead a society that will insist on:

- An increasing emphasis on the quality of life rather than on the quantity of goods produced or owned

- Moving away from independence toward a concept of interdependence among individual institutions and nations
- Living in harmony with nature rather than working to conquer it through technology
- A trend away from the concept of competition toward a concept of cooperation
- De-emphasis on technological efficiency in favor of social justice and equity as primary social goals
- Self-development of an organization's individual members instead of the dictates of organizational convenience
- Participatory management rather than dogmatism and authoritarianism
- Reinstallation of the work ethic—not as an unavoidable and unpleasant duty but rather as a principal means of self-fulfillment
- Recognition of leisure as a meaningful activity in its own right[13]

This list underscores the need for nontraditional leaders for the future. Surprisingly, though, these leaders will also need to possess and advocate "traditional" values that are seemingly out of vogue at the moment:

- Incorruptible personal integrity
- Respect for the property of others—this returning value will be coupled to an increasing quality of life in a world of declining quantity
- Reassumption of and social stress on individual responsibility versus "let the government or someone else do it"
- The desire to develop a clean and orderly society—a demand born of three factors: desire for a higher quality for life; a decrease in the availability of material goods (quantity in life); and social pressures brought about by the increasing numbers of people on earth

If our institutions of higher education are able to set students on pathways to achieve these goals, they will also have a positive influence on the balance of society. These students who will be our future leaders will also carry their well-defined value systems into the homes they establish, will insist that priority be given to high-quality elementary education for their children, and will support and strengthen our religious institutions.

A unique opportunity is open to our universities and students today to become leaders of our society in its continued transition, and to help reconcile the differences that will exist between the goals of the individual and those of society in the years ahead. Our universities can lead the way in this endeavor, and in so doing we can bypass the often predicted dehumanizing society of 1984; then, by the year 2000 we may have achieved a people's republic in the truest sense of the word.

REFERENCES

1. J. M. Winski, "By 2000, Prevention of Starvation May Be Chief Global Concern," *The Wall Street Journal,* Mar. 25, 1976, p. 1.
2. George P. Shultz, *Leaders and Followers in an Age of Ambiguity* (New York: New York University Press, 1975), pp. 23–47.
3. Jonathan Spivak, "Population of World Growing Faster than Experts Anticipated," *The Wall Street Journal,* Apr. 12, 1976, p. 1.
4. Ibid.
5. Jonathan Spivak, op. cit., *The Wall Street Journal,* Mar. 25, 1976.
6. Ibid.
7. The Royal Bank of Canada, *Monthly Letter,* Montreal, Canada, April 1976, pp. 2–3.
8. Ibid.
9. Todd Fandell and Charles Camp, "Transportation in 2000 to Rely on Equipment Much Like Today's," *The Wall Street Journal,* Apr. 1, 1976, p. 1.
10. Alfred L. Malabre, Jr., "U.S. Unlikely to Be as Big—or as Rich—as Analysts Thought," *The Wall Street Journal,* Mar. 15, 1976, p. 1.
11. Leonard L. Berry, "Corporate Leadership in the Age of the People," *Atlanta Economic Review,* May-June 1976, pp. 4–7.
12. George Odiorne, "Some Comments on Input-Output Relations in Non-Profit Bureaucracies," in Lewis Benton (ed.), *The Management of Non-Profit Organizations* (New York: D. C. Heath, 1975), pp. 123–128.
13. Leonard L. Berry, op. cit., p. 6.

11
THE ROLE OF ENERGY MANAGEMENT

ELLA GRASSO
Governor of Connecticut

Experience is the best of all schoolmasters, only the school fees are heavy.
Thomas Carlyle

The nineteenth-century British essayist outlined in simple yet vivid words the price to be paid for experience. The experience of the period 1973–76 in relation to the fuel crisis can serve as a valuable "schoolmaster" if public servants will reflect on what did and did not happen as a result of that difficult situation. The people of the United States were forced to question a way of life that permitted vast quantities of energy to be consumed in extremely wasteful ways. That questioning drove home the fact that most Americans have shown little or no respect for the natural resources that provide their supply of energy.

In the discussion of management for the future, energy serves as an important focus. It is a relatively new breed of problem that cuts across all fields of human endeavor. The cost of energy influences the course of an entire economy, including the availability or lack of jobs. Energy controls a nation's flow of transportation and serves as a guide to the type of housing and commercial construction that is feasible. Management of energy resources offers a vehicle for the development of public policies that will have far-reaching effects on all aspects of national life.

As governor of the state of Connecticut, I clearly understand that if unsolved, the problem of energy management will pose a formidable road-block to a healthy business and industrial future. Integrated into the overall state planning process, energy management can serve as a potent impetus to growth and a valuable guide to the spending of taxpayers' dollars. In Connecticut, the oil embargo that began in the fall of 1973 offered a crash course in the uses and abuses of energy as well as the role government must play in the management of policies and programs to deal with an energy crisis. The embargo taught the people of our state about an uncomfortable dependence on petroleum in general and imported petroleum in particular. The lesson included skyrocketing fuel prices that affected the costs of all kinds of consumer goods.

Nationwide, the oil embargo decreased the supply of petroleum by 14 percent in January 1974. Similar reductions followed in subsequent months. The gross national product dropped by well over $10 billion with a corresponding increase of approximately 500,000 men and women in the ranks of the unemployed. The people of Connecticut and the United States were also given a jarring example of the use of natural resources as a tool of international diplomacy. As a result of the Arab-Israeli war in 1973, Arab members of the 13-year-old Organization of Petroleum Exporting Countries (OPEC) agreed to convert crude oil into an economic weapon. Arab oil was embargoed to Western nations, especially those which supported Israel. The United States was at the top of the embargo list. In addition, the OPEC nations announced that they would henceforth unilaterally determine the posted price of crude oil.

The result of the new policy was an increase of 70 percent in the price of Arab crude as of October 17, 1974, accompanied by a cut of 5 percent per month in exports. Early in 1974 the Arabs relented somewhat in their dealings with many nations, but not with the United States. The embargo on shipments to our nation was continued, and increased prices were retained. Those prices had tripled and in some cases quadrupled for American consumers. Consumer prices throughout the United States climbed rapidly. Fuel shortages engendered long lines of impatient motorists at service stations. A new demand for sweaters was created by those who kept their home thermostats turned down to conserve the limited supply of home heating oil. Politicians blamed oil company executives for shortsightedness. Oil company executives blamed politicians for lack of leadership. Consumers blamed oil company executives and politicians for failing to solve the problem.

The daily flow of verbiage did little to clarify the basic facts of the crash course on energy imposed on the people of Connecticut. They learned the basic fact that Connecticut, a small and densely populated state with no native fossil fuels, relied heavily on oil for its energy. While the United States collectively relied on petroleum to satisfy about 45 percent of all energy needs, Connecticut was almost 80 percent oil-dependent. When the price of oil went up, the cost to most of the states was tripled for less than half of its energy, but the cost to Connecticut was more than tripled for four-fifths of its energy.

As is often the case in an emergency of this magnitude, the states turned to Washington for help. As winter approached and the effects of the embargo penetrated all parts of the United States, the Federal Energy Office was created by executive order. During the winter of 1973–74, the Energy Office directed the allocation of petroleum products throughout the nation. Energy Offices established in each of the 50 states participated actively in the distribution program.

By the spring of 1974, it was obvious there would be a continuing need to allocate energy resources and develop energy strategies for the future. For this reason the Federal Energy Agency was created in June 1974. While the executive branch in Washington was attempting to deal with the energy crisis through administrative action, Congress was adopting the Emergency Petroleum Allocation Act. It was a stopgap measure that did little to solve the long-range energy problem faced by our nation.

In 1976 the Federal Energy Policy and Conservation Act was approved by Congress. The act was adopted after almost every energy-related issue was subjected to extensive compromise, but it was regarded as a small, first step toward a national energy policy. During 1974–76 greater attention was focused on the development of alternate energy sources to reduce our dependence on an oil supply governed by foreign powers. To stimulate that development, the 25-year-old Atomic Energy Commission was dismantled in January 1975, and its functions divided between two new agencies.

The Energy Research and Development Administration (ERDA) was given the overall responsibility of generating alternate energy sources, including nuclear power. The Nuclear Regulatory Commission (NRC) was assigned the role of regulating the nuclear industry. Specific tasks included the licensing of nuclear plants, upgrading disposal techniques, and improved safety and security standards at nuclear-fuel-processing centers throughout the country. By 1975, however, the impact of the Arab oil embargo had been diluted by the availability of increased fuel supplies. The sense of urgency so evident during the winter of 1973–74 was gone, and there no longer appeared to be an energy crisis.

The attempts by the federal government to manage fuel shortages created by the Arab embargo were paralleled in Connecticut. In December 1973, primarily in response to the embargo, the state administration created the Energy Emergency Agency. As the name suggests, the agency was designed to handle crisis situations, including response to demands for relief from service-station operators. Just as the Federal Energy Office was transformed into a broader-based Federal Energy Administration, Connecticut's Energy Emergency Agency was transformed into the Connecticut Energy Agency, with increased emphasis on public education and planning for the future. The new state agency was charged with developing policy options. At the same time, a Connecticut Energy Advisory Board was created to draw on the expertise and commitment of the private sector. The Connecticut Energy Agency supplied the advisory board with energy supply-and-demand projections. The advisory board, in turn, digested the projections and recommended programs to meet future needs.

During 1974, even though public concern about energy shortages waned, the need became obvious to incorporate energy considerations into the overall planning responsibility of state government. It was clear, given the experience of the disastrous economic effects of the oil embargo, that energy cost and supply were inevitably intertwined with the future of business and industry, transportation, and the quality of the state's environment. With the assistance of the Connecticut General Assembly, legislation was developed early in 1975 to establish the state Department of Planning and Energy Policy (DPEP). I signed the legislation in July 1975, inaugurating a new chapter in the Connecticut effort to manage its energy future.

Energy emergency procedures initiated during the crisis of the oil embargo were retained in the new agency on a limited, standby basis. Research and policy development emphasized during 1974 were also retained and expanded. However, the importance of DPEP was its function as a vehicle for integrating energy into the long-range planning essential to the progress and growth of Connecticut.

The task was formidable because Connecticut suffered in 1976 from the same malaise that affected the rest of our nation. The supply of energy was no longer regarded with alarm by the majority of our people. The easing of concern occurred even though United States reliance on imported petroleum was more than 40 percent higher than it was before the Arabs imposed the oil embargo in 1973. There were a number of reasons for this discontinued sense of urgency. Energy supplies and prices stabilized during 1975. Disinterest spread among the people as an overwhelmingly Democratic Congress which took office in 1975 was unable to reach any agreement with a new Republican president on a meaningful energy program.

More and more public attention was focused on inflation and the business recession. Even though the oil embargo had contributed heavily to these economic trends, people were more concerned with solutions than with the origins of the trends. The public's attitude of disinterest in energy problems was a reflection of the inaction in Washington. Put another way, if Washington was not worried enough to initiate bold, new programs to meet future energy needs, why should the public be concerned?

For example, an interest developed in Connecticut early in 1975 to require minimum efficiencies for certain household appliances and appropriate labeling to inform consumers of efficiency ratings. Throughout the year, it appeared that Congress would enact this kind of legislation to preempt state action. As a result, Connecticut legislative initiative was put aside. Because of the difficulty in securing needed federal action in the field of energy management, Connecticut and other concerned states initiated their own programs. Aside from the creation of DPEP, Connecticut embarked on a number of regional approaches. Most of the states along the Atlantic seaboard, from Maine to Florida, are oil-dependent, and several major decisions taken at the federal level are known to have been designed to maintain that dependence.

Federal decisions, for example, discouraged refinery capacity in New England. Officials in Washington believed such capacity would alter the long-standing role of New England as a shock-absorber area in a fluctuating fuel flow situation throughout the United States. As a shock absorber, the northeastern states were utilized to absorb excess domestic production in times of fuel surplus or import more oil than usual in times of deficient domestic production. When the impact of the oil embargo struck the United States, many officials of these states asked whether their part of the country should be asked to bear a disproportionate share of the burdens imposed on an entire nation. Their answer was "no," and the response was strong enough to promote a sturdy bond among these states with a common and continuing interest.

Joint pressure from the northeastern states was responsible for the Entitlements program created under the Emergency Petroleum Allocation Act. The program was based on the fact that some oil refiners relied more heavily on crude oil from domestic sources than others who paid significantly higher prices for imports. The Entitlements program equalized oil prices to consumers by equalizing refiners' costs regardless of the mix of domestic and imported crude. The individual states also brought about the success of the set-aside program which guaranteed equitable distribution of existing fuel supplies to assure that hardships were minimized or avoided. The collection of data also became of prime interest to individual states. That data serve as the basis for analyzing federal initiatives. This type of joint participation in the decision-making process is vital to the success of future federal-state relationships.

Energy management of tomorrow must be based on a number of existing factors. The overriding factor is that the United States is the largest energy consumer in the world. At the time the Arab oil embargo was initiated, energy consumption in the United States was increasing at the rate of 5 percent per year. The rate of usage had doubled in 20 years, and projections indicated another doubling in the next 20 years. With 6 percent of the world's population, the United States consumed 33 percent of the world's energy supply. Per capita energy consumption in our nation was eight times the average of the rest of the world.

While consumption was increasing rapidly at the beginning of the embargo, domestic production of energy had slowed considerably in the United States. For example, it had been 23 years since our nation was energy self-sufficient. Coal production in 1973 was at the same level as in 1943. Exploration for domestic crude oil had leveled off in 1970 and declined consistently after that. Natural gas had been consumed faster than it had been discovered since 1968, leading to increased dependence on liquefied petroleum gas and imported synthetic natural gas. In 1973, 35 percent of the petroleum consumed in the United States was imported, whereas the ratio of imported crude in 1960 was 15 percent.

The use of automobiles was becoming more and more widespread. The trend was a natural outgrowth of the population dispersal that was taking place throughout the nation. As the quality of life in core cities deteriorated, suburbs mushroomed. With fuel prices low and supplies seemingly inexhaustible, automobiles provided the flexibility required for suburban living. In 1950 the average number of cars in Connecticut was one per household;

in 1976 the average was nearly two. The United States automobile industry in 1976 produced two cars for every baby born, and there were more licensed drivers in America than registered voters. The rush to using automobiles left in its wake a sadly neglected railroad system. In 1959 more than 106,000 miles of railroad track were traveled throughout the United States. By the time the oil embargo began in 1973, only 28,000 miles of track were operational. Similar shrinkage was evident in other forms of mass transportation.

Buildings and homes were constructed with little or no regard for energy consumption. Builders of mass-produced homes often cut corners on insulation. If glass walls added a certain esthetic value to office buildings, it was usual to install bigger and stronger climate control systems to warm tenants in winter and cool them in summer. The air-conditioner business mushroomed, adding to fuel consumption in automobiles and electricity consumption in homes and offices. The expanding rate of energy consumption was accompaned by almost no public concern that the well would ever run dry. When the impact of the oil embargo struck during the winter of 1973–74, the dangers of our rate of consumption that had been lurking beneath the surface of American society burst into view with shocking reality.

Connecticut, with its weighted dependence on petroleum, was paying energy bills 1.5 times the national average. The necessity of balancing our state's fuel mix was given priority status by officials of state government. However, the range of solutions available to our state was limited, and the management of our energy future would have to be tailored to fit resources available to the citizens of Connecticut. There are no fossil fuels in our state. Therefore Connecticut and all the New England states can look forward to retaining their unenviable position at the end of the fossil fuel pipeline.

New exploration was undertaken in the outer continental shelf off the Atlantic Coast, but there was little hope that this exploration would provide substantial benefits to New England. If significant discoveries were made, New England could expect only to share the resources with the rest of the nation. Existing limitations on the supplies of petroleum and natural gas could therefore be expected to continue. Repeated suggestions that oil refineries be built in Connecticut and elsewhere in New England drew mixed reactions. Some New England states indicated a willingness to locate a refinery within their borders. Connecticut was unconvinced. Until a secure source of crude oil could be assured, a refining capacity for Connecticut or any other New England state seemed premature. Connecticut's particular geographical location appeared to make it a poor choice based on environmental considerations. In addition, economic studies conducted for our state indicated that the products of any such refinery would not necessarily be earmarked exclusively for use in New England. Also, there would be little if any economic benefit to consumers in the six-state region.

Along with the unavailability of additional petroleum resources, energy suppliers were pessimistic about chances for increased dependence on natural gas. The alternatives—liquefied petroleum gas and synthetic natural gas—were expensive and largely imported. These qualities made synthetic gas an unattractive alternative. Connecticut could not look to major hydroelectric projects for power because of a lack of suitable sites. The use of coal for electrical generation was also a remote possibility primarily because of the extraordinary transportation costs involved. The movement of massive amounts of coal and ash was not feasible on the existing debilitated rail system. In addition, the burning of coal posed major environmental and health hazards that would have to be overcome before this fuel could be utilized on a large scale. In the mid-1970s the fledgling technologies of solar and windmill power were too expensive and untested to be of practical value in the near future. Connecticut, with federal assistance, sponsored solar-energy projects in a housing project for the elderly and a state armory, but it would take several years of experience once construction was completed to determine the economic value of this energy resource.

The most practical alternative to Connecticut's petroleum dependence at this time was nuclear power. In 1976 nuclear plants generated more than half of the state's electricity, but this share reduced Connecticut's petroleum dependence only by 6.5 percent. At the same time, nuclear power was plagued by regulatory, procedural, and capacity problems. Very real dilemmas existed in the transportation and storage of radioactive waste as well as siting and safety risk factors. Based on known reserves and current projections, the domestic supply of uranium appeared to be inadequate. Additional reliance on nuclear power could very well create the same kind of dependence on foreign uranium suppliers as our state and New England had faced in the past with foreign petroleum producers.

Taking all these factors into account, Connecticut's goal of achieving a balanced fuel mix would take a long time. While basic decisions were being made on new technologies that would be economically, environmentally, and socially acceptable, emphasis would have to be placed on energy conservation. One of the priorities of my administration was the development of viable alternatives in transportation where 99 percent of the fuel used was a refined petroleum product. Energy management dictated a major state effort to promote alternatives to private automobile travel.

The state Department of Transportation encouraged major employers to institute car-pooling programs among their workers. The department utilized available data processing resources to assist motorists to locate and join car-pool programs. The department also conducted a vigorous program of commuter bus operations in major metropolitan areas. As of the summer of 1976, more than 20,000 Connecticut citizens were involved in car-pool programs, and the ridership in 18 commuter bus operations averaged approximately 27,500 per week.

Major strides were also made in the revitalization of our railroads to provide another viable alternative to private automobile usage. Reorganization of the depressed railroad industry throughout the Northeast resulted in creation of AMTRAK rail passenger service and ConRail. Connecticut cooperated with the new organizations in the development of special schedules, reduced fares, and public education programs to encourage the use of trains. The success of these programs would depend ultimately on the extent of modernization of facilities, improvements in service, and public willingness to utilize railroads in the overall effort to conserve energy.

Energy conservation in buildings and homes was also given priority attention. In the residential and commercial sectors, for example, petroleum accounted for more than half of our state's annual energy consumption. More than three of every four existing buildings will still be in use when our citizens enter the twenty-first century. Active retrofitting programs were therefore encouraged to reduce substantially the energy required to heat, cool, and light homes, stores, schools, and churches. During 1976 Project Retro-Tech was initiated throughout Connecticut, with the help of federal funds, to help the owners of more than 550,000 single-family dwellings reduce energy usage.

The project made homeowners aware of the need for effective insulation. It helped them analyze sources of heat loss in their homes, provided instruction for do-it-yourself projects, and encouraged other needed work by contractors. Courses for homeowners were taught at various facilities around the state and toll-free telephone service maintained for a five-month period during the fall and winter of 1976–77. The service offered residents information on insulation, retrofitting, and energy management, where and when courses were being taught, and guidance for the organization of Retro-Tech courses for individual groups.

The DPEP, which coordinated the Retro-Tech program, also worked closely with business and industry to develop improved techniques for the reduction of energy usage. In the year and a half period beginning in January 1975, 18 major companies and organizations had succeeded in achieving cuts in energy usage of more than 30 percent. One company, the Olin Corporation of Stamford, was honored in May 1976 for achieving a 36 percent reduction, the equivalent of 6662 barrels of number six fuel oil each year.

If the Connecticut program of energy management is to be successful, the efforts of state government must be intensified in the three major areas of fuel resources: acquisition, allocation, and conservation. The primary responsibility for acquiring and stimulating the growth of domestic energy resources rests with the federal government and the private sector. Since Connecticut has no fossil fuel or uranium reserves of its own, our state must lend its voice and expertise to national programs designed to develop energy resources that are free of foreign influence.

In the area of allocation, energy management requires Connecticut to pursue individual and regional efforts. These efforts must be designed to ensure that no one sector of the United States is required to bear a disproportionate burden of any national energy policy. At the same time, as reliance on foreign energy supplies is reduced, fairness demands that those areas of our nation heavily dependent on imported petroleum must in some way be accommodated until alternate sources of energy can be developed at reasonable prices.

In resource conservation, state government can demonstrate commitment and leadership through promotion of efficiency and encouragement of recovery programs. In addition to the concentrated efforts by Connecticut in the fields of transportation and conservation, the state embarked on a potentially far-reaching recovery plan. The Connecticut Resource Recovery Authority was created to develop regional projects to collect solid waste and convert it into energy sources.

Energy management made significant progress in Connecticut in less than two years. The program was born in the crisis of the Arab oil embargo and honed by the painful lessons of waste and poor planning. The techniques of coping with an energy dilemma stemming from humankind's dependence on a finite resource are still in their infancy. Substantial advances have been accomplished, and the outlook for the future is encouraging. Moreover, energy management is proving to be an experience that, in the words of Carlyle, "is the best of all schoolmasters"—for its impact is broad and its influence far-reaching.

The management of a changing and expanding economy is intertwined with the management of our energy needs. Progress in the field of energy can be applied to the economy to ensure an orderly and productive growth of our society in the years ahead. The English philosopher Herbert Spencer wrote that "progress . . . is not an accident, but a necessity. . . . It is a part of nature." The necessity we face is to manage our affairs for the benefit of future generations. The necessity is a challenge we welcome.

12

LEADERSHIP OF THE SPIRIT:
A Present and Future Need

THOMAS R. HORTON
IBM Director of University Relations,
International Business Machines Corporation

If you do not think about the future, you cannot have one.
John Galsworthy

It is not merely management which the future requires, but leadership of a very special kind. In pondering tomorrow's needs, this essay reviews predictions made by those who study the future. Since forward vision can at best be dim, one must be wary of depending heavily upon specific forecasts about the shape of tomorrow's world. Still, such predictions and speculations serve to trigger useful trains of thought, even though most futurists' forecasts are wide of the mark. One prescription is for the need of future leaders to have the capacity to deal with the unexpected. The development of management techniques and methodologies are then surveyed. The past's contribution to management theory and methodology is rich and varied. Yet methodology has its limits, and in the race between problem complexity and solution by methodology, complexity seems to be clearly in the lead.

Though management in some ways is becoming a scientific endeavor, it is still a very human one. This article suggests the need to emphasize and further develop the human element. The importance of the quality of managers' ideas is traced through each level of a particular, nonprofit management hierarchy. Ways are suggested to encourage the development of the reflective manager, the man or woman who is able to turn an idea over and around in several dimensions to seek its most appropriate perspective. Means are suggested to assist in broadening the perspective of future managers through exposure to experiences beyond their immediate horizons.

Finally, a clear distinction is drawn between "management" and "leadership," and some proposals are made concerning the latter: the development of systems which can more effectively seek out, identify, and nurture future leaders; rigorous research on the nature of leadership; and the possible development of leadership institutes, inspired by the success of the French *Grandes Ecoles,* which would be charged with the national task of finding and encouraging potential future leaders.

THE FUTURE AS GUIDE

I wonder if the soothsayer laughs when he sees another soothsayer.
Cicero

Perhaps it is anxiety which causes human beings to try so desperately to foresee the future. A major part of a manager's concern must be the future, since this is the period in which the consequences of decisions and actions will become known; not trying to anticipate possible futures would be foolhardy in the management of any enterprise, profit or nonprofit. But the recent boom in futurology and the growing custom of convening conferences of otherwise sensible people to issue statements about the shape of the future and recommendations as to what must be done as a result of that forecasted shape, raise the question as to whether such officially proclaimed futures can be looked to as useful guides by management.

Paleolithic caves doubtless housed primitive futurologists. Later civilizations gave priests the task of reading the entrails of sacrificial animals, since the future was revealed as a religious experience. More recently the process has been given some scientific respectability. It is not unusual for technological forecasts to be found in reputable scientific journals. Nor has the field of management escaped this futurist orientation. In 1960, on the occasion of the tenth anniversary of the Graduate School of Industrial Administration of Carnegie Institute of Technology, a convocation of scholars was held to discuss management in 1985.[1] Since that post-Orwellian year is fast approaching, it may be instructive to look back on some of the forecasts and assumptions that were in fashion in 1960. One assumption was a vast increase in leisure time; employment would be available to virtually all who wanted it. Today there is plenty of enforced leisure time, for lack of jobs. By 1985 the computer, said one of the conferees, will have developed the ability to solve almost the entire range of problems which are solvable by humans. It will have learned to apply judgment and insight and, in fact, will have become a thinking machine; as a result, humanoids will have replaced humans in many management roles since they will have surpassed humans in ability. One of the basic questions at that 1960 conference on the future of management was whether there would be any role left for middle managers in 1985, since computers will have overtaken their capabilities and jobs.

Looking back from today's perspectives, a business executive or college president, pressed by inflation and entangled in the increasingly sticky web of government regulation, may wistfully wish that the computer *had* become an efficient, steady middle manager; but the fact is that the most difficult of his or her problems are human problems, most of which will yield to no less than human solutions.

In the mid-1960s another prestigious group, the Commission on the Year 2000, was organized to reflect on society's future and to make recommendations. The usual technological predictions were made—more reliable weather forecasting, some weather control, new sources of power, interplanetary travel—and again a world of steady employment, increasing affluence, and leisure were foreseen. The growth of the megalopolis, for example, the great urban stretch extending from Virginia to Massachusetts, was forecast.[2] Indeed, in the field of higher education it was anticipated that great university cities would develop by the year 2000.[3] (Perhaps these cities would have been spawned by the urban universities to be established as a result of the recommendations of the Carnegie Commission on Higher Education which reported a few years later.)

Today an observer wonders whether the latest conventional wisdom concerning population shifts to the Southern Rim, or Sunbelt, will result in a southward displacement of that megalopolitan growth. University administrators, observing the strains now being felt by the City University of New York system, may be tempted to wonder whether the university cities in the year 2000 will be built upon the ruins of that system.

Perhaps the most widespread recent publicity on futures was given to the forecasts made by the Club of Rome's project on the predicament of mankind, outlining the inevitable consequences of continued and uncontrolled population and economic growth.[4] The popularity of *The Limits to Growth* underlines humankind's fascination with its future. The Club of Rome issued a statement in 1976, four years after its first pronouncement, claiming that it is *not* growth which is the problem (though that is indeed considered still a problem), it is the *lack* of growth which would yield a more enduring hurt, since growth is essential if the world's poverty is ever to be overcome.

As still another example, it was thought by prominent scientists about 20 years ago that one very desirable course of action would be to find some way to double the production of engineers and scientists, particularly at the Ph.D. level.[5] This increased supply of educated technological brainpower would then be unleashed to solve society's problems. But the long effects of "stagflation" in the seventies have resulted in unemployment even in this well-prepared sector of the labor force. Yet another major technological forecast, issued less than a decade ago, based many of its predictions on a fundamental assumption that energy costs would steadily decline.

The important and rapid emergence of women into nontraditional roles throughout American society seems not to have been forecast even dimly by recent committees of seers. This is understandable since such committees have rarely had more than token female representation. It is clear that futurists' predictions must necessarily fall short of reality. Yet they do serve to stimulate in an important way new trains of thought and new perspectives about the present. While such predictions are less than useful as a guide to what future management will require, they do suggest the need for a flexible leadership capability, a capacity to cope with surprise.

THE PAST AS GUIDE

Every age of the world has increased and still increases the real wealth, the happiness, the knowledge, and perhaps the virtue, of the human race.

Edward Gibbon

In ancient times, simple forms of management knowledge sufficed. Most engineering and scientific projects such as the construction of the observatory at Stonehenge or the Egyptian pyramids had relatively simple project goals, though both represented enormous achievements in terms of coordinated and purposeful human endeavor. The history of the great armies of the world and the development and institutionalization of the Roman Catholic Church, to name only two examples, required remarkable organizational insight.

Research in the field of management, however, is relatively young. It was only two centuries ago that Adam Smith made his monumental contribution which established the field of modern economics. The industrial revolution demanded the development of new forms of organization and managerial technique and gave rise to what has come to be known as "modern management." Whether the father of this school is James Montgomery, Robert Owen, or Charles Babbage, the pace of mechanization made it necessary that intellect be focused on the manufacturing process and the worker. Still, the modern era of "scientific" management, heavily weighted toward quantitative considerations, is an even more recent development. The seminal contributions of Frederick Winslow Taylor were made scarcely a century ago. Adding an interdisciplinary flavor, political philosopher Mary Parker Follett brought an entirely new perspective to the concepts of leadership and management control.

Looking back over a lifetime of historical writing, Will and Ariel Durant devoted a chapter of *The Lessons of History*[6] to the subject of economics and commerce. The one lesson which seems most clear is that over the long course of history, every economic system has sooner or later had to rely upon some form of the profit motive. Productivity and economic growth have depended utterly upon human incentive, operating within the workings of the market. The distribution and delivery system of public goods and services in the long run can be no healthier than the system of private initiatives which generates the needed funds. Today management techniques developed in the private sector are being applied to the public sector, and in fact each has contributed much to the growing list of management methodologies.

Some methodologies, such as Peter Drucker's Management by Objectives (MBO), have had wide application across both sectors—in manufacturing organizations, banks, retail establishments, school systems, and even religious orders—with considerable success. Another widely heralded but perhaps less widely used technique is PPBS (planning-programming-budgeting system) whose early promise caused it to be applied with mixed results to a broad range of private and public activities. Designed for well-defined, tangible activities such as weapons system budgeting, PPBS has been less effective as a budget planning tool in the public schools. The critical path method (CPM), originally a contribution from private technological industry, was rapidly followed by the U.S. Navy's performance evaluation and review technique (PERT), which called upon statistical probability theory and used computer runs to produce detailed scheduling and control documents.[7] Soon computer specialists had developed modeling and simulation techniques for a great variety of enterprises in an attempt to help reduce the burden of management, so that decision making became a choice among programmed alternatives. Terms such as minimax (or maximin), stochastic analyses, dynamic correction, risk forecasting, and anticipation data became a part of the management school lexicon.

With such a vast array of management theory and technique one might expect successful solutions to even the most difficult management problems. At the very least their informed use should give management an early-warning device against serious trouble. Yet in recent years a great automobile company produced as product a $250-million marketing failure; the largest privately financed transportation system in the world went bankrupt; a leading aerospace company required an emergency governmental subsidy of vast millions of dollars in order not to become bankrupt; a serious underestimate of usage was made by the leading communications utility, causing severe degradation of service which required special corrective efforts; major oil companies failed to anticipate the political actions of Middle Eastern leaders; large New York City banks staggered under the burden of high-risk loans and unforeseen effects of the economy; nationwide investment scandals occurred; financial near-collapse of New York City became imminent; the U.S. Postal Service developed management problems which will yield to no easy solution. This list could be readily expanded with examples from both the public and private sectors.

Good management clearly requires more than brilliant technique. It is not that systems analysis and operations research have failed us. Rather, the complexities of circumstances seem to have grown beyond our ability to mesh the mechanism to the problem effectively. Certain techniques appropriate to one task are inappropriate to others. For example, major universities effectively call upon management science to assist in portfolio management, class scheduling, even simulation of tenure alternatives. Less appropriately, the stern disciplines of formal planning techniques have been applied to the task of department budget allocation at some small and fragile liberal arts colleges. In some cases good techniques have been applied poorly to public sector problems for lack of training.

The application of sophisticated methodology to the management of hospitals, cultural institutions, and voluntary associations is still to be felt in full force. Today there are almost 20,000 men and women studying at graduate or professional schools of public administration or management who have expressed their intent to apply their knowledge and administrative skills to organizations outside the private sector. In time the results of this relatively new phenomenon can be better judged.

So far the past's contribution to management has been discussed only in terms of technique and methodology. However, a much richer heritage exists, in examples of human leadership. Any scholar of management could compile a list of figures who have towered above others in such major fields as government, business, finance, technological enterprise, education, and civil rights. The exercise of attempting to compile such a list illustrates the wide range of personalities who have provided leadership. For example, contrast the style and personality of President Thomas Jefferson with that of Theodore Roosevelt; Elizabeth I with Queen Victoria; or Henry Ford with Alfred P. Sloan, Jr. Perhaps one of the more profound truths which the past offers for application to future management is that there is no standard management model or style of leadership. Perhaps the future may require yet new styles. Since one's vision of the future is so dim, perhaps all that can be safely recommended is the maintenance of a management attitude which is attuned to and eager to benefit from the infinite diversity of human character.

THE PRESENT AS ABSENTEE

The time is out of joint.
Hamlet

When observing the management decision process in action—whether decisions are formed through meetings, evolved through exchanges of memoranda, or issued by fiat—one is struck by the heavy but unseen influence of the past and, at times, the apparent absence of the present. For example, the board of trustees of a private hospital may decide to launch a major capital campaign to expand its number of beds, just at the time that the birthrate is precipitously falling. Although analysis will indicate clearly a high probability of increasing numbers of empty maternity beds becoming available, the campaign will be launched with suitable fanfare. Trustees of a small college which is enjoying a temporary increase in enrollment (due perhaps to a public university enrollment "cap" being legislated) and hence facing a temporary shortage of dormitory rooms may decide to borrow heavily for new construction, in the very face of indisputable evidence that future enrollments are likely to decrease. These are examples of decisions which seem to be made by a process of accretion or by the inexorable force of slow-motion momentum. If in such circumstances a board member wishes to challenge the wisdom of the proposed expansion plan, he or she may be rudely challenged by the majority and treated almost as a traitor to the cause: "Listen, don't you believe in the future of this institution?" or "Honestly, I thought we were all together on this; we have been leading up to this decision for the past four years, and I say we must move forward now, and I call the question!" Such management decisions seem to be entrapped in a kind of time warp. Like Billy Pilgrim of *Slaughterhouse Five,*[8] the objecting board member is whiplashed between the past and the future. If the board member objects that plans made in the past perhaps should be reviewed in the present, he or she is told that the future demands no less than the decision which has been proposed. If he or she then questions *future* projections of needed hospital usage (or forecasted college enrollment trends), the board member is referred to the exponential growth of the past as indisputable evidence of a need to build toward the future.

This time-warp phenomenon of decision making is not limited to the board level. All of us know the type of manager whose mental set or outlook is firmly affixed to the past, for example, the middle manager who defends his or her position on the basis of the fact that "We have always done it this way." A past-oriented manager of this type often reports to another of the same type (since in fact the former was chosen by the latter on the basis that "We've always selected people of this background for that particular job"); and a hierarchy of three or more managers of this backward-looking orientation can stifle almost any organization. Sometimes the decision process seems to become stuck in a gluey viscosity, as the decision finally emerges in slow motion, independent of the needs of the present. In this process a decision may be reached after its need has vanished and possibly when it is no longer even appropriate.

Just as disturbing is the exclusively future-oriented middle manager. This is the person who completely ignores the past, skips lightly over the present, and shoots toward the future from an intuitive hip, with this typical justification for a decision: "I am sure that such and such is going to happen, so we simply have to do it this way." When such and such fails to happen, the decision may or may not have been the right one.

A member of a Congregational church may find it a sobering exercise to review the minutes of past meetings of the church's official board over, say, a five-year period. Such records may abound with examples of actions taken on the basis of misunderstood, misstated, or missing rationales. A facile committee chairman or minister may learn to manipulate the committee by arguments which shift deftly between the past and the future, sliding over the present without touching it at all. Although one may ignore the present reality in the decision process, its validity and consequences cannot be escaped.

One would not expect the present to be overlooked or confused with the future by professional experts in accounting and financial mangement. Yet, newspaper coverage of the New York City budget crunch uses such terms as backloading, front-filling, and stretch out, terms which apply to shifts of time in fiscal transactions and slippages in the time by which the budget must be balanced. One reason for New York City's massive financial crisis in the first place was the practice of blurring the lines separating successive fiscal years. By borrowing from future revenues and papering over past and present fiscal obligations, one can develop a sort of time-warp accounting. But the consequences of the present reality will intrude into the future.

An example of a methodology designed to help keep the present in focus is the set of management tools developed by Charles Kepner and Benjamin Tregoe.[9] The application of their concepts and techniques is instructive and can be a clarifying act. The process of asking such questions as "*When* a condition first existed, *where* it was first noted, *what* other conditions had changed and exactly *when?*" is not compatible with "time-warp management," as it forces the present reality onto center stage, brightly lighted. Systematic methods such as these have been applied beyond problem solving to complex decision making and even to objective setting. Perhaps more important than any methodology or technique, however, is the development in management of a deep devotion to "reality thinking," in which the present is very much with us at all times. Perhaps this is just another way of describing the need for aware, tough-minded leadership.

REFLECTIVE VERSUS REFLEX MANAGEMENT

The brain is an organ of last resort.
John Dewey

A highly desirable management trait is responsiveness. However, this is sometimes misunderstood to mean simply quickness of response. Although certain tasks (such as catching a person who has jumped from the window of a burning building) require instantaneous and firm response, this is not the usual, day-to-day requirement of a manager. The quality of a response is often more important than its speed. Speed may test alertness and reaction time, but quality of response calls for intellectual analysis and mental testing. Moreover, even the highest level of response capability is not a sufficient talent to define the superior manager, who must have, in addition, the ability to set direction and to inspire *others* to respond.

Let us look for a moment at characteristics of the several levels of management needed to deliver one specific desirable outcome. Choosing as example something outside the normal experience of most managers in business, let us consider the management hierarchy involved in a successful performance of a great symphony orchestra. As a first essential, experienced, qualified instrumentalists must be found and recruited, since a first-rate performance is unlikely to come from musicians of lesser rank. As in any team effort, some sense of community or shared goal must be nurtured. Rehearsals must be scheduled. The positioning of the major sections—strings, woodwinds, brass, percussion—must be accomplished in terms of the acoustics and visual effects of the hall.

Yet even if all of the necessary myriad of details are attended to, there still can be no truly superior performance without the leadership of a superior conductor during rehearsals and performance. The conductor, to survive in that role, must have musical knowledge and intuition of a level sufficiently high to command the respect of the great variety of instrumentalists who must be led. The conductor is teacher and learner, but foremost, a leader. Although he or she must have the capacity to react very quickly during the concert, it is not speed of reaction which is critical to acceptance and success, but rather the ability to extract superior performances from the instrumentalists and to blend them into one great instrument, the orchestra in gestalt. A popular textbook on conducting technique opens with the bald statement that the most important requirement of a conductor is the ability to inspire the performers.[10] The process of great conducting is the drawing forth from each performer of his or her utmost capability simultaneously with all others in such a way as to produce an overall effect which is pleasing technically, emotionally, and intellectually. Strict obligations exist to the composer, performers, and audience. The sound must be acceptable to the music critic as fresh and crisp, creative in interpretation, yet true in every sense to the concepts and instructions of the composer. Such perfection at times may appear to result from a sort of "participative conducting"; yet the conductor must be clearly in charge. Hans Richter said of his conducting:

> . . . it has even happened that in spots I allowed myself to be led by the orchestra, fully aware that the instinctive, spontaneous, unconstrained utterance frequently flowing from an intelligent body of players offers the true clue to the spiritual content of a composition. I would not hesitate to call this the genius of an orchestra. This of course is not intended to convey the impression that I do not desire and succeed in exerting my own will without indulgence. It is only that I wish to be spared the knout, the club, through which some conductors try to subjugate the free unfoldment of an independent-thinking ensemble. Whoever seeks to subject the orchestra inflexibly to his exclusive will is no true musician.

Hans Richter is the conductor of whom Claude Debussy wrote: "he conducts as dear God would conduct if He had learned conducting from Hans Richter."[11] Successful orchestral conducting requires an intense concentration on detail and, more important, the ability to synthesize. There is a wide agreement that it is the quality of the conductor's thought process (the *ideas* that are conveyed to the orchestra) which gives the leader's baton its authority.

Carrying the management analogy further, a symbiotic relationship between the conductor and the orchestra's concert master may add to the success of a conductor and the ensemble's performance. The willingness of the conductor to stand aside and delegate fully to a master violinist the task of setting the mood or ambience of a particular phrase requires the same sort of judgment and courage that a business executive makes when a decision is made not to intervene in a particularly important decision which is being handled by a subordinate. Perhaps the confidence tacitly shown in this way draws forth an extra measure of quality which otherwise would be absent.

In any enterprise there is a dividing line which separates mere management from true leadership, a recognizable distinction between quite adequate and superior. The leader strives for the higher quality; as Handel told a distinguished listener after the first London performance of *The Messiah:* "I should regret it, my Lord, if I only *entertain* people; my aim is to make them better."[12] It is this spiritual quality which a superior conductor seeks to produce through the application of worthwhile ideas to the recreation of the composition. Yet the task of transforming the potential of the score to a kinetic musical experience neither begins nor ends with the conductor, celebrated as that person may be. As we have seen, the conductor is dependent on the concert master and performers. In addition, all are dependent on the orchestra company's general manager, without whom there would be no schedule, no audience, no hall. The conductor is free to conduct partly because of a shield of protection from business matters and other distractions. Salary negotiations, union disputes, arguments over season ticket price structure, meetings on acoustical problems of the hall, gentle removals from the orchestra of musicians who are no longer able to play well—these are the everyday grist for the general manager's mill. This is also the person who is primarily responsible for the selection and care of the conductor. Essential to the general manager's success is a keen and informed musical taste; yet the conductor's ego must be nurtured even at times of profound and substantive disagreement. No less essential is financial ability, since no symphony orchestra in the world makes money.[13] Caught between the orchestra members and the community, a general manager of a metropolitan orchestra must deal with still another body, the board of directors. This group of civic-spirited volunteers may include some people whose chief interest in membership is the prestige it brings. Others may have a passionate interest in music and a concomitant desire to help the manager and the conductor produce the finished product. The general manager in this circumstance becomes a buffer, to protect the autonomy and musical integrity of the orchestra. One hopes for some members who serve to convey the needs of the orchestra to the community and the spirit of the community to the general manager. Through a supportive exchange of ideas and viewpoints, the board can do more than merely exercise its legal role of trusteeship. It can play an affirmative role.

Yet board members have no authority as individuals over the orchestra. The board of directors acts only as a body, in concert (no pun intended). So finally there is the board chairman whose job is to see that the whole enterprise achieves harmony and performs with some distinction, whose task is essentially one of helping to create a climate of trust and spirit of shared goals. The chairman must try to isolate and overcome misunderstandings and dissonance of viewpoints. The role of board leadership is partly to convey ideas, partly to shape them. The board chairman's role is very different from that of the general manager, conductor, concert master, or solo instrumentalist, yet there is one common requirement at each leadership level in this musical enterprise—the requirement for quality of reflective thought and a willingness to have one's ideas tested and challenged by others whose mental capacities and tastes merit respect.

Richard Strauss told young conductors: "If you cannot control the orchestra by the quality of your ideas, you don't belong in front of it."[14] This may apply just as well to the efforts of all managers as they attempt to conduct and direct their diverse enterprises. Clearly, at each level of management of an artistic enterprise such as this example, the value added comes from reflective thought and questioning: What did the composer have in mind? How would this movement sound if the violins attacked with more energy? Would the effect be better if the tympanists were moved higher? Would attendance increase or decrease with a different membership structure? Should programming be influenced by the community's requests or shall we educate and elevate the community's musical tastes? It is obviously not the speed of response to such questions that will affect the orchestra; it is the *quality* of response, and this comes from the turning and testing of hypotheses, reflections, and mental simulations of the results of decisions.

This capacity for reflection seems to be closely tied to the capacity for leadership. To study a leader, one should look at those who are led. A willingness to be led implies that something of value is being provided by the leader. Often that something is an understanding or a new perspective about the task to be performed. Surely the qualities of reflective leadership are essential for management in the future.

FOCUS AND PERSPECTIVE

Every man takes the limits of his own field of vision for the limits of the world.
Arthur Schopenhauer

Whatever techniques and conceptual methods are employed, one imperative of future management is to keep reality in sharp focus. An analytical, process-oriented capability is needed to grasp the essentials of a problem and probe to its heart and find its best solution. Other traits, such as courage, may be absolutely essential at certain times, but clarity of mental view is the sine qua non at all times. Management training and development courses designed to teach and extend this capability should be encouraged. Less easy to teach than problem analysis are breadth of vision and capacity for perspective.

Perspective of viewpoint usually results from a heightened awareness of worlds other than one's own. The middle manager whose whole life is his or her job, whose social acquaintances are fellow company employees, whose annual vacations over a 10-year period cannot be distinguished one from another has a certain limited perspective, set of values, and horizon. A top executive who limits his or her exposure to other top executives with similar social and political views limits personal growth and perhaps the growth of the business enterprise as well. Such an executive is sometimes said to need a sabbatical for refreshment and "battery recharging," and at times this may be effective. Extended travel, temporary transfer to a very different part of the company, participation in management seminars, and other ideas are frequently tried as a remedial sort of treatment. One wonders whether some preventive application of continuous refreshment might be better.

In American society, opportunities abound for intellectual refreshment. Some executives find they can mentally shed their problems by taking on difficult but quite different problems of voluntary social agencies. Hospitals, schools, colleges, museums, choral groups, bands, religious service organizations such as the Salvation Army, parks, zoos, youth agencies, alcoholic and drug counseling or rehabilitation centers, sheltered workshops for the handicapped, political parties, churches, homes for the aging, and other agencies need management skills and insights of a high order.

A hazard of such volunteer work is that an executive may quickly be pigeonholed into an accustomed pigeonhole: a corporate treasurer assigned to be a university treasurer or a marketing vice president asked to lead the development committee. This may not provide the desired change of pace or view and may be less than beneficial to the agency as well. A second hazard is that one may find that the executive director of the agency wishes to restrict the board's exposure to mundane matters of business and the routine of the budget cycle, keeping from the board the program and personality of the organization. Even worse, the new board member may be surrounded by familiar, corporate faces. If either of these conditions stand, this is no sabbatical or opportunity for new perspective but rather more of the same. Many volunteer agencies do exist which give the executive volunteer the opportunity for one-to-one contact with members of a new human community, the challenge of dealing with an unfamiliar point of view, the chance to broaden perspective, to live in two worlds. Many other types of mind-expanding opportunities surround us—formal education in new fields; a vacation spent in an intellectual atmosphere such as the Chautauqua Institution, Aspen Institute for Humanistic Studies, or on a college campus; travel to some obscure spot where tourists seldom tread; or any other *designed* and *new* experience, as opposed to the acceptance of the usual, ever-narrowing life experience as it may present itself, unplanned. The quality of management benefits from an awareness of the broad milieu of human experience. The future demands that we work harder on this problem than we appear to be doing today.

The central contribution of an expanded awareness of worlds or cultures other than one's own is in the realm of values. Any attempt directly to teach values becomes a sort of ideological or didactic experience. Ideally, values should be learned, rather than taught, through rich and deep exposures to life, literature, theater, and the arts. J. Douglas Brown[15] claims that no one without a keen sense of tragedy should have authority over others and recommends Shakespeare as mentor. In the long run, management needs the development of a deep, human intuition. Values cannot replace scientific management techniques, which will be needed in the future; one hopes for a future management which is skilled in this science but dedicated to its humane application.

LEADERSHIP FOR THE FUTURE

It is not strength, but art, obtains the prize; to be swift is less than to be wise.
Homer

So far, certain essentials have been isolated: a willingness to confront reality, a natural capacity to reflect, a willingness to search for and question values through broadened perspective. Harder to define is the greatest need: the *essence* of leadership. Though difficult to define, it is instinctively recognizable—it is the difference between the merely well-trained performer and the artist, the learned educationist and the educator, the politician and the statesman, the manager and the leader. A sufficient future supply of management capability is assured: business schools are filled to brimming with eager candidates. Leadership is the more pressing need.

What are the essentials of leadership? Let us list at the outset intelligence, technical mastery, physical vigor, capacity for interpersonal relations, integrity, and courage. Having said that, we still search for the spirit or essence of the leader. It is the author's belief that this quality of leadership springs from a much deeper well, an inner capacity found somewhere beyond the psyche, from a source very close to the "self" or the soul of a person. Until this almost esoteric quality is better understood, it is unlikely to be capable of being taught. Perhaps it never can be. Yet it is needed in future management. What is *not* needed is some pedestrian analysis of the qualities of leaders, as selected by opinion survey, and a subsequent production line to turn out trained, imitation leadership. Rather, the superior, subtle quality of leadership must be identified and encouraged to emerge slowly from the very center of potential leaders. This process may require more tolerance for individualism (a positive concept) and even eccentricity (not so positive) than many modern organizations can comfortably display today.

A true leader develops and inspires quality of commitment not always found in a professional manager. Organizations as well as individuals display (or fail to display) this characteristic. This is akin to the life spirit, and it must be nurtured. If the creative seed die, this human or organizational life force withers away. It is easier to identify this quality than to produce it. In an egalitarian society the idea of establishing centralized leadership academies or institutes to encourage the early selection and training of those with supreme capacity for leadership may not be practical. The *Grandes Ecoles* of France which train small numbers of highly selected students for top administrative posts in government, industry, business, and the arts may not be a practical possibility in this country.[16] Yet, this suggestion should not be too readily discarded. Thomas Jefferson spoke of democracy of opportunity and aristocracy of achievement. The American *Grandes Ecoles* could be modeled on this ideal.

One wonders whether the current academic and industrial management selection mechanisms tend to "select out" some of the very qualities that an ideal mechanism should "select in." As an example, consider the college presidential search committee which seeks a president with academic attainment and managerial capacity, one skilled in fund raising, alumni and community cultivation, and on and on. Since in any population so few exist who can claim top capacity in each of these categories, a compromise decision must eventually be made. The final decision may be to select as candidate the person with at least adequate demonstrated capability in each of the categories and no distinction in any of them, rather than one who is absolutely superb in one category and eager and able to learn the others. The real question, of course, is which of the two has greater leadership capability, and since this depends upon the milieu in which the leadership will be exercised, one is not likely to know until the job is in fact filled.

One wonders also whether the sieve of conventional management resource and executive development programs of today are wholly successful in identifying and nurturing candidates with the spark of leadership (a study of the top leaders in history will show them to have been people with highly individualistic traits and personalities) or whether instead it is the classical, above-mediocre, "well-rounded" person, precisely fitting some comfortable mold, who is being identified and labeled "manager for the future." No specific prescription seems possible, nor is a solution in terms of management science formulas likely to exist, simply because of the nature of leadership. But there are some points which might be pondered:

- The need to develop identification systems which act more as nets reaching out than as sieves or filters, "selecting out"
- The necessity for broadened perspective at all levels, through planned visits to "other worlds," other cultures
- The need to conduct rigorous research on the qualities of leadership and their origins
- The possibility of developing national or regional leadership institutes, inspired by the success of the French *Grandes Ecoles,* to be charged with the task of competitively selecting men and women of the very highest potential, and developing those talented few to be an important source of future leaders
- Most of all, the need to reflect deeply and thoughtfully on these matters as the future unfolds

NOTES AND REFERENCES

1. Melvin Anshen and George Leland Bach (eds.), *Management and Corporations 1985* (New York: McGraw-Hill, 1960).
2. Herman Kahn and Anthony J. Wiener, "A Framework for Speculation," *Daedalus,* Journal of the American Academy of Arts and Sciences, Summer 1967, pp. 711–716.
3. Stephen R. Graubard, "University Cities in the Year 2000," *Daedalus,* Summer 1967.
4. D. H. Meadows et al., *The Limits to Growth,* A Report for the Club of Rome's Project on the Predicament of Mankind (New York: Universe Books, 1972).
5. Harrison Brown et al., *The Next Hundred Years* (New York: Viking, 1957).

6. Will Durant and Ariel Durant, *The Lessons of History* (New York: Simon & Schuster, 1968).

7. CPM was the contribution of the DuPont Company; its relationship to earlier graphic project management methods is described in: D. Wren, *The Evolution of Management Thought* (New York: Ronald Press, 1972). PERT developed through the efforts of Lockheed's Missile Systems Division, Booz, Allen, and Hamilton; and the expertise and experience of the U.S. Navy.

8. Kurt Vonnegut, *Slaughterhouse Five* (New York: Dell, 1969).

9. C. H. Kepner and B. B. Tregoe, *The Rational Manager* (New York: McGraw-Hill, 1965).

10. Brock McElheran, *Conducting Technique* (New York: Oxford University Press, 1966).

11. Karl Krueger, *The Way of the Conductor* (New York: Scribner, 1958), p. 243.

12. Ibid., p. 12.

13. Thomas Thompson, "The Importance of Being Fleishman," *The New York Times Magazine*, Apr. 11, 1976, p. 36.

14. Karl Krueger, op. cit., p. 31.

15. J. Douglas Brown, *The Human Nature of Organization* (New York: Amacom, 1973).

16. The *Grandes Ecoles* are a family of higher professional institutions established to train students, selected by national competitive examination, in various career fields. Courses of study for various kinds of government service are provided by the *Ecole Nationale d'Administration*, the *Ecole Polytechnique*, and others; professional business education is the speciality of the *Ecole des Hautes Etudes Commerciales;* and additional *Grandes Ecoles* provide training in other fields such as aeronautics, mining, telecommunications, music, and the dramatic arts. Parallel institutions are the *Ecoles Normales Supérieures*, whose curricula include a broad spectrum of courses spanning the sciences and the humanities.

13

GOVERNMENT'S ROLE IN ECONOMIC MANAGEMENT

JACOB K. JAVITS
United States Senator from New York

There is an ongoing and vital debate in this country over the role of government in economic management. Since the 1930s there has been a quantum jump in the involvement of government in the economy of the United States, with government as participant, partner, regulator, insurer, financier, and consumer with business. In the 1960s we reached the peak of our belief in the ability of government to solve virtually every problem with sufficient money and governmental machinery, and now we seem to have reached the opposite conclusion: that government cannot handle any problem well and is itself the problem rather than the answer. This latter view may have short-term election appeal to those frustrated by the complexity of our society, but it is not a serious answer to genuine problems.

I believe that one of the major challenges we face as a nation is preservation of the essential elements of the free enterprise system in a world tending toward greater concentration of power in government. Management in the future will have to take increasing account of the role of government in its affairs and be willing to undertake ventures with government where appropriate. Government must become more sensitive to its enormous impact on business and the economy and more attuned to methods of regulation that achieve their purposes without causing business to break down. There are exciting possibilities for a new partnership between business and government through a more rational and systematic approach to our problems.

We have labeled this approach "economic planning," and the concept is embodied in a bill (S. 1795)—entitled the "Balanced Growth and Economic Planning Bill"—that Senator Hubert Humphrey and I introduced May 21, 1975. (Unfortunately, it died in Congress.) The ideas in this legislation could as easily be called "economic management" or "policy planning," though we chose to confront the issue directly. The label applied is not particularly important; the concept is.

The idea that the United States government requires a consistent and rational means for considering the interrelationships of our problems is gaining wider acceptance. The Humphrey-Hawkins bill seeking to legislate "full employment" adopts a large element of planning from the Humphrey-Javits bill, and the issue promises to become important in political debates. We need a mechanism that will provide an overview of the issues, yet be capable of analyzing the components. This is not a magic solution to intractable problems or a means of raising the government to new levels of competence. It is an attempt to apply new tools, developed largely in the business world, to serve the needs of the nation. Two elements of planning require explanation here: why we need planning, and what issues must be addressed in developing a satisfactory planning mechanism.

WHY WE NEED PLANNING

It is important at the outset to keep in mind a crucial distinction between a *planned* society, such as the centrally planned economies of Eastern Europe and the Soviet Union, and a *planning* society, in which planning seeks to invigorate the market or strengthen social goals inadequately provided for by the market. Our goal is to introduce a larger element of planning in the approach to national issues, not to supplant the market.

The last few years have occasioned a sharp rise in our perceptions of world interdependence. The United States had been relatively self-sufficient for many years in food production, natural resources, oil, and technology. Our market was so large that exports were relatively unimportant to our total growth, and were almost a by-product of U.S. technology. The United States thus grew accustomed to its preeminence in the world and its ability to influence the course of other nations which exerted no reciprocal effect.

Events of recent years have begun to alter our position in the world, though we have not fully faced up to the changes. Since the early 1960s there has been a dramatic increase in the number of independent countries, resulting from the end of colonialism. Initially little more than economic appendages of European powers, these countries have now developed their own economic and political philosophies. We see the results in the United Nations and other international agencies: a strong trend toward nationalism, statism, and socialism. Many of the institutions developed by the United States and its wartime allies have been altered materially by the participation of these new nations, and in some cases the United States and its allies are beginning to lose or have lost control over their direction.

The economic consequences of these trends are clearly evident in such recent international economic forums as the Seventh Special Session of the UN General Assembly on international economic issues, which met in September 1975 in New York, and the UN Conference on Trade and Development (UNCTAD) held in Nairobi, Kenya, in May 1976. The triggering event that welded the developing countries into a cohesive bloc (though there remain very substantial differences among the developing countries) was the oil embargo of 1973. Though the poorest of the developing countries were hardest hit by the price increases that accompanied and followed the oil embargo, the action of certain members of OPEC (Organization of Petroleum Exporting Countries) demonstrated for the first time the great power of the oil producers. It was an example they thought worthy of emulation by other developing countries, and the Integrated Commodity Program and Common Fund proposed by the developing countries at UNCTAD was the culmination of several years' work on the issue.

The growing effort of the developing countries to alter the world trading system that has provided such great benefits to the industrial nations since World War II has also been directed at foreign investment in the developing countries. Nationalization of raw material and oil-producing companies has substantially altered the terms of business in these countries. Socialist governments in many developing countries have limited the opportunities for investment and have created a climate of hostility to multinational corporations, many of which are American.

Among the OECD (Organization for Economic Cooperation and Development) countries a different attitude prevails, especially on questions of trade and investment among themselves. However, the revelations of corporate bribery and corruption have forced governments to take a stricter attitude toward the multinational corporations. Some industrial nations, more dependent than the United States on raw materials from and exports of finished goods to developing countries, can be expected to take a more sympathetic view of their demands. At the same time, there is now greater synchronization of business cycles among all countries, especially the industrial countries. The recent worldwide recession was substantially worsened by the simultaneous drop in the economies of all the industrial countries. This synchronization demands more frequent consultations among the leaders of the OECD countries.

The world is moving toward a greater economic interdependence, however bedeviled it may be by economic nationalism. The United States is becoming more dependent on foreign oil, not less so. Our need for foreign raw materials is increasing, and foreign markets are becoming more important for the prosperity of U.S. business. The scope for private foreign investment, without host country participation or home country encouragement or supervision, is diminishing. Commodity markets will be altered by the spread of commodity agreements. Greater planning activities by all governments may impinge on U.S. interests and require increased international cooperation.

Many Americans find some of these trends dismaying. They long for the simpler past when world events did not press in so closely, and when the prevailing world philosophy was close to our own market economy individualism. It is hard for us to understand that what has brought prosperity to the United States has not done so elsewhere. The challenge facing us is adaptation to changing circumstances with concurrent retention of our political values and economic strength. These trends will force our government into a more active role to protect its own interests. This can best be done through planning that takes into account the greater dependence of the United States on the world economy and the consequent need for greater interaction.

Besides the pressures pushing the United States toward planning in its international environment, strong domestic reasons argue for planning. Some major national problems cannot be solved by reliance on traditional market forces or macroeconomic policies of the federal government; in such cases planning will be decisive. These include very high unemployment of youth and minority groups, urban decay in older cities, environmental pollution, a disjointed and inadequate transportation system, and the role of technology in our lives. Business faces significant problems of capital formation, inflation, industrial concentration, worker alienation, and consumer dissatisfaction. These problems are both social and economic, and there is little reason to believe that they can be dealt with satisfactorily by the market mechanism alone. Planning would permit consideration of social needs instead of relying solely on market forces.

The authors of the Planning Bill do not intend it to supplant in any manner the market system, but on the contrary to invigorate it and permit other factors to be taken into account in decision making. Some adversaries of planning oppose any government involvement in the economy because it has the potential of diminishing their individual freedom to operate. This involves balancing social or economic costs to the society against individual economic freedom, a judgment that often requires legislative determination. Planning does not decide such questions but it can inform the decision makers of the options. The absence of planning does not prevent government from intervening in the economy: witness export controls and wage and price controls. Nor would a planning mechanism necessarily make government intervention more likely; that would depend on economic conditions and the views of officeholders. But it would offer a chance to systematize government and coordinate its often inconsistent policies.

Economic decision making is concentrated in large corporations, many of which have annual sales figures that exceed gross national products of several countries. These corporations are often impervious to normal market forces. They can actually raise prices while demand is declining, and use advertising as a powerful force to create new demands for products which may be of questionable utility and value.

Government is involved in our economy because of its complexity and the economic concentration of industry. The United States is faced with significant environmental and resource limitations for the first time, because the market has treated many of the undesirable side effects on air, water, and the environment as "costless." Finally, the public demands a more vigorous pursuit of national interest objectives. Informed citizens are no longer willing to allow economically self-interested groups to dominate public policy. These trends can be better dealt with by indicative (voluntary) national planning. All require a public policy carefully developed and attuned to the realities of our times. It is appropriate to outline the main features of the indicative planning process as envisaged by the Planning Bill as presently written before considering a checklist of the issues that must be considered in any discussion of a federal indicative planning mechanism.

The Planning Bill establishes a three-member economic planning board in the executive office of the President. The board is charged with preparing a long-term national economic plan which would be submitted to Congress every two years. Long term in this context means a plan of four-to-six-years duration, with longer-term analysis for sectors with long lead times. The plan would be reviewed and approved by a council on economic planning, composed of major executive branch department heads dealing with economic policy. When the President submits the plan to Congress, he also transmits copies to each governor, so state and local participation in the review of the plan is made possible. An advisory committee and sectoral advisory committees involving participation by representatives of the private sector are established to advise members of the board on the plan.

The Joint Economic Committee is responsible for coordinating congressional comments on the plan, and would be given authority to report a concurrent resolution of both Houses of Congress approving, modifying, or disapproving the plan. If the concurrent resolution disapproves the entire proposed plan, the President must revise and resubmit the plan. If any portion of the proposed plan is disapproved by Congress, that portion may not be implemented by the executive branch. The plan would be indicative only; it would not be legally binding on the government or private sector. The President would be expected to hold the executive branch agencies responsible for policies conducive to implementation of the plan. Separate legislation would be required to implement aspects of the plan in the absence of existing legal authority.

ISSUES TO BE ADDRESSED ON PLANNING

I propose at this point to analyze the indicative planning concept to determine what elements are necessary for a suitable indicative planning mechanism. In other words, what issues must be addressed by Congress in legislating on such planning. A major question is the form that planning ought to take. Will it resemble the indicative planning of France, the primarily macroeconomic planning of Norway, or the centralized planning of the Eastern European countries? The answer is none of the above. But certainly not the centralized planning of Eastern Europe, which has replaced the market as the central economic mechanism. The form of U.S. planning will be unique: a truism, but also a recognition of the special characteristics of American society and economic organization. The large state-owned sectors present in almost all European countries are lacking here. The federal character of the U.S. government requires much more extensive local variations and inputs. The presidential structure of government and the constitutional checks and balances prevent a unitary approach to planning.

The heart of the question on the form of planning is whether it will be coercive or indicative (voluntary). The Planning Bill answers that question clearly by not granting the planning agency power to enforce a plan. The plan would guide the legislative and executive branches in the development of legislation, but would not alter the procedure by which laws are made. The plan is a blueprint; it is not a law. Once having adopted a plan, the government will be measured by its success in carrying out the proposals contained in it; but the plan must be seen as a tool, not as an end in itself. Besides, the purpose of planning is to expand freedom, not to diminish it.

It is important to decide whether the planning process will focus on one goal, with other subsidiary goals, or on a variety of goals, thus establishing a more neutral process. This decision is crucial; for example, the Humphrey-Hawkins bill focuses on full employment as the primary goal, with everything else relating to it; while the Humphrey-Javits bill follows the second course and sets out a variety of goals. Arguments may be made for either approach. The Humphrey-Hawkins approach singles out full employment as the most important national goal and bends the entire planning process to that end. I do not quarrel with the importance of that goal, but I feel that planning ought to be a more neutral tool. The concentration on full employment runs the risk of excessive politicization and may set the planning mechanism off on an exclusive course of job creation to the detriment of a balanced approach to a range of problems. Planning is such an important issue that it should be addressed on its own merits. The inclusion of planning within an employment bill (Humphrey-Hawkins) tends to obscure the issues that ought to be brought out.

A related question is the breadth of the issues to be considered by the planning agency. Should the agency look strictly at economic issues such as those addressed in the report of the Council of Economic Advisors, or should it range across social, political, military, and economic issues? At one extreme the planning agency could do nothing except construct input-output tables and economic models, or act as a data collection and dispensing agency. Those functions may be useful but hardly justify the effort to establish a planning function within government. Planning is largely an economic exercise, but it should not be so narrowly technical that it cannot be meaningful to legislators and informed members of the public. At the same time, planning ought to be a tool to improve the economic performance of the country and to permit the consideration of social costs in economic decisions. However, it cannot cover every social or political issue without usurping the normal functions of government. It is virtually impossible to separate the social and political implications of various actions from the strictly economic—which are the main thrust of U.S. business—but the line of division of responsibility ought to be clear: the political and social aspects should be dealt with by Congress, but the planning agency can provide alternatives and analyses that will assist Congress in making its choices on the basis of complete information. The effectiveness of the planning agency will depend significantly on how precisely its objectives are defined, and how careful it is to separate its economic analysis from social judgments.

In addition, some consideration should be given to the manner in which the recommendations of the planning agency are presented. Should a single though well-designed course be presented by the agency, or should several alternatives be presented so Congress can choose the one it thinks most appropriate? For example, the cost of various unemployment targets should be presented so Congress would know the rough costs of the alternatives. Since political viewpoints are likely to be linked to each alternative, the final choice of the appropriate alternative is likely to be a political decision. As the plan is being considered by Congress, it will be subject to the same pressures encountered by normal legislation, and its final shape will reflect the viewpoint of the dominant coalition in Congress.

The location of the planning agency and its relationships to existing agencies are important issues. The Humphrey-Javits bill establishes a separate agency within the executive office of the President, which would prepare a plan and present it to Congress for consideration. Within Congress the joint economic committee would coordinate the congressional response to the plan, with technical assistance from a new division in the Congressional Budget Office designed to deal with long-range planning. The Humphrey-Hawkins bill adds the planning function to the President's Council of Economic Advisors. The Council has a planning mandate under the Employment Act of 1946, but this function has atrophied over the years as the Council has concentrated on short-term economic analyses. Other suggestions for the location of a planning agency are the establishment of an independent board such as the Federal Reserve Board, an agency similar to the various regulatory agencies, an arm of Congress such as the Congressional Budget Office, or the general accounting office within an institution such as the Smithsonian Institution where it would become a high level "think tank," or scatter the planning function among the existing agencies.

I think there are two important issues here: how far to inject or remove the planning function from the political process, and how to increase the chances for agreement and cooperation between the President and Congress. There already exist so-called think tanks which analyze complex issues of government: the Rand Corporation, Brookings Institution, the Council on Foreign Relations, and so on. Their important role does not need duplication by a new government agency also removed from the political process. We are looking for an agency which will inform political decision making. This requires proximity to the President without the day-to-day involvement of program or regulatory administration that is the function of the executive departments and regulatory agencies. Without a close relationship to the

President the recommendations of the planning agency will carry little weight; yet proximity also implies that the agency may be politicized by the President. The same could be said for a location within Congress. This is a paradox we must face: the greater the independence of the agency, the less likely it is to influence public policy directly.

No planning mechanism can be expected to resolve political differences between the executive and legislative branches. But a planning process that begins in the executive branch—the logical choice for the development of coherent economic programs—and then moves the consideration to Congress, its specialized committees, and a technical arm within the Congressional Budget Office can identify the issues and signal the areas of difference. Further, the planning process as conceived in the Humphrey-Javits bill would involve the private sector as a major partner through advisory committees and also other levels of government (state and municipal), which would have the opportunity to comment on the plan. This would provide buffers to temper the potential political differences. The important point is to set up a process that will establish priorities and will enable the executive and legislative branches to focus on them.

I have emphasized the *process* rather than the static concept of establishment of an agency. I do not regard the end product of the process as a plan, a neatly bound document setting out fulsome and high-minded goals that can be promptly forgotten. Rather, the plan is a working document whose purpose is to achieve political agreement on various goals and to provide means to reach accord. It is the process itself and the results which flow from the process that are important.

I recently had the pleasure of participating in a conference with Senator Maurice Lamontagne of Canada, who discussed most perceptively Canada's experience with planning. I was struck by one well-phrased thought. He said: "It can be argued that effective planning cannot be achieved in Western democracies because governments have to be elected and that the systematic pursuit of distant goals is incompatible with frequent elections." He believes that the conflict between distant goals and frequent elections is largely a symptom. The real incompatibility is between planning and special interest groups promoting factionalism.

This brings us to the issue of the relationship between planning and the private sector. Private sector compliance with the plan would be voluntary, but there is great scope for mutual cooperation between the private sector and the planning process. The Humphrey-Javits bill contemplates the organization of sectoral advisory boards to provide input to the planning agency. Sectoral problems in major industries or broader problems that cut across industry lines could be handled by consultation and study by advisory boards. It is not contemplated that targets would be set for output by industrial sectors, as certain opponents to planning fear. Instead, the planning agency would examine long-term constraints on production, with the idea of recommending solutions for raw material shortages, capital formation problems, and production bottlenecks. Long-term supply and output forecasts would enable the private sector to obtain additional information needed to improve the operation of the market. In addition, the plan would provide business with a more accurate picture of probable government action over time, a vital need for long-term corporate planning. A fine sense of balance will be necessary in the relations between the planning agency and the private sector: a recognition of the problems of business without becoming a captive of business, a receptivity to business counsel without altering the proper arm's-length relationship between business and government. Lack of implementation powers is a significant safeguard for the integrity of the planning process.

Thus far this discussion has emphasized plan development rather than plan implementation. The latter must be given equal attention if plan development is to be more than an economic exercise in a vacuum. Plan implementation includes the enactment of separate legislation to put elements of the plan into action, executive rule making under existing authority, executive branch compliance by Presidential request, and voluntary action by the private sector. A significant function of the planning agency will be monitoring the progress and problems of implementation. Congress will need frequent reports on implementation progress. The agency will need to be especially sensitive to the failures of implementation to determine where the plan is unrealistic, unworkable, or out of date. The underlying idea is that the plan is a working document, not a rigid, doctrinal instrument to be followed at all costs. The intent should not be to force the plan to work, but to use it as a flexible tool for improving the economic functioning of the country.

Senator Lamontagne's troubling argument about the inconsistency between planning and the political process in a democratic society haunts our discussions on planning. Do we have the political will to solve our long-term economic and social problems, especially when those problems may require unpopular sacrifice and cut across short-term and narrowly focused interests? Our inability to reach agreement on our long-term energy policy and our lack of political will to control firearms are examples of the frustration that planners will face.

I have argued frequently that planning does not give us a key to the solution of problems when the political will is lacking. To the extent that we falter because of misinformation, misconceptions about alternatives, or lack of understanding of the factors at work shaping our economy and the world, the planning process can help us. To a large degree the question is whether external pressures will force us to use more rational methods for the resolution of critical problems. The longer we delay the use of the planning process, the greater the danger that the pressure will build for drastic actions that could undermine our basic freedoms.

14

INDUSTRIAL DEMOCRACY:
A New Challenge for Management

JAMES M. JENKS
President, Alexander Hamilton Institute, Inc.

American executives are faced with an extraordinary challenge to what they presently perceive as management's prerogatives. Rising rapidly over the horizon is the concept of industrial democracy, an idea alien to what many managers consider the American way. However, U.S. industry's crying need for greater productivity, flying in the face of dramatic changes in the work ethic, narrows our choices for managing workers and work. Democratizing business enterprises may not be the sole solution, but many experiments—here and abroad—that involve workers in responsibilities management has thought of as its own, have paid off handsomely. I believe that involving workers in decisions on how work should be done is an important factor in management for the future. Despite many cracks and potholes that will need to be filled in on the road to more democracy in business, I predict results favorable for management and worker alike.

What is industrial democracy? One writer on labor affairs describes it as a form of worker involvement that attempts to give employees a sense of direct participation in making their jobs more satisfying while maintaining necessary efficiency. In a real sense, it is putting into practice in industry many of the democratic principles that have been used in America politically for 200 years. Many factors at work in our society are important for managers to understand. The ones I consider most important in connection with democratic management for the future are:

- The decline in authoritarian management
- The changes in peoples' attitudes and values
- The different conditions of work today
- The distance we have already moved toward more democracy in business
- The things managers should know and do to prepare the way

AUTHORITARIAN MANAGEMENT DECLINES

Most experienced workers already know how to do their jobs better than does management; even better, in many instances, than the persons who most closely supervise their work. Recently, in connection with a study on motivation, the personnel manager at an aluminum forging company told me he realized that, "One problem of worker motivation in the company is a combination of poor work design and built-in resistance by the line foremen to any change." He concluded that the worker operating the machine knew more about the job than the industrial engineer or the foreman. "But," he said, "nobody was listening to what the worker was trying to explain." In short, authority often leads to unwarranted feelings of superiority and deafens supervisors and managers to workers' suggestions for improvement in work methods.

The roots of our authoritarian management structure extend back into the murky voids of history. Whether authoritarian management grew out of the age of feudalism or was adapted from a militaristic discipline, it received a tremendous shot in the arm from the American pursuit of efficiency. Time and motion study was developed around the turn of the century by the father of scientific management, Frederick W. Taylor. His methods and those of other efficiency experts since then examined tasks bit by bit, motion by motion, to find the one best way to get a job done. These experts sought peak productivity from workers through scientific management of tasks. In addition, other developments designed to increase efficiency called for division of labor and work simplification. Perhaps the clearest and most easily understood example is the assembly line.

These developments in the United States came at an opportune time. Immigration was at its height. Millions of workers poured into the United States eager to accept any job under nearly any conditions to get settled in a land of such great promise. In short, Taylor had the docile labor force needed to plant the seeds of efficient work methods and have them sprout and grow. Taylorism occurred at the right time and in the right place. His was a monumental contribution to the rapid development of efficient industry in our country. Taylorism worked well with obedient and surplus labor. It also strengthened further the authority of management. The fact that managers and industrial engineers discovered how to increase efficiency quite naturally bolstered beliefs that only managers could make the right decisions concerning how work should be done. The quiet acceptance by immigrant labor of their place, which was in accord with the traditions of the societies in Europe from which most of them came, further widened the divisions between management and workers. The structure of industry, at least partly as a result, grew evermore autocratic. Only one great movement—labor unionism—might have offset the growth of authoritarian management in the first half of this century. It did not because labor leaders felt that their own growth depended on at least two things: a strong authoritarian hold on their members and an adversary relationship to management. Any democratizing of industry during this period, labor leaders thought, would have undermined their own organizing efforts.

So developments of the first 60 years of this century implanted beliefs in worker submission to management and worked against worker participation. So strongly has the notion of managers' right to manage become ingrained in our society, it will take the balance of this century for that belief to become unraveled, no matter how beneficial to management such nullification may be. Most of today's managers find repulsive the idea of sharing their rights with workers.

THE WINDS OF CHANGE

These factors sustained an undemocratic business organization structure in the midst of the world's most democratic and industrially successful nation. But there has been a relaxing of attitudes as management has sought ways to increase output per worker other than by applying the discipline of "stopwatch efficiency." The Hawthorne experiments at Western Electric during 1929 showed that paying attention to workers led to increased productivity. In the 1950s human relations was the name of the game. One time, at Caterpillar Tractor Company, I was talking with a first line supervisor when he received a telephone call from "Louie." Louie turned out to be Louis Neumiller, then chairman of the board. Using first names was one of Caterpillar's ways of improving human relations.

Social scientists, such as Abraham Maslow, influenced industry in the 1950s. They persuaded many managers that people had a hierarchy of needs—from physical comfort as the basic need to other layers of needs that must be satisfied before self-actualization will occur. Frederick Hertzberg became the guru of job enrichment in the 1960s. Many companies that have enriched jobs by using his theories have increased productivity.

Management, while still resisting changes in its right to manage, has moved further along the road to industrial democracy than many managers care to admit. So far, for the most part, management has itself made the rules for human relations, job enrichment, worker participation, and other methods of increasing worker involvement in the determination of how the work will be done. Codetermination of work—that is, a democratic approach whereby managers and workers jointly decide how work will be done—has been tried in only a few companies in the United States. But its momentum is building and what it means must be learned as a foundation of management for the future.

Resistance to further democratization of industry is crumbling. And it will lessen further in the next quarter century, not because of overwhelming pressures from labor or government to change. It will diminish because a new generation of managers and workers, with new attitudes toward work, will be taking over America's industrial complex. It will be a quiet revolution. But it will be no less startling in its ultimate effects, no less important for management for the future than the famed industrial revolution and the era of scientific management. It will have results that yesterday's managers and even many of today's would say, if asked, that they could not tolerate—but one that tomorrow's managers will welcome (except for those few who do not remember that the "good old days" really were not all that good) when it finally comes to fruition.

WHY PEOPLE ARE DIFFERENT

The United States is still the most open and free society in the world. Of all countries, it is the one where democratizing business enterprises might have been expected to have occurred first. For industrial management to have remained an authoritarian institution in the midst of such a society would be a curiosity, were it not for the accidental coincidence of industrialism, mass immigration of docile labor, and scientific management. It has taken a half century for these factors to work themselves out in the United States. They are working themselves out to the distress of the advocates of the old order of no change, but with the potential for another giant step forward for our society.

What are some of the present-day factors that lead me to conclude that industrial democracy is inevitable and will pay handsome rewards to employers and employees alike? A person would have to be nearly totally isolated from the world to be ignorant of the fact that the generation of prime-age workers, say those between 18 and 36, have attitudes and values dramatically different from their parents. The "generation gap" may have been celebrated too much in the press and on TV. Nevertheless, changed attitudes of the "now" generation (or, as my daughter calls it, the Pepsi generation) are something that managers must work with and understand if there is to be management in the future. The "now" generation in the United States is the best-educated work force that any country, anywhere in the world, at any time in history has ever seen. Even allowing for a possibility that the quality of education may have been diluted by the enormous burdens that too rapid expansion thrust upon our educational institutions, more people in this generation have been exposed to longer periods and higher levels of education than those of any previous one.

That alone would have caused a change in attitudes and values. Compounding that fact, however, is the cruel hoax that equates more education with infinite opportunities for satisfying (and monetarily rewarding) work. It is a sad truth that under all economic systems, opportunities for satisfying work are finite, not infinite. Many people were concerned some 25 years ago with raising so high the expectations of the underprivileged people of the world that when these expectations could not be met, rebellion of the have-nots against the haves would result. That may still prove to be true, as shown by the unrest in Africa and in the subcontinent of India. But, ironically, partly because of the overselling of education, it is our present, privileged, prime-age workers who have rebelled about their conditions of work, their lack of say in how their job should be done, and what jobs they should be assigned to. We now see coming true the shopworn beliefs of those workers who have always been sure that they could run the business better than their bosses. Today it is true; many workers are better educated and more intelligent than their bosses. Many do know how the job could be done better with resulting benefits for the business as a whole.

The present generation may possibly be overeducated. It is probably miseducated. There is a serious mismatch between available jobs and available workers. In the depths of our most recent major recession there were jobs for janitors, hospital workers, and servants. But the attitudes of the Pepsi generation left it with few members willing to fill such positions. Another factor that changed attitudes and values of the "now" generation, and makes a work force that cannot be productively managed by using the management practices of the past, was the stress of the Vietnam war. Every generation in modern times had its own war to contend with. But with the possible exception of the Civil War, none of our other wars had been as stressful to combatants and noncombatants alike as Vietnam.

All soldiers are reduced to the same states of anxiety and fear after the first shots are fired their way. To that extent, there is no difference between being shot at in a "good" war or a "bad" one. But whereas we entered other wars with high ideals, patriotic fervor, flag-waving, and varying degrees of enthusiasm to save the world, or remember Pearl Harbor, we crept into the Vietnam conflict. Fully half our population opposed it. We put our soldiers under the severe stress of wondering why they were in the predicament even before they came under fire. In addition, the noncombatants of the generation felt stress from avoiding the draft or protesting violently against our involvement.

On the one hand, serving in a no-purpose war produced stress, both before and during combat. On the other hand, ducking service produced emotional stress. Is it any wonder, then, that members of a generation so exposed should revolt against authority? Or that they should carry their feelings over into the work place where, once again, they are enmeshed in conditions over which they have no control? Or that having once been alienated by an authoritarian government, they are again alienated by authoritarian management? Are not these conditions that would propel the "now" generation to embrace more firmly than ever the idea of democracy—of having some say over how their jobs should be done? Indeed they are.

To top off the reasons why a generation of people are different in their attitudes toward work and in their values, one has to look at the affluence of the country in which the Pepsi generation grew up. In the 1930s their parents dreamed of a car in every garage. Now two-fifths of all families have two cars. Half of all homes in America have two TV sets. Home ownership is not reserved to the rich as it was in the twenties and thirties. It became the standard American way during the time when the generation grew up. Half of today's high school graduates go on to higher education; fewer than 20 percent of their parents did.

Recently, a colleague recalled overhearing his parents discuss (this was during the Great Depression) the fact that they must postpone buying a new car. Today parents rarely discuss postponing the buying of anything. Creditamericard has made instant acquisition of material goods possible as the TV antennas sprouting from tenements attest. How could any generation's attitudes and values be unaffected by such affluence? They cannot and have not. The Pepsi generation's discontent with doing things in the future as they have always been done in the past just will not happen—in social matters, government, or the ways businesses are organized and managed.

WHY CONDITIONS ARE DIFFERENT

Much has been said about dehumanizing work causing dissatisfaction among workers, increasing absenteeism, and lowering productivity. The promoters of scientific management did much to dehumanize work, at least by present-day standards. But when one contrasts work methods that grew out of the Taylor era to conditions in the sweatshops, steel mills, and coal mines existing before scientific management took hold, one can hardly say that work was more humane before Taylor than after. No, it is what the worker expects and perceives as humane or dehumanizing that counts. Much work today is dull, repetitive, boring, and monotonous—but only in terms of perceptions and what workers have been led to expect.

The machine age and technological improvements—such as sound buffering and air conditioning—have made working conditions far superior to what they were only a generation ago. Using conveyors to move things around the factory may depersonalize the work place, or "defatigue" work, as one writer sardonically puts it. But workers in the early part of this century, whose tasks were also dull and repetitive, seldom complained of boredom. Noise, pollution, heat, and physical effort resulted in exhaustion too complete to allow room for thought about how mind-numbing jobs were. Workers of that era were simply too tired to be bored. In addition, sophisticated methods of producing often equally sophisticated goods and services (the computer does produce services as anyone who has recently purchased an airline ticket knows) has increased frustration among workers. Today's workers are far more dependent on and less knowledgeable about what their coworkers are doing than was true yesteryear.

The computer operator may be separated by only a pane of glass from the programmer who "instructs" the operator's machine. The operator can actually see the programmer do his or her work and is totally dependent on the output. Yet the logic that goes into programming may be completely beyond the grasp of the operator—it certainly is a mystery—resulting in a feeling of alienation and frustration. A generation ago people who worked "cheek by jowl" learned enough of each other's skills to understand what the other was doing and to act as a substitute in case of need. It is frightening for a person, such as a computer operator, to watch a programmer go through mysterious steps that are far more complicated than the output the operator uses.

The increase of women workers and managers has changed working conditions. Even though it was only in 1975 that the percentage of women in the U.S. work force equaled that achieved in 1945, the war effort was the cause of the high number of women working then. But women in the labor force today are different. They are not like "Rosie the riveter" of World War II fame. They are, by law, entitled to equal pay and equal opportunity. They are increasing their numbers in management. It is worthwhile asking, aside from the question of whether women will perform as well as men (for that is not open to question), how their views of how managers should manage and how their attitudes and traditions will affect the practice of management for the future.

No matter how chauvinist, male or female, one may be, no one denies that women have played a subservient role during the history of mankind. Indeed, that is one of the most violently voiced of their current complaints. As a result of the role they have played, women have not been indoctrinated as authoritarians as men have. Therefore, they may well refuse to adopt the male-made authoritarian management system. Indeed, a case can be made that they will rebel against it, once their numbers among managers have increased. Their attitudes, as every man knows, cannot be taken for granted. Women may provide the cutting edge in the movement for democratizing management in the United States.

There is one other aspect of the "now" generation that needs to be mentioned. The prime-age worker generation constitutes a distinct bulge in our population statistics. The younger section of this group are the war babies, the product of the jump in the birthrate that began in 1946 and persisted until the birthrate began to decline 20 years later. The people in this population bulge, who now form a surplus of entry level workers, are mismatched by education and expectations to jobs available. They are discontented with their lot but unwilling to settle for just any kind of job or organization of work. They question authority and are aware of their power. They are moving along the time line to positions of greater influence and power.

Those persons in the population bulge who are slated (doomed?) to remain workers will have their influence on how jobs are done. More importantly, those who are in or will move into management hold many of the same values and attitudes as the worker element. We are said to grow less radical as we grow old. But are ideas any longer radical when they are held by the majority? The managerial elements of the people in the population bulge will soon form a majority. They will play a crucial role in determining exactly the type of industrial democracy that must be the inevitable result of present motive forces.

People are different. Conditions are different. We can play the game of quoting newspaper headlines that say "Russians are a threat to Jewish minority" and reveal that the headline appeared 50 years ago. We can quiet the fearful by feeding them the palliative that the more things change, the more they stay the same. But when we take that posture, we risk deluding ourselves and being surprised when a predictable result comes to pass. Because people are different and conditions are different does not mean that different is bad. Different is bad only when one views it that way. Different can be good, as today is better for the majority of people in this world than was yesterday. Let us look at who benefits from change and why. Let us see how we can manage for the future so that future management will produce handsome results for all.

MANAGEMENT MOVES AHEAD

One of the assurances that people like me who forecast the future have, is the certain knowledge that the only truly predictable fact about the future is that it will differ from the past. It takes no real courage to make predictions. It only takes some fortitude to withstand the assaults of those who are desperately anxious to avoid change and quite eager to make savage attacks on the seer. The forecaster raises questions that the antiforecaster has not considered and for which the latter may have no answers. The forecaster has the advantage over detractors of knowing the starting line for his or her thoughts and the directions in which they are going. This is much the same advantage that the split end in football has over the defensive secondary. He knows when, and in which direction, he is going to make his cut, and the corner backs and safeties do not.

The forecaster can often unleash a torrent of criticism simply by his or her choice of words. Not long ago Harvard Business School Professor George Cabot Lodge described the newest American ideology as "communitarism." Perhaps it was the choice of the label, whose first seven letters are the same as communism, that brought heaps of unwarranted abuse on Professor Lodge's head. For while there have been "pinkish" teachers on the Harvard Square side of the Charles River, few doubts have been raised about the presence of left-wingers on the Business School's side of the river, much less such an invasion of the citadel of capitalism by a Massachusetts Lodge. So while the self-appointed defenders against change cannot be easily faked out, history tells us that their tenure is short, that things do change, and that change has brought more benefits than has immobility. And so it will be in the management of business in the years to come.

In this country, at least, the words industrial democracy have rung a discordant note. To illustrate: A visiting editor told me that she had recently interviewed the owner of a large business who said that he would shut down his company completely if industrial democracy ever took hold in the United States. His misunderstanding of the term, of the forces in motion, of the resilient power of the American managers is so complete that, for a person who has gained his high position, one has to be as impressed as much with his ignorance as concerned with his threat.

Industrial democracy has already arrived. It has been successfully and happily inserted in the American way of management in many companies, albeit at times under disguise. Some examples: A multiplant company has one of its plants located in a Midwestern state. The location is truly middle America, the heartland of conservatism in our country far removed from the liberalism and "wild-eyed radicals" of either coast. Industrial democracy is practiced in this plant, though it may not be called by that name. The results have been reduced absenteeism and less turnover of labor. Productivity has ranged from equality with or higher levels than other plants where this concept is not yet at work. Less scrap, lower maintenance costs, and higher output gains are also reported.

What is the system of management at this plant? It is far from the traditional, authoritarian model which has been the hallmark of American industry, as well as the management method used at this company's other operating units. Management first took steps that resulted in a renewal of the work climate at this plant. Management wanted worker participation in job design and decision making to be spontaneous. It is axiomatic, of course, that spontaneity must be met with responsiveness by management. It was. Not all workers at the plant wanted greater job involvement and where they did not, it was not forced on them.

The basic organizational structure was retained to take care of what might seem to be a dual system of management—partly old, that is, structured by managers; and partly new, structured by workers with management. Management's posture has been one of providing response to those workers who wanted job involvement while accommodating the desires of those who wanted no change. By way of illustration: one maintenance man wanted the right to order his own cleaning supplies instead of going through the purchasing department. The other maintenance men did not want the bother of ordering and paperwork. Both parties were accommodated by management. Employees also participate in decision making, even the hard decisions of layoffs during slack periods. Not only does discussion take place on the floor of the plant about such decisions, the choices between two courses of action are often put to a vote. The voting booth is symbolic of the democratic process in action.

Another example: An engineering company, during a period of rapid growth, expanded into office space in seven different locations, some as much as 25 miles apart in the city of Los Angeles. This resulted in duplicated services, poor communications, high expense, and inconvenience. The company anticipated more growth. It needed more office space and a solution to the problems created by having the headquarters people scattered in different buildings in the city. A company task force studied several locations, any one of which would allow the entire headquarters to be consolidated in one building. The choices were put to a vote of the employees. The move was made to the site that received the majority of the vote. This is clearly another example of the democratic process at work in business.

At a factory in West Virginia, maintenance of the aluminum reduction pot lines was being handled on a "crash" basis. When a breakdown occurred, the maintenance department rushed a crew to the area of the breakdown to get the pot lines operating again or to remove the cause of the mechanical breakdown to the repair area for rebuilding. Maintenance crews were kept on a standby basis around the clock since the pot lines operated 24 hours a day. The workers on the day shift believed, however, that by working in five day turns to provide coverage around the clock, the necessary maintenance could be done by them alone. Workers bid on the type of work they preferred—either minor maintenance on the line or major rebuilding in the shop—rather than being assigned to specific maintenance tasks. They worked without supervision, used their own judgment in setting priorities for maintenance to be performed (as opposed to being given a set schedule), and kept their own time records. This is another instance of industrial democracy in action, even though it is not called by that name in the company.

As a result of this involvement of workers in what jobs they will do and how they will do them, the pot lines are in operation a much higher percentage of time than under the old system that had been dictated by management. Management is pleased with the resulting cost savings. The workers, too, are pleased. In an attitude survey they revealed that they have a much closer feeling of identification with the company. The outcome has clearly brought benefits to management and workers alike.

WHERE MANAGEMENT GOES FROM HERE

If I have not made it clear, let me say I do not think of industrial democracy as a tragedy which we must resignedly accept and learn to enjoy. Certainly some managers, whose minds are set in concrete, may find that attitude the easiest one to take. Nor do I feel the way one famous economist did when he was accused of defeatism in his writing about the future of capitalism. He said that when one receives a report that a ship is sinking, it is the spirit with which the report is received that determines if it is defeatist. If the crew merely sits down and does nothing, their perception of the event is one thing. But if they rush to the pumps, it is entirely another thing. I do not think there is any need to rush to the pumps. There is no question of saving management from sinking. Rather, I feel strongly that all managers should man the oars to pull this ship of ours in the right direction in as rapid a fashion as is possible.

It is an old cliché that America is the land of opportunity. Whereas in Europe the industrial democratic movement has been spearheaded by government, we have a great opportunity for enlightened management to lead the way in the United States, to usurp the role of big government which, if we abandon the opportunity, will surely move toward another layer of obfuscating bureaucrats whose meddlesome mission will be further control of the industrial complex. Lest my opinion that management should lead in the move to industrial democracy seem a contradiction in terms, let me hasten to point out that political democracy does require leadership in order to do its work. So does industrial democracy. I am simply saying that management should be the leaders in this democratic process, rather than government. Labor unions, too, will have to participate, though they have not shown any great interest in doing so. Unions can also "man the oars" in those segments of the labor force that they have organized. Unions do not represent all workers. But all workers have managers.

Management must seize the initiative while the opportunity is still there. Otherwise it will find itself on the defensive, particularly against big government but more probably against the powerful and potentially destructive combine of government and organized labor. I do not say that taking the initiative means that management should dictate the terms of industrial democracy. That would indeed be contrary to democratic processes. One-sided (management alone) imposition of its form of industrial democracy would in fact be a contradiction.

We have in America an industrial structure that works. It has built the most powerful industrial nation in the world. It has created unparalleled affluence even though pockets of poverty and misery remain. Like any structure, however, it can be made better, stronger. Our industrial structure can be the foundation, or the cornerstone, of a new and better one. We should, after all, still seek to improve the quality of life for everyone. Improving the quality of life depends, for many people, upon quantity—more food, more housing, more goods, more services. That is particularly true for people living on the fringe of existence. But there is more to quality of life. We can easily provide greater quantities of goods for the few at the expense of the quality of life for the many. The trick is not to make it an exclusive process. It can be inclusive. Therein lies the question of conditions of work—primarily for workers but also for many managers who find their jobs less than fulfilling now.

The common thread that management must use to sew together the various patterns that make up jobs is to include the sense of direct participation in making jobs more satisfying and more fulfilling. That will require a reversal of the polarities of power. Some reversal, some diminution of the adamant assertions of management's rights and workers' rights has already occurred, as shown in the illustrations of industrial democracy that I have previously given. If the power from each pole is not diffused, big government will step in, establishing itself as the sole arbiter of the way democratization will proceed or allowing itself to be attracted to the vote-getting magnet of big labor.

WHAT MANAGERS SHOULD DO

If one accepts the premise that management should grab the reins in the drive to greater democracy in business, one must agree that managers should be accountable for making it work. Leadership without accountability becomes dictatorial. I have said much about how workers are different and conditions are different. And it is true that management has also begun to change, slowly and surely. But aside from the slow, surface manifestations of evolving management, there are some fundamental changes in attitudes that managers should make, some fundamental things that managers should do.

It is important, I believe, for managers to forget their class distinctions. They must get on with the task of moving American industry forward as free enterprise, free from institutional domination by big government, big labor, big business, and the latest arrival among institutional powers, big education. All large, well-organized institutions have a way of limiting freedom of expression that is so essential to the democratic process. The most striking feature of class distinctions in industry is the difference between the trust shown factory workers and that shown white-collar, nonmanagement workers. Certainly labor unions, with their insistence upon an adversary relationship with management, have played a part in perpetuating a dual value system, based on mistrust of factory workers. The differences show up in the way wages are paid, hours are kept, and dozens of work rules that make up false and unnecessary class distinctions between factory and office workers.

Managers must change to a single value system from the present dual one. Fundamentally, this means an attitude change. But here are some tangible steps managers should take:

- Stop designing policies for the few employees who need them. Consider the feelings of the majority of people. For example, punitive work rules regarding lateness or absenteeism threaten the conscientious worker. They do nothing to deter the person who is chronically late for work, or the worker who is always absent on the opening day of the hunting season. Just the fact that such rules exist causes resentment, especially when they are applied uniformly to nonexempt workers in the plant, and haphazardly, if at all, to exempt workers in the office. Where such policies do exist, start reversing them.

- Build respect for the employees' work place—the plant floor or the general office. Many managers point with pride to their open-door policy. They say that anyone can come to see them at any time. But they fail to realize that when people come to see them, those people feel like Dickensian characters, approaching hat in hand. The plant floor is the workers' office. As one writer puts it, replace the open-door with an open-floor policy. Certainly, managers can conduct part of their business at the employees' "office" as well as at their own. Managers will benefit not only from their exposure to the workers but by their exposure to the work place.

- Include an appropriate cross section of workers in meetings, especially those in which discussions held or decisions made directly affect the workers and their conditions of work.

- Get involved in matters of current social interest such as ecology, minority matters, consumerism. The broadening effect of such involvement, beyond developing a community of interest with those being managed, will help managers understand the psychology of motivation. Motivation, some critics say, is manipulation in disguise. The point is not to learn how to motivate people, so much as it is to learn what sources all people draw on for self-motivation.

- Give reasons for rules. Safety, for example. It is not really enough to say that "government safety regulations require this rule." Or that ignoring a safety rule will be hazardous to the worker's health. Explain exactly the causes and effects that make any rule necessary.

- Study the American union movement. Take every opportunity to learn why union leaders act as they do. Unions will be crucial to making the changes in our system that are necessary to increase democracy in business. The first step will be to overcome the adversary relationship that unions hold as paramount and substitute for it a cooperative approach. The ends of union and management are much the same, in the final analysis, no matter how differently they sound when articulated. But neither party can see the other's views about how to achieve these ends.

- Study the experiments in industrial democracy that have already taken place in Europe. We do not need to import Europe's ideas. Indeed, to do so would put government in the driver's seat, where it is firmly in control in Europe, and have it mandate our system. That is exactly what we need to avoid if we are to create the American model of democracy in industry. There is no reason to build our model from scratch and ignore the lessons already taught any more than our founding fathers ignored the Magna Carta when they wrote the Bill of Rights.

- Involve workers in the designs of their jobs. It is ridiculous on its face to assume that all wisdom resides in the minds of a managerial elite. The Japanese have shown us that participation in decision making works well, not because many heads are better than one but because far better definitions of problems come when they are viewed from all possible angles. Once problems have been clearly defined and everyone in the group has participated in the definition, implementation of the decisions reached comes swiftly and easily. Participation by people in the decision process eliminates communications barriers and hastens understanding of the ramifications and results of decisions. The people who will carry them out already know their roles and, at least partly, how to play them.

American management has many great advantages to create a new, democratically based industrial society. The most important of these is our own 200-year-old successful experiment with political democracy. That gives us a tradition and a heritage that no European society, or any other society, has ever had, and a foundation on which we can base democratizing our businesses. Beyond our traditions, we have the advantage of freedom from the constraints imposed on European countries by their heritage of feudalism, the most authoritarian management structure that has arisen since Roman times. That heritage may well be the reason why only the powerful weapons of government could force adoption of a measure of industrial democracy in some of the countries of Europe.

Above all, however, it is management's frame of mind, and that of the individual managers who make up the managerial group, which will be most crucial to a successful outcome for an improved, democratic business model, American style. One overriding factor that all managers must keep in mind is this: No management policy, public or private, that runs counter to societal trends has ever succeeded. The socioeconomic trends that have developed, particularly those that grew out of why people and conditions are different, are clearly discernible. Those who seek to block what people want will ultimately fail. Those who try to direct people's desires will succeed. Democratic businesses, economies, and societies are not improvements over other systems simply because democracy is an ideologically splendid or socially acceptable value. They succeed because they work better.

15

WHAT IS THE FUTURE OF THE CORPORATION?

REGINALD H. JONES
Chairman and Chief Executive Officer, General Electric Company

I think there is reason to be concerned whether the corporation as we know it—the characteristic institution of our American enterprise system—will survive into the next century. Great social and institutional changes are taking place that will necessarily affect the corporation, especially the larger firms that are the core of our nation's industrial system. We in management are no strangers to change. The corporation has survived and prospered precisely because it *is* highly adaptable to changing circumstances. In fact, corporations are perhaps the principal agents of change in the United States, with a highly successful record as engines of human progress. It is not by coincidence that the United States created the first and only trillion-dollar economy in the world. That is the result of our traditions of political and economic democracy, in which the profit-and-loss–disciplined private corporation, rather than the government, is the primary economic instrument. One would think that an institution which has been so spectacularly successful would have an assured future—at least for another century or so. But curiously, it is almost impossible to find any prophet who sees much of a future for the investor-owned corporation.

WHAT THE PROPHETS SAY

Even the most friendly futurists, such as Daniel Bell, Herman Kahn, and Peter Drucker, forecast trouble. As the economy shifts from goods to services, in terms of occupation and output, we become a "post-industrial society." And the question futurists ask—and management must answer—is whether the post-industrial society will also be a *post-business* society.

Other prophets are less generous. More than a century ago Karl Marx predicted that capitalism would collapse of its own inner contradictions, to be superseded by socialism or communism. Many people around the world still accept this as a historical necessity and are working to move history along by one means or another. The gloomy historical philosopher Oswald Spengler, writing of the "decline of the West" at the beginning of this century, prophesied that our civilization is doomed to end with a great final struggle between money and power—business and government. And the inevitable outcome, he said, will be the triumph of Caesarism, raw power triumphant over economic and political democracy.

Recently, the prophets have taken a different tack. John Kenneth Galbraith and Richard Goodwin believe that the bureaucratic necessities of operating an industrial system—the disciplines it imposes on all concerned—will inevitably cause the major corporations to be absorbed by the state, the central planning and controlling bureaucracy. Then there is the consummate pessimism of Robert Heilbroner. He predicts that the pressures of human population on the earth's resources will inevitably bring us into a system of worldwide rationing and control, wherein such bizarre oddities as private enterprise and private decision making—at least with respect to industrial resources—simply could not be allowed. Thus the challenge extends to *all* industrial democracies, to their economic *and* political structures.

These are observations of intelligent and serious men, and they are not to be ignored. I believe they tend to overstate the weaknesses of the private enterprise system and underestimate its creative power and adaptability. Nevertheless there *are* bureaucratic tendencies; there *are* worldwide trends to planned economies; there *are* crises that make the public yearn for strong, authoritarian controls.

EXAMINING THE VULNERABILITIES

My purpose here is not to predict the end of the corporation—far from it—but to surface some of its vulnerabilities, a subject I think especially important for those with managerial responsibilities. Absorbed as we are with the day-to-day tasks of running successful businesses, we cannot ignore the dangers to the survival of the system itself. Preserving and strengthening the best economic system ever developed is one of our greatest responsibilities to future generations. With this responsibility in mind, let us examine some of the vulnerabilities.

A Shift in Values

The deepest challenge comes from a basic shift in the values and beliefs that undergird our society. The counterculture is not a passing phenomenon. The values that have supported and vitalized our business system—belief in rationality, objectivity, efficiency, self-discipline, thrift, hard work—seem to be losing their power. Science and technology, once universally admired, are becoming objects of suspicion.

The shift in values is not confined to the young. As C. Jackson Grayson pointed out in *Harvard Business Review*,[1] both labor and business nowadays often seek to reduce competition, not encourage it. Increasingly, Americans distrust the market system and demand that government step in to assure them economic benefits. Much of the public has come to feel that controls—in other words, central planning—are not only desirable, but superior. Grayson concludes, "We are very near the point where further centralization will change our present system into one that can no longer perform its function efficiently." And at that point, the sustaining rationale for the private corporation disappears.

Financial Starvation

Another serious vulnerability is the possibility of financial starvation. Corporations cannot survive without a steady infusion of capital investment in new plants and equipment and new technology. Without this, the system runs down, loses its competitive capability in the world, and fails to satisfy the economic needs of society. American business today is suffering from several decades of underinvestment. Ever since the Great Depression, public policy has systematically favored the stimulation of demand, redistribution of wealth, and growth of government services—and given the needs of producers much lower priority. Now we pay the piper.

Between 1976 and 1985, it is estimated that the capital investment needs of the private sector will be on the order of $4.5 trillion. That compares with $1.5 trillion invested in the past dozen years. Where will that enormous amount of private capital come from? With real profits declining, the tax structure weighted against new equity, and business going deeper and deeper into debt, the possibility of a capital shortage is not academic. Major corporations with serious financial problems have been reluctantly turning to the government as financier of last resort. Perhaps that seems a long step from regarding government as the financier of first resort. But if consumption-oriented tax policies continue over time to dry up the sources of voluntary savings and investment, the United States will turn increasingly to public financing, and the power to tax could ultimately become our primary source of capital. And that, of course, would be the end of capitalism and private enterprise.

Uncontrolled Inflation

Another and related vulnerability that must be faced is the possibility that today's chronic inflation, if not brought under control, could lead to political and economic chaos. Dr. Kissinger has solemnly reminded us of the disruptive social and political effects of inflation and the vulnerability of the Western democracies. On the other hand, excessively stringent measures to stop inflation lead to down-spiraling recessions. Thus we always walk an economic tightrope between inflation and recession.

Either of these problems, getting out of hand (as they nearly did in 1974–75), could conceivably lead to demands for major changes in our economic system, with some form of socialism brought into being under the guise of emergency reform measures. The top 100 corporations—the most visible targets for control—would be the most vulnerable in such a situation. That is one reason why we cannot regard a harsh recession as an acceptable solution for our problem of inflation.

Planned Economies

Yet another area of vulnerability is the fact that American corporations are increasingly obliged to compete on the international scene with state enterprises and state-controlled economies. How can individual companies hope to compete effectively against the power of national treasuries and their ability to tax the people to cover their inefficiencies or advance political objectives?

As more and more of the world turns toward planned economies, using the whole resource base of a nation like one single economic enterprise, Americans might, in self-defense, find themselves drifting in the same direction. The temptation to join the march toward government planning and control may be stronger than we think. Various legislative proposals for national economic planning have already been introduced in the Congress under powerful political auspices.

Another variation of this theme is the trend toward socialism in Europe. Unlike the United States, the labor movement in Europe has a Marxist tradition and is trying in several countries to gain control of private industry through the use of political power. In an excellent book entitled *British Nationalization 1945–73,* R. Kelf-Cohen points out that the nationalization of Britain's basic industries was not brought about by a great national desire for socialism, but by pressure from the trade unions—the dominant elements of the Labour Party—to attain better control over the management of these industries.

The labor movement in the United States, unlike its European counterpart, has not formed a political party. It has been content to work—very successfully—within the traditional two-party system. Furthermore, American unions are for the most part strong supporters of the private enterprise system. Nevertheless, if the European trade unions, with their strong Marxist orientation, were to push Europe still further into socialism, this could not fail to affect the Unites States in the long run.

Regulation to Extinction

But the most insidious vulnerability, and the one most likely to change the major corporations into mere arms of the government, is the slow, evermore entangling web of regulations by which the power of decision is being transferred from the boardroom to federal agencies in Washington. I need not recite here the the long litany of statutes and regulations by which the federal government tells business what it may and may not do. The threat of federal charters and the licensing of corporations would be the last straw. Every one of these regulations is introduced as a protection for the public, and every one is said to be adopted for our own good. The cumulative effect is what we must be concerned about.

Public policy for decades has favored growth of the public sector over the private sector. Expenditures by all governments in the United States—federal, state, and local—amounted to 10 percent of the gross national product in 1929. They have increased every decade and in 1975 reached 36 percent of the economy. If the long trend continues, they will be about 50 percent before the end of the century. The question is—when government is such a pervasive element, at what point do we cease to have a market-oriented, private-enterprise economy? We have, of course, a highly mixed economy at the present time, and the distinction between public and private enterprise is being blurred. As Professor Galbraith put it in *Atlantic* Magazine in 1967, "It requires no great exercise of the imagination to suppose that the mature corporation, as it develops, will eventually become a part of the larger administrative complex associated with the state. In time the line between the two will largely disappear. Men will marvel at the thin line that once caused people to refer to General Electric, Westinghouse, and Boeing as *private* business."[2]

IS IT WORTH SAVING?

What are we to make of all this? If it is all so inevitable, should we plan accordingly? If the major corporations—the core of our private enterprise economy—are ultimately to be controlled or absorbed by the federal government, should we cynically start positioning our companies for power roles in the bureaucracy to come? Or do we have, in our private enterprise system, some freedoms and values that must be preserved for future generations?

I am sure I know management's answer. Historians tell us that situations of freedom are rare and not very long lasting in the 5000-year history of civilization. What we have developed in the United States—political and economic democracy—has never been developed elsewhere on such a scale. It would be to our eternal dishonor if we were to let it be destroyed. There is more at stake than the private enterprise system. If too many of our economic liberties are lost, our political and civil liberties will follow. A government that controls our economic life will soon control the rest of life. Freedom is indivisible. This is, of course, an old story. But then, so is socialism. The struggle between liberty and tyranny, people and governments, is a very ancient struggle, and every generation must work out its own accommodation.

BEWARE THE ELEPHANT

None of us expects to return to the laissez-faire doctrine in which government plays no significant role in the economy. That day is gone. Nor can we afford the kind of divisive adversary relationship between government and business that so frequently has us working at cross-purposes. Rather, we need a relationship built on mutual respect and support for common objectives. On some technical projects where the risks and costs are too large for individual corporations, business and government will have to work together if the job is to be done. We will need more governmental support for economic objectives overseas—a really effective foreign *economic* policy. But as one of my associates says, "Beware of getting into bed with an elephant. If he ever rolls over, you've had it."

We will need to have a proper understanding about who does what, with government determining national objectives and policies, and private enterprise getting the economic work done. Though both business and government serve the public, we must insist on maintaining the essentially private, market-oriented character of the corporation and try to reverse the long, uninterrupted trend of expanding the government sector at the expense of the private sector of the economy. How can this be done? My purpose in this article has been to examine the vulnerabilities, not to present a plan for salvation. But certain principles would seem to be basic.

Develop a Constituency

First, business must develop a constituency of hard-core supporters. As Irving Kristol has pointed out, "No institution in our society can endure without a constituency—a substantial number of people who are loyal to the institution and who will quickly rally to its defense when it is in trouble. Yet the modern corporation is just about the only major institution of our society which does not have such a constituency. . . . Constituencies are not born but created—and once created, they need constant cultivation. Politicians understand this, but corporate managers do not."[3]

Kristol stresses the share owner constituency, but I think it is larger than that. Our natural constituency is the middle class which not only invests in but works in and buys from the corporation. These are the people with a direct economic and political stake in the corporation's success. We in management need to cultivate their loyalty, engage in serious two-way communications, and specifically ask for their help when we need it. All of us are aware that this is more easily said than done, or we would have done it long ago. So-called economic education programs for the public have failed miserably, and programs to sell the free enterprise system like you would sell soap are an insult to the people. In my view, we will have to win our constituency issue by issue, like any successful politician, demonstrating how specific proposals will affect the lives and pocketbooks of the people whose support we need. People do not want lectures. They want answers to problems and assurance that we really care about the things that concern them.

Voluntary Action to Prevent Regulation

Another basic principle is to resist unnecessary governmental interference with business decision making. This is one principle that every businessman and businesswoman seem instinctively to understand, but unfortunately we have too often been purely reactive, forever in a defensive posture. The best defense is a good offense. We must anticipate public criticism and take the necessary action to make regulation unnecessary. In retrospect, it appears that industry did not anticipate the strength of public feeling that could be aroused on the subjects of safety and environmental pollution. The auto industry particularly has been hurt by legislative overreaction.

Energy conservation and consumer information are areas in which the danger of excessive regulation runs high today. An ounce of prevention here will be worth a *ton* of cure. Industry must take the initiative in developing *voluntary* standards such as the energy-efficiency ratings of the air-conditioning industry, and move out front with effective programs of consumer education. Or if legislation is needed or inevitable, as in the case of pension reform, industry can help to assure a sensible outcome by coming up—on its own—with legislative proposals responsive to the real problems. It is the excesses, the needless and heedless use of governmental power, that must be avoided—primarily through voluntary action that anticipates public concern.

Conscious Evolution

But more important than resistance to excessive regulation is the positive performance that wins and holds the support of our constituencies. The American public, the sum total of all our constituences, is highly pragmatic. It supports institutions that deliver the goods. Thus the basic strategy for corporate survival is to anticipate the changing expectations of society and serve them more effectively than competing institutions. This means that the corporation itself must change, consciously evolving into an institution adapted to the new environment.

PLURALISTIC SOCIETY

Consider the changes. It is quite clear that the United States can no longer be called "a business society," as we were from about the Civil War to the end of World War II. Today we are a pluralistic society in which many competing groups and institutions strive for power and influence. Thus more decisions will be made and more resources will be allocated by political processes rather than the market economy. We must adapt to that. Moreover, as I mentioned before, the U.S. economy is primarily engaged in the production of services, not goods. Though the production of food, materials, and manufactured products is still this country's basic strength on the world scene, six out of ten Americans are engaged in the services sector, and that will increase to seven out of ten in the 1980s. Higher priority is being given to such things as health care, education, municipal services, travel, and recreation. Does this mean that the post-industrial society will also be the post-business society? Not at all. For one thing, industry has a big challenge to provide the equipment that will make the growing services sector more productive. And with some imagination, corporations can provide—as businesses—many of the services now provided by government and other institutions. This too means adapting to a more political climate.

WORLDWIDE OPPORTUNITY

Looking further ahead, we see that the easily available sources of energy, food, and materials on this planet are being used up. Unless the world wants to settle for a regimen of shared poverty, we will have to tackle the economic and technological task of developing the more difficult secondary sources. For example, nuclear power instead of oil, intensive farming of submarginal land, farming and mining the sea, and development of substitutes for scarce metals. These are tasks of economic development for which the private corporation has shown itself to be eminently suited, though it will require adaptation to a new relationship with governments in all nations.

And while the United States may be entering its post-industrial phase, most of the nations of the world are striving to reach the industrial level. Who is the best qualified to provide the know-how, the technology, and the organizational skill required in the developing nations? The initiative has already been taken by corporations, many of which are now operating on a world scale. There are many critics of the so-called multinational corporations, but as Peter Drucker points out, "Business is the only institution capable of being multinational. . . . The nation is too small a unit to make rational economic decisions."[4] If the gap between the rich and the poor nations is to be narrowed, the business corporation has the best chance of succeeding because it is the most effective international institution we have.

NEW DIRECTIONS

These, then, are some of the directions in which the corporation should be evolving:

- Toward a new and more productive relationship with government
- Toward competing more effectively for influence and resources in a pluralistic society

- Toward business ventures in the fast-growing services sector
- Toward the development of new technologies and new sources of food, fuel, and raw materials
- Toward economic development on a world scale to help narrow the gap between rich and poor nations

These are noble and self-justifying purposes, but they do not assure the successful future of the corporation. For we have many points of vulnerability, as I have tried to show. The sportswriter Damon Runyon once wrote, "As regards the human race, it's 9 to 5 against." At this juncture most of the prophets seem to give the same odds against the long-term survival of the corporation. But we have all seen the underdog emerge as the winner because of the will and energy to prevail. That is the challenge: in the words of William Faulkner (in his Nobel Prize acceptance speech in Oslo), "not merely to endure, *but to prevail.*"

REFERENCES

1. C. Jackson Grayson, *Harvard Business Review,* November–December 1973.
2. John K. Galbraith, *Atlantic Magazine,* October 1967, p. 37.
3. Irving Kristol, *The Wall Street Journal,* Oct. 14, 1974.
4. Peter Drucker, in Herman Kahn (ed.), *The Future of the Corporation* (New York: Mason & Lipscomb, 1974), p. 61.

16

EXPANDING COOPERATION FOR GLOBAL ECONOMIC DEVELOPMENT

HENRY A. KISSINGER
Former United States Secretary of State

The endeavor of independent nations to advance global economic development, and so to better the quality of human life on earth, is one of the most important enterprises in history. Our goal is nothing less than to shape an enduring structure of international collaboration that offers peace and prosperity, equal opportunity and dignity to all peoples. Mankind has always yearned for peace and a just international order. In our time these twin goals have becomes a realistic possibility. Their attainment will require us to meet challenges whose scale eludes the grasp of individual nations, whose complexity mocks the slogans and solutions of the past, and whose pace outstrips the measured processes of traditional diplomacy.

There is before us all the imperative of world stability—the task of resolving conflicts, reducing tensions, and resisting the encroachment of new imperialisms, new oppressions, and new dangers. For this undertaking the United States, together with other nations, has assumed a heavy responsibility. Beyond it lie our positive aspirations. The American people are a humane people. We know that stability is not enough; peace must extend mankind's reach for a better life. In the Declaration of Independence of the United States, the seminal document of our national existence, we have

Adapted from a presentation before the Fourth Ministerial Meeting of the UN Conference on Trade and Development on May 6, 1976, at Nairobi, Kenya. Published with permission.

written that " . . . all Men are created equal . . ." and entitled to " . . . Life, Liberty, and the Pursuit of Happiness. . . ." This pursuit brought me to Nairobi—to advance on behalf of President Ford and the U.S. government the great cause we all hold in common.

In the long sweep of history, the future of peace and progress may be most decisively determined by our response to the necessities imposed by our economic interdependence. This is the challenge which we have assembled here to address—the urgent need for cooperative solutions to the new global problems of the world economy. These issues dominate the agenda of the evolving relationship between North and South, the industrial and the developing countries.

- They are issues of economics—of an effective system of trade, monetary relations, and development assistance and of ensuring that the prosperity of some nations does not come at the expense of others.
- They are issues of politics—of how nations deal with each other and of how we can construct an international order that promotes peace.
- They are issues of morality—the recognition that economic might does not make right.
- They are issues of justice—the awareness that the well-being of our peoples depends upon an international system fair and open to all.

The modern age and our common morality insistently demand respect for human dignity and the fulfillment of the human personality. But a world in which poverty and misery continue to afflict countless millions would mock these imperatives. The daily preoccupation of men and women would be the harsh necessities of survival; the energies of nations would be consumed in hatred and rivalry. We must build, instead, a world of cooperation and widening human opportunity reflecting the fundamental interdependence of our destinies.

Today the accelerating forces of modernization—technological, economic, social, and political—link the peoples of the world as never before. They can intensify conflict or they can provide us with unprecedented possibilities to advance our common aims. All nations are part of a global economic system. If that system is to flourish, it must rest on the firm foundation of security, fairness, and opportunity to all who wish to participate—rich and poor, North and South, consumer and producer. It must embrace the interests of all if it is to be supported by all. President Ford sent me to Nairobi to help bring about a constructive and cooperative relationship between the developed and the developing countries over the remainder of this century.

The Ministerial Meeting of UNCTAD was the first of its kind to be held in Africa. This was altogether fitting, for Africa's importance in world affairs is growing. And African countries have an especially high stake in a successful conference leading to concrete progress. No continent has been more vulnerable to worldwide economic instabilities. No continent suffers so cruelly when crops fail for lack of rain. No continent endures a heavier burden when commodity prices fluctuate violently. And no continent has more to gain from the organized cooperation of all nations to promote economic and social progress and to ensure a greater role for the developing nations in the world's economic deliberations.

This is a continent of proud traditions and new nations, of rising aspirations, and of determination in the face of monumental challenge. Here it can—indeed it must—be demonstrated that people of all races and colors can live and prosper together in peace with equal rights and mutual respect. I was privileged to be a guest in Africa and to enjoy the extraordinary hospitality of its people and leaders. I have greatly benefited from my discussions with African statesmen, and I have learned much about the concerns and hopes of the peoples of Africa. The nations of this continent can be confident that the United States is prepared to cooperate with them in their great struggles for justice, economic progress, and freedom from external intervention.

The U.S. delegation came to Nairobi to achieve, with representatives of other nations, a major step forward in international cooperation. We began the conference at a moment of opportunity. The world economy was recovering from a deep recession—my own country perhaps most rapidly. Increasing American demand for products of other countries will make a major contribution to recovery around the world. Many obstacles to sustained economic growth remain; but there are convincing signs that we have surmounted the worst part of the economic crisis and that before us, if we act with wisdom and energy, is the opportunity for a new and prolonged period of prosperity. This, therefore, was a decisive moment which offered us a brief, but special, opportunity to reinvigorate and improve the world's international economic system. This was the time to free the world from disruptive cycles of boom and bust and to enhance the opportunities of the developing countries.

The United States, better than almost any other nation, could survive a period of economic warfare. We can resist confrontation and rhetorical attacks if other nations choose that path. And we can ignore unrealistic proposals and preemptory demands. But the historic opportunity which was at hand would slip away. It was up to us, as the spokesmen of nations meeting in this world forum, to reach beyond the doubts and temptations of the moment toward the permanent international interests of us all. In so doing, we could take courage from the knowledge that the means exist to achieve a brighter future. It lies within our power to shape a world where all people can live in dignity and aspire to progress.

I urged that we hold before us as the goal of the conference, and of the dialog between developed and developing nations, the motto of the Republic of Kenya: "Harambee—work together for the good of all," and suggested that we begin by building on the positive accomplishments of the Seventh Special Session of the UN General Assembly in September 1975. At that meeting the industrial and developing nations, in an encouraging demonstration of consensus, put aside ideological confrontation, declared their common purpose of moving forward cooperatively, and adopted an agreed agenda for action. On behalf of President Ford, I called upon the conference to accelerate the efforts and continue the cooperative spirit which began them. The United States pledges its dedication and willingness to cooperate over the decades ahead. We do so with an open mind. We want to hear the ideas and proposals of other nations, to exchange views and to forge a fresh consensus.

THE STATE OF OUR EFFORTS

Let me first review what our nations together have achieved since September 1975. We agreed at the Seventh Special Session to take measures to help ensure basic economic security against cycles that devastate export earnings and undermine development. In January 1975 the International Monetary fund (IMF) expended its compensatory financing facility as we had proposed, to make available several billion dollars to stabilize export earnings. In September we pledged to accelerate economic growth by improving developing countries' access to capital and new technology. To these ends the United States, other industrial countries, and several oil-producing countries have begun to marshal increased capital and technological and human resources to promote development. Negotiations have been completed to increase World Bank capital by $8 billion; we will contribute our fair share to a $6 billion increase in the resources of the Inter-American Development Bank; we will contribute to an expansion of the African Development Fund; we are actively participating in discussions on replenishment of the Asian Development Fund and Bank.

At the special session the world community dedicated itself to improving trade and investment in key commodities. International solutions have already been achieved on several key commodity issues, including the successful negotiation of coffee and tin agreements. Progress is also being made in expanding the world's supply of its most vital commodity—food. And finally, at the special session, the world community made a commitment to meet the special needs of the poorest countries which have suffered the most from recent economic dislocations. We have made significant progress by providing financial and technical assistance to increase food production and by introducing new measures to help relieve crushing balance-of-payments problems of the poorest nations.

These achievements are only the beginning of the process. We are now in the midst of what may well be the most extensive series of international negotiations on trade, finance, commodities, and development in history—involving more nations, addressing more issues, and affecting more people than ever before. In particular, we can advance our work in four key areas:

First, we must make renewed efforts on commodity issues, including the problems of resource investment and trade. Commodities—energy, food, and other primary products—are the building blocks of growth and prosperity. For many countries development of resources is the key to industrialization, employment, decent incomes, and healthy diets. All nations need adequate supplies of primary products and fair compensation for their production. Solving the complex of these issues is a critical test of our ability to work together systematically to expand the world's wealth for the benefit of all.

Second, we must design a far-reaching long-term program to accelerate technology transfer. The quantity of capital investment by itself does not assure sustained development. There must be, as well, continuous improvements in productivity that only new technology and trained local manpower can bring. Comprehensive efforts are crucial; the subject deserves high priority and comprehensive efforts will be required.

Third, we must deal with serious balance-of-payments and debt problems which face a number of developing countries. Rising import costs—caused in large part by higher oil prices and reduced export earnings due to recession in industrialized countries—have created unprecedented international payments problems. An improved world economy will automatically ease the problem for many countries. Nevertheless we must continue to seek means of assistance for the particular problems of certain developing countries.

Fourth, we must continue to respond to the special and urgent needs of the poorest countries. Helping these nations will demonstrate not only the capacity of the international economy to serve all countries equitably, it will also reflect our collective sense of responsibility. Let me now suggest specific new approaches for dealing with each of these four problems.

A COMPREHENSIVE APPROACH TO COMMODITIES

Commodity exports are critical for development. The non-oil-producing developing countries rely on primary products for nearly two-thirds of their export earnings. Yet production and export of these resources are vulnerable to the whims of weather, the swings of worldwide demand, and new technology. Cycles of scarcity and glut, underinvestment and overcapacity, disrupt economic conditions in both the developing and the industrial world. It has become clear in recent years that a piecemeal approach to these issues will not suffice. The UNCTAD Secretariat has made an important contribution to meeting these problems in its integrated commodity program. While the United States cannot accept all of its elements, there are many parts which we are prepared to consider.

The United States proposes its own comprehensive approach to commodity issues. It reflects many of the objectives contained in the integrated program and our desire for constructive action on all aspects of the challenge. It contains the following elements:

- Ensuring sufficient financing for resource development and for equitable sharing in their benefits by the host nation
- Improving the conditions of trade and investment in individual commodities and moderating excessive price fluctuations

- Stabilizing the overall export earnings of developing countries
- Improving access to markets for processed products of developing countries while assuring consumers reliability of supply

Adequate Investment

Most of the world's raw material production, in fact, takes place in the industrial countries. But if development is to take hold, a special effort must be made to expand the production and exports of primary products of developing countries. Such a program must overcome the following problems:

First, we must deal realistically with the political and economic problems which are diverting investments from developing to developed countries. For paradoxically, resource development is often discouraged by the very countries which are most in need of it. Nationalization and forced change in the terms of concessions in some developing countries have clouded the general climate for resource investment in the developing world. Social and political uncertainties have further complicated investment prospects. As a result, commercially viable projects have been postponed, canceled, or relocated; and capital, management, and technology have been diverted to production of higher-cost raw materials in the industrialized world. Second, in the next decade alone the total requirements for global investment in resources will be massive. Individual projects will require unprecedented sums of capital and complex financial arrangements. The time required between the beginning of a project and its completion is increasing. All these factors compound the political uncertainties and further inhibit rational investment. Third, there is no one institution that can work comprehensively to facilitate resource development, particularly in energy and minerals, or to promote equitable sharing of its benefits.

If present trends continue, serious misallocations of capital, management, and technology are inevitable. The costs of raw material and agricultural production will escalate. Many potential producers will be unable to attract adequate capital. All countries will pay the price in accelerated inflation and retarded growth—with the poorest countries suffering the most.

To overcome these problems, the United States proposes the establishment of an International Resources Bank (IRB). This new institution would promote more rational, systematic, and equitable development of resources in developing nations. It would facilitate technological development and management training in the developing countries. It would help ensure supplies of raw materials to sustain the expansion of the global economy and help moderate commodity price fluctuations. The IRB would mobilize capital for sound resources development projects by assisting individual resources projects to secure direct financing and issuing bonds which could be secured by a specifc commodity. Alternatively these bonds could be retired through delivery of a specific commodity. "Commodity bonds" of this type could greatly improve conditions of supply and market access and help developing countries to stabilize export earnings.

To enhance confidence for both host governments and investors, the IRB would begin operations with a capital fund of $1 billion. It would participate with foreign investors and the host government in project agreements specifying the conditions of the investment on a basis acceptable to all parties. Such an agreement could include a formula for production sharing and arrangements by investors to help develop the managerial, technological, and marketing capabilities of the host country. The bank would support guarantees of both investor and host nation performance in accordance with conditions established in the project agreement.

To ensure effective coordination with other public institutions, the IRB could be associated with the World Bank group, in a form to be worked out by the participating countries. It could operate in close collaboration with—and render even more effective—other institutions such as the World Bank and its associate, the International Finance Corporation, and the Inter-American Development Bank as well as the UN Revolving Fund for Mineral Exploration. The IRB proposal offers many advantages and new concepts:

- Its facilitating role as third party with the host country and the foreign investor will encourage conditions for project development consistent with internationally accepted standards of equity.

- The IRB mechanism provides multilateral guarantees of the performance of both the host nation and the foreign investor in accordance with the project agreement—thereby reducing the noncommercial risks. This cannot fail to promote greater flows of investment capital for resource projects on reasonable terms.

- The proposal contemplates production-sharing arrangements under which the foreign investor is assured of an established percentage of total production with disposition of the balance to be controlled by the host nation. This allows the host nation to share in production from the outset, providing it with the basis for further processing of the raw material should this prove to be economically feasible.

- Commodity bonds would be a fruitful new international instrument for forward purchases of commodities. They could contribute to earnings stabilization. They would also provide added assurance of market access for the host country and supply access for the consumer.

- Finally, through the IRB, modern technology would flow into developing nations. The two key elements required for development—management and technology—are provided by the foreign investor directly in a new form of capital investment. The trilateral agreement could include provisions for the progressive acquisition of technology by the host country and thus contribute importantly to the process of technology transfer.

We consider the IRB to be an innovative and significant response to the basic needs of the developing nations and the international community. It will be a major advance in the sharing of benefits and responsibilities between industrialized and developing nations. It will help ensure the essential flow of capital, management, and technology into resource development under conditions acceptable to host governments. And it will enhance the predictability that is essential to attract capital investment. We hope other countries will join us to design and establish this global institution.

Improvement of Commodity Markets

We are all conscious of the problems the world economy has faced recently in this area. Within only two years the tight supply and astronomical prices of many critical materials have been followed by a period of declining prices. Many economies have been severely shaken, and several countries have suffered balance-of-payments crises. Drastic price changes affect the developing countries most severely, playing havoc with foreign exchange earnings and development plans. And because raw material production projects require years to develop and involve high risks, volatile prices tend to lead to erratic patterns of investment. There are a number of ways to improve commodity markets—long-term contractual arrangements, better exchange of market information, improved distribution, more efficient production methods, and better storage and transport facilities.

We agreed with the UNCTAD Secretariat that buffer stocks deserve special attention. For those commodities where buffer stocks are feasible, sharp fluctuations in prices can be moderated by building stocks when markets are weak. And adequate supplies at reasonable prices can be assured through releasing stocks when markets are tight. The United States believes that buffer stocks can be financed from a combination of sources—direct contribution by the participants, export taxes, commercial borrowing guaranteed by the countries participating in the buffer stock or through the existing facilities of international institutions. Should existing sources prove inadequate, we would also be prepared to consider the IRB as a supplemental channel for financing a particular buffer stock. In these ways we are convinced that adequate international financing for buffer stocks can be assured within the context of the specific commodity agreement under which the stock is established. Clearly the United States would not want a buffer stock in which we had agreed to participate to fail for want of adequate financing.

The United States has pursued a constructive approach to other aspects of the commodities problem. We have joined with producers and consumers of key commodities to agree on measures to improve and stabilize markets. We have signed commodity agreements on coffee and tin, and we will participate in negotiations on sugar. We viewed cocoa as well suited to a buffer stock arrangement but were disappointed in the agreement negotiated a few months ago which we believe is unlikely to improve the functioning of the cocoa market. If other parties are interested, we stand ready to renegotiate this agreement. The United States recently participated in the first meeting of producers and consumers of copper. We look forward to the establishment of a permanent producer-consumer group.

Agricultural raw materials need serious attention as well. Those that face declining markets from growing competition from lower-cost producers and synthetics can benefit from market promotion, research to improve productivity, and marketability or diversification into other products. We recommend that producer-consumer forums dealing with individual commodities focus on such possibilities. We urge that the World Bank and the regional development banks give high priority to funding projects for these purposes.

Today the United States proposes these additional measures: First, let us reach agreement on a definite timetable for the study of specific commodity problems of interest to developing countries. We are prepared to initiate concerted consideration in producer-consumer forums of measures to improve the stability, growth, and efficiency of markets for all key developing countries' commodity exports. Particular attention should be given to the formation of groups for bauxite and iron ore. Second, since many of the poorest countries are dependent on these products for export earnings, we urge the World Bank and regional institutions to sponsor projects to improve production efficiency and markets for jute, sisal, and other hard fibers—or to facilitate diversification into other products to reduce excessive reliance on them.

Finally, any program of resources development must emphasize the two most vital international resources—food and energy. Forecasts of good harvests must not lull us into letting the progress begun at the World Food Conference slip away. At that conference nations agreed to work toward a system of world grain reserves to improve food security, increase support for agricultural research, develop programs for nutritional improvement, and increase agricultural development in low-income countries.

We urge other countries to join us to make the concept of world food reserves a reality, increase support for agriculture development in poorer nations, and provide necessary food aid. In energy we strongly support the efforts of oil producers and consumers from both the industrialized and the developing world to achieve cooperative solutions at the Conference on International Economic Cooperation (CIEC). We urge that our proposal for an international energy institute—which would help developing countries take advantage of their domestic energy resources—receive priority attention.

Stabilizing Export Earnings of Developing Countries

At the Seventh Special Session, the United States listed as its first priority the need to ensure economic security for the developing world. We continue to believe that the world economic system must provide the developing nations greater security from the worst effects of fluctuating prices, recession, inflation, and other economic shocks which they are helpless to prevent or avoid.

We are gratified at the rapid implementation of our proposals to the special session for the far-reaching expansion of the International Monetary Fund. These innovations make available billions of dollars in new financing to offset steep declines in export earnings. The most significant step forward has been the IMF's agreement to liberalize its compensatory financing facility. As of now roughly $800 million from this improved facility has been provided. If this rate continues, more money will have been lent this year from the facility than the entire amount provided over the last 12 years.

Another major advance has been the establishment of an IMF trust fund to help meet the balance-of-payments needs of the poorest countries. While many developing countries have received substantial benefits from the compensatory financing facility, low-income countries, whose export revenues depend on one or two commodities, often need additional financial help to meet balance-of-payments problems. To assist the poorest countries, the United States has proposed that the trust fund provide concessional financing to poorer countries to offset declines in earnings from an agreed list of particularly significant commodities.

Moreover the United States would be ready to join others in a review of the adequacy of the trust fund's resources, should they prove inadequate to stabilize earnings and thus provide general balance-of-payments financing for low-income developing nations. We especially urge those oil-producing nations with strong reserves to contribute to the trust fund's lending capacity.

Expanding Trade in Resources and Processed Goods

Trade has been an engine of growth for all countries; for many developing countries it is the most critical vehicle of development. The United States has taken a number of initiatives to meet the special needs of developing countries. We have reduced global trade barriers, especially those affecting processed goods; provided preferential access to our market for many exports of developing countries; worked in the multilateral trade negotiations (MTN) in Geneva for reduction of barriers in tropical products; and recognized in our general trade policy the special trade needs of developing countries.

We now have these challenges: We must maintain the momentum in reducing world trade barriers. We must focus especially on reducing barriers against processed goods, which retard developing countries' efforts to industrialize. We need additional international arrangements to assure reliability of supply, for the steady flow of new materials is vital to every country.

To maintain momentum in reducing trade barriers, industrial countries of the OECD (Organization for Economic Cooperation and Development)—despite the strains on their economics from higher energy costs and recession—have pledged themselves to avoid restrictive trade measures. The United States intends to join with other developed countries in a renewal of that pledge at the next OECD ministerial meeting. In addition, at the multilateral trade negotiations now taking place in Geneva we will pay special attention to the interests of developing countries, particularly in such areas as processed exports, tropical products, and nontariff barriers.

The institution of a generalized system of preferences (GSP) by the United States, combined with the preference systems of other industrial countries, has opened significant trading opportunities for developing nations. Our own preference system already covers more than 2700 items from nearly 100 countries. The annual trade value of these items is roughly $2.5 billion. We are examining the possibility of including additional products.

The United States will give priority support to the UN Development Program financing of a joint GATT–UNCTAD (GATT—General Agreement on Tariffs and Trade) program of technical assistance to developing countries. This will help those countries take full advantage of the preference schemes of industrialized countries by finding the most productive areas for new and increased exports and the best techniques of marketing their products. In addition, intensive negotiation is now underway in the MTN on tariff treatment of tropical products—including processed goods and manufactures—that are of particular interest to developing countries. The United States intends to implement negotiated tariff reductions in this area as soon as possible once the tropical product package is agreed on.

In keeping with the Tokyo declaration, the United States believes that the MTN negotiations on rules concerning nontariff barriers must give greater attention to the needs of developing countries. For example, the United States believes that a code to govern the use of countervailing duties against export subsidies should recognize the special conditions facing developing countries. We will urge that the special needs of developing nations be taken into account when new international rules pertaining to offsetting action are being developed.

With respect to new rules on safeguard measures against injury from imports, we will consider special treatment for less-developed countries which are minor suppliers or possible new entrants into the U.S. market. We recognize, too, that developing countries have interests in other reforms of the trading system which are not presently under negotiation. We will respond to these views with an open mind. We are confident that with goodwill on all sides constructive agreement can be reached on specific reform issues within the time frame of the multilateral trade negotiations.

The reduction of tariffs against the exports of processed raw materials from developing countries is especially important. Lowering these barriers would provide fresh opportunities to expand and diversify exports, particularly in cases where tariffs now escalate with the degree of processing. To this end the tariff reduction proposal which the United States has made in the MTN will not only result in significant tariff cuts but also will reduce tariff escalation. We expect that developing countries will regard this as an incentive to positive cooperation in the current negotiations.

If more open market access is one pillar of an expanding international trading system, greater reliability of supply is another. Without reasonable assurance from producer countries that they will not arbitrarily interfere with exports, importers must turn to other sources. Consumers will then bear the cost of less efficient production, unreliable producers, the cost of lost markets, and reduced foreign investment.

There is an urgent need to analyze methods to improve reliability of supply. We urge that work begin promptly in the GATT to determine whether an international code on export controls is feasible. Such a code should define more clearly the circumstances under which countries may legitimately apply export controls. It would reduce the uncertainties for consumers and exporters; and it would mitigate some of the political damage to relations between countries when restrictions are imposed on exports. The United States will also continue to seek commitments of reliable supply in the context of specific arrangements negotiated for individual commodities.

This four-point program—a new International Resources Bank, a case-by-case effort to improve conditions of trade and investment in primary products, stabilization of export earnings, and improved market and supply conditions—recognizes that these issues are linked; yet it permits pragmatic and flexible treatment of specific problems. The approach I have described is a major effort by the United States to deal on a comprehensive basis with commodity issues. It is workable; it is achievable; it is a program which meets the needs of developing and developed nations alike. We urge favorable consideration and rapid collective action.

TECHNOLOGY FOR DEVELOPMENT

Let me now turn to another area of major concern—the application of technology for development. Technology is at the heart of the development process. It enables people to extend their horizons beyond the mere struggle for existence. Technology draws the fullest measures from the finite resources of our globe. It harnesses the intelligence of human beings and the force of nature to meet the needs of mankind. For two centuries technological progress has been fundamental to rapid industrial growth. A central challenge of our time is to extend the benefits of technology to all countries.

There are a number of impediments to a rapid and effective technology transfer from industrialized to developing countries. First, in many cases technology from industrial countries may not fit the real needs of developing countries. By and large the challenge is not to transfer a carbon copy of existing technology but to develop new technology and technological institutions that are most relevant to the conditions of individual developing countries. Second, developing countries often lack adequate information and expertise to identify the technology which best meets their needs. Third, there is often a shortage of the trained manpower needed to select, adapt, and effectively manage technology. Fourth, technology often cannot be separated from capital and management. Hence it is one element of the overall investment process. And to be successful, technology must be applied within a framework of government policies which facilitate and nourish the process of technology transfer.

The task, therefore, is not simply the turnover of formulas or blueprints. We must pursue a comprehensive approach which provides a broad range of programs and incentives to transfer both technology and the fundamental skills that will give it root and effectiveness. To promote this, the United States proposes a five-point approach:

First, to adapt technology to the needs of developing countries, the United States supports the establishment of a network of research and development institutions at the local, regional, and international level. We need to strengthen global research capacities for development and to expand intergovernmental cooperation. Therefore, we propose the following:

- An International Industrialization Institute should be established to encourage research and development of industrial technology appropriate to developing countries. A founder's conference involving all interested countries should be convened "with all deliberate speed."
- The Energy Commission of the Conference on International Economic Cooperation should establish an International Energy Institute to facilitate energy research and the application of energy-related technologies to the special needs of developing countries.
- We should extend existing networks for applied research in the fields of agriculture, health, and education. The creation of new institutions must be accompanied by measures to help the process of technology transfer. To improve cooperation between industrialized and developing countries, the United States proposes new programs in three fields of advanced science, to which we are prepared to make major contributions of knowledge and experience—in satellite technology, water resources development, and oceans technology.
- Satellite technology offers enormous promise as an instrument for development. Remote-sensing satellites can be applied to survey resources, forecast crops, and improve land use in developing countries. They can help to foresee and evaluate natural disasters. Modern communication technologies, including satellites, have large untapped potential to improve education, training, health services, food production, and other activities essential for development. Therefore, very shortly the United States will make available to interested developing countries demonstrations of the various applications for development of the experimental *ATS-6* communications satellite, the Landsat remote-sensing satellite, and high-resolution photography. We are prepared to cooperate with developing countries in establishing centers, training personnel, and, where possible, adapting our civilian satellite programs to their needs.
- The United States will play a leading role in applying water resources technology to such objectives as improving the quality and productivity of agriculture and developing new industry. We will play an active role at the UN Water Conference to be held in March 1977, putting forward practical measures to share our knowledge and experience.

- The technology necessary to mine the deep seabed, manage fisheries, and exploit the vast potential of the oceans is rapidly being developed. The United States has made major advances in this field. We plan to invite scientists, managers, and technicians from different countries to participate in our scientific projects. And we strongly support provisions in the Law of the Sea treaty which will provide incentives for sharing of deep-seabed technology appropriate to developing country needs.
- Finally, there is a pressing need to develop new ways to use technology to improve the basic condition of the poor. The United States is increasing the technical component of its development programs to provide basic nutrition, health, and education services.

The second element of our program is to improve the amount and quality of technological information available to developing countries and to improve their selection of technology relevant to their needs. We will support the efforts of the UN International Center for Exchange of Technological Information to provide comprehensive information on the capabilities and facilities of national and regional information services. For its part the United States will inventory its national technological information resources and make available, both to developing countries and to the UN Center, consultants and other services to improve access to our national information facilities. These include the National Library of Medicine, the Division of Scientific Information of the National Science Foundation, the National Agricultural Library, and the Smithsonian Information Service.

The United States also supports the proposed UNCTAD advisory service to strengthen the ability of developing nations to effectively identify, select, and negotiate for technology most appropriate to their requirements. We support the concept of regional advisory services under UNCTAD auspices to provide expertise and resources to the technology requirements of particular regions and countries. These regional centers could act as conduits for the activities of other programs and institutions for the application of technology to developing countries.

Third, to nurture new generations of technologists and technology managers, the United States proposes a priority effort to train individuals who can develop, identify, and apply technology suited to the needs of developing countries. To this end, training competent managers of future technology should be central objectives of the proposed International Industrialization Institute and the International Energy Institute. For its part the United States will encourage universities, research institutes, and industrial training schools in the United States to create special institutes and curricula for technology training for the developing countries; we will provide for and assist their sister institutions to developing countries. We invite other developed countries to join us in this effort.

Finally, the United States proposes that appropriate incentives and measures be devised to curb the emigration of highly trained manpower from developing countries. For the benefits which developing nations derive from trained technology managers are of no consequence if they leave their home countries. In this connection the U.S. government will encourage the formation of a technology corps, which will parallel our executive service corps in organization and operation. This will be a private, nonprofit organization to which corporations and universities would contribute highly skilled personnel experienced in the management of scientific and technical operations. They will work with and help train local manpower in specific development projects.

The fourth element of our approach is to make the process of transferring existing technology more effective and equitable. New technology in industrialized countries resides primarily in the private sector. Private enterprise is in the best position to provide packages of management, technology, and capital. To enhance that contribution, both industrialized and developing countries must create an environment conducive to technology transfer. The United States recommends that voluntary guidelines be developed that set forth the conditions and standards of technology transfer which encourage, facilitate, and maximize the orderly transfer of technology.

The proposed International Resources Bank also contains features which can enhance the ability of developing countries to manage technology and thereby encourage its transfer. In the trilateral agreement with the host nation and the IRB, the foreign investor would generally undertake to provide both management and technology. The investment project could, by mutual agreement, include the obligation to progressively transfer some of the technology to the host nation over the period of the agreement—as well as accelerate the developing of the country's capacity to manage such technology.

The flow of technology in the channels of world commerce can be diverted by restrictive practices. Some practices may directly limit the transfer of technology; in addition, where technology is transferred, restrictive provisions on trade in high technology products can limit its benefits for others. The United States proposes that international attention be focused on the full range of these practices, with a view to their reduction or elimination.

The fifth element of the U.S. program is to set goals for achievement before and during the UN Conference on Science and Technology for Development, now proposed for 1979. The United States strongly supports this conference and its objectives. Preparations for it provide a major opportunity for both developed and developing countries to review their responsibilities for the sharing and use of technology. To speed our preparations, the United States will convene a national conference in 1977, bringing together our best talent from universities, foundations, and private enterprise. They considered the broad range of technological issues of concern to the developing world. They helped mobilize American resources to assist developing countries to meet their research requirements. And they were encouraged to prepare detailed American proposals for the conferences and institutes I have described. We recommend also that the OECD nations urgently study the possibilities of a greater contribution by all industrialized nations to overcoming the problems of technology transfer.

This five-point program represents the most comprehensive effort ever put forward by the United States to deal with the challenge of applying technology to development. We invite the ideas and proposals of all member nations. Working together, we can see to it that this age of technology will improve the quality of the lives of all of our peoples in a manner undreamed of by previous generations.

BALANCE-OF-PAYMENTS AND DEBT PROBLEMS

Rising import costs caused in large part by higher oil prices and reduced export earnings resulting from recession in the industrialized nations have generated unprecedented international payments deficits. Though global economic recovery has begun, many countries will face persisting deficits. A major institutional effort must be made if these countries are to avoid severe cutbacks in their imports and consequent reductions in their economic growth. There are three priority areas:

- We must ensure that flows of funds for development projects are neither reduced nor diverted by short-term economic problems. In addition, long-term financing must be increased and its quality enhanced.
- We must enable private markets to continue to play a substantial role in providing development capital. For many countries private capital flows are, and will continue to be, the principal form of development finance.
- We must see to it that the domestic economic policies of all our countries are sound. They should not place undue pressures on payment positions by unnecessary accumulations of debt. And we must give particular attention to those countries unable to avoid critical debt problems.

Resource Flows

We have been heartened by the immense effort made since the Seventh Special Session to assure adequate balance-of-payments financing for less-developed nations. Especially important has been the expansion of the International Monetary Fund's lending facilities. These efforts should help ensure that sufficient balance-of-payments financing is available on an aggregate basis to developing countries.

But emergency lending cannot be a substitute for effective and high quality foreign aid. Though most foreign assistance from the United States and other donors is provided on highly concessional terms, much can be done to improve the quality of resource flows. In many cases the conditions of assistance restrict its financial and developmental impact; one example is the tying of aid to procurement in donor countries which can reduce its value. The United States therefore will urge the OECD Development Assistance Committee to develop arrangements for the reciprocal untying of development assistance.

Private Capital

For many developing countries, particularly those in the midst of industrialization, private sources make up the bulk of development capital. Of the $35 billion balance-of-payments deficit of the non-oil-producing developing countries in 1975, nearly half was financed by private capital flows. Without this contribution, the consequences of the mammoth deficit would have been unmanageable. The IMF/IBRD (International Banks for Reconstruction and Development) Development Committee is studying a wide range of measures to ensure that international capital markets continue their imaginative adaptation to the needs of developing nations.

In addition, negotiations on the replenishment of the International Finance Corporation (IFC), which we proposed at the Seventh Special Session, have been completed. The IFC is actively engaged in examining the U.S. proposal for international investment trust to mobilize portfolio capital for investment in local enterprises. The United States gives its full support to these efforts.

Debt Problems

Many countries have had to resort to short-term external borrowing to finance their deficits. Debt payment burdens are mounting; a number of countries are experiencing serious problems in meeting their debt obligations. Generalized rescheduling of debts is not the answer. It would erode the credit worthiness of countries borrowing in private capital markets. By tying financing to debt, it obscures the significant differences among countries and prevents an appropriate focus on those in most urgent need. And it would not be fair to those nations which have taken strong policy measures to reduce their obligations.

The debt problem must be addressed in relation to each country's specific position and needs. The United States stands ready to help countries suffering acute debt service problems with measures appropriate to each case. The procedures must be agreeable to creditor and debtor alike. The device of a creditor club is a flexible instrument for negotiations. To improve the basis for consideration of balance-of-payments problems of particular developing countries, the United States proposes that the CIEC Finance Commission or another mutually acceptable forum examine the economic and acute financing problems of developing countries.

THE POOREST COUNTRIES

The needs of many nations in the developing world are great, but the special requirements of the poorest countries are massive. This conference has a collective moral responsibility to respond to this challenge. We must devote major efforts to improve programs for the poorest countries and to devise new ones where necessary for, without adequate assistance, the poorest will be condemned to continuing poverty and helplessness. We must increase resource flows, improve their terms, and enhance their quality. And aid must be given on softer terms, because the poorest countries are by definition unable to service debt except on a highly concessional basis.

Resource flows to the poorest countries must be freed from restrictions on procurement sources and the financing of local costs which distort the design of projects, waste resources, and cause excessive reliance on imported equipment. The IMF trust fund now being established will importantly ease the immediate balance-of-payments problems of the poorest countries.

For the longer term a substantial replenishment of the International Development Association is imperative. The United States will, as always, meet its commitments to this vitally important source of assistance. And we look forward to generous OPEC (Organization of Petroleum Exporting Countries) support for this important institution. Thus the United States has already taken a number of steps to assist the most needy countries. We will do more.

- To meet the urgent needs of the Sahel region, we are actively participating in the deliberations of the "Club des Amis du Shale." In addition, we have proposed that an urgent study be undertaken on ways not merely to ease the drought but to end the water shortage by mobilizing the great African rivers, not to perpetuate relief but to initiate basic reform.

- The U.S. Congress has already authorized a contribution of up to $200 million for the International Fund for Agricultural Development. We look forward to the June Plenipotentiary Conference which has been called to sign the agreement; and we urge others to contribute generously so that the $1 billion target can be met.

- We have secured authority under our Foreign Assistance Act to finance all total costs of aid projects in least developed countries when necessary to ensure their success.

- Seventy percent of our bilateral development assistance is now programmed for countries with per capita GNP of $300 or less.

- For countries whose per capita GNP is less than $500, we strongly support proposals to increase their share to over 80 percent of all UNDP (UN Development Program) grants. One-third of this should go to the least developed countries in this category.

- We pledge a major expansion of our efforts to develop integrated systems for basic community health services. These will combine medical treatment, family planning, and nutritional information while making full use of locally trained paramedical personnel.

In the 1976 Law of the Sea negotiations in New York, the United States made a detailed proposal that revenues from deep-seabed mining and resources exploitation be shared with the international community, especially for the benefit of the poorest countries. This is a substantial effort. It must be complemented, however, by improvement in the terms of bilateral assistance to the poorest countries. To this end the United States proposes that all donor countries agree to provide all development assistance to the relatively least developed countries on the UNCTAD list on a grant basis.

The United States will seek authorization from Congress to provide all development assistance to the poorest countries on this basis. We already have congressional authorization to convert repayment of a portion of our loans under PL-480 to grants under certain circumstances. Taken together, these two steps will significantly increase the grant element in our bilateral assistance programs. Human suffering and human deprivation are not questions of ideology or bloc politics. They touch the elemental needs of mankind and the basic imperatives of universal moral values. We must not fail to do our duty.

CONCLUSION

Economic development is a task of many dimensions. Whatever may be our differing perspectives, the United States believes that a number of conclusions stand out clearly: Development is a mutually reinforcing endeavor. There is nothing permanent about the distinction between the developed and developing worlds. Developed countries thrive and advance most surely when the international economy grows vigorously and steadily. As the United States sees other nations develop and industrialize, we feel renewed confidence in the world economic system and in our own economic future. Sustained growth and development require that we work together cooperatively.

Development involves mutual responsibility. International cooperation cannot be one-sided. The strength of the industrial countries must be regarded as a trust for the progress of all; the developing countries only hurt themselves if they weaken that strength through contrived scarcities, cartels, embargoes, or arbitrary seizures of property. At the same time the developed countries have an obligation to do their utmost to spur development. Our efforts here must take into consideration the concerns and the contributions of all countries—developed and developing, producer and consumer, East and West, North and South.

Development is a process of change and innovation. It must respond not only to rapidly changing technology but also to the evolution of political attitudes. The old relationships of donor and recipient are increasingly paternalistic and anachronistic to the recipient; they may also come to seem a one-sided burden to those who have long been donors. We must fashion a new sense of cooperation that is based on the self-respect and sovereign equality of all nations. Each nation must find its path to development which allows it to retain its self-respect and identity, its culture, and its ideological preference. But development itself is not a function of ideology—it must unite practical solutions and a philosophy of international cooperation. It cannot grow from doctrines of confrontation and the exploitation of despair.

Development is a human enterprise. It is the talents and efforts of individuals which make development a reality, and it is they who are its ultimate beneficiaries. Our first aim is the minimum essentials of life—food, clothing, shelter—and the relief of human suffering and monotony, debilitating illness and ignorance, and demeaning servitude to others. Then development must look beyond survival to provide opportunities for education, greater personal freedom, and individual dignity and self-respect. Finally, development must deal with the quality of life—the dignity of the individual, personal freedom, and equality of opportunity regardless of race, religion, sex, or political belief.

The magnitude of the task before us will require unprecedented international collaboration. No nation alone can surmount—and only together can all nations master—what is inescapably a global challenge of historic proportions. But we are not confronted by overwhelming odds or by intractable obstacles. We have it in our power to achieve in our generation a rate of economic advance that has no parallel in human experience.

In each age men and women have striven for greater prosperity and justice and dignity. Yet always in the past there have been setbacks; history has recorded a surfeit of misery and despair. Our age is the first where we can choose to be different. And therefore we must. If we succeed, this decade could be remembered as a turning point in the economic and political evolution of mankind. The new institutions and mechanisms we create could be perceived as building blocks of international cooperation that strengthened the world's sense of community. The implications for world peace, as well as for economic cooperation, are vast.

The United States proceeds from the conviction that both morality and practical interest point in the same direction—toward a dedicated enterprise of cooperation. If we are met in a cooperative and realistic spirit, we are prepared to offer our national capacities in support of a historic extension of the global economy and global development. So let us get down to business. Let us make this task a priority of all our foreign policies. Let us set our sights high, but let us not make our desire for the ideal block achievement of the attainable. Let us reach agreement on practical steps that improve the lot of our fellowman. We owe our people performance, not slogans; results, not rhetoric. The United States extends its hand to those who will travel with us on this road to a more humane and bountiful future. Let us travel it together.

17

MANAGEMENT TOWARD THE YEAR 2000: The Challenges and the Opportunities

EDWARD M. MAZZE
Dean, W. Paul Stillman School of Business, Seton Hall University

Every professional manager knows that to be successful, he or she must adjust to a dynamic business environment. "Futurism," the art of describing tomorrow on the basis of what we know today and of assessing current trends, is gaining enormous attention. The reason for this interest is to try to predict conditions in reasonable detail and to evaluate how outcomes depend on current choices. The term "breakthrough" is frequently used to indicate new discoveries. We often lose sight of the fact that new developments are the result of painstaking work by many people over a long period of time. Recognition is given only to the final, tangible development. The telephone, radio, TV, and computer were not "invented" at a specific moment in time. They were "developed" from an accumulation of knowledge (old and new)—an assembly of data, experimentation, and final development. To speculate on what management will be like in the future, one must understand management as it is today. If there were one word which best describes the future, it would be change. And change results in new problems and challenges for managers to face.

POPULATION OF TOMORROW

The original forecast by the federal government for population in the year 2000 was 305 million; but because of the declining birthrate, the latest estimate is about 283 million. Other predictions put the population in the year 2000 somewhere in the range of 235 to 300 million. The United Nations (UN) in 1966 issued population projections to the end of the century for the world as a whole, and for specific economically developed and developing areas. These projections indicate that if present high fertility and declining mortality rates continue, world population will reach 7.5 billion by the year 2000. The UN also calculated three additional projections—termed high, low, and medium variants—predicated on a birthrate that declines along with the mortality rate. The high variant gives a world population, in the year 2000, of 7 billion; the medium variant, 6.1 billion; and the low variant, 5.4 billion; this assumes a decrease in birthrate in the developing areas. Life expectancy will increase for both males and females, according to projections that show the 1967 level of 67 years for males rising to 69 years by the year 2000 and the female level rising from 74 to 75.

PEOPLE AND MANAGEMENT

Two trends affect the quality of the population in the United States in the future: higher education for millions of people, with no less than 50 percent and as many as 75 percent of high school graduates going on to college; and better socioeconomic status for millions of women. By 2000, it is predicted that almost all families with heads of households between 20 and 30 years of age in the United States will include one or more college graduates. These families will constitute a mass of affluent, highly educated adults—an intellectual and economic elite available for management positions in both profit and nonprofit organizations. The second trend that will affect the availability of people for management positions is the breakdown in traditional roles between the sexes. For example, the women's liberation movement has had a major impact on society for laws to eliminate discrimination against women. It is predicted that women's educational achievements and earnings will rank alongside men's in the near future. The number of women working has grown 35 percent in the last 10 years compared to 9 percent for men. There are now 32 million women in the work force, and the number is expected to hit the 40-million mark by 1980. Numbers alone do not tell the story; it is not only how many women are working but what they are doing. Many women are entering job categories heretofore closed to females.

An increasing demand for women and men in professional and technical fields will eventually open the presidential suites of companies to scientists and engineers. Also, minority groups will find greater job opportunities in middle and top management.

LIFE-STYLES

The future will bring about a change in life-styles, values, and attitudes. The life-style of "being an individual," "being me," or "doing your own thing" is seen as the dominant one of tomorrow. Another change in values is the decreased emphasis placed on achievement or making it to the top. People are interested in task accomplishment or getting things done, but they are more interested in doing things which are satisfying to themselves.

People will have more leisure time because the working day of the future will be shorter. Today there is a yearly maximum of 240 workdays; this may go down to 175 days by 1990. The workweek is getting shorter and there is more flexibility in the workday. Companies are experimenting successfully with three- and four-day workweeks that permit employees to decide when they want to start and stop work as long as they put in the hours required to get the job completed. More leisure time and shorter workweeks will lead to new challenges for managers.

FUTURE PRODUCTS AND TECHNOLOGY

The majority of scientific discoveries and products used today have been developed within the twentieth century. The rate of introduction of new products has been increasing rapidly and will speed up more in the coming years. The number of inventions in the next 10 years is projected to equal the total number of those in the last 30–35 years. The work of scientists in future years will produce more technological change. In medicine, for example, it is predicted that all of people's physical ailments, including aging, will be significantly reduced by the end of this century. Organ transplants and mechanical devices will become commonplace as a means of prolonging life. There is even the possibility of chemical manipulation of human intelligence and memory.

As the population increases, there will be greater demands for integrated transportation systems to move people and products. By the year 2000, such innovations as the hover principle and more monorail systems and automated control systems for automobiles will be in use. Bulk cargo will be moved by ocean freighters powered by nuclear energy and pipelines. The most economical transportation medium for low-value, heavy, durable bulk cargo over long distances will be cargo carriers equipped with flotation gear that can be dumped into the proper ocean current. A new type of surface transportation will be the "air truck," an aircraft that will feature relatively low speeds with short-range and high-life capabilities.

Communications will see wider use of videotape cassettes and the laser beam. By the year 2000, most offices will have a communication core possessing the present capabilities of the telephone, radio, TV, computer, and facsimile—all linked by switching systems from office to office as well as to central points. Technology will provide businesses with increasingly efficient, flexible, cheap communication with no limitations on distance. Transmission of pictures and texts and the distant manipulation of computers and other machines will be added to the transmission of the human voice on a scale that will eventually approach the universality of telephoning.

Some of the products and innovations listed below will be available by the year 2000:

- Common use of individual power sources for lights, appliances, and machines
- Three-dimensional TV
- Mechanical and chemical products for improving analytical ability
- New uses for tunnels and underground buildings
- Nuclear excavation and mining
- Automated universal credit, audit, and banking systems
- Conference TV similar to conference telephoning
- Inexpensive design and manufacture of one-of-a-kind products through computerized analysis and automated production
- Direct electronic communication with the brain
- Personal "pagers," perhaps two-way pocket telephones
- Artificial moons and other methods for lighting large areas
- Maintenance-free machinery that lasts a long time
- Small, long-lasting, battery-operated TV receivers that cost less than $20

Changes in technology affecting the population, life-styles, businesses, and products will lead to new challenges for management to solve. For example, a highly developed science and technology may lead to a hazard of mass destruction through nuclear and biological weapons. Replacement of manual and routine labor by machinery will cause exacerbated unemployment. Advances in communication and transportation will result in increasing air, noise, and land pollution. Introduction of efficient production systems may bring about a dehumanization of ordinary work.

TOMORROW'S MANAGEMENT

The management philosophy of the executive will change by the twenty-first century: he or she will be more concerned with managing "alternatives" than resources; availability of resources will be taken for granted. Computer technology will also change the way of managing. A new method of managing is envisioned where management skills will be adapted to highly centralized, mechanized, and computerized techniques. This will lead to a universal system type of management.

The focus of management has already shifted from a things first, people second philosophy to a people first, things second emphasis: that is, the Age of People. This is illustrated by the fact that management techniques have been applied to such nonbusiness areas as health services, population control, recycling of solid wastes, prison industries, and fund raising. Management opportunities in government at the state and local levels are growing. The Age of People includes a major value change in society, with the challenges of the nation's ghettos, women's liberation, environmentalists, and other influences needing attention by business people. It is an age in which people are concerned with the quality of life, ethnic pride, and dignity. Business is expected to repay a long accumulated debt to the physical environment. The traditional concept of the assembly line is being challenged. More middle-aged adults are leaving high-paying jobs for a simpler life. Vast urban regions are beginning to develop into integrated industrial areas.

Today's approach to management is really not adequate to reflect the transitions taking place. We can foresee three changes in management in the future.

1. *New Industries:*
A wide range of new industries will develop as corporations move into sectors previously serviced by public agencies. In addition to the education, health, and public safety markets, opportunities will arise from the return to private enterprise of transportation, resource recycling, garbage collection, pollution control, and welfare services.

2. *New Technologies:*
Science and technology will be encouraged with relatively few limitations.

3. *Service Orientation:*
Manufacturing organizations will provide more information and services to their consumers.

Six additional types of changes will affect the character and role of management in the future:

1. Changes in manufacturing problems. The future promises a wider variety of complex products to meet the specific needs of both industrial and consumer users.

2. A more sophisticated buyer will have a better understanding of products and will have higher expectations as to quality and performance.

3. Environmental changes in resources available to management. Improved data processing and communication will provide the manager with better and more up-to-date readings on the environment in which he or she is working.

4. Increased business size and responsibility. Organizations of the future will be larger and more complex.

5. More emphasis on government control. There are many ways in which the government can initiate change by legislation and moral persuasion.
6. Acceleration of the process of change. The increasing pace of change in the future places greater responsibilities and challenges on organizations to operate in a dynamic environment.

The role of management is changing. What individuals manage, how they manage it, for whom they manage it will be influenced by such matters as the economy, legislation, and technological advances.

CAUSES AND EFFECTS

Management deals with the achievement of objectives by utilizing the resources available. The introduction of scientific methods in management has replaced traditional, and frequently unplanned, routine with intelligent planning and methodology. In future years, the emphasis in scientific management will move from adaptation to change to active anticipation and planning for change. The increasing size of organizations has taken management out of the realm of activities that can be handled informally by a few people and into the range of more formalized procedures. It is making management more of a science than an art.

The term science often means something irrefutable, a collection of laws that are both immutable and products of ratiocination. The word science means "knowing." When the term "scientific management" is used, the connotation is that some definite laws are available to provide a substitute for hunch or guesswork. Thus, we have encouraged debate on whether or not management is a science, since its laws are artificial and often change. Veneration of science generally comes from people with little scientific background. No one knows what electricity is. Many hypotheses have been developed to explain it. Our most useful knowledge consists of empiric laws developed from experimentation. People working with electric power know Ohm's law, $E = IR$, or voltage equals current multiplied by resistance. This law applies only to a limited number of conditions and does not explain electricity; it only gives a means of simple calculation of many electrical problems. Albert Einstein, with his theory of relativity, seriously undermined much of earlier work, including Isaac Newton's. As we probe space further, we may find yet other variations we do not understand. Less than 30 years ago many scientists held the theory that if any object achieved the speed of sound it would be destroyed. Today we exceed the speed of sound many times.

Should we expect management to become a science with immutable laws? A body of knowledge about management is and has been under development since the beginning of mankind. It is much more difficult than natural science because part of the subject concerns people. Despite some theorists who claim to have reduced all human thinking to a set of equations that can be duplicated by computer, many feel this is oversimplification and humans are still unpredictable. Much has been learned about managing people, but perhaps much more important than what has been learned is a change in attitude that is often referred to as "enlightened" management. This enlightened concept has two prongs: the accumulation of information on the behavior of people under certain conditions and a greater acceptance of social responsibility for those at the bottom. The latter sociological aspect, which is applauded and whose continued development is desired, is an attribute of humanity at large, not of management.

Management is more properly concerned with the behavior of people. This concept can be simplified if we apply the line of thinking used in the physical sciences: the relationship of cause and effect. Many of our physical laws were developed out of experimentation. When it was found that with certain causes, the same effect was obtained and that a variation in the causes would produce certain variations in effect, a law was developed. We explain that when two parts of hydrogen are mixed with one part of oxygen under certain conditions of temperature and pressure, the gases disappear and water results. We then postulate chemical laws that apply in principle to many things without our actually knowing exactly what happens or why. Dmitri Ivanovich Mendeleeff developed the periodic table from which the existence of certain elements was predicted before their isolation. In other words, an order in physical science was demonstrated and has been proved, but why? This is a point at which, for many people, religion takes over and a supernatural guiding intelligence is postulated.

Cause and effect also relate to management problems, but the number of variables is much greater. Individual people differ, and many social and political theories are in vogue. It is more than possible that temperature, humidity, cosmic radiation, and other factors of which we presently have little knowledge also affect human beings. The greatest problem is identifying both causes and effects and their interrelationships. New York City reports an increase in crime in the summer. Is it the temperature, the greater percentage of time people spend outdoors, the amount of sun available, the fact that school is over? The answers to these questions are not always apparent. Possibly the collection of data over a period of time may shed a little light on the causal relationships.

Much of the confusion in management comes from the variety of causes and effects. What labor once denounced as paternalistic, it now demands in union contracts. If every new contract results in a nearly total victory for a particular union in a particular plant or industry, should anyone be surprised if at some future time a refusal of management results in a strike? If the cost of labor continues to mount to the point where management can better afford to install automation and so eliminate certain jobs, should labor be surprised? If these displaced people become relief recipients and taxes rise, should anyone be surprised?

There is a new frontier and there will be a continuous breakthrough in the science of management. What is primarily needed is more careful analysis of cause and effect without emotion. The solution of many of today's problems in management may be more legislation, merely the passage of time, or better education of all concerned in the laws of cause and effect.

SCIENTIFIC CONTRIBUTIONS

The behavioral and managerial sciences have moved from a state of infancy to where they now provide useful analytical concepts and empirical knowledge for decision making. They do not provide easy solutions to management problems in general, but are useful for offering techniques to handle specific problems. The behavioral and managerial sciences provide theories, methods, and research findings, and a strong potential for more empirical knowledge, analytical concepts, and models which are valuable for reinforcing the science of management. In 1959 Thomas H. Carroll, vice president of the Ford Foundation, made the following statement concerning interdisciplinary contribution to management knowledge: "In all likelihood the social and behavioral sciences will be applied increasingly to problems of business administration. The relevance of economics has always been apparent, but the application of other social sciences, particularly psychology, sociology, and social anthropology, are still in the pioneering stage." Today the contributions from these sciences are reported widely in management literature. However, considerable danger can exist in unrestrained borrowing from other fields the findings, generalizations, and techniques developed to answer other problems in other contexts. The borrower is in danger of seeing something in simple terms that in reality is very complex.

In the last 20 years, behavioral and mathematical techniques applied to decision making have caused a revolution in the technology of business administration. Like most new techniques, they have gained acceptance on the basis of a number of special applications. There is still room for many more worthwhile applications. Management, as a specific discipline, developed almost entirely within the past 75 years.

MORE MANAGEMENT BY OBJECTIVES

Research has shown that most people operate at only 20 percent or less of their capacity. Improving productivity is a major concern of the manager today and will have greater importance in the future. Many people never get around to setting specific goals for themselves. Goals provide a direction to move toward, they set "ideals" so that results can be compared to some predetermined needs, and they are targets to assist individuals in being more productive. Individual sets of goals are unique: none are exactly the same because they are the results of many human factors. They develop from an individual's attitudes, habits, personality, skills, and environment.

If we look to the benefits of management science in the public sector, there is reason for optimism. The use of management science techniques is widespread enough, rewarding enough, and intense enough to have created a momentum that will not stop. The wall built by the early administrators against the use of these new techniques is crumbling away. The 1960s saw the beginning of new approaches to management decision making in industry; the 1980s will in all probability be the era of management science in all sectors—private and public. The underlying premise has been that there are clear and present opportunities for wide applications of management science tools in the public sector. The government is the biggest of all economic activities, and resources are limited. Improved management is necessary and will be requested in the future.

INTERNATIONAL MANAGEMENT

In the last 30 years, six major changes have taken place in international business. These changes are: the growth of common markets; the opening up of trade with countries operating under different economic systems; the emergence of new countries; the development of multinational corporations; the easing of conditions for doing business abroad; and the improved economic conditions of all nations. These changes have created a need for a more scientific approach to international management.

As a company's activities become multinational, the nature and extent of its management problems change. Operating an enterprise in the global marketplace creates a variety of problems. Problems arise in coordinating and integrating company operations to fulfill overseas profit objectives. The firm that makes overseas commitments in terms of human resources, know-how, or finances cannot treat its operations abroad as an isolated part of the company's business. There are some basic similarities between international and domestic business transactions. However, there are also some dissimilarities due to language, climate, distance and communications, laws, marketing and business sophistication, people and their characteristics, social and business customs, business standards, and differences in national monetary systems and economic policies.

With an increasing number of companies becoming multinational, a new role has been assigned to international management which goes far beyond the task of selling, manufacturing, or financing a product abroad. This new role is threefold. First, it concerns the coordination of international activities on a worldwide scale. Second, it involves economic education for people in the foreign country. Third, it concerns integration of the company's programs in an international environment. More professionals with international management skills will be needed in the years ahead.

AMERCIAN MANAGEMENT AND ECONOMIC DEVELOPMENT

The majority of people in the world are poor because of low per capita income, high rate of illiteracy, and increasing population rate. Poverty is a major obstacle to economic growth. Because a country is poor, it does not develop; because it does not develop, it remains poor. Even as we reach the year 2000, there will still be a major gap between rich and poor countries. The factors conducive to economic development are availability of natural resources, accumulation of capital, increases in the scale or specialization of production, availability of trade, and technological progress. A country is considered to be developing economically if it expands output, puts profits back into industry, and evidences some technological change. Governments of developing nations can increase output by using various measures to encourage investment from within the country or from external sources.

The role of American management in economic development has been and will continue to be a sharing of its know-how and technology with managements in foreign countries. A large number of foreign executives were trained in management at American universities. This transfer of technology has caused a commercial revolution in the developing country, which is the first step toward the industrial revolution needed for effective economic development.

WHERE DO WE GO NEXT?

The focus of management has shifted over the years from using intuition to solve problems to a behavioral-management science approach. This is illustrated in part by the fact that management is becoming more scientific and managers are now recognized as professionals. In addition, management technology is being applied to such areas as public administration and multinational businesses. The material in this article reflects some of the transition taking place. Yet, there are still many challenges for managers to face in the future, such as:

1. The need to measure management productivity. Presently, there are no productivity measurements that could stand close scrutiny in this area.
2. The range of new constituencies needing management know-how; for example, the energy industries.
3. A "truth-in-research" approach for collecting, analyzing, and using information for decision making.
4. A more unified approach to training managers, particularly for the non-profit sector of the economy.

Management for tomorrow must have greater knowledge. It has to be prepared for continual adjustment to new conditions and must be able to set benchmarks for measuring performance.

18

Control: Past or Future

WILLIAM H. NEWMAN
Samuel Bronfman Professor of Democratic Business Enterprise, Graduate School of Business, Columbia University

Managerial control offers great opportunities for improving the effectiveness of private and public enterprises. Long pushed aside by the excitement of planning and the challenge of organizing, refinements of controlling have received comparatively little attention. Too many people think of managerial control as only a repressive, negative activity. Like taxes, control is often regarded as an unavoidable burden. The negative viewpoint arises in large part because of inadequate design of managerial controls and inept use of those we have.

This paper attempts to place control in a different perspective. The basic contention is that controls will have more impact when they are: oriented toward the *future* rather than the past; and designed to influence *behavior* of people who take action. The presentation is intended to be conceptual, but with enough examples so the concepts are more than abstractions. Three distinct types of control are identified and their behavioral impact examined. Then, to give operational meaning to the future orientation of such controls, the selection of predictors and their incorporation into a control system is discussed. The viewpoint is that of a manager who is concerned about effective behavioral response to his or her control design.

This paper is adapted from sections of chaps. 1–3, *Constructive Control* (Englewood Cliffs, N.J.: Prentice-Hall, 1975) and published with permission of the publisher.

DEFINITION OF CONTROL

The word "control" has diverse meanings, ranging from financial ownership to a throttle on a motorboat, and from hidden power to psychological influence. However, we shall center our attention on managerial control—*the series of steps a manager takes to assure that actual performance conforms as nearly as practical to plan.* Confusion can be avoided by *not* using control loosely to embrace power, authority, influence, and leadership. These and other factors contribute to desired results, but if we include all of them in the concept of control, the term becomes so broad it loses any clear meaning.[1]

Managerial control always includes evaluation and feedback. The evaluation may occur at various stages and the feedback may go to different people. But the cybernetic idea of a process involving appraisal (perhaps a prediction) and a response to that appraisal can be found in all control situations. The appraisal alone is not enough. A fire siren never put out a fire; nor has an on-line computer printout secured a new customer. Only when some person responds to the signal, or takes action in anticipation of it, does a managerial control become effective. An adjustment in behavior is crucial.

BASIC TYPES OF CONTROL

Control efforts can be made much more effective by recognizing three different types of control:

1. Steering controls
2. Yes-no controls
3. Post-action controls

The essence of *steering controls* is that results are predicted and corrective action taken before the total operation is completed. Flight control of a spacecraft aimed for the moon, for example, begins with trajectory measurements immediately after takeoff and corrections are made days before actual arrival. We do not wait for a record of a hit or a miss to start controlling. Similarly, control of labor relations requires more than strike and turnover statistics; instead, someone has to evaluate the current situation and predict what is likely to happen if the present course is continued. If an unsatisfactory gap is discovered between the *prediction* and our desired goal, corrective action should be initiated.

Under *yes-no controls,* work may not proceed to the next step until it passes a screening test. Approval to continue is required.[2] Yes-no controls are essentially safety devices. The consequences of a faulty parachute or spoiled food are so serious that we take extra precautions to make sure that the quality is up to specifications. Avoidable expense or poor allocation of resources can also be checked by yes-no controls. If we could be confident that our steering controls were effective, the yes-no controls would be unnecessary; unfortunately, steering controls may not be fully reliable or may be too expensive, so yes-no controls are inserted.

In *post-action controls*, work is completed and then results are measured and compared to a standard. The typical budgetary control and school report cards illustrate this approach. Post-action controls, by definition, seem to be too late. The work is already completed before it is measured. Actually, post-action controls do serve two purposes. They provide inputs for reward systems and help tie rewards (or punishments) to measurable objectives. Also, post-action controls provide planning data if similar work is undertaken in the future.

All three types may be needed to control a department or major activity. But steering controls offer the greatest opportunity for constructive effect. The chief purpose of all controls is to bring actual results as close as possible to desired results, and steering controls provide a mechanism for remedial action while the actual results are still being shaped.

Positive Response to Steering Controls

The great virtue of steering controls is that most people regard them as helpful rather than as pressure devices. If the goal is accepted, the various feedbacks are treated as aids in achieving that desired result. Even granting that sometimes a control report conveys unwelcome news and prods a person to extra effort, the warning is constructive in tone. Coming before work is completed, the signal is seen in terms of action needed rather than personal evaluation. Since steering controls provide inputs early enough for the main actors to use the data in their own decisions, their personal involvement in the control cycle is high. And this close involvement in the control process adds to the positive response.

Goal acceptance is crucial. Unless the astronaut wants to get to the moon, or the salesperson wants to increase sales, reports of deviation from course and of potential obstacles are merely static. And an unreasonable par can sour the reaction to the latest word about, say, competitors or planned shipping dates. Steering controls generate a positive response only when the people on the giving and receiving ends of the control effort are steering in the same direction.

Who steers is also an issue. Outside regulation of detailed operations annoys persons who see themselves as experts in that area; consequently, self-regulation is more welcome. This suggests that steering controls should be translated into action as close to actual operation as possible. The positive response to the control activity then spreads among operating personnel.

Neutral or Negative Reaction to Yes-No Controls

Yes-no controls set hurdles to be crossed. They ensure that quality standards are met, that a proposed action is within budgetary restraints, and the like. For the "professional" who takes pride in his or her work, being able to clear such hurdles easily may provide reassurance. But the check is only whether work is good enough to pass. If it is better than standard, little or no praise is given; if it is below standard, the work is rejected. And rejection of work often creates delays and resentment. On balance, when yes-no controls demand attention, they proclaim bad news.

Negative feelings about yes-no controls are often increased when: (1) a person is unable to achieve other goals because work is blocked by this hurdle; (2) the par is felt to be unreasonable, for example, the budget is too tight or the requirement for a salary increase is too strict; (3) the standard is vague and unpredictable[3] (as, for example, in determining the legality of a contract, the impact of a public relations release, or the qualifications of a person for promotion). Unpredictable standards are particularly troublesome because people lack guidelines on how to prepare for the control. If the standards applied to separate cases appear to be inconsistent, charges of favoritism and politics will follow.

Such reactions to yes-no controls can be reduced, first, by making clear the need for the control to meet basic objectives of the company or department. Both the aspect being measured and the par should be traceable directly to a basic objective. Second, acceptance is improved by making the measurements as objective as possible and insisting on consistency in their application.[4] These steps will rarely make the control popular, but they will cut down frustration and build a feeling of fair play.

Post-Action Controls as Score Cards

In a strict sense, measurement and evaluation after work is completed cannot alter what is already done. Like Monday-morning quarterbacking, talking about what might have been will not change history. Nevertheless, control reports serve as scorecards, and people are concerned with that record. A comparison of final results with desired results, that is, post-action control, may be useful in one or more of the following situations:

1. In a continuing flow of repetitive operations—such as producing shoes or processing social security payments—evaluation of today's results may suggest changes for tomorrow's operations.
2. When somewhat comparable (but not identical) activities will be undertaken in the future, comparison of actual results against targets may suggest an opportunity to improve the process that will be used in the next cycle. For example, a failure of last year's sales to come up to budget may suggest more advertising next year. But note that in both the above situations we are using an assessment of the actual results from past efforts to signal the need for somewhat different efforts in the future. The payoff comes from improved operations in the future.[5]
3. If "rewards" (medal, bonus, discharge, praise) based on actual results have been promised, measurement of the results must be taken and the

appropriate rewards made; this is necessary to build future expectations about the close relationship of actual results and rewards. The aim is psychological reinforcement of the incentive scheme. Here again, the payoff from the reinforcement lies in future behavior.

SELECTION OF PREDICTORS

The preceding analysis suggests that effective managerial control is largely based on predictions of results, not on actual results. If a cholera epidemic, an electric power failure, an uninspired symphony performance, an inflationary price rise, a wage bill 20 percent over budget, or other off-target results actually occur, the time for control action has already passed. What is done is done. We cannot reverse history. Instead, we try to anticipate what is likely to happen and, on the basis of these forecasts—these predictions—take corrective action which we hope (predict) will help bring actual results close to the control target.

Since effective control requires prediction of actual results, a crucial element in each control design is finding one or more good predictors. In practice, such predictors, or sensing devices, are as diverse as the desired results they forecast. The following list merely suggests the array of possibilities.

1. *Input Measurements:*
The level of some key input may predict the actual results of an operation. For example, orders received foretell shipments at a later date; inquiries from customers often predict orders; a knowledge of the level of a customer's inventories may forecast inquiries. Payroll changes provide insights into future labor expense. Purchase contracts for parts give cues as to future costs and shipping dates.

2. *Success of Early Steps:*
The ease or difficulty of completing early steps and the revelation of unanticipated difficulties are frequently used to predict final results. Thus, the completion of engineering specifications and other implementation plans provide a basis for revising the estimated cost and delivery date of a nuclear power plant. Early reviews of a theater play or a book, like the initial reception of a new product, give strong clues to longer-run popularity.

3. *Sophistication of the Process:*
The degree of sophistication and skill with which an operation is conducted provides another basis for predicting results. In schools, for example, preparation of clear lesson plans throws some light on the likelihood of a good learning experience. The number of "cold calls" by an insurance agent has a bearing on the volume of business the agent is likely to write during the following months. In a food plant, the attention to moisture content foretells the quality of cornflakes that will be produced the next day. In observing

how any process is performed, we try to identify variables most likely to "cause" differences in final results.[6]

4. *Symptoms:*
Though symptoms do not directly affect actual results, they can be useful predicting devices. Tardiness and absenteeism reflect worker morale and may forecast low labor efficiency. Even more subtle, building vibrations enable one production vice president to sense machine shutdown and production delays long before reports appear. Traffic noise helps an urban couple predict whether their guests will be late.

5. *Assumed Conditions:*
All expectations of desired results are based on assumed operating conditions—such as high government spending, no labor strikes, expansion of competitors' capacity, and the like. Careful monitoring of these key assumptions may indicate an external change which will help or hinder the achievement of results. Here, attention is on necessary conditions.[7]

Considerable ingenuity is needed in finding good predictors for use in control. Obviously, the sooner—and the more reliably—a wide gap between desired results and predicted results is recognized, the greater will be the opportunity to take corrective steps.

Feedback and Corrective Action

With luck and perseverance we will uncover several different ways of predicting what is likely to occur in each of the desired result areas. The question then arises which of the available predictors to use. Since one predictor may give us early but erratic signals, whereas another warns of external trouble, and a third is late but comprehensive, a composite of several feedbacks is often needed for balanced control of a key target.

Guides for Selecting Predictors

The characteristics desirable in a composite feedback scheme are: promptness, reliability, coverage, reasonable expense, and simplicity.

1. *Promptness* is critical. E. H. Schleh concludes, "Above all a management control system must be current."[8] The possibility of successful corrective actions with a minimum of resistance is enhanced when the need for adjustment is discovered before a lot of personal effort has been invested and current facts are forgotten.

2. *Reliability,* while subordinate to promptness, is obviously desirable. False leads waste executive effort. So, when possible, a predictor which occasionally is erratic should be coupled with some kind of confirmation

test. Thus, when the small-craft warning goes up, the experienced sailor keeps a closer watch on the movement of clouds.

3. *Coverage* also warrants attention. A long line of customers, for example, may flag serious inventory and production problems; a low number of grievances may indicate satisfied workers. But such predictors give only a partial picture; other aspects of the total situation must be checked. A more comprehensive review may occur less frequently, or with a lag, but it does help maintain balanced effort. With a narrow index, temptation to manipulate just that one factor always exists.
4. *Expense* of measuring varies widely. An index of new orders may be easily compiled from records kept for other purposes. Field interviews with users of our product are much more expensive. And the cost of testing pharmaceuticals for side effects in human beings rises to still another order of magnitude.
5. *Simplicity* is a virtue. Too many reports can swamp the system. Unimportant information diverts attention from the main goals; frequent needling is irritating. So for many dimensions "satisfactory" conditions should not be reported. Feedback should center on key variables or major shifts in the work environment. Steering can then focus on goals we wish to maximize and on serious obstacles.

All these considerations—promptness, reliability, comprehensiveness, expense, and simplicity—are involved in deciding what information should be sent to whom and how often. But until someone acts on the information, control has not been achieved. Evaluation and corrective action are essential concluding steps.

Confirm and Elaborate the Warnings

Many predictors used in a control system are not fully reliable. Thus, a jump in absenteeism caused by a flu epidemic may be a false alarm with respect to morale; a surge in inquiries about services may reflect unusual publicity on a popular TV program rather than genuine interest of potential users. So before we act, someone should take a hard look at all the evidence bearing on the change in expected results.

In addition to confirming that previous expectations are no longer valid, the manager under pressure wants to know what *is* likely to happen if no modifications are made. How serious is the prospect? Cold weather that portends high activity for fuel dealers, for instance, may merely call for adjustments within the normal capacity of the distribution system; but the prospect of an acute fuel shortage requiring the rationing of supplies—and perhaps the closing of schools, theaters, and plants—triggers quite a different set of responses. Corrective action is based on a more thorough evaluation of what lies ahead.

Possible Corrective Actions

That popular control illustration, home heating, is extremely simple. When the thermostat detects a need for a change, only one action is possible—turn the furnace on, or off if it is already running. Most managerial control situations are vastly more complicated and hence not suitable for automation. The measurements are multidimensional, the opportunities are unique, and practical alternatives have not been predetermined. Instead, an array of new possible solutions must be devised.

The "cause" of a departure from normal will suggest alternatives in a stable operation.[9] But in dynamic settings, possible alternative actions range over shifts in resources, modified ways of operating, changes in incentives, new alliances—inside and outside the organizational unit. Significantly, however, a scanning and predictive control scheme that gives early and relevant warnings provides the manager with more leeway in utilizing these various corrective options.

CONCLUSION

The kind of control suggested in the preceding pages contrasts rather sharply with that described in most of the literature on managerial control. The bulk of past writing focuses on post-action controls or yes-no controls; procedures which make use of existing records are featured. While such controls can be useful, they lack the forward-looking, behavioral emphasis needed in our dynamic world. The concept of steering control is not new, as witnessed by the various examples cited, but it deserves far more attention. Future oriented control is a significant management resource that still awaits full development.

NOTES AND REFERENCES

1. This definition of control is consistent with the common usage among U.S. managers. There is sufficient variation, however, to warrant careful listening when the term is used. For example, R. N. Anthony finds the distinction between planning and controlling hard to draw, and then compounds the confusion by using "management control" to embrace both planning and control which occur between strategic planning and routine operations. (See *Planning and Control Systems*, Harvard Graduate School of Business Administration, 1965.) In contrast, A. S. Tannenbaum considers all sorts of influence in his *Control in Organizations* (New York: McGraw-Hill, 1968). H. Smiddy and his associates at General Electric Company tried to sidestep the confusion—and the negative connotation of controlling—by emphasizing "measuring" as one of the four basic management processes (along with planning, organizing, and integrating), but this formulation has not gained general acceptance. The present analysis seeks to enrich and sharpen the meaning of a recognized word rather than use old words in unfamiliar ways or invent a new jargon.

2. In the quality control literature the term "acceptance control" is often used for this type of check. In financial control expressions such as "clearance" or "required approval" are common. In all such arrangements the standards required for acceptance are assumed to be clear. The purpose of the check, to use Herbert Simon's terminology, is to satisfice rather than optimize.

3. The problems of developing acceptable budgetary goals are well treated in G. H. Hofstede, *The Game of Budget Control* (London: Tavistock Publications, 1968), chaps. 8–9. This book is probably the best behavioral study of responses to controls available.

4. Occasional exceptions will, of course, be necessary. In fact, people working under the system may strongly advocate exceptions—to achieve justice or meet an emergency. But exceptions have little meaning until we have established a stable, predictable social system as a base.

5. Note that analysis and evaluation for purposes of future planning need not stick to a control format of predetermined standards and feedback. The aim of the analysis is to help devise better plans, whereas control is predominantly concerned with restraining and motivating behavior toward selected objectives.

6. Sophistication in performing work is often the primary measurement applied to staff activities such as law or even personnel because the consequences are so intangible. In these situations, however, controls are typically post-action—with little effort to utilize manner of working as a predictor.

7. F. J. Aguilar, *Scanning the Business Environment* (New York: Macmillan, 1967), discusses the formal process of environmental scanning by a business enterprise, but he does not explore how such monitoring can be tied to control activities.

8. E. H. Schleh, *Management by Results* (New York: McGraw-Hill, 1961), p. 179. G. S. Odiorne says, "Prompt feedback is far more important in changing behavior than intensity of feedback." See G. S. Odiorne, *Management by Objectives* (Pitman, 1965), p. 167.

9. See C. H. Kepner and B. B. Tregoe, *The Rational Manager* (New York: McGraw-Hill, 1965) for an analytical technique for uncovering causes of deviant results in a stable situation. The focus in this book is on decision making; many of the suggestions can be easily transferred to the corrective action phase of control in standard operations.

19

BUSINESS MANAGEMENT IN AN AGE OF CHANGE

DAVID P. REYNOLDS
Chairman of the Board
and Chief Executive Officer,
Reynolds Metals Company

. . . the first job of a business manager is to convert social needs into profitable opportunities.
Peter Drucker

I like this Peter Drucker quotation, and I think it is going to be even more true of the challenges and opportunities business managers will have in the years ahead. My father used to have a similar saying: "He succeeds best who helps others succeed." This philosophy has been a key to the dramatic growth of our company, and has gained validity with each passing day.

Converting social needs into profitable opportunities is bound to become much more challenging and exciting as we move into future years. Although many of our traditional options are disappearing, science and technology are opening a vast field of new options. And human priorities and aspirations are changing at a rapid pace. Our ability to provide the goods to fill the needs of society—and to anticipate the needs—is therefore going to require increased human resourcefulness in the years ahead. Some theorists say we have changed to a "post-industrial," or service, economy. But we cannot overlook the fact that we are still very basically a goods-producing economy, and that performing this function with more intelligent utilization of raw materials and energy is going to be critical to our future well-being. I believe we have the capacity to grow and to improve the quality of our life and our environment. The foundation of this growth rests on our basic needs for food, shelter, and clothing—not to mention the hardware needed to expand our horizons and accomplish new goals.

In addition to being an adept innovator, tomorrow's business manager will also have to be a person of exceptional courage and commitment. Some of our most important social, technological, and business advances have been accomplished against tremendous odds. As the world and the issues we face grow ever more complex, this characteristic will become paramount in a manager serving the needs of society successfully. Tomorrow's business manager will not be able to rely much on history and will have to become expert in making value judgments based on current events and the huge mass of data and statistics available. In a world increasingly dependent on specialists, the successful business manager will need both good rounding, as a generalist, and a keen sense of the public pulse.

Decisions in the future will have to be made against a time frame that is growing longer and longer. Even today, for example, a decision to build a million-kilowatt single-unit power station must take into account that the probable time required from initial conception to full operation of the plant is about eight or nine years. Assembling the skills necessary to get a job done is also a slow process.

On July 4, 1776, King George III wrote in his diary: "Nothing of importance happened today." In the latter twentieth century we live in a world where communication is instantaneous, and where the potential for elaborate and sophisticated communications systems boggles the mind. It is an era in which news media are not content with things as they happen, but try to scoop each other before they happen. Complex issues are squeezed into a few televised sentences or a few printed paragraphs. All this is making it increasingly essential that a business manager be a skilled communicator—available, clear-spoken, open, and candid.

By the same token, the hostility that too frequently has existed between business and the university, and between business and government, has been wasteful of our time and resources. Substantial contributions to the common good can be accomplished by improved communication among all three parties, and business managers can do a service to society by taking a leadership role in this important area. Business managers are beginning to realize they no longer can afford to play their old, passive communications role, or delude themselves that they are communicating when they are only talking among themselves. We have a tremendous task ahead of us in coordinating the use and development of all our resources: space, material, financial, human. Business has an expertise in this area and can make a strong contribution.

Our economy today is laboring under the heavy financial burden of a "catch-up" phase in environmental controls. There is great concern, with some justification, about the amount of expenditures going into nonproductive as opposed to productive facilities—especially at a time when delays in productive expansion could create problems for society in coming years. There are many worthwhile but frequently divergent goals we would like to reach. In managing for the future we need to strike a balance between our goals, so that one is not accomplished at the expense of another.

The story of my company's development of the aluminum can in many ways illustrates a number of the points I have covered here briefly. We saw the can as a package that would meet the needs of society better than anything on the market. It would do a better job of protecting product quality, its light weight would save on transportation costs and energy, it would be competitive, it would be a neater package that consumers might prefer. However, if I had taken the proposal to the Harvard Business School, I would probably have been laughed out of the classroom. The market was strongly dominated by other materials, and can makers had no real incentive to change. The odds were tremendous. It took a lot of courage, but we were convinced we had a better package that would fill a need and offer a profitable opportunity.

I remember one of our early attempts to introduce the package. We had been working to prove that aluminum was a better material for frozen orange juice, but were frustrated by the can manufacturers who put a premium price on the aluminum can. As a result, our idea was not getting anywhere. So we purchased some conventional can-making equipment, installed it in a trailer, and headed for Florida. There we called in the entire Florida citrus industry to witness the truck-based production operation to prove aluminum cans could be made competitively. The demonstration was successful. The can makers eliminated the price premium and the citrus industry began studying a conversion to aluminum.

At this point we were faced with our next major problem. We knew the decision of the industry could go either way. Because of long lead times, if we waited on customer commitments for the coming packing season, we would never be able to meet the can makers' production schedules, and would have been set back another year. So we took a calculated risk. In the two months prior to the citrus packaging season, we rolled almost 7 million pounds of special sheet needed for citrus cans—without any firm orders from the can makers and without a clear reading from the industry regarding their commitment to aluminum. As history now records, our gamble paid off, and before the season was over we had shipped our inventory and more. Almost 1 billion aluminum cans were used by the citrus industry that season—with Reynolds supplying the lion's share of the metal. To me, this experience is a good example of the courage, commitment—nerve, if you will—that must be put behind an idea, big or small, to bring it to reality.

To make the commercial, environmental, and energy-saving advantages of the aluminum can available to the beverage market, we developed a whole new way of making the container. The innovative, drawn and ironed two-piece design, consisting of a cup and a top, made the can competitive for the beverage market. Today—as a result of further design and production improvement—the can weighs almost 25 percent less than when it was first introduced. Recently we introduced a nondetachable opening tab which makes the package more sound environmentally. Management's job is never done, and frequently a good idea can be further refined or improved to meet the needs of society.

The can's greatest environmental advantage is its recyclability. If we could recycle every aluminum can sold, we would make a significant contribution to the reduction of litter and solid waste, especially as aluminum gained a larger share of the can market. Such a recycling program would also have other advantages for society: it would help conserve natural resources, save 95 percent of the energy needed to make new aluminum, and save capital investment in new aluminum-making facilities that would be needed to make a comparable amount of the metal. Recycling aluminum on such a scale obviously would be a monumental undertaking. But the concept and its possibilities fascinated me. It was again a classic situation in which social needs could be converted into a profitable opportunity. From the outset, our objective has been to recycle—on a money-making basis—100 percent of the used aluminum consumer products which might end up as litter or solid waste.

In January 1967 we launched a pilot recycling program in Miami, Florida, designed to prove our contention that the aluminum can could be collected and recycled on a massive basis. We worked with two charities, asking the public to collect aluminum cans and other household aluminum scrap and to donate them through service-station collection points as a contribution to the organizations involved. We quickly found that the public is not motivated by voluntary contributions to charity; though we made many mistakes, we also learned many valuable lessons in Miami. Tomorrow's business manager, maybe more so than today's, will have to learn that you cannot be afraid of failure, but you have to know how to profit from it. Knowing how to handle the bumps is an outstanding trait of a successful manager. Adversity is frequently the wellspring of great accomplishment; if people have never had a temporary failure or a setback, they have not set their goals high enough.

In 1968, with the program continuing in Miami, we took a different approach with another pilot recycling operation in Los Angeles. This time we offered to pay the public ten cents per pound—about one-half cent per can—cash on the barrel head. This proved to be the motivation required. The success of this concept in California has been the basis for our recycling program, which is now nationwide in scope. In addition to our own permanent centers, we operate a fleet of mobile units which take aluminum recycling to the people—literally—in small towns, in metropolitan suburbs, and along the byways throughout America. Individuals (many on a full-time basis for retirement income), children, college students, schools, clubs, and other organizations are combing the countryside for the valuable commodity. Some have set up regular collection routes at taverns and restaurants, or bring in a bag every several weeks from their own home collection.

The program has been tremendously successful. By the end of 1975 we were recycling aluminum at a rate equivalent to 50 percent of the cans we make—which put us halfway to our goal of 100 percent. We have also reached the point where the operation is on a sound economic basis. It has been a good business venture, a social need turned into a profitable opportunity, a positive management contribution, and an excellent new source of aluminum.

As our consumer recycling program was growing, we began working with state and local government agencies responsible for solid-waste handling, private refuse concerns, and other companies, providing technology and market assistance oriented to recovering aluminum and other nonferrous metals from refuse. Today the mining of solid waste is no longer a dream. Systems are in operation or under construction in many areas of the country. While aluminum and other nonferrous metals make up less than 2 percent of the solid-waste mix, the high scrap value of these metals contributes tremendously to the economics of municipal refuse-processing plants, which must compete economically with the lowest cost disposal alternatives. Of more particular concern to our corporate interests is the fact that solid waste is generated in such high volume in this country that the 1 or 2 percent aluminum content amounts to more than 3 billion pounds of reusable metal each year.

As municipal processing plants come on stream, we are entering into contracts to buy aluminum from this valuable source. We also were instrumental in building a new home of recycled materials—aluminum, paper, glass, fiber, iron, plus industrial waste products—to demonstrate the marketability of these products in conventional construction. The home was sold as a private residence, and today looks no different than other homes in its neighborhood. It was an idea ahead of its time—but its time surely cannot be far off. Again, it is an example of the kind of innovative leadership business management must take in pointing the way for society in the future.

There will be times in the future, as there have been in the past, when even the most magnificent examples of human resourcefulness will fall short, at least on a temporary basis. And there will be times when we will find ourselves with conflicting goals, all of equal value. It is at this time that some painful decision will have to be made, so balanced progress can be achieved without unnecessarily lengthy delays that are detrimental across the board.

As mentioned earlier, we are today in a tremendous catch-up period on pollution controls. Surely no sensitive, intelligent person can help but appreciate the value of this effort to preserve the clarity of our air and the beauty of our rivers and streams—now and for future generations. On the other hand, pollution controls are using financial resources that could be used in many other ways, not the least of which are productivity improvement and job creation. As a result, we may find ourselves in the near term in a situation where we will have to stretch out the priorities given pollution control. I hope not. But more than ever we need leaders in all segments of society who can see all sides of a question so we can all benefit from and literally live with the outcome.

As a manager looking to the future of my own industry, I see aluminum's greatest opportunities in four areas of basic human need—transportation, shelter, energy transmission, and food packaging and distribution. In transportation, aluminum's light weight, strength, corrosion resistance, and formability can make an important contribution in everything that is designed to move, particularly the automobile. The proper use of aluminum can greatly reduce the weight of a car and thereby increase mileage per gallon of gasoline. Typically, a single pound of aluminum used in an auto part produces an immediate and direct weight saving of 1.5 pounds when substituted for traditional materials. This, in turn, saves another three-quarters of a pound by allowing lighter structural supports.

In building and construction, the energy situation will provide a greater opportunity for aluminum to help make buildings of all kinds more durable and energy efficient. The ability of the proper combination of aluminum building products to reduce heating, air conditioning, and maintenance costs has been documented. Additional energy is saved in the shipping and handling of lightweight aluminum building components. In the field of energy transmission, aluminum is the basic workhorse. The world will be increasing, one way or another, its energy sources. Aluminum transmission and transportation equipment will play a fundamental role for one basic reason. Aluminum is the most economical conductor of electricity.

In packaging—especially the packaging and distribution of food—aluminum can be of particular service to society. As the food needs of the world's growing populations become more critical, aluminum will be called on in many forms—from storage silos to large shipping containers, from beverage cans to meat and vegetable packages—to help protect and distribute the very sustenance of life and human energy. It has been estimated by the UN Food and Agriculture Organization that at least one-fourth of the world's food disappears between the field and the table—a prey to rats, insects, fungus, and mildew. Much of this waste is due to inadequate packaging. This is intolerable in a world where millions are hungry. The use of aluminum can help eliminate this waste and also save significant energy in the shipping and distribution of food.

I mention all these applications as examples of ways in which one industry, one material, can help us solve some of the world's problems. Some applications make use of technology we have had for some time, others involve new technology.

As stated at the outset of this chapter, I am very excited about the coming period in business management. The opportunities to convert needs into opportunities will exist on a scale unknown to us before. In summary, I think the successful business manager of the future will have to be four people rolled into one:

1. *Visionary:*
Far-sighted, able to see the interrelationships of actions internally and externally, able to sense the public pulse, a long-range planner

2. *Enlightened:*
Keenly knowledgeable as a generalist, alert to new options, imaginative enough to innovate, a good communicator

3. *Productive Conservationist:*
Able to conserve yet expand the value of our resources, and to develop untapped resources, both physical and human

4. *Courageous:*
Committed to forge ahead against the odds with ideas that respond to the needs of society

I have great confidence in both the future course of business management and the managers of today. Business has an impressive record for getting things done, for innovation, and for accomplishment. Its management has a growing sense of the interdependence of all sectors of our society and a keener sensitivity to their needs. Because of the accomplishments and capabilities of business, we too often expect the superhuman of its leaders—as we do of leaders in other fields—and therein lies some of our discontent. We have every right to expect the future business manager to push human resourcefulness and courage to the limit in meeting human needs and opportunities. My father, a poet as well as a business manager, wrote these lines:

We abhor the beaten path. Not for us
The cowbell or the curfew. We shun
The smooth highroad strung
With signs of warning and safety signals.
We dare the dark to reach the dawn.

20

THE NEW DIMENSIONS OF MANAGEMENT

WILLIAM J. RONAN
Former Chairman,
The Port Authority of New York and New Jersey

Worldwide recognition of the importance of management per se—the critical role of the art and science of management—came only in the aftermath of World War II. Previously, to be sure, management philosophy, methods, and performance had been the object of major attention in certain industrialized nations, particularly the United States. However, it was in the rebuilding of war-ravaged economies and in the effort to assist new nations achieve economic as well as governmental stability that management was given its more appropriate place in the sun.

The awareness that how governments were managed; how the expanding social services were managed; how enterprise was conducted was as important as the availability of resources, financing, and manpower; all brought a new appreciation of the role of management itself. Indeed, in the extension of military and economic assistance through various international aid programs, help was not only proffered in management information and training but in some instances was made an intrinsic, if not a requisite, part of the aid package. Management as a discipline—as a quasi-profession—had made the jump from the business enterprise arena to the governmental and voluntary organization areas prior to World War II. From the "scientific management" pioneering of Frederick Taylor and his contemporaries, the field of management had grown into a formidable body of information distilled from experience and an organized series of precepts and approaches with as much, or more, validity as those of longer-established professions.

Management in the second half of the twentieth century is accordingly a developing discipline and a focus of attention in the free enterprise world, the socialist world, the semi-state-planned economies, the developed world, and the developing world. It is a significant factor in the international world—in the international and regional organizations established among the nations for a wide spectrum of purposes. Management may be defined as the purposeful utilization of manpower, money, energy, technology, and materials to accomplish collective objectives. The objectives may be to produce goods and services, construct works, raise money, make profits, achieve economic plans, maintain law and order, balance competing interests, assure national or international security, conduct research and development, or audit performance. This litany does not specify or detail all the myriad possible objectives. It serves to show, however, the universality of the management problem.

The foregoing definition of management is disarmingly simple. But analysis of the terms in present-day application and future prospects serves to indicate the complexity and the vastly expanded spectrum of management. The task of utilizing manpower, money, energy, technology and materials in the present world is far more complicated than heretofore. The outlook for the future is for greater rather than lesser complications.

MANPOWER

In the area of manpower, the tasks of staffing enterprises are a far cry from the simple tasks of the pre-World War II years and eons away from the early decades of this century. The development of recruitment, testing, placement, classification, compensation, and other personnel procedures has given management more effective methods for dealing with matters involving the work force. But the social and political milieus within which the personnel phases of management must now be conducted are very different. Additionally, there has not been enough experience to give management a sense of certainty regarding them. The antidiscrimination laws and equal opportunity statutes and their implementing regulations set forth appropriate social objectives. They complicate the task of management. No longer is the task only to find the best person (not man) for the job. The task is to provide opportunity for and not discriminate against: veterans, minorities, women, the handicapped, the aged, and, in some instances, homosexuals, ex-criminals, and ex-addicts, whether of drugs or alcohol.

The task is made no easier by the far more important roles played by unions, the organization of shop supervisors, white-collar workers, and a fair amount of what used to be called "middle management" personnel. Moreover, the professional groups within business and government have also found it necessary to form or join unions or organizations having similar bargaining power, whether called unions or not. Accordingly, management now deals with the organized demands of doctors, nurses, teachers, lawyers, writers, laboratory technicians, and many others. In societies where the individual practitioner is isolated and with little, if any, bargaining power, the only resort is to join a group sufficient to exert pressure on his or her behalf.

Management not only contends with these groups but frequently finds itself caught in their competing and conflicting interests. The number and variety of jurisdictional disputes has added to the burden of the managers. And the penchant of the stronger groups—whether union or professional—to limit the segments of the work processes which they will discharge creates additional cost and performance problems. The professional nurse in the hospitals of today performs only a portion of the tasks done by the nurse of yesteryear. The compartmentalization of portions of the flow of work in the factory or in the field has had a longer history and continues to challenge management efforts for productivity.

These forces slow the introduction of new technologies and automation and postpone the early reaping of their full benefits. The problem is one not only of the free, or enterprise, economies but of the semiplanned economies and socialist countries as well. A group visiting a socialist nation where an automated rail rapid transit system had been developed was surprised to find two men in the motorman's cab—one monitoring the operation and the other opening and closing doors. When asked why *two* men—when even one had nothing to do except in an emergency—the manager of the system replied, "We are negotiating with the trade union organization to phase out the second man." The introduction of drug therapy in the treatment of the mentally ill made dramatic changes in the whole program of therapy and the need for psychiatrists or institutional staffs. Curtailment of the number of psychiatrists on a hospital staffing table, however, involved a considerable struggle with similar arguments about reliability of performance of the new technology and the safety to both customer (patient) and the general public.

Management faces a continuing struggle to overcome the inertia in work classifications and rules which stand in the way of productivity advances due to technological changes. In this respect, the older industrialized nations confront a competitive challenge from some of the newer industrialized nations. These nations not only offer wage competition, but rigid craft, skill, and professional traditions have not significantly taken root. New technology with the most modern equipment can, accordingly, be run by general operators and served by general mechanics without the inflexibilities and inefficient compartmentalization of the older industrial societies. Clearly, one of the tasks of management is to strive to bring technology, plants, equipment and work-force practices into line with modern competitive reality. To do this in the older and established industrial societies will take a major cooperative effort, not the least of which will be convincing business, labor, political leadership, and the general populace that the higher standards of living and social improvements rest importantly on competitive productivity.

Concomitant with professionalization is the arrogation to professional members sole privilege of legitimate practice of a wide spectrum of activity—most of which really does not require professional expertise. Management is thus confronted not only with the rigidities that such professionalism entails but with a limited pool of qualified manpower for the tasks and inordinate costs as well. The administration of hospital and health care programs provides striking examples of these problems. Licensure laws and professional canons have protected thc practitioner first, the patient second, and the paying public third. The overly restrictive regulations have been serious deterrents to the employment of such paraprofessionals as nurses' aides, members of the medical corps, vocational nurses and physicians' assistants.

So costly and restrictive have current activities become that it has been suggested that the health care institution should be licensed and have wide freedom under general guidelines to set requirements and assign its employees. In wartime the military services have shown that assistants—paraprofessionals—can maximize the time and talents of highly trained specialists by relieving them of many routine duties. In a world of limited numbers of and with so pressing a need for professionals, the challenge to management to move in these directions will accelerate in the future.

Another personnel factor in the present and emergent worlds is ethnicity. Whether it takes the form of replacing white Europeans with blacks in various nations of Africa, or developing Malaysian labor to compete with Chinese; whether it involves French-speaking versus English-speaking groups in North America, indigenous Indians in Mexico and other parts of Latin America, Hispanics and blacks in the United States, or various ethnic groups in the Soviet Union; ethnicity presents major social and political problems importantly involving management in all these societies. On the international scene, the elimination of the colonialism of the past has brought a new nationalism and a new emphasis on ethnicity. The world has yet to evolve to the point where individuals are measured as individuals. Currently, there are strong currents stressing ethnic differences rather than homogeneity. The time when individuals will stand as individuals in a society of mankind—true homogeneity—is still remote. Accordingly, management faces unprecedented training and upgrading responsibilities and justification to political and social groups for its personnel practices, yet has the task of producing goods and services at a level of efficiency.

The integration of women into the work force is an accomplished fact in most industrial nations. The process will be accelerated and women will undoubtedly play increasingly more significant roles in virtually all areas of labor and the professions and in management itself. This involves no special or traumatic changes. The transition of women from the home to factory, office, politics, and management is in full swing. Their talents in all these areas have become not only socially acceptable and desirable but essential for the kind of world that is evolving.

For the aged, the juvenile not adapted for further education, and the handicapped who can work, there remains a challenge both to management and society. The establishment of part-time jobs, segmentation of tasks that can be effectively performed, and integration of these special talents into a program of productive results is a task that management can perform, but there are political and social elements requiring definition or clarification if they are to be successful. The concepts of employability, social welfare eligibility, and management responsibilities are all involved. Indeed, the concept of "retirement" in the industrial world and the concept of youth employment may well see significant changes in the years ahead.

MONEY

The financial aspects of management have wider range and significance in today's world. First, business finance has become more complex. The intricacies of financial relationships in conglomerates, multinationals, and traditional corporate businesses require new management knowledge and understanding. To management's basic traditional drive for profit is now added the element of tax losses carried forward, the acquisition of businesses for the tax benefits they may provide rather than the profit they offer, and other ramifications growing out of changing tax concepts and tax losses. The role of depreciation in business accounting and the differing treatments of inventory give management new tools for the conduct of enterprise. They also make the tax counsel and the accountant—plus the outside auditors—far more crucial collaborators in the management process than heretofore.

Other outsiders actively influence and, in a sense, also participate. Major enterprise has always relied on its commercial and investment bankers. Now it has "assistance" not only from bankers but from the Internal Revenue Service or its equivalent and government agencies, such as the SEC, that regulate security issues. If a major enterprise is involved in foreign commerce or international transactions, it encounters exchange controls, problems of currency convertibility, and taxation problems both in its home base and its business places abroad. In many of these areas, because of the shifting economic and political currents, monitoring of the governmental offices having responsibility becomes a crucial element of management intelligence.

Indeed, the relationship between enterprise, on the one hand, and general government, on the other, has become more interrelated in the market economy nations than heretofore, except in wartime. Government fiscal policy and the credit policies of the central banking institutions command attention from the management of large, intermediate, and small enterprises. The enormous direct effects of government spending—for military purposes; public works; a multitude of economic assistance programs in agriculture, transportation, and other areas; and social welfare programs which impact significantly on purchasing power of the consuming public—are all important in corporate strategy, production, and marketing planning. So significant is the stake of enterprise that a substantial portion of the time of chief officers of large corporations is devoted to following government fiscal policy and purchasing, appearances before legislative and executive governmental bodies regarding government business, and a considerable public relations effort in the democratic nations to inform and help influence the general public regarding these matters.

Virtually all major enterprises have their government specialists on the management team. This is not the traditional lobbying effort, though that continues on an intensified basis and still involves outside trade association and paid lobbyists. It is rather the regular employment of experienced personnel who know the intricacies of government processes. Their input on government policy can be as important as the intelligence they report back from their continuing association with the administrative bureaucracies of the government departments and the legislative aides as well.

The dependence of enterprise on government has some reverse echo in public dependence on enterprise for its contribution to national employment, income, foreign exchange, and national security. Events in Western Europe, England, Japan, and the United States in the past few years have underscored the significance of this reverse dependence. Such names as Citroen, Volkswagen, Leyland, and Lockheed come to mind. Clearly, if there is a significant national dependence on particular enterprises, the strategy of enterprise management becomes a concern not only of shareholders but of government itself. The impact of the bankruptcy of a large enterprise can have so widespread or ripple effect that government has an immediate concern. Management efforts to leverage this dependency to overcome corporate deficiencies or economic failures are familiar. They are fraught with risks that do not always pay off. In the United States the demise of the Penn-Central is a case in point, as is the collapse of the Franklin National Bank and the failure of W. T. Grant and Company.

The phenomenon is by no means limited to the market enterprise nations. The socialist states have their own commercial, industrial, and financial enterprises whose relationship to central planning and general government involves management considerations on both sides. A Soviet bank suffered severe losses in a part of the Far East—sufficient to be embarrassing both to the bank itself and the U.S.S.R. Failures of managements of key enterprises to meet their commitments to general government in socialist societies are from time to time reported in their press.

ENERGY

The energy quotient has vastly increased significance with the great rise in energy costs and energy outlook generally. In many areas of the world cheap energy was taken for granted and energy supplies assumed to be available and secure. Decisions by management in the energy field obviously can have critical impact on the costs and productivity of enterprise. The task facing enterprise management is not enviable. Government energy policies appear to be still in a state of flux. At the same time, the supply of liquid fossil fuels and natural gas appears to be limited, so new energy sources must be phased in at some point. Given the ramifications of shifts likely in energy, the crucial significance of management decision or indecision is apparent. The move by the American automobile industry to the smaller compacts with lesser fuel consumption, following the Arab oil embargo, did not prove to be attractive to the domestic market. The industry had not made a wholesale shift so it was prepared to push the production of the large, heavier vehicles with high gasoline consumption.

In the era of cheap energy, it has been more economical or convenient to bring energy to the labor force and the confluence of other materials. Management will increasingly face the question whether to locate facilities closer to or at the sites of the energy supply. The movement of industry (other than directly petroleum in character) to oil-rich lands is not only contemplated but is now underway in modest proportions. But here again, management decisions involve broader considerations. Oil-rich nations of the Middle East, for example, have neither the labor force nor the skills to mount such extensive industry as their energy resources could support. Therefore, they face the prospect of importing foreign labor with all the social, economic, cultural, and political concerns that entails.

TECHNOLOGY AND MATERIALS

Technological development has a twofold aspect in the expanding spectrum of management. First, through electronic data processing, computer technology, and other electronic devices, information available to management—on production, costs, inventory, finance, and marketing—now provides a wider intelligence base for decision making. The whole area of forecasting has been revolutionized and management controls enormously strengthened. In the public and enterprise sectors, the understanding and utilization of computer and other electronic technology in the decision making and audit-appraisal aspects of management is essential in the complexities of the developed societies.

The other aspect involves the rapid rate of technological development and change that impacts upon virtually all aspects of the production of goods and services. Whether to continue with the state of the art or push the current state of the art or take a leap into new technology obviously entails a grave responsibility. Success in a bold leap to new technology can put one nation far ahead of another in military hardware and strategic influence. Such a technological success by an enterprise can mean another Xerox; failure can mean another Rohr Industries problem when the gamble on aerospace capabilities rapid transfer to urban rail transit did not pay off.

Associated and integrally related with technology is the whole matter of materials: their selection, acquisition, and utilization. Competition among materials has never been greater and it will become more rather than less so. Advancing research and development, scarcities of some materials and abundance of others, prices of materials, and possibilities of substitutions of new materials offer enormous room for new products, services, and levels of performance. The task of management in judging the timeliness of innovation, substitution, staying put or getting out of products and processes has never been more important. At the rate of current development it will continue to be crucial. Examples of successes and nonsuccesses are all around us. The time span from propeller to turboprop, jet, fan-jet and supersonic commercial aircraft was less than 30 years. Look at its impact on the aviation industry from aircraft fabrication to operation.

COLLECTIVE OBJECTIVES

Clearly, the objectives of organizations have been modified, caught as they are in the dynamics of economic, social, technological, and political change. However, the basic or bare elementals persist. The purpose of most organizations is, first, survival. Second, they seek to continue to be viable. Third, they seek to renew themselves and to grow—if not in size at least in influence. Indeed, the concept of growth has been so much a part of the world's history for the past 50 to 75 years, that it is difficult to contemplate an era of no growth or a time when purposive drive to improvement was not a canon of society and most organizations therein. The idea of progress has spread from the West to the entire globe. It has motivated the capitalist, the socialist, the communist worlds. It has encompassed the Buddhist, the Hindu, the Moslem, as well as the Christian and Judaic peoples. It is a part of the Third World.

The Club of Rome and the no-growth advocates have had a leavening influence on the drive for growth, and environmental considerations and resources availability have emerged as more essential considerations than heretofore. But the impetus for growth will continue. The Club of Rome has itself recognized the likelihood and essentiality of growth. Management has been primarily growth-oriented. The presumed purpose of management is to maximize the potential of the organization to serve the collective objectives that created and continues it. The ecological movement, the conservation movement, and even the impact of the no-growth movement are not likely to change the growth orientation of management. These elements, however, provide new considerations for management as they add new dimensions to the decision-making processes.

MANAGEMENT FORMS AND DYNAMICS

The broadened spectrum of management responsibilities, the increased input required for decisions, and the widespread and crucial impact of decisions have had their imprint on management itself. The impact of decisions has spawned a vast array of "staff" services ostensibly to assist the decision-making "line" executives and has proliferated housekeeping, or auxiliary, services as well. Management itself, as a consequence, has become more complicated.

The complications involved in decision making and the far-reaching effects of decisions have led to more collective executive arrangements, whether formally recognized or not. The institutionalization of offices such as the Office of the Chairman or the Office of the President is a manifestation of the process. In government it has been developed to the point where decisions by the President, cabinet officers, and governors of large states rarely involve participation by the incumbent but are made by staff associates in the official's name. This phenomenon is more widespread in government than in other enterprises because of the constitutional, statutory, and political factors involved. In the private and voluntary sectors decisions "down the line" are more acceptable to the clientele served.

In the private sector "group executive" arrangements have developed. These are enterprises run by a collegiate executive—with more than one "president." The purpose has been to assure consideration and to get the consent of more than one individual for major corporate decisions. This type of enterprise has also been adopted by directors who were unable to choose an individual as the chief executive officer. Furthermore, it has had the effect of creating a collective responsibility for decision rather than pinpointing it on one individual.

The difficulties encountered in structuring management are reflected in the wide variety of organizational patterns and the profusion of titles in corporate statements and organizational descriptions. Where the title president was once reserved for the one chief executive, many organizations have numbers of presidents such as group presidents and regional presidents. Even the title chief executive officer has its complications, as there are establishments that have chief executive officer for finance, chief executive officer for operations, and so forth. The complexities of organization below the top executive levels have led to the recognition of staff specialization in organization per se and have supported a wide and ever-expanding variety of outside management consulting firms to assist in structuring the hierarchies and ordering the processes for effective operation.

MAJOR MANAGEMENT CHALLENGES

Given the broadened spectrum, the complexities, and the widespread impact of decision, the difficulties of getting decision, stimulating action, and placing responsibility are compounded. In virtually all aspects of activity—governmental, private, and voluntary—bureaucracies have had to be created to encompass the areas involved. And the bureaucracies themselves become a formidable force both to the outside worlds of their customers, taxpayers, service recipients, patients, or whatever, and to the cadre of management executives supposed to direct them.

The problem of bureaucracy—that is, energizing the bureaucracy, getting action, placing responsibility for failure to act as well as for overt action—is worldwide. This is a major challenge for management across the globe. It is one of the banes of planned socialist societies. It threatens increasingly to stifle initiative and productivity in the enterprise societies. Management must cope with the problem and devise new approaches to meet and surmount it. At stake is achievement of the collective purpose for society itself.

In the recent two-hundredth anniversary of the United States, the commemoration lost sight of one of the single most important elements in the Declaration of Independence. That document was a clarion call for political, economic, and religious freedom against remote and nonresponsive bureaucracy. The new dimensions of management must embrace this revolutionary concept if the world is really to progress.

21

COMPULSORY ARBITRATION REVISITED: The Relevance of the Public Sector Experience to Private Sector Management

ERIC J. SCHMERTZ
Professor of Law, Hofstra University Law School

There is a tendency to perceive collective bargaining, the most visible part of labor-management relations, as a microcosm in which issues may be thought of and dealt with as analogous to matters familiar to us from the ordinary events of the world at large. The device may be employed for many purposes: it may be an aid in setting a perspective for the analysis of a problem; it may provide a means of explaining or rationalizing a conclusion. Thus, for instance, many arbitrators are inclined to think of discharge—and to refer to it in their writings—as "industrial capital punishment." If there is any validity to this kind of analogy, then similiarly it can be said that collective bargaining is the diplomacy of industrial relations and, to paraphrase Clausewitz, the strike is the pursuit of that diplomacy by other means.

General Clausewitz's sanguine view of war as a last step—an acceptable and necessary step—in the practice of diplomacy is typical of the nineteenth century, which produced carefully designed rules and conventions for the uses and conduct of wars. This cynical acceptance of war as an inevitable and perhaps even necessary condition of life in the world may be compared to the acceptance if not the usage of the strike as a fixture in labor-management relations and to the development of an entire body of law which assumes that strikes will occur, permits that occurrence, and only regulates or prescribes how and when the strike may be used and what may or may not be done in its conduct. As in war, there is little attention to the strike's effect on the parties involved or the "citizenry" caught up in it. But the twentieth-century development of war to levels of ultimate destructiveness and the related efforts—tentative, experimental, and of only limited success—to end wars or limit their use, also find an analogy in the collective bargaining microcosm. The strike is regularly referred to as "economic warfare."

Yet a recognition is gradually developing that the strike, in present-day contexts, is disruptive and destructive; that its continued use imposes unacceptable losses both on management and labor; that it may be an economic luxury many industries can no longer afford; and that regardless of whether it takes place in the public or private sectors the welfare of the affected public can be equally jeopardized. Over the last three decades virtually all private sector collective bargaining agreements have provided for and utilized arbitration as the means for final resolution of disputes over the application and interpretation of those agreements during their term. As a consequence, by joint agreement of management and labor, a vast but private adjudicatory system has developed in the United States for the settlement of grievances. The acceptability of that system to both management and labor, and its success in achieving its purpose of eliminating the strike during the life of the contract, are now beyond question or dispute. Indeed, it has become an inseparable part of our private sector collective bargaining and contract administration processes.

For about the same period of time, however, the use of arbitration to resolve bargaining deadlocks over the terms and conditions of the collective agreement—when direct bargaining between management and labor for a first or successor contract fails—has been anathema to both sides. Indeed, I think it safe to say that there has been no other issue on which management and labor have been so much in agreement, with shared and equal intensity, and for so long a period of time. Hence, while the well-accepted and widely employed grievance arbitration system has virtually eliminated strikes, lockouts, and other interruptions of normal work schedules during the term of the collective agreement—as the quid pro quo for the contractual "no strike" clause—management and labor have rejected its use as a substitute for the strike when they are unable to negotiate a first or successor contract.

In my judgment, the reasons long held by both management and labor in support of this latter position are either not or no longer true, or the conditions on which they are based have so significantly changed as to warrant a reappraisal of the validity of that position. The reappraisal need not be "agonizing." In my opinion, in the decade ahead, the private business community of the United States will take a fresh and objective look at, and will assume a more pragmatic and affirmative attitude toward, the use of arbitration or some comparable adjudicatory system to resolve collective bargaining deadlocks over the terms and conditions of contracts, when direct bargaining fails.

Let me be precise. I am talking about agreements to arbitrate that are mutually, privately, and voluntarily arrived at by the parties as part of their negotiations, either at the time the deadlock arises or as an institutional part of their contractual agreement to cover such future situation. I am not talking about, nor do I advocate, compulsory arbitration of contract terms mandated by legislation or by executive or other governmental fiat. Rather, my proposal—and what I see in the decade ahead—is a pragmatic use of arbitration to resolve contract terms, based on the private agreement of the parties involved, either for ad hoc issues or as part of their continuing contractual relationship. If it be "compulsory arbitration," let it be termed "compulsory arbitration voluntarily agreed to," meaning of course that both sides are legally bound to the process agreed to until it is mutually revoked, but that the threshold agreement to use and be bound by the process is for the free and voluntary determination of the parties and not imposed on them by governmental regulation. The parties are then free to make adjustments in the process as needed, redefine its use and applicability, and discard it if it proves unworkable. In short, the compulsory arbitration forum should be something initiated by the parties and thereafter retained as part of their exclusive jurisdiction, to be dealt with as they see fit; a governmentally imposed system would deprive the parties of this essential control and flexibility.

Ironically, the impetus and rationale for a fresh and objective look at an adjudicatory system for the resolution of labor-management bargaining disputes comes from the public labor relations sector, which for many years lagged legally and institutionally behind the private sector in unionization, collective bargaining, and contractual relationships. The long held and unchallenged distinctions between the public and private sectors which have supported the sharply contrasting rationales for the prohibition of strikes in the former and the generally full and free use of the strike in the latter, are the very notions now subject to challenge. Contemporary analysis suggests that there are less relevant differences between the two sectors than originally thought. Thinking the "unthinkable" logically follows, namely, whether the strike in both sectors cannot be equally counterproductive, injurious to the parties involved, and inimical to the public welfare. And if the use of arbitration or other comparable adjudicatory systems as the alternative to the proscribed strike in the public sector have produced fair, reasonable, and responsible settlements of new contract terms—especially based on relevant criteria important to management such as "ability to pay" and "increased productivity"—why would such a system not be suitable to the private sector? I submit, based on my experience, that the public sector arbitration system has produced and continues to produce precisely those commendable results. Whereas private sector collective bargaining continues to be based for the most part on economic warfare with the strike a key if not an ultimate weapon in that free-for-all struggle, and with less regard for (and no legal obligation to consider) the merits of the issues in dispute, the public sector arbitrator is required to base and justify his decision or recommendation on such rational and relevant standards as:[1]

- Comparison of wages, hours, fringe benefits, conditions, and characteristics of employment of the public employees involved in the impasse proceeding with the wages, hours, fringe benefits, conditions, and characteristics of employment of other employees performing similar work and other employees generally in public or private employment in New York City or comparable communities

- Overall compensation paid to the employees involved in the impasse proceeding, including direct wage compensation, overtime and premium pay, vacations, holidays, and other excused time, insurance, pensions, medical and hospitalization benefits, food and apparel furnished, and all other benefits received

- Changes in the average consumer prices for goods and services, commonly known as the cost of living

- The interest and welfare of the public (including ability of the employer to pay)

- Such other factors as are normally and customarily considered in the determination of wages, hours, fringe benefits, and other working conditions in collective bargaining or in impasse panel proceedings

From the standpoint of management in the private sector, and with full appreciation of how jealously it guards its prerogative to decide conditions of employment and not abdicate that responsibility to an "unaccountable" third party, can it still be said that the traditional bargaining process with a resultant strike or lockout (the latter is more illusory than real as a management weapon) will produce a settlement more responsive to the financial condition of the company involved, its competitive position, and its position in the marketplace than an arbitrated decision, without a strike, based on the criteria enumerated and the evidence submitted by both sides material to that criteria? While a directly negotiated settlement without a strike is still the preferred result (and even that is subject to reexamination where the parties are markedly uneven in their bargaining strength), I am no longer persuaded that management should continue to hold unconditionally to the view that a directly negotiated settlement *with* a strike would still be preferred to privately agreed-to, or privately institutionalized, arbitration of unresolved contract terms.

Aside from the philosophical and early legal theories that public employment was a "privilege" and that strikes by public employees were acts of disloyalty and contempt against the Crown (under English common law) or the government—and hence proscribed—contemporary reasons for prohibiting strikes by public employees include: (1) the essentiality of the services they render; (2) the effect that cessation of those services has on the public; (3) the fact that the government or employer is not a "for profit" organization and is less able to pass the cost of labor settlements onto the "consumer" (in the form of higher taxes); and (4) the fact that government, responsible for the delivery of governmental services, cannot "take a strike" or put the union to the "economic test" to the extent and under the same circumstances and intent as a private employer—nor, as a practical matter and for the same reasons, can the public employer utilize the "lockout."

But are the distinctions real? Is a strike by employees of a private bus line on one avenue of a city less of an inconvenience to the public than a strike by bus drivers of city-owned buses a few blocks away? Is a strike by public employees working for the Parks Department, or those who paint bridges or repair streets, more damaging to the public interest than a strike by employees of a private milk company, food chain, or cemetery? Is a strike by municipal hospital workers any more critical to the welfare of hospital patients and the public than a strike of workers similarly employed in private hospitals and nursing homes located in the same municipality? Is a strike by public school teachers or sanitation workers that much more inimical to the public they serve than a strike at private newspapers, parochial schools, or private carting companies, or by over-the-road truckers or home heating oil deliverers? Strikes by fire fighters and police officers, considered by many to have no comparable counterpart in the private sector, may well be the exceptions that prove the rule, or at least the exceptions that raise doubts about the broadly based views on the public welfare distinctions between private and public employment.

Can a private industrial enterprise, in fierce competition with others, including foreign competition, realistically absorb a lengthy strike and shutdown, or increased costs, any more than a municipality or state? Are ability to pay, comparability with other employees similarly situated, quality and quantity of productivity, and other relevant and rational standards any more or less applicable to the public or private sectors of our economy, to the unions, or to the employers and employees in both?

If to ask these questions is not to answer them, they serve at least to make us reexamine the so-called distinctions between the public and private sectors on which I believe the acceptance of compulsory arbitration in one, and the rejection of it in the other, is principally founded. Specifically, if the distinctions are not real—or are no longer as valid or compelling as before—it is logical to question whether there is any longer a viable reason to reject out of hand the use of arbitration of interest disputes in the private sector as a voluntarily agreed-to substitute for the strike.

Thoughtful management is becoming increasingly aware of the capital losses related to the idling of plants, loss of business during a strike period as well as the permanent loss of customers who find and remain with other suppliers. Responsible labor leaders also recognize that the strike weapon is a two-edged sword. If business today is conducted to a considerable degree on borrowed capital, it is equally true that the wage earner in this last quarter of the twentieth century depends, for the maintenance of life-style and standard—to a far greater degree than wage earners in the first and second quarters of the century—on mortgage loans, credit purchasing, and other forms of borrowing and is ill-prepared for a strike, long or short. Yet if demands of wage earners, and union demands on their behalf, are justified in whole or in part, there should be a sensible and impartial method of granting those demands instead of putting wage earners through the economic adversity attendant to the strike. Conversely, if their demands or those of the union are excessive, unrealistic, or economically unsound, a similar forum should be available to make those determinations without putting the employer through the same adversity. The fact is that in a society and economy based as thoroughly as ours on anticipation of continued prosperity and growth, and on obligations undertaken on the basis of such assumptions, the potential losses and hardships inherent in all but the most temporary interruption, suspension, or reduction of income are greatly magnified.

Employment of the alternative process of arbitration of contract terms was given its greatest impetus by the phenomenally rapid growth of collective bargaining in the public sector. By 1975, some 37 states had laws providing for collective bargaining for public employees. In most jurisdictions, strikes by public employees are forbidden and only seven states authorized any form of public employee strike. Various devices have been employed to correct the imbalance in bargaining power thus created and also to provide ways of resolving impasses in public sector bargaining. Among these, final and binding interest arbitration has been one of the devices most commonly used. Twenty-two states have enacted legislation providing for arbitration of contract negotiation disputes for some or all of their employees. This is not to say that the advent of interest arbitration has been universally hailed in public sector bargaining, or that its continued use is unopposed. A common additional criticism of the process—the argument frequently offered in opposition to institution of final and binding arbritration as part of a system of collective bargaining—is that it is antithetical to the entire concept of collective bargaining. Those who resort to this argument point out that collective bargaining is a process of negotiation in which the two interested parties, in direct confrontation, are forced to evaluate one another's demands, reevaluate their relationship, reexamine their own respective positions, and search diligently for areas of compromise in a joint and cooperative effort to find a mutually acceptable basis for the continuation of the relationship. It is claimed that the specters of the strike and the lockout are major factors in promoting the good faith effort of the parties in finding such compromise in a process in which each is also bent on upholding its own self-interest to the fullest extent possible; and it is argued that the introduction of interest arbitration to the process has a precisely opposite effect. The contention is that either or both parties may feel free to approach the bargaining process in a spirit of intransigence and to withhold ultimate bargaining positions where it is known that the result will be, not a strike or lockout, but rescue by third party neutrals. These critics usually offer, in addition to their advice, the prediction that institution of a system of interest arbitration will be followed by a progressive and rapid breakdown of "real" collective bargaining.

Experience, where it exists in sufficient degree to warrant analysis and the drawing of conclusions, appears to refute these arguments fairly fully. In the more than five years that New York City has employed final and binding arbitration of all bargaining impasses, 392 separate contracts have been negotiated. Of these, only 29—less than 7.4 percent—reached the point of impasse at which third party intervention was required. It is interesting to note, moreover, that although the New York City system provides an additional step in which the impasse panel's award may be appealed by either party to the impartial board—the Board of Collective Bargaining, which administers the system—only eight such appeals have been filed.

In short, the existence of final and binding arbitration as part of the labor relations structure has neither caused an abandonment of the bargaining process nor, where it has been utilized, has it resulted in a high proportion of awards that were not mutually acceptable to the parties. The latter fact disposes of another argument frequently offered in opposition to the use of interest arbitration, namely, that it will work consistently to the disadvantage of one or the other of the parties. In the public sector, the opponents are almost invariably on the management side since, in most jurisdictions, the alternative of the strike is not available to labor. In this connection, it is particularly interesting to note that in New York State which, unlike New York City, uses final and finding arbitration only in police and fire negotiations, among the hundreds of police and fire contracts throughout the state, arbitrated fiscal provisions were quantitatively, though fractionally, lower than negotiated settlements. The record shows, in other words, that the views expressed by some management representatives, that interest arbitration inflates union gains, are unfounded. If the costs of public employee wage settlements and other benefits have been excessive, the problem is not traceable to the process of final and binding arbitration, nor to the arbitrator or neutral adjudicating the issues. Rather, it can be easily and readily documented that if some wage settlements have been high or if the fringe benefits such as pensions have become excessive, this has been the result or product of direct bargaining or legislative action, not the consequence of arbitration. Indeed, cannot this be a logical lesson for the private sector employer? Have not employers agreed to settlements they considered greater than the facts warranted, and perhaps more than they thought they could afford, because the only alternative was a strike? How would they have done if the issues were submitted to arbitration? Based on our experiences, where arbitrated settlements in the public sector have been fiscally conservative, and certainly less innovative or precedent setting than directly bargaining settlements, the arbitration process to resolve even such sensitive issues as wages, fringe benefits, and pensions, is not to be feared by private management.

The New York City Office of Collective Bargaining, an independent, tripartite agency responsible for the supervision of labor relations between the city and most of its public employee unions, is a leading public sector labor relations forum in the United States. The 10-year experience of the agency, which includes the use of binding arbitration (that is, "finality" of impasse panel decision) should be of particular interest to private management representatives since it provides some clear insights on how the arbitration process works, in practice, as contrasted to the essentially speculative shibboleths and prejudices traditionally associated with the subject.

One serious if not outrageous misconception is that neutrals, when it comes to interest arbitration, are not neutral at all but are somehow predisposed in favor of the union demands, and that management cannot expect its interests, problems, and needs to be recognized or dealt with effectively. The system of impasse arbitration in New York City has followed no such pattern. From the number of cases in which resort to the process took place, the number of cases in which both parties affirmatively accepted the decision, the relatively small number of cases in which statutory appeals were taken, and the de minimus number of cases (2 out of 392) in which management entered such an appeal, it can be reasonably concluded that the impasse arbitration system produces results satisfactory to both the employer and the unions in most cases, and to the employer in more than 99 percent of all cases. That impasse panels have been aware of and concerned with the problems of management is more than a matter of inference and conjecture. In award after award, impasse panels have shown a marked concern with and understanding of not only management's needs in collective bargaining, but a highly developed sensitivity to the special problems of government as the employer. This awareness has had its most striking demonstration during the fiscal crisis in New York City and during the period immediately preceding the general declaration of that crisis.

It should be noted, in fact, that impasse panels were dealing with union demands as though a crisis had been declared many months before any official action was taken by the municipal government to cope with the problem. Thus, in an award issued in January 1975, eight months prior to enactment of any fiscal emergency legislation, an impasse panel adjudicating wage demands of licensed practical nurses in the municipal hospital system wrote:[2]

> **The Panel also makes note of the current series of articles in the New York Times regarding the adverse financial condition of the [City]. . . . However sympathetic [the panel] may be to the arguments advanced by [the union] and however much [the panel] may recognize the hard work and contribution made by the [unit employees] to the health care services rendered by the City, [the panel] cannot consider that this is a time, when the principal employer is considered to be "bankrupt," to grant greater financial recognition to this unit of employees. . . .**

In a February 1976 decision, an impasse panel decided against awarding pay increases based on a wage offer *by the employer* during the course of negotiations prior to impasse, pointing out that "[the union] at its peril, elected to resist a negotiated pay settlement" and that the offer by management need not and would not be equaled by the arbitrator. The panel explained its rejection of the union's contentions on this point, in pertinent part, as follows:[3]

> **One of the major factors to be considered in all current pay increase disputes in City government is of course the unremitting fiscal plight of the City. It is a time when consideration of pay cuts dominate all public discussion of City employee salary levels and possible alternatives to expense reductions through further layoffs of personnel.**

As early as 1973, impasse panels were conditioning wage increases on the inclusion in bargaining agreements of productivity provisions aimed at increased efficiency and the reduction of real costs to New York City government and, in turn, the taxpayer. In November 1973 I served as chairman of the impasse panel which ended the only strike of fire fighters in the history of New York City. My colleagues were Dean Michael I. Sovern of Columbia Law School and Professor Thomas Christensen of New York University Law School. In this bitterly contested matter, the panel kept its award within the wage guidelines established by the Cost of Living Council and stipulated that the wage increases (5.5 percent) were conditioned on the implementation of specified productivity improvements. Demonstrating its concern in that case for the maintenance of a balance between the demands it considered legitimate and the bona fide problems of and constraints on management relating to the delivery of such vital government service, the panel said:[4]

> . . . we feel keenly our responsibility to justify wage improvements with substantially offsetting gains in productivity. . . . The wage increases we recommend are not only within the [national economic stabilization program] 5.5% guideline but are also geared to and dependent upon the substantial productivity gains recommended by the panel under the heading Productivity and Economies of Operation.

An additional and significant factor in that award was the panel's treatment of the matter of the contract length. In light of an imminent change in administration, the panel wrote:[5]

> . . . with a new administration only weeks away from taking office, we cannot foresee what changes may be in the offing, and we have no sense for what can be prudently recommended in the way of improved benefits for the fiscal year 1974 . . . [the new administration] should not be bound for an extended period of time to conditions mandated by an impasse panel before whom it had no opportunity to appear.

The view illustrated by that language, and characteristic of impasse arbitrations generally, is that the procedure is an extension of the bargaining process and that the panel works with the parties and the realistic issues confronting them, not in judgmental isolation. The foregoing examples are representative of what has been going on and are not sui generis exceptions. If the arbitrators and the arbitration system in the public sector is demonstrating that measure of care, prudence, and responsibility in deciding interest cases involving large sums of public money, what support is there for the irresponsible notion that arbitrators would be partisan, indulgent of unsubstantiated union demands, or unmindful of management's needs and problems in the private sector? It should be noted that the arbitrators serving in the public sector are private practitioners of the arbitration profession who gained their initial experience from the private grievance arbitration system, who continue to serve there as well, and who remain sophisticated and knowledgeable about private sector collective bargaining.

Further reference to arbitrators and the arbitration profession is in order. A few hundred "professional arbitrators," who devote all or a substantial part of their time to this, handle the bulk of arbitration cases in the United States. I know of no more conscientious, intelligent, dedicated, and ethical group. Their continued success and acceptability rest on their continued impartiality and competence. As they are mutually selected by the parties in virtually every case, either ad hoc or as impartial chairmen, their capabilities, knowledge, and sense of fairness and justice are put to the test with each case. While awards of arbitrators occasionally are successfully vacated by appeal to the courts for error or exceeding authority, I know of not one instance in which a professional labor-management arbitrator has been found to have been corrupt, to have committed fraud, was willfully biased, or engaged in any other willful misconduct in the course of official duties. The profession functions "in a fishbowl" and has lived up to the confidence and trust the parties have placed in it and in each of its members.

The new arbitration work in the public sector represents a challenge to the arbitration profession. It had devoted itself, for the most part, to grievances and to the application and interpretation of existing contracts in the private sector. It had little experience in "legislating" new contract terms of employment according to the arbitration, fact-finding, and impasse panel requirements of the public sector. The profession has met the challenge. Its members have become knowledgeable in handling statistics, budgets, actuarial data, economic indexes, and all the other complex factual matters connected with terms and conditions of the employment relationship. The experiences in New York City and elsewhere where public sector laws or procedures employ neutrals to decide or recommend on unresolved contract terms, proves unquestionably that the professional arbitrator is fully competent to handle bargaining issues and that the simplistic and undocumented dogma—expressed most often by management representatives—that arbitrators lack the familiarity with their industry or the business experience to understand and intelligently deal with complex bargaining issues, has proved to be simply another untruth, now shattered.

Additionally, for the same reasons, our experience has laid to rest the erroneous notion that arbitrators lack a sense of responsibility for the settlements they order or recommend, because, unlike the parties, they do not "have to live under the contract." The sensitivity and awareness of arbitrators to this very fact and charge has made them keenly responsible, indeed conservative, in what they order. As previously noted, their "track record" has been more prudent, more traditional, and far less precedent setting than what the legislatures and the parties in direct bargaining have done with conditions of employment. In sum, I think it nonsense—and contrary to every relevant evidentiary indication—for private sector management to fear or view the arbitrator as unsophisticated, inexperienced, lacking in responsibility or restraint, or devoid of the requisite intelligence and ability to deal with the problems at hand. Arbitrators have made the transition from three decades of private sector grievance arbitration to the "new action" in public sector disputes over contract terms, and are fully capable of completing the cycle by serving effectively and constructively in the arbitration of private sector contract disputes, when such services are needed and requested.

Whether interest arbitration, if used in the private sector, will prove as productive as it has been in public employment, remains to be seen. Misconceptions notwithstanding, there are relevant differences between the private and public sectors, and any attempt to translate literally from one to the other runs the risk of superficiality and dislocation. That does not mean, however, that experience in one sector cannot be instructive in the other, and, in practice, most public sector labor relations boards and agencies have drawn heavily on well-settled principles of labor law established in the private sector. It seems probable that with the passage of time the reverse will be true and that developments in public sector bargaining will have impact upon private sector practice. For instance, if both management and labor in the private sector reach the conclusion, suggested above, that the strike has become too costly and destructive and that it would be mutually beneficial to find an alternative, the search may be greatly assisted and advanced by the fact that such alternatives have already been sought, found, and thoroughly tested in the public sector, and have been shown to work well.

Experimentation with many variations of the basic process of interest arbitration will be increasingly instructive. Currently in use in various jurisdictions are such offshoots as "last-best offer" arbitration in which, before the close of hearings, each party presents a total package proposal to the panel which must choose the one that finds greatest support in the record. A variation is the system in which the panel may adopt the final position of either party, on each issue, on an item-by-item basis. Another matter of interest to parties considering the adoption of interest arbitration will be the different forms of arbitration panels, the various methods of designating panels, and the type and scope of the powers exercised by such panels in the various circumstances in which they have been used. Panels may be made up solely of neutrals or may be tripartite in composition. As in grievance arbitration, they may be appointed in the contract or designated by an outside agency such as the American Arbitration Association. A panel may be authorized only to hear and determine in one jurisdiction, but in another the panel may have the power to mediate with consent of both parties where circumstances indicate that such action might be productive. In short, a wealth of material on the experience of government management and public employee unions with these processes will be available. With appropriate adaptations, well-established public sector practices should be readily applicable to private sector collective bargaining. Whether or not such cross-pollination will actually occur remains to be seen. It is also as yet unknown when, if at all, a broad-based movement away from the strike in the private sector will occur. But that the need has already been felt and acted on in some areas of the private sector is well known.

New York City's newspaper industry has been plagued by strikes for the last quarter century. During that time, an industry which supported 15 daily newspapers in 1900 and 10 in 1950 has shrunk to 3 that are printed and published in the city. It is not suggested that these conditions are attributable solely to strikes or even to labor conditions generally. But the crippling 114-day strike of 1962–63 and the atmosphere of crisis bargaining which has permeated each new contract negotiation since then was and has doubtless been a significant contributing factor. In any case, the parties themselves—the newspaper industry and certain unions with which it deals—gave such weight to these factors in examining the ills of their industry that in some of their most recent contracts they have included provisions for the use of binding arbitration in the resolution of future bargaining disputes. Too little time has elapsed for any evaluation of the effects of this step to be made. The fact that it was taken at all is of significance, however, in the context of this discussion.

Of even greater significance are similar developments in the steel industry. The roller-coaster quality of labor-management relations in that industry is well known. This has not even involved an actual strike since 1959. But the traumatic effects of the 116-day strike of 1959, in which 100,000 employees were laid off—some for as many as seven or eight months—and which imposed incalculable short-term and long-term losses on the industry, continued to be felt throughout the next decade in the form of crisis bargaining and massive stockpiling by steel users. Thus, after the losses experienced in 1959 in trade which turned to, and to some extent stayed with, foreign suppliers or which converted permanently to other materials such as aluminum, the industry was subjected, during the 1960s, to stockpiling demands from customers laying in three-month supplies in anticipation of possible strikes.

This required the cyclical opening of marginal facilities and scheduling of extraordinary amounts of overtime by steel companies prior to settlement and corollary plant shutdowns and employee layoffs immediately after agreements were reached. The unbroken repetition of this cycle with every contract negotiation during the 13 years following the 1959 strike led to the execution, in March 1973, of the industry's so-called Experimental Negotiating Agreement (ENA), in which binding arbitration of unresolved items of contract negotiation was substituted for the strike. Prior to its first test in contract negotiations, the agreement was the subject of litigation in which a group of employees sued the companies and the union claiming that the ENA, by forfeiting the right to strike, compromised a basic and necessary right and power of the workers. Having survived this legal test in Federal District Court for the Western District of Pennsylvania before Judge Hubert Teitelbaum, the ENA had its first practical test in the 1974 negotiations in which the parties expressed their satisfaction with its effects by writing it into the new agreement for application to the 1977 negotiations. It has been hailed by leaders of both labor and management in the steel industry, as well as by outside observers, as a major achievement toward stabilization of this internationally competitive, but basic industry.

The sports world found the process useful. To avoid disruptions to team play by individual "holdouts," and to ease fan irritation with salary disputes between players and their teams, the baseball owners and the players' association agreed to a last-offer arbitration system of salary disputes. Though suspended after two years of use, reports of the newly negotiated contract between the owners and the association indicate that the salary arbitration system will be reinstated with the next season.

In 1976 the Weekly Labor Arbitration Report of the Bureau of National Affairs stated that a no-strike agreement providing for binding arbitration had been reached between the Air Line Pilots' Association and Braniff Airways and between the Airline Employees' Association and National Airlines. Under the agreements, if negotiations for a new contract fail, the National Mediation Board will provide the parties with lists of arbitrators from which an arbitrator will be selected to resolve the bargaining deadlock by arbitration. Again, these are only representative of a slowly growing list of industries experimenting with or giving consideration to the use of a privately agreed-to and privately administered system of arbitration of bargaining deadlocks, as part of their private industrial relationship.

In summary, it cannot be supposed that the strike is about to fade from the labor scene or that it will ever disappear completely in a free society. Indeed its lawful abolition is neither desirable nor advocated. Instead, thought should be given to a movement toward adoption of means other than the strike to resolve bargaining impasses. I think that movement will occur on a gradual basis, initially in private industry, where it is recognized that survival requires acceptance of an alternative to the strike, or where conditions hospitable to strike action—good profitability, little competition, nonessentiality of the product or service to the public—are no longer present. If there is a gradual acceptance of interest arbitration in private industry, the effect may be comparable to what grievance arbitration has done for the private sector, and what compulsory arbitration has done for public employment—a sharp reduction in the exercise of the right or power to strike, not because the strike is proscribed, but because it is replaced by a workable alternative.

NOTES AND REFERENCES

1. Paragraph 1173-7.0 (c) (3) (b) (1,2,3,4,5) of the New York City Collective Bargaining Law. Chapter 54, New York City Charter. The term "impasse panel" is legally synonymous with "arbitration."

2. *Licensed Practical Nurses v. N.Y.C. Health and Hospital Corporation.* OCB docket number I-113-74.

3. *Research Scientists Association v. N.Y.C.* OCB docket number I-122-75.

4. *Uniformed Firefighters Association v. N.Y.C.* OCB docket number I-105-73.

5. Ibid.

22

THRIFT INSTITUTION MANAGEMENT: Tomorrow and Today

IRA O. SCOTT, JR.
Vice President,
Savings Banks Association of New York State

Long-term forecasting, political or economic, is patently easier than short-term. Tracking trends leads to extrapolations. The nature of the eventual resolution of contemporary confrontations is often apparent. The long-term viability—or lack thereof—of existing institutional arrangements can usually be assessed with considerable confidence in the near-term. Hence, the long-term viability will be dealt with in summary fashion.

In the nirvana of thrift institution development, the more backward variety remaining in the Western world will have achieved the status of the Scandinavian model, in which regulatory laissez-faire applies to thrifts and commercial banks alike. The Swedish and Danish banking laws, for example, do not distinguish between stock commercial banks and mutual savings banks. Specialization within the two industries occurs as a result of management choice, not governmental decree. American thrifts will in the future, as their Scandinavian counterparts do now, continue to specialize in home finance. Commercial banks will continue to specialize in commerce. Thrifts will also be viable institutions.

The author gratefully acknowledges his indebtedness to William A. Beasman, Gordon S. Braislin, Joseph C. Brennan, Vincent H. Crawford, Stephen Feldman, Albert B. Hooke, John J. La Falce, Leonard Lapidus, Maurice Mann, Garth Marston, Robert D. Mettlen, John T. Morgan, Joyce Orsini, John W. Raber, Monte Radack, Abraham Serfaty, John D. Walsh, G. Dale Weight, and Alan A. Walters.

Now for short-term viability: American thrift institutions today are hemmed in by the most primitive form of housing finance existing in free market economies. Token progress is being made. Grudging entry for the thrifts into the payments mechanism is being tolerated. De minimus asset flexibility is being introduced with severely restricted consumer lending authority. However, the asset side remains—from the point of view of the future of the private sector in housing finance—dangerously inflexible in the face of what will likely be more frequent and accentuated episodes of inflation[1] generated, hostile economic environments. American thrifts cannot be assured of a significant role in the future of U.S. housing finance by continuing to "borrow short and lend long."

REG Q ISSUE

Some years ago, those in authority decided that residential housing should be given a relatively high priority among our nation's economic goals. The level of priority those public officials had in mind exceeded in their view—and realistically so—the level that would eventuate as a market response. Hence, the device of setting different interest-rate ceilings on the deposits of different institutions was selected as the means whereby the anticipated market response could be outdistanced. Such was the origin of the Reg Q (Regulation Q) differential. The selection of this qualitative, or direct, type of control had nothing whatsoever to do with questions of equity or parity, as these objective standards might be applied to financial institutions. Reg Q was a means to an end. In retrospect, all can agree that it has not worked miracles. Housing is still a "prince or pauper" industry.[2] But more housing is financed today in the United States than would be financed without Reg Q, *given the constraints imposed on the mortgage instrument by those who set the national housing goal.* Essentially, this meant that 26-million housing units should be supplied during the decade 1969–79, and *financed by long-term, fixed-interest-rate instrument of indebtedness.*

Emphasis is being given to this rather obvious point, because the lack of attention it has received explains what must seem to many the unusually bitter controversy that attends the entry of the thrift industry into the market for household financial services. Much attention has been given in the "broadened powers" debate to questions of competitive balance between commercial banks and thrift institutions. However, few contemporary economic controversies have entailed such a waste of energy and resources.

To focus on the essence of the problem and put questions of equity and parity where they should be—outside the debate—competition between *two commercial banks* will be considered. That is, two commercial banks—rather than one commercial bank and one thrift—form the basis for the relevant comparison. Selection of two commercial banks casts aside all questions of equity and parity. No detractor or heckler can cite the merit of broadened powers, the issue of tax status, or the question of mutual-versus-stock form of organization.

Commercial bank C (for commercial) does a normal commercial banking sort of business. It makes 90-day loans to finance inventories. If it is chartered in an agriculture area, it may even extend its seed or cattle loans to a one-year maturity. Lucrative corporate customers get *term*-loan accommodation. This may exceed one year in maturity, but with a rather important proviso, a *floating* prime. Consider next commercial bank H (for housing). This bank has invested over one-half of its resources in long-term, fixed-interest-rate mortgage loans. Now how do C and H fare in an inflation-ridden economic environment? This, of course, is a rhetorical question. Clearly, all the ills which beset the American thrift industry today will also visit themselves on commercial bank H.

The fundamental issue is the competitive position of the two industries, that is, whether the two industries will be allowed to compete for capital and to manage capital on an equal basis. To clarify this point, continue to suppose there were no thrifts. Suppose there were only two kinds of commercial banks, types C and H. Clearly, if those in authority want to preserve the private sector's role in home finance, special measures would have to be taken to shore up the position of commercial bank H. In fact, Reg Q has been the chosen instrument. It is noteworthy that the House Sub-Committee on Bank Supervision and Insurance, under the leadership of Congressman Fernand St. Germain of Rhode Island, recently offered to give housing-oriented commercial banks the benefit of the Q differential.

In sum, borrowing short and lending long is not a viable arrangement for home finance in the United States today, regardless of whether a lending institution is called a mutual thrift institution or a stock commercial bank. Some form of capital allocation device, such as the Reg Q differential, must be provided. The thrift industry needs the Reg Q differential because it enables the thrifts to compete more effectively for funds against the commercial banks. Reg Q ceilings limit the cost of funds to the thrifts and therefore have a favorable effect on earnings. Ceiling limitations, of course, restrict the freedom of the thrifts to compete with the market. But for a variety of reasons, not all monies leave the thrifts when market rates exceed Q ceilings. Moreover, those—both in and out of authority—who suggest that the elimination of the Q ceiling will solve the problem of disintermediation do not know whereof they speak. Such a simplistic solution does not go to the heart of the problem. *The elimination of Reg Q does not eliminate the problem of borrowing short and lending long.* In the final analysis, it is a question of *earnings*, not ceilings.

Without the Q differential and ceilings, the thrifts would need a flexible asset structure to generate earnings in periods of high interest rates necessary to enable them to compete with the commercial banks and the market. Thus, it is not the existence of ceilings but a limitation on earnings that serves as the ultimate cause of disintermediation. This fact is dramatized by the British experience in 1973. In the United Kingdom, the building societies account for most of the private sector's contribution to housing finance. These societies regularly adjusted their mortgage lending rates as the rates they were required to pay on their deposits were changed. As would be expected under such a regimen, the British building societies never experienced disintermediation. Involuntary losses of deposits only came about in the fall of 1973, when Prime Minister Heath put a ceiling—*not on deposit interest rates*—on mortgage interest rates. To reiterate, Great Britain did not have a Reg Q. What they suddenly got was, in effect, a long-term, fixed-interest-rate mortgage. And they began losing funds in a manner matched only by the outflow of deposits experienced repeatedly by U.S. thrifts. Again, it is a matter of *earnings*, not ceilings.[3] And thrift institutions will not be able to generate the earnings necessary to sustain a fully competitive position until they are permitted not only to borrow short, but to lend *short* as well.[4]

HOW HAS THRIFT MANAGEMENT BEEN DOING?

To buttress the argument, some reference to the record will be made next. (All tables mentioned will be found at the end of this chapter.)

Tables IA and IB show data on market share. Data are available for October 1972, 1973, and 1974. It will be recalled that the 50 basis-point differential was reduced by one-half—to 25 basis points—in July 1973. In Table IA, the share of market for consumer time and savings deposits at depository institutions is given for selected years and includes $100,000 certificates of deposits (CDs) for individuals. Between 1972 and 1973, the commercial bank share declined. By 1974, however, it had practically stabilized. Thrift institutions, as a class, showed an increasing share. This pattern was accounted for wholly by the S & L's (savings and loans), for the savings banks share declined.

Several comments are in order. First, the relative stability of the commercial bank share after July 1973 can be accounted for by two factors. The reduced differential improved the appeal of full-service banking offered by the commercial banks. In addition, the superior earnings position of the commercial banks gave them an advantageous competitive position in bidding for over $100,000 deposits (see Tables III, IV, and V). A second observation focuses on the geographical characteristics of the two components of the thrift industry. The savings banks industry is basically regional, concentrated in New England and the mid-Atlantic states. The rest of the United States is, for the most part, in the hands of the S & L's. This means that the savings banks industry is in close proximity to the sophisticated money market centers of the northeastern section of the country. Indeed, as the record shows, the savings banks industry is the bellwether of the waves of intermediation and disintermediation that fan out across the land from the great northeastern money markets. The S & L industry remains, to an important degree, relatively isolated—and hence insulated—from the competitive forces of the money market. The experience of the two components of the thrift industry is compared in Table II.

Table IB presents data similar to that shown in Table IA, except that $100,000 deposits are excluded. In this case, all deposits are subject to Q ceilings. The commercial bank share does not show the same stability as that in Table IA. But the decrease in market share slows markedly in the second period. The thrift pattern is much the same as before, with the S & L's running up substantial gains and the savings banks exhibiting a definite decline in market share.

In Table III, time series of net income are compared for the three industries. These statistics speak eloquently of hardships experienced by the thrifts as they finance long-term, fixed-interest-rate mortgages with short-term deposits, while the commercial banks are able to match the maturities of their assets and liabilities. The standard deviation[5] of changes in net income for mutual savings banks is 65; for S & L's, 27; and for commercial banks, only 7. The geographical factor undoubtedly again goes a long way toward explaining the difference between the S & L's and savings banks.

The effective tax burden is also an important factor which contributes to the erosion of the competitive position of thrift institutions. In Table IV, total federal, state, and local tax liability—as a percentage of net income—for the three industries is compared. Over the period observed, the tax burden for commercial banks has declined. For thrifts, the tax burden has increased.

It all "comes home to roost" in the bottom line. Table V depicts net worth/deposit ratio for the three industries. For the period studied, the thrifts are again in a disadvantaged position. And again, the relative fixity of the asset structure is a significant factor in explaining these discouraging results. And there is no surcease. Repeated bouts with the capital market in an inflationary state bring costly waves of disintermediation. During periods of money market ease, the reverse flow of funds cannot readily be margined by the thrifts. Cyclical swings in the U.S. economy thus find the American thrift industry uniquely vulnerable, a story which is told in eloquent fashion by the trends depicted in Table V.

DEFENSIVE STRATEGIES FOR THE THRIFT MANAGER

For all the criticism heaped on Reg Q by the commercial banking industry, Q evidently has not protected the thrift industry from a worsening capital position. What, then, can thrift management do, confronted as it is by declining net worth ratio, absence of variable rate or essentially short-term, home-finance mortgages, and an eroding effectiveness of Reg Q?

Specifically, the thrift manager today must do two things: first, strive to reduce risk exposure; second, endeavor to increase earnings potential. Reduced risk exposure can be gotten through a better balance between the maturity of assets and liabilities—that is, either by increasing the maturity of the institution's liabilities or by reducing the maturity of its assets. To improve earnings, the thrift manager does best by borrowing cheap—attracting all the deposit liabilities which available capital can margin at the trough of the interest rate cycle—and by lending dear—investing at the peak of the interest rate cycle. The optimal solution in a world of uncertainty can be approached only through a series of approximations. These approximations may be reduced to the following guidelines for management:

1. Increasing attention should be given to profit maximization as opposed to growth and other objectives. Four corollaries follow from this precept:
   a. Social or community-minded ventures cannot be financed without having available previously generated profits from which to finance them.
   b. A manager should avoid the objective of managing the largest institution in town to grow itself into liquidation.
   c. Interest rates paid for deposits and other sources of funds should be flexible in both directions.
   d. Ultimately, the wherewithal to margin growth must come from earnings. For example, an institution whose earnings prospects are nil will be unable to float an equity issue.
2. Calls on capital should be economized through:
   a. Reduction in the average maturity of assets.
   b. Increased investment in trading and service type operations. If management takes these crucial steps, it will be in a much better position to increase the return to capital.
3. Since asset acquisitions and liability incurrences necessarily imply interest rate forecasts, these forecasts should be made explicit.
4. If market and legal constraints permit, debenture capital sources should be tapped to margin profitable growth.

Some of these guidelines or tentative precepts for today's thrift manager will be discussed further. To begin with—and this cannot be overemphasized—the manager must understand that the company's continuation as a viable institution is the primary responsibility. The only way an organization will remain viable and continue in existence as an independent entity will be to achieve and maintain sufficient capital and reserves to provide protection against losses and to margin profitable growth. Again, the only way those reserves will occur is to produce sufficient net income. If the manager cannot or will not grasp this fundamental principle, it is only a matter of time before the institution will be absorbed through merger or acquisition.

As we all know, the problem of borrowing short and lending long at fixed rates in an inflationary economy can result only in rapidly disappearing profit. To avoid this fate, today's manager must shift sight from the permanent mortgage portfolio target to the loan origination and underwriting objectives.[6] Garth Marston has publicly admonished his members for holding an increasing share of the residential mortgage market and not setting up their own mortgage banking profit centers.[7] On an earlier occasion, Maury Mann, in a similar context, preached the same gospel to his Savings & Loans listeners.[8] Additional leading advocates are William A. Beasman, The Savings Bank of Baltimore, Maryland; Daniel T. McSweeney, McSweeney & Associates, Newport Beach, California; and David L. Smith, Glendale Federal, California.

Financial institutions which engage in real estate lending and have a high yield on assets are heavy originators of loans for a fee. It is a proved fact that those which originate loans are more profitable than those which purchase loans. The churning of funds involved in a repeated origination and sale of loans will increase the return to a fixed amount of capital and, at the same time, protect the institution from the impact of inflation on the short-term cost of money. To implement this approach, the institution must make loans which are salable. A secondary market exists for loans that conform to the underwriting criteria established by such government agencies as Federal National Mortgage Association (FNMA), Federal Home Loan Mortgage Corporation (FHLMC), and Government National Mortgage Association (GNMA). For loans that do not conform, attention must be paid to requiring a due-on-sale clause and lending on properties where a reasonable expectation of an early move exists.

The real estate loan mix must also be a prime consideration, since multifamily and commercial loans tend to have a higher yield than single-family residentials. The existing portfolio can be upgraded through promotion to persuade existing mortgagors to borrow more money by rewriting the first mortgage, writing a second mortgage, or taking out a consumer loan. Low capital investment opportunities that may improve the overall return on capital include real estate syndications of limited partnership investors, property management, insurance agencies, accounting and data processing services, investment counseling, land development joint ventures, and property ownership and leasing.

Next to asset management, a particularly weak aspect of present-day management practice concerns the role—or lack thereof—of interest rate forecasting. Thrifts tend to invest their large deposit gains in long-term assets at the time the deposits are received. By doing so, they are speculating that long rates will not rise, in spite of the fact that such deposit gains occur at the *trough* of the interest rate cycle. When the same institutions disinvest in long-term assets, they are speculating that long rates will not fall. Yet such disinvestment tends to occur at the *peak* of the interest rate cycle. Since such investment behavior is precisely the worst that is possible, there would appear to be substantial prima facie evidence of a need for introducing explicit forecasting techniques.[9]

A final word on the net worth position and the problem of existing low-yielding assets, which is a difficult but not insurmountable obstacle to improving earnings performance. Assets which yield less than returns currently available in the marketplace may be expendable. When confronted with the proposition that they should be sold, some managers respond: "But they can only be sold at a loss." Such a statement implies that avoiding a sale somehow avoids a loss that indeed already exists.[10] In any case, the institution's earnings—and future net worth position—under certain systems of taxation, can be enhanced by replacing low-yielding assets with currently available higher-yielding assets.[11] If the institution's capital/deposit ratio is already at the legal minimum, either the capital position must be strengthened through the issuance of subordinated debentures, or the supervisory authorities must be persuaded that future benefits warrant today's "costs."

EPILOGUE

Finally, I will make a brief comment regarding the thrift manager as a human being—his or her attitude, outlook and conception of reality. When the Q differential was larger and institutions could easily maintain a comfortable spread, no unusual management skill was required. Today's managers face a different kind of world. Today it is the marketplace, tomorrow the commercial banks, and before we know it, the world of the great retail chains, the consumer durable manufacturers, and the credit card companies. Today's manager must want to manage. Free enterprise will force creativity and new services. Today's manager must be aggressive, must have vision. Too many are people who can only read regulations. Management needs people who challenge the system, analyze the problem, and move aggressively to its solution. The weaker manager will resist operating in a competitive environment and will be eliminated. The strong will survive, and the consumer will be better served through the greater competition that results.

The most difficult task confronting today's manager is to acquire the personnel capable of implementing the policies necessary to assure a future for the thrift institution. Entering mortgage banking, nationwide loan origination and placement of loans, commercial lending, construction lending, consumer lending, liquidity management, and interest rate forecasting, all require specialists not often found internally in today's thrift institutions. The manager must resist the thinking that encourages "giving the $25,000-a-year person a chance" (just because this individual has been with you for 10 or 20 years, and even though you have serious doubts concerning his or her ability to handle the assignment) when the job requires a $50,000-a-year person having the expertise necessary for success. To break out of old thought patterns when dealing with the market for people is even more important than setting aside traditional responses when dealing with the market for money.

Table IA
SHARE OF MARKET CONSUMER TIME AND SAVINGS DEPOSITS*
AT DEPOSITORY INSTITUTIONS
OCTOBER 1972, 1973, 1974
(Amounts in $ billions)

	Commercial Banks		*Thrift Institutions*		*Totals*		*Commercial Banks*		*Savings Banks*		*Savings & Loans*	
Year	*$*	*%*	*$*	*%*	*$*	*%*	*$*	*%*	*$*	*%*	*$*	*%*
1972	144.7	33.2	291.7	66.8	436.4	100.0	144.7	33.2	89.7	20.6	202.0	46.3
1973	152.0	32.4	317.7	67.6	469.7	100.0	152.0	32.4	94.9	20.2	222.8	47.4
1974	160.2	32.3	335.6	67.7	495.8	100.0	160.2	32.3	97.3	19.6	238.3	48.1

*Includes $100,000 certificates of deposit held by individuals, not subject to Regulation Q ceilings. Deposits held by businesses are excluded.

SOURCES: Federal Reserve Board, Member Banks' Time & Savings Deposits Surveys, October 1972, 1973, and 1974; National Association of Mutual Savings Banks; and Federal Home Loan Bank Board.

Table IB
SHARE OF MARKET CONSUMER TIME AND SAVINGS DEPOSITS*
AT DEPOSITORY INSTITUTIONS
OCTOBER 1972, 1973, 1974
(Amounts in $ billions)

	Commercial Banks		*Thrift Institutions*		*Totals*		*Commercial Banks*		*Savings Banks*		*Savings & Loans*	
Year	*$*	*%*	*$*	*%*	*$*	*%*	*$*	*%*	*$*	*%*	*$*	*%*
1972	135.6	31.7	291.7	68.3	427.3	100.0	135.6	31.7	89.7	21.0	202.0	47.3
1973	133.4	29.6	317.7	70.4	451.1	100.0	133.4	29.6	94.9	21.0	222.8	49.4
1974	135.0	28.7	335.6	71.3	470.6	100.0	135.0	28.7	97.3	20.7	238.3	50.6

*Excludes $100,000 certificates of deposit, not subject to Regulation Q ceilings, and all deposits held by businesses. The proportion of large time to total time deposits of member banks were as follows: 42.4 percent in 1972; 56.1 percent in 1973; and 63.1 percent in 1974.

SOURCES: Federal Reserve Board, Member Banks' Time & Savings Deposits Surveys, October 1972, 1973, and 1974; National Association of Mutual Savings Banks; and Federal Home Loan Bank Board.

Table II
NET DEPOSIT FLOWS AT MUTUAL SAVINGS BANKS AND SAVINGS & LOAN ASSOCIATIONS
(Amounts in $ millions)

	Selected Periods of Disintermediation						*Selected Periods of Reintermediation*			
	April 1969–June 1970		*July–Sept. 1973*		*April–Sept. 1974*		*Jan. 1971–Dec. 1972*		*Jan.–Dec. 1975*	
	$	%	$	%	$	%	$	%	$	%
Mutual savings banks	−1,380	−2.10	−1,867	−1.95	−3,793	−3.86	+11,144	+15.57	+4,754	+4.81
Savings & loans	+5,388	+4.04	+489	+0.22	+3,240	+1.36	+60,637	+41.42	+43,121	+17.75

SOURCES: National Association of Mutual Savings Banks and Federal Home Loan Bank Board.

Table III
VARIABILITY OF NET INCOME OF DEPOSITORY INSTITUTIONS
1965–1974
(Amounts in $ billions)

	Commercial Banks		*Thrift Institutions*		*Mutual Savings Banks*		*Savings & Loan Associations*	
Year	*$*	*% change*	*$*	*% change*	*$*	*% change*	*$*	*% change*
1965	2515		1004		223		821	
1966	2684	+7	831	−20	177	−21	654	−20
1967	3142	+17	708	−15	94	−47	614	−6
1968	3426	+9	1094	+55	223	+137	871	+42
1969	4335	+27	1259	+15	213	−4	1046	+20
1970	4837	+12	1068	−15	164	−23	904	−14
1971	5286	+9	1701	+59	344	+110	1357	+50
1972	5654	+7	2208	+30	479	+39	1729	+27
1973	6579	+16	2328	+5	478	0	1850	+7
1974	7091	+8	1800	−23	317	−34	1483	−22
Standard deviation		7		32		65		27

SOURCES: Federal Deposit Insurance Corporation and U.S. League of Savings Associations.

Table IV
EFFECTIVE TAXATION OF DEPOSITORY INSTITUTIONS
1970–1974
(Federal, State, and Local Taxes as Percentage of Net Income)

Year	*Commercial Banks*	*Thrift Institutions*	*Savings Banks*	*Savings & Loans*
1970	26.6	27.3	32.2	26.0
1971	23.9	25.2	27.0	24.8
1972	21.7	27.4	28.0	27.2
1973	19.7	29.0	29.7	28.6
1974	19.1	31.4	33.8	30.8

SOURCES: Federal Deposit Insurance Corporation and Federal Savings and Loan Insurance Corporation.

Table V
NET WORTH/DEPOSIT RATIO OF DEPOSITORY INSTITUTIONS
1960–1975*
(Ratio in Percent)

Year	*Commercial Banks*	*Thrift Institutions*	*Savings Banks*	*Savings & Loans*
1960	9.13	8.66	9.77	8.02
1965	9.46	8.21	8.90	7.89
1970	10.22†	8.12	8.00	8.19
1975	10.01†	7.11	7.70	7.06

*Data are for the end of December except for 1975, which are for the end of June.

†The net worth component includes reserves on loans and securities to make it comparable to data for the thrift industry. Data for these reserves were not available for 1960 and 1965.

SOURCES: Federal Deposit Insurance Corporation; National Association of Mutual Savings Banks; and Federal Home Loan Bank Board.

NOTES AND REFERENCES

1. For purposes of this discussion, "inflation" should be taken to mean "unanticipated inflation." The most serious problems facing the thrifts today would, of course, vanish were continuing economic stability to be achieved.

2. Obstacles such as rising construction costs and overbuilding have impeded progress toward achieving national housing objectives.

3. Cf. Ira O. Scott, Jr., statement before the Joint Economic Committee, presented Oct. 3, 1974, and published in *Financial and Capacity Needs,* Hearings before the Joint Economic Committee, 93d Cong., 2d Sess., Oct. 1, 2, 3, and 10, 1974 (U.S. Government Printing Office, 1974), pp. 171–184.

4. From a macro-response point of view, it is interesting to note that anti-inflationary policies might receive broader support from the electorate were mortgages forced to bear the burden of inflation practically immediately through an upward adjustment in mortgage rates of interest.

5. This is a statistical measure of variability. Specifically the standard deviation is

$$S = \sqrt{\sum_{i=1}^{n} \frac{x_i - \bar{x}}{n}}$$

where x_i = percentage change in net income

$\bar{x}$ = average of percentage changes in net income

n = number of observations

6. Through correspondence with Bertil Sjöstrand, President, Stockholms Sparbank, the author has learned that this, the largest mutual savings bank in Sweden, holds only 35 percent of its assets in long-term mortgage paper, while emphasizing the origination and sale of loans as a line of activity.

7. See Garth Marston, *The Savings and Loan Industry in 1976,* an address delivered before the Annual Meeting of Stockholders, Federal Home Loan Bank of Chicago, Apr. 21, 1976; and the press notice of the same speech in *American Banker,* Apr. 23, 1976.

8. See Maurice Mann, *The Future of the Thrift Industry,* an address delivered at the Annual Convention of the National Savings and Loan League, Oct. 26, 1975.

9. Cf. Leonard Lapidus and Patrick Page Kildoyle, *Liquidity Management at Mutual Savings Banks in New York State,* remarks before Group I Banks of the Savings Banks Association of New York State, Oct. 25, 1973.

10. This is the kind of loss, by the way, which more and more supervisors, with an assist from the Financial Accounting Standards Board, seem intent on making quite explicit.

11. Some tax advantage is necessary for a profitable switch. Given identical quality and a common final maturity, it is impossible to gain through a switching operation. The present value of the original (low coupon) security is

$$P_o = c\left(\frac{1 - v^n}{i}\right) + 100\, v^n$$

where c = coupon amount

$v = \dfrac{1}{1 + i}$

i = market rate of interest

The present value of the new (high coupon) security is

$$P_n = c\left(\frac{1 - v^n}{i}\right) + 50\, v^n$$

where the high coupon rate equals twice the low coupon rate. Then

$$P_o - P_n = 100\, v^n - 50\, v^n = 50\, v^n$$

23

TIDES AND SHALLOWS

JOHN E. ULLMANN
Professor of Management and Marketing,
Hofstra University

There is a tide in the affairs of men
Which, taken at the flood, leads on to fortune;
Omitted, all the voyage of their life
Is bound in shallows and in miseries.
On such a full sea are we now afloat
And we must take the current when it serves,
Or lose our ventures.

Shakespeare
Julius Caesar, Act IV, Scene III

The future of management would be easy to assess if its major task consisted only of administering enterprises or institutions in a steady state, with no significant challenges from without or within and limited essentially to peaceful paper shuffling or button pushing. Such operating conditions are rare, however, and when managements believe them to exist, such judgments are usually wrong; "steady-state" administration, when practiced, usually means that the management cannot recognize stagnation when it is taking place right under its nose. Thus the future which the managers of our public and private sectors will have to cope with and, to a large degree, create, depends on their ability to respond to changes. Whether their response, in turn, will lead to a pleasant or unpleasant future depends on the competence with which managements as a group have responded to the evident pressures for change, with all their attendant disturbances, that are all around us nowadays.

One area of change is central to this discussion. It is the creation and use of technical innovation. This point may appear obvious but actually the policies followed by business managements belie it, as we shall see later. To be sure, the importance of technical innovation is well established among economists. In 1939 Joseph Schumpeter asserted bluntly that " . . . innovation is the outstanding fact in the economic history of capitalist society and . . . is largely responsible for most of what we would at first attribute to other factors." While Schumpeter's definition of innovation extends over non-technical fields as well, the role of technology has become the central one in innovation. Its treatment is the esential criterion of managerial performance and, one should add, it requires of management a far greater technical expertise than is often met with in this age of diversified conglomerates which were often assembled only for financial advantage—and short-run advantage at that. The old doctrine of managerial transferability, in other words, has become progressively less tenable and with its decline, the possibilities of changing managerial performance by altering the internal structure have likewise diminished. Modern industrial affluence, such as it is, owes its existence far more to new products and production methods than to changes in managerial techniques.[1]

Furthermore, unless managerial treatment of technical innovation is improved, the prospects are of epidemic failures of public and private institutions. We have already learned that entities considered impregnable can collapse, from businesses whose names were household words to empires. Indeed, many more would be in this situation if everything insolvent were actually thrown into bankruptcy. As it is, a lot of activity goes on because the creditors choose to ignore the insolvency, live in hopes, and, in the meanwhile, accept prettily engraved paper as a substitute for real assets. The Eurodollars are an example, being in essence checks that will never be presented for payment—and, of course, there are many national currencies in similar shape.

The problem has part of its origins in simple complacency. Modern industrial society has long taken as an article of faith that technology continually produces innovation and that, if a problem exists, a "tech-fix" will promptly be created to solve it. This view is accepted by friends and foes of technology alike. Its humanist critics picture technology as the source of new products which somehow always end up indifferent to environmental damage, safety, and at times the very survival of humanity. Even its patrons among the industrial and governmental managements have taken to worrying so much about the consequences of the alleged technical cornucopia that, in the early 1970s, they took up "technology assessment" which, by defining the impact of future technical developments, was to protect us all from our excess brilliance.

Unfortunately that exercise turned into a spectacular counting of unhatched chickens. The issue is not nearly as much what technology keeps unloading on us in the way of embarrassing riches, but why it is failing to solve so many clearly identifiable and pressing problems. Indeed, the way this failure is still largely ignored is itself an eloquent indicator of the quality of managerial performance. With one major exception and a few minor ones scattered here and there within the industrial sphere, tech-fix has turned into "tech-fizzle." Compared to the recent past, the supply of new products is drying up and such derived effects of good technology, as the improvement of productivity, have slowed to a glacial pace. The promising leads of the late

1950s in energy and transportation have not been followed up significantly and it is just in these areas where the needs are most acute.

It should be obvious that successful managements will have to help provide the means of reorganizing our lives on more efficient lines, to supply necessities and comforts as well as a civilized social order, while using raw materials more economically. That problem is only slowly being defined, let alone solved. There is an impressive body of evidence for the existence of the tech-fizzle. A simple comparison between the achievements of the periods 1945–60 and 1961–76 makes the point. In the earlier period, the new products included most of the antibiotics, oral contraceptives, and steroids; a dozen or so new plastics and fibers of major importance such as polyethylene, orlon, dacron, and synthetic rubbers; frozen foods; detergents; aerosols; passenger jets; a new way of making steel; the computer in its basic form; most electronic automation systems; transistors; the nuclear power systems now used; power assist systems for automobiles; a new generation of pesticides; black-and-white TV and then color; and many more innovations. Even allowing for the fact that some of these rested on theoretical and prototype work done earlier, and that several served to open a deplorable number of Pandora's boxes, the record is a remarkable one.

The list of projects under serious development about 1960 is also impressive. There was a hydrogen-oxygen fuel cell good enough to power an agricultural tractor. Intensive work was proceeding on seawater desalination; methods using heat, freezing, and membranes were all being studied. There were extensive experiments on solar power and an experimental power plant working with the temperature gradients of seawater was built in Abidjan on the Ivory Coast. The use of waste heat from power generation to desalt seawater was, in fact, so intensively investigated that articles discussed learnedly the pricing policies for the power and the water. Perhaps most important in the long run, fusion power was first studied in those days and some of the first experiments in plasma containment date back to that period.

After about 1960, effort in all these areas slackened. Several virtually disappeared from the literature, and anyone taking up once more some of the energy-related projects after the crisis of 1973 found the records of the earlier work followed by a prolonged sleep unmatched since the castle of Sleeping Beauty. For example, the United States established with much fanfare an Office of Saline Water, but its appropriations dried up and its existence quickly became vestigial. Fusion research likewise took a backseat and well-known scientists in the field found themselves unable to get significant grants for continuing their work. It should be noted that very expensive equipment is required for fusion research, but even humbler help was very hard to come by.

One would therefore be unable to make up an even remotely comparable list of innovations, either successfully launched or in the final stages of development for the years 1961–76. Solid-state devices displaced tubes and replaced the conventionally wired components with integrated circuits. The result has been an enormous reduction in size and power consumption of much electronic equipment, though only the calculator qualifies as a new product which may soon, by using the microprocessor, or "computer on a chip," merge with the computer itself.

Such major areas as medicine, however, have been unable to record new discoveries of the kind that made the 1940s and 1950s so exciting. No major disease has yielded in the face of new drugs. The creation of vaccines against viruses is, to be sure, almost routine now. The measles and rubella vaccines were developed in much the same way as those against polio in the 1950s. But virus diseases as such are still incurable and the medical profession is still, by and large, reduced to hoping that the virus will be self-limiting and practicing prophylaxis against secondary infections. Cancer, strokes, heart disease, hypertension, arthritis, and diabetes are, at best, "managed" by some new methods, and, in some cases, benefit from new diagnostic aids.

The most discouraging aspect of the decline in innovation has been actual retrogression in many once innovative industries. Surveys of the age of American industrial equipment show that it is steadily getting older, more so than that of almost all other industrial countries. Moreover, many industries really have no choice but to hang on to their existing equipment until it collapses totally or they expand. The new equipment is mostly a larger but otherwise only slightly slicked-up version of the old (a point to which we will return later) and very expensive to boot. Its purchase cannot be justified purely as a replacement of obsolescent but functioning equipment because the difference in performance is simply too small to provide a significant financial return.

In general, product development has suffered from this period of neglect. New products frequently illustrate a point made by the writer several times in the past,[2] that changes are made mainly to save manufacturing cost and not in the interest of the operational performance or economy of use of the product.

In the absence of viable challengers, some old and increasingly dysfunctional products overstay their welcome. We are, for instance, no nearer to an alternative to the internal combustion engine than we were 20 years ago when various battery and similar systems were first seriously proposed in a modern context. When new projects are finally finished, they are invariably late and their costs so much more than budgeted that they will probably never pay their way. The BART transit system of San Francisco and the Metro of Washington, D.C., are examples of combined technical incompetence and bad management which will make both of them permanent public charges. A similar debacle is that of the "people mover." These simple personal transit systems are, in essence, trolley cars with elevator controls; yet two attempts to build such systems, in Morgantown, West Virginia, and in the Dallas–Fort Worth airport, proved disastrous. Long shutdowns, cutbacks, lawsuits, and accidents plagued both systems. It is particularly significant that these failures concerned electric traction and that they occurred in the land of Edison, George Westinghouse, Charles Van der Poole, Leo Daft, and Frank Sprague, who practically invented it about the turn of the century.

A no less significant phenomenon is to be found in the constant managerial complaints by manufacturers and public utilities over their inability to meet legally mandated environmental, safety, and efficiency standards. The regulations now in force are almost invariably the result of a long history of unconcern over the damage done by their enterprises, so that the current complaints are a confession of technical incompetence and failure to provide the necessary resources for solving the problem. Nuclear power, for instance, is handicapped by the failure and embrittlement of structural materials by neutron flux.

For a long time, analyses such as the foregoing were dismissed as arbitrary and selective value judgments and, indeed, it was difficult to secure a significant audience for such views. By and large, the attitude of business managements to the bearers of bad news owes a great deal to the Egyptian Pharaohs who executed them. Some of the implications of the decline, moreover, are highly embarrassing to public policymakers. The decline of U.S. research is now, however, well documented by a study of the U.S. National Science Board.[3] Its salient findings include the following:

Research and development expenditures fell from 2.9 to 2.3 percent of gross national product between 1967 and 1974, a relative decline of 20 percent. The proportion spent by the U.S.S.R. and West Germany surpassed that of the United States in that period. After rising slightly in the early 1960s, the proportion of scientists and engineers in the population engaged in research and development declined slightly since 1968 and again was overtaken by the U.S.S.R., with Japan, West Germany, and France rapidly gaining. The United States has traditionally run a favorable balance of patents, that is, of foreign patents to U.S. nationals minus U.S. patents to foreign nationals. That surplus has shrunk by about 30 percent since 1968. National research and development expenditures have remained constant in terms of 1967 dollars since 1968. Finally, "radical breakthroughs" declined to half their share of total innovations between the periods 1953–59 and 1967–73, as measured in a survey in which respondents *themselves* classified innovations into improvements of existing technology, major technological advance, and breakthroughs. Further evidence of the decline of innovation results from the analysis of the improvement of productivity. Throughout manufacturing, productivity (output per labor hour) has improved over the years, though its rate of growth has slowed down and, for a time in 1974, actually showed a decline for the first time since statistics on the subject have been collected. Surely, apart from this lapse, this bespeaks progress!

Unfortunately, there is strong evidence that, rather than technical progress, productivity has been increasing because the production units have become bigger, that is, management took advantage of economy of scale rather than of technological or other changes which really meant doing the job more efficiently. It takes the same human effort to push the start button on a large machine as on a small one and big machines often cost less per unit of output than small ones. A recent study under the direction of the writer tested this association in 15 industries, ranging from steel, coal, and agriculture to automobiles, shoes, and apparel. In each case, we examined the changes in the average size of production unit as well as the flow of innovation and the productivity of labor. The central finding was that though there is wide variation in innovation, with a few industries having innovated extensively since 1945 while others remained almost unchanged, economy of scale is universally found to coexist with productivity improvement.[4] Where physical market constraints restrict further growth of plants and machines, productivity improvement stops and, in some cases, the industry proceeds to cut costs by moving jobs abroad.

There are several cases where the limits of size have been reached or where a hitherto steadily rising rate of input of nonlabor factors has reached a point of diminishing return. For example, continuing increases in the rate of energy use or of fertilizer in agriculture have failed to produce increases in crop yield in recent years. Serious concerns have been expressed on the subject by the American Academy of Sciences, with special reference to the overwhelming importance of American agriculture to the global food supply and to the position of the United States in the world.

In another example, labor productivity in open-pit coal mining had been improving steadily, in step with the evermore enormous size of the shovels and draglines used to mine the coal. However, the feasible size of this machinery depends on the depth of the actual coal seam and this is provided by nature. Nothing is gained by using a giant machine on a relatively shallow seam; only more waste material is scooped up. Accordingly, the maximum size of open-pit mining machinery was reached about 1968, and ever since productivity has been declining. To be sure, the industry claims that tighter laws requiring it to restore the mined-out land result in increasing labor time, but this should always have been part of the equation.

The steel industry furnishes another example. The United States was extraordinarily tardy in introducing the new steel processes such as the basic Bessemer (L-D process) or continuous casting—an omission itself indicative of poor management of technological resources. Again, however, the production units kept getting larger until they reached a limit set by the American steel market. As a result, the U.S. steel industry has expanded its capacity only very slowly and has not been able to take advantage of economy of scale which, as noted, turned out to be the "best" way to improve productivity. By contrast, its Japanese competitors, having a much faster growth rate, were able to build blast furnaces and integrated steel mills of much larger size and therefore with lower costs. The slow growth and economic difficulties of the U.S. steel industry, and the much worse troubles of the British industry which have similar roots, are thus strongly related to the paucity of innovation, other than making everything bigger.

The U.S. automobile industry has similar troubles. Since 1960, progress in special-purpose computers and solid-state controls have facilitated the construction of ever larger transfer machines which are the conveyor-linked systems of machining and assembly stations used in the manufacture of automobiles and their major parts, such as engines and frames. As for the "business end" of these machines, that is, for the components that actually do the work, significant improvements in tool materials date back to about 1950, and so does the addition of inspection stations. The automatic exchanges of worn tools began to be used only shortly thereafter. At any rate, the record is again one of slowdown in significant innovation and so the industry in part fell back on one of its old and deplorable standbys, the speedup. Strikes and job actions resulting from the brutal work pressures were the result, even though these abated somewhat, as the industry slid into the depression of 1974. Its inflexibility, moreover, made the industry unable to respond to the demand for small cars which made itself felt after 1973. The U.S. industry thus did not bring out its own cars, using in the main older designs from its European subsidiaries. By the time their production had been organized, with the accustomed dinosaurian slow motion, the boom had passed and much of its benefits had been reaped by West German and Japanese producers, even though the currencies of both these countries had been grossly inflated in value relative to the U.S. dollar.

The conclusion to be drawn from the experiences of these and other industries is that increasing size has been substituted for *real* innovation and technical progress, and that this is a progressively less viable strategy in a world in which raw materials are becoming shorter in supply. For all its self-congratulatory claims, industrial management is not at all well poised to respond to the challenges posed by these new trends.

We might note at this point that one reaction of the "conventional wisdom" to these analyses is that the United States can afford to let manufacturing drift abroad, because, after all, we have become a "service economy," that is, one in which the largest group of workers is employed in industries other than manufacturing, agriculture, or raw materials generally. According to this model, the United States would retain the "high technology end" of manufacturing and help to manage the foreign hewers of wood and drawers of water at their labors. This can only be charitably described as preposterously wrongheaded. First, there is no way in which the United States can keep the benighted foreigners in their stations in this way. The progress made in the foreign computer industry is a case in point. Second, high technology is not conspicuously profitable until the product has entered manufacture—and that is just the time when it is "supposed" to start emigrating. Third, reliance on foreign sources of supply or, worse still, on "coupon clipping" from foreign patent and process licenses, poses awful security problems and removes the sources of profit from the control of the managers, whatever solemn assurances are offered to the contrary. Fourth, "service" occupations cover a multitude of sins and only a small proportion of them correspond even remotely to their original definition of "the human care of human beings." Rather, they encompass all government activities; a Gulag camp guard or Chilean torturer would qualify for membership as would the vast bureaucracies which often seem so dedicated to the prevention of progress. Much of this activity expends its efforts in internal linkages, that is, people send each other memos and keep each other busy and nothing discernible is done for the outside world except, of course, for battening on it financially. For the most part, it is almost impossible to measure the productivity of service jobs (mainly because the output cannot be measured), let alone improve it. Included in the group are also many business enterprises in a variety of fields which serve other businesses in areas not related to any physical output and are thus economically equivalent to government bureaucracies.

Finally, considering all those Americans who are to show the managerial flag among the lesser breeds, have the proponents of this model ever taken a look at just about everybody's immigration laws? Have they taken note of the jungle of immigration visas, work permits, residence permits, changing regulations, and quotas, with which governments have surrounded themselves? One must suppose they have not, for otherwise this factor alone would rule the idea out of court.

Nevertheless, such considerations underlie much of the movement of American manufacturing abroad. Traditional innovation has dried up at home and so the thing to do is to migrate toward reservoirs of cheap labor and if this means going to countries where striking may carry the death penalty, as in South Korea and Singapore, then this is a circumstance to be accepted. But all this is exactly the kind of policy that has brought the multinational corporations which can establish their own factories in the cheap labor countries into the political bad odor in which they often find themselves nowadays.

The location of business activity is, in fact, an area in which business and government often work at cross-purposes, unless, as in the United States under the Nixon-Ford regime, the very concept of public planning for such purposes is anathema. In the United States, for instance, it is almost hysterically fashionable to move away from the established industrial areas of the North and Middle West into the so-called Sun Rim, that is, the tier of states along the Southern border of the United States and a few among the next row further inland. This migration has reached the stage where it is called "The Second War Between the States: A Bitter Struggle for Jobs, Capital and People"[5] and where it may reduce large sectors of the United States in the North to permanent poverty, while, at the same time, overload the new promised land with people and activities too numerous to be sustained by the resources of the region, most notably water.

The region is, however, the epicenter of political conservatism, hostility to unions, poor protection for workers and consumers, and resistance to federal standards in business and employment. Large corporations tend to favor small governments to deal with, for example, state governments in the U.S. context. It helps to even things up a bit; these smaller units of government have shown themselves to be highly "flexible" in the past (so much so that a sizable number of their functionaries, having met up with unfeeling public prosecutors, now find themselves as enforced guests of their former employers). Whatever other reasons exist for these migrations, a major reason has certainly been the desire of business to respond in some cost-cutting way to the decline of real innovation by moving elsewhere in the country.

Incidentally, the process is by no means the "natural" flow of economic activity predicated on free enterprise models or "rational" economic decisions. Rather, it is actively encouraged by tax incentives, arbitrarily low tax assessments, sale and lease-back arrangements for factories which may be financed by bonds carrying the full faith and credit of their communities and then rented at far below the market, and so on. Businesses may weigh their decisions carefully, but at times there is quite a heavy thumb on the scale.

We should note that similar problems beset other industrial countries. The *Mezzogiorno*, the Italian South, is an area where vast investment has been poured in, but much of it appears to have been wasted or found itself in industries which were not labor intensive in a land notorious for its high unemployment rate. The issue in Northern Ireland is, in part, jobs for all. There are two major industries in the area: linen has been ruined by synthetics and cheap labor competition elsewhere; shipbuilding, apart from war times, has not had a decent order since the R.M.S. *Titanic*. In Wales and Scotland, to cite another British problem, continued lack of industrial development, high unemployment, and poverty have helped spark a nationalistic upswing. It is particularly so in Scotland where visions of independence—of a Northern Kuwait, subsisting in affluence on oil and Scotch—have made themselves strongly visible. Both within Britain and Italy, the lack of really new activities and an overall stagnation of the national economy have served to turn the cause of prosperity for those now poor to trying to rob Peter to pay Paul, that is, to moving existing enterprises to where the living is easier and thus to move unemployment around rather than reduce it.

There is one area of human endeavor which has been conspicuously immune from this chronicle of gradual decline and stagnation. In fact, if ever there was a case of countercyclical prosperty, this is it. The area is, of course, armaments and military spending generally. For years now, arms spending in the United States has exceeded all corporate profits before taxes. Thus, if businesses paid no taxes, or anything to their owners, or retained anything in the business, the total would still not be enough to meet the defense budget which, therefore, has to account for a substantial proportion of federal tax receipts. Indeed, if the social security and other trust funds are taken out of the budget (which they must be, being financed by separate contributions and legally earmarked only for their stated purpose), wars—past, present, and future—account for 52 percent of the federal budget. This has bought, inter alia, 8900 long-range nuclear weapons, though from 200 to 400 would be enough to destroy a third of the population of the U.S.S.R. and three-quarters of its industrial capacity. These are the facts of overkill and distorted priorities. The issue is not a recent one, of course. Bernard Shaw[6] put it this way in 1903:

> **. . . in the arts of life, man invents nothing; but in the arts of death he outdoes Nature herself and produces by chemistry and machinery all the slaughter of plague, pestilence and famine.**

. . . There is nothing in Man's industrial machinery but his greed and sloth: his heart is in his weapons . . . Over . . . battles the people run about the streets yelling with delight, and egg their Governments on to spend hundreds of millions of money in the slaughter, whilst the strongest Ministers dare not spend an extra penny in the pound against the poverty and pestilence through which they themselves daily walk.

The last sentence is surely an accurate description of the actions of the U.S. Congress in 1976 which voted, in part, more money for armaments than even the Pentagon wanted, but whose attempts to help with school lunches, education in general, and job creation ran into Mr. Ford's vetoes. And, of course, it is overkill which puts such actions beyond the bounds of rationality and well within what Harold Lasswell has called the psychopathology of politics. To be sure, there have been and are forces in the United States which oppose thése policies, but they have had conspicuously little help from the managements of businesses, even when those not only did not benefit from but were actually harmed by the war economy.

The last point—the damage done by the war economy—is an extremely important one. There are three salient issues. First, much of the military effort has been justified against its critics by pointing to the alleged "spin-off" that is, the commercially useful by-products of military research and weapons development. While it would be absurd to argue that there has not been any such diffusion, its importance is really very small indeed. For example, a favorite example of the spin-off advocates used to be the ceramic heat shield of missiles which would, one was told, produce better cookware. But the flow was actually in the opposite direction in that existing ceramic technology was used to make heat shields and, anyway, not even the most retarded cooking school dropout would require a casserole which could be heated to 2000°C. In another case, lasers are now used to spotweld detached retinas, but the main focus and support of laser research is its potentially destructive purpose as a "death ray." Not even its potential as a way to fusion power is being explored with comparable zeal. Finally, the whole spin-off notion is operationally absurd from a managerial viewpoint. A nonmilitary example makes the point clear: heart valves are made of a material similar to that of girdles, but nobody suggests that the way to better heart valves is to do more girdle research. No responsible manager would endorse so circuitous a way to the future.

The spin-off examples which can really be substantiated sometimes miss the point. For instance, much new technology on telemetering of vital functions has resulted from space mediine. Intensive care units in hospitals owe a certain debt to these techniques. However, the point of medical care is surely not just hardware but active human attention; the issue is finding doctors and nurses giving that kind of care, instead of the positively veterinarian detachment so often found in reality. It is not so much telemetering information as being able to act on it and cure the patient, and there, as we said earlier, innovation has been lagging.

The development of the spin-off products also raises another issue. Military research and development have introduced some appallingly bad habits into research management. They include indifference to costs and a demand that product research be paid for separately by government instead of being a regular business expense. There is a need for"'supporting services," including a proliferating bureaucracy. There are new and narrow specialties which are difficult to convert once the need has passed, and much work is based on assorted hairsplitting over existing specifications which may become positively theological in intensity.

The same shortcomings, notably the indifference to costs and the bureaucratization, have carried over into other aspects of product development. As a result, military or space discoveries have to be practically reinvented as part of their commercial development. We would not be getting electronic calculators for $7.99 if the circuit chips carried Pentagon price tags. For these reasons it is absurd to claim usefulness in other areas for the management method of military-space contracting. "If we can build all those missiles and put a man on the moon, why can't we . . ." —that's how that refrain sounds. But the main difference between these efforts and others is that there money does not count. There was no way of deciding a "fair price" for putting a man on the moon and thus no central economic parameter, other than what the American public could be politically persuaded to swallow. By contrast, new methods of generating energy or transportation or ways to desalt seawater must compete with established and existing sources, and the competition is in large measure simply on price, even though other considerations may partially supersede it. This holds even for medical treatment, for instance, in kidney machines and clotting factor therapy for hemophilia.

In fact, military firms do not, in general, behave as in a conventional profit model. Since the traditional decisions of private enterprise—what to make, how to make it, in what quantity, at what price, and with whose money—are largely set by government in such firms, what is maximized is sales rather than profit.[7] Meanwhile, in 1971–72 some 68 percent of federal research funds were allocated to military and space work[8] and those, let it be noted, were lean years followed by fatter ones, what with MIRV and MARV missiles, the B-1 bomber, Trident submarine, and cruise missiles. These projects have made preemptive demands on the nation's engineering talent. The large proportion of engineers working for the military (which exceeds 80 percent in some areas) has effectively closed the supply of engineering talent to other fields, such as energy, in which it would have contributed more to the nation's real security than piling on more overkill. One of the more disgraceful legislative records concerns the fate of "conversion" legislation, designed to cushion the transfer of engineers and scientists to nonmilitary specialties once contracts are finished. No such laws ever emerged from congressional commmittees, even though they have been routinely introduced ever since Sen. George McGovern's first bill in 1963. Contractors for the military are in fact discouraged from undertaking such planning; and, let it be added, some of their managements admit to their incompetence in nonmilitary fields and with good reason. When a contractor evidently emancipates itself from dependence on military jobs, the firm is regarded as one of the "undeserving poor" for further contracts. A more humbe stance—laced, as we have heard recently, with some strategically placed gifts—appears to be more profitable.

That such mismanagement of the nation's most strategic talent resources is tolerated, especially by the business community, is no doubt related to the extraordinarily durable myth of war preparations as a source of prosperity.[9] Americans remember that the renewed depression of 1938 was aborted in part by war preparations (the more imaginative New Deal programs having run their course by that time). The Korean war produced no such effects, however, and as for the Vietnam war, it was, among other things, the worst disaster for world capitalism since the 1930s. The war was, as Mr. Wilbur Mills once admitted in his days of power and glory, financed by deficit spending because if taxes had been raised instead to pay for it, popular support would have evaporated even sooner than it did. As it was, the inflationary effect of deficit financing bore a heavy responsibility for the round of inflation that began in 1969 and which led to the ham-handed compensatory promotion of the depression of 1974–75 whose end, at least with respect to the disgracefully high unemployment rate, is not in sight. Moreover, the United States did not enforce any control over currency transfers. European countries accepted and held dollars, ultimately in the form of Eurodollars which, as we noted earlier, resemble rubber checks. Thus inflation was exported to boot and foreign countries were induced to pay in part for the Vietnam war by having dollars which were later devalued. Presently, deflation and unemployment crossed the Atlantic as well, producing further strains in Europe. The near-miss of the Italian Communists in the 1976 elections, Britain's drift into bankruptcy, and unpleasant authoritarian rumblings in West Germany and France are cases in point. The orderly fixed current exchange rates have meanwhile been replaced by a "float" in which currencies are not regarded merely as exchange media for the purchase of goods and services but as investment media. And so the Arabs dump sterling and buy Swiss francs with the result that Britain's inflation goes into high gear and the Swiss franc rises to 46 cents U.S. and thus prices Switzerland out of its exports and, to a great extent, even out of American tourism. All this is a far cry indeed from the happy prosperous days of Rosie the Riveter in World War II. And yet the delusion persists.

Major weapons programs are touted primarily for their effects on jobs which in turn are carefully broken down by congressional districts. The amount of largesse per favorable vote is thus known in advance and, given the current unemployment, makes for powerful pressures even on members of Congress who would otherwise be politically opposed to the programs. The B-1 bomber was a case in point. The concept of this $90 billion project owed much to the "nothing like a well-bred horse" sentimentality of the old horse cavalry afficionado; after all, even with the enormously inflated officer corps, it is hard to find too many chiefs jobs, commanding a bunch of machines like missiles. What with such shaky military need its boosters tried to sell the project as a source of jobs even though a study by the prime contractor's own economic consultants showed that housing would have provided 70,000 more jobs for the money. During the 1976 vice-presidential debates Senator Mondale's votes against the B-1 were called "killing jobs" by his opponent, Senator Dole.

Such analyses showed that the "multiplier effect" of nonmilitary jobs is substantially greater than that of the arms jobs. Work which creates more industrial activity or which satisfies a real demand is intrinsically more productive of jobs than arms work which does neither. In June 1977 President Carter scrapped the B-1 bomber, amid loud clamor over the job impact. The shock, however, was mitigated by new work on the cruise missile, the neutron bomb, and the MX "subway" missile. Like the Hydra of old, the arms race sprouted three heads where one had been chopped off and so the overkill boondoggles continue.

There are several additional reasons to explain why the innovation problems described here will not soon be remedied. First, there are three schools of thought which suggest that we should not or cannot make a serious effort. The first is the elitist view that "we don't even need all these wretched innovations," as it was once put to the writer by a protagonist of this viewpoint who was, however, careful to single out TV and jet planes as examples, rather than antibiotics. But such views are not only subjective, they suggest that science can be turned off in some way, to everyone's benefit. The argument is not whether we need or do not need, but what gets the support and the preferences, and that is where we have been going wrong.

This view is really the same as more or less giving up. It was echoed very strongly in President Ford's remarks at the economic summit conference of San Juan on June 27, 1976, that the industrial countries had "overcommitted" themselves economically to improve social conditions and raise their citizens' standard of living.[10] People, in other words, have been having it too good. This, of course, is nonsense, gven the social problems of all the participating countries, and, in any event, such views are politically untenable unless accompanied by proposals for a true sharing of hardships within each society. The fact is that we are faced with a variety of problems in resource use, resource efficiency, and ways of living for which excellent approaches to solutions exist—provided we do not waste the intellectual resources required for their solution on other things.

There are also those who maintain that we *should not* innovate because we have sinned and deserve to be cut back, for the benefit of other countries, or the poor, or the physical world, or whatever. It is interesting that this approach tends to come from the political left, but leads to the same result as the conservative approach espoused by Mr. Ford—"it's too good for 'em." One successful book along these lines projects a future much like that of the antiutopias of science fiction but gives detailed instructions for a bucolic last stand for the provident and affluent, very much in the old "backs to the wall and save the last bullet for the little woman" tradition of the days of Empire. Finally, there are those who, inspired by the apocalyptic projections of Arnold Toynbee and his followers, regard the "decline" as irreversible—a sort of toilet flush of history. Their reasoning also leads them to last stands and such. One would not have to consider such views in as much detail were it not for the fact that they appear to have a following precisely among groups of intellectuals who should be the last to give up the struggle.

A second set of policies which run counter to potential improvement in the innovation field is to be found in the attitudes of business executives themselves. In many industries, one has the impression that managements spend more effort in the publicity media explaining that something cannot be done than in serious research. Part and parcel of this approach is the endless lobbying effort against mandated changes in operation, followed by administrative and court challenges, inordinate delays, enormous costs, and mountains of paper. One would certainly not in any way wish to see due process of law abridged, but it should be recognized that such exercises have produced a lot of bureaucracies *on both sides.* These tend to live in a sort of symbiotic relationship, or at least in one of antagonistic cooperation, like prizefighters required to bash each other periodically, according to set rules, so that the public goes on supporting them.

In this connection, one facet of conventional wisdom deserves reexamination. It is that, in the affluence of the 1950s and 1960s, managements have reconciled themselves to the existence of unions and social legislation, as in safety, the environment, employment conditions, and the like. Nothing could be further from the truth—as clearly shown by the Republican election campaign of 1976, similar resurgences of the Right in Europe, and Mr. Ford's remarks in San Juan. This is usually called the "swing of the pendulum" because the trends toward social legislation have "gone too far," or the inevitability of "going two steps forward and one step back." As to the former, there is no method of predicting the amplitude or frequency or whether the pendulum even exists; if it does, let us see now, what is a 10-year swing into misery as a proportion of your remaining active and healthy years? And on the "two forward, one back" procedure, that one originated as a penance for Christian pilgrims; there is no previous record of its being touted as a sound method of getting from A to B.

Thus, the current gutting of higher education which is taking place in the United States and, in different form, elsewhere in the West, is looked upon as a correction of this kind. Nothing could be more disastrous. As it is, in the United States natural science and engineering graduates have declined as a proportion of all graduates and remained stagnant in actual numbers.[11] Moreover, for a variety of reasons, the standard of preparation has been declining,[12] so that more remedial work than previously is required at the university level precisely when the amount of knowledge to be imparted is greater than ever. The number of new scientists thus bears some resemblance to the arithmetic of the late Benito Mussolini, who in 1938 cut his army divisions from three regiments to two so that he could still tell the world he had 60 divisions when in fact he had about half that number. It is excellence which brings good innovation, not mere competence, and that is a frail flower in an atmosphere of student "processing" amidst cutbacks. Some good scientists, moreover, still find it hard to get jobs, and for those who lose them later in life, the impact is still catastrophic. The reason for this waste is that it takes the formulation of sound objectives, good organization, and adequate investment; and, though there have been some improvements since the Nixon regime, there is still no real commitment.

In advocating these changes in our research organization and design, one need not presuppose any sweeping changes in society; a reorientation of priorities is what is mainly needed. Capitalist and communist countries have been equally remiss in this;[13] indeed, the military emphasis is even stronger in the U.S.S.R. The Tu-144 supersonic jet booms its way across Siberia, but the potatoes cannot be delivered to Moscow with efficiency. The job, however, must be done. As we consider housing, energy, transportation, production design, and health, the list of unmet needs is almost endless. Such lists will not be presented here, however, because without a proper commitment, they would be as relevant to our needs as a child's "Dear Santa" letter. We have arrived at our current sad state for several reasons set forth here among which the misuse of technology and science for military purposes is the principal and most destructive one. Unless and until we recognize that neither investment nor talent can be wasted in this way, we shall not be able to meet our challenges—the "tides" of our epigraph—and we will surely "lose our ventures" as a result.

NOTES AND REFERENCES

1. Consider, for instance, quantitative methods of business analysis: how many businesses *really* and *regularly* use mathematical programming, decision theory, inventory modeling, statistical quality control? Those in the field, including the writer, are still preaching to the barely converted.

2. For example, J. E. Ullmann and S. E. Gluck, *Manufacturing Management* (New York: Holt, Rinehart and Winston, 1968), p. 22; J. E. Ullmann, "Some Economic Aspects of Automobile Safety Devices," in *Passenger Car Design and Highway Safety* (Mt. Vernon, N.Y.: Consumers Union of the United States, 1962), p. 248 ff; J. E. Ullmann (ed.), *Product Innovation in Selected Industries* (Hempstead, N.Y.: Hofstra University Press, 1967).

3. National Science Board, *Science Indicators, 1974* (Washington, D.C.: National Science Foundation, 1975), pp. 4, 5, 16, 33, and 106.

4. J. E. Ullmann, *Productivity, Innovation and Economy of Scale* (in progress).

5. *Business Week*, May 17, 1976, pp. 92–98.

6. G. B. Shaw, *Man and Superman* (Baltimore: Penguin, 1952), pp. 145–146.

7. J. Gorgol and I. Kleinfeld, *The Military Industrial Firm* (New York: Praeger, 1972).

8. National Science Board, op. cit., p. 6.

9. For an extensive discussion of this issue, see S. Melman, *The Permanent War Economy* (New York: Simon & Schuster, 1973).

10. The New York *Times*, June 27, 1976, p. 1.

11. National Science Board, op. cit., pp. 134–135.

12. For a recent substantiation, see F. E. Armbruster et al., *The U.S. Primary and Secondary Schools* (Croton-on-Hudson, N.Y.: Hudson Institute, 1976).

13. It was long thought that the elimination of the profit motive would usher in an era of invariably beneficient science; but, in his desire to be sympathetic, even so excellent a Western scientist as J. D. Bernal had to swallow Trofim Lysenko as part of the heavy hand that has lain on the not very productive Soviet science establishment. See J. D. Bernal, *Science in History* (London: Watts, 1954), pp. 666–669.

24

GLOBAL ECONOMIC PROBLEMS AND TRANSNATIONAL CORPORATIONS

KURT WALDHEIM
Secretary General of the United Nations

When considering global economic problems, there is often a belief that there exists somewhere, if it only could be found, some new formula, concept, or plan which would resolve all the problems confronting the world. Sometimes it is as if another John Maynard Keynes, or a modern Thomas Jefferson, is eagerly awaited to suddenly lighten the darkness and point out such a path. But, unfortunately, no such simple answers exist. In this complex world, leadership can be based only on a better understanding of the nature of each individual crisis. In this process the contributions of all—politicians, government officials, business and academic communities, trade unions, and concerned citizens—are needed now to find a solution. Otherwise, the world's problems will continue to increase until they become completely overwhelming.

One of the main functions of the United Nations (UN) is to evaluate global issues in a manner which will lead to constructive and mutually beneficial negotiations on difficult problems. Even when these appear to be almost insoluble, this negotiating process has a value of its own. It keeps the effort to tackle issues alive, and it also acts as a safety valve for emotions and frustrations which otherwise might explode in harmful and dangerous ways. This basic fact about the UN is sometimes overlooked because of the very natural public desire to see positive results achieved with speed.

Over the past 30 years the UN has forged an instrument which is now very different in many respects from that which was envisaged in 1945. To ignore this hard-won experience would be as foolish as if the ancestors of Americans had determined, 30 years after the American Revolution, that there was no point in continuing with a system which had failed to fulfill all the glittering ambitions of 1776. The question, therefore, that presently confronts the World Organization is whether it can be adapted, and if need be reformed, to meet new imperatives.

The economic system established at Bretton Woods proved, for a considerable period, to work well for the growth of the industrial countries. It enabled them to shake off the effects of World War II much quicker than anyone had imagined possible. But as the process of decolonization accelerated and new nations emerged, an increasing awareness developed of the scale of the imbalance between the industrialized and the developing nations. Although progress could be recorded in almost all countries and all sectors, and in spite of a great deal of bilateral and multilateral assistance, the gulf between the affluent few and impoverished many has continued to widen. All available indications are that unless fundamental policy changes are made, the situation cannot be corrected in the foreseeable future.

Looming above everything is the virtual certainty that the population of the world, which has recently passed the 4-billion mark, will double in the next three decades. The world has barely begun to plan and organize itself for that situation. Today some 500 million people live on the edge of starvation. Throughout the developing world there is a chronic shortage of basic needs, particularly health, education, and social services. How are the unborn billions to be fed, educated, housed, and employed when the situation is already so desperate for so many? The complaint of the Third World has been that the old economic system was advantageous for the few and inequitable for the many. In current circumstances it may also be argued that the old system is now not even adequate for the affluent nations. This is the real significance in the new awareness that the developed world also has a stake in the emergence of a more efficient and equitable international economic order.

Obviously, in evolving new approaches, care must be taken not to discard those elements in the old which have proved to be valuable and efficient. It is a matter not of destroying a system, but of making the best use of the old and incorporating new ideas, techniques, and approaches to resolve global economic problems. It must be recognized that what is really in contention is a situation which is in its nature economic, but which has much wider practical implications. In the past the world, and consequently the UN, was sometimes paralyzed by the great ideological and political disputes between the East and the West. Today it is faced by the possibility of a polarization between the rich and the poor, which could have very similar consequences.

There are various new ingredients in what is not, after all, basically a new situation. Individually, many of the poorer nations may be small and powerless. Collectively, they not only represent the majority of the world's population but also have an important part of its natural resources. Their situation is not altogether unlike that in the United States when the trade unions, individually weak, drew together in large groups and created a power which they had never had before. That the poorer countries are now organizing themselves for negotiation and a collective approach is not surprising. Done in the right way and in a spirit of cooperation, this concerted effort among developing countries should be viewed as a positive development which can contribute to the integration and stabilization of the world community, just as the development of trade unions proved to be essential to the functioning of industrial societies.

This is what has been happening in recent years. In fact, this trend has been increasingly apparent within the UN. Since the early 1960s it was this new cohesiveness which made it possible for developing nations to focus the attention of the world on the great global economic and social problems of the day. Other manifestations of this initiative were apparent in the UN world conferences on trade and development, environment, population, food, the role of women in society, industrialization, the law of the sea, and human settlements, as well as in the debates at the sixth and seventh special sessions of the General Assembly on the establishment of a new international economic order. As a result of these negotiations, the need for a new approach is now universally accepted. Of course, there remain major areas of disagreement, but the debate on principles has been carried so far that if the present momentum is maintained, serious negotiations could now achieve an important breakthrough in some areas of international relations, which have been the subject of so much dispute and frustration in the past.

As part of this process of reappraisal, it is not surprising that much attention today is devoted to the role of the transnational corporations. It is important to emphasize that the involvement of the UN in this delicate and complex problem was not born of hostile attitudes, but was created out of a real desire to improve the contribution of transnational corporations to national development. Moreover, it is increasingly recognized that this is a problem which cannot be left simply to the normal processes of bilateral negotiations between governments and corporations.

It became clear during the 1960s that the internationalization of production was emerging as one of the most pervasive components in economic relations between countries, surpassing in financial terms the intranational transactions which characterized the classical operation of world trade. It was evident that such a dynamic phenomenon could not and should not remain outside the purview of international institutions which had effectively developed means of monitoring, and to some extent regulating, other aspects of economic activity. It is understandable that there should be concern in many quarters about the effect of global corporate strategies on national economies. These are often evolved and directed from a central headquarters in a major industrialized nation and have as their basic objective the maximization of global production and profits. Such policies, which do not necessarily coincide with the national plan, policies, aspirations, and sensitivities of many nations, especially those at an early stage of their development, are of particular concern to developing countries, where substantial new investments usually have a very considerable impact upon the societies into which they are introduced.

What is at stake, therefore, is not only development objectives, but the chosen style of development. There are often wide divergences between the basic policies of large corporations and those of the nations in which they operate. Reconciliation between these objectives is often possible and, given the universal desire for rapid development and the potentialities offered to this end by transnational enterprises, areas of joint advantage may be frequently discovered. But the conditions of association must be very carefully pondered by both parties, and the proper insertion of any project in the framework of national plans must always be scrupulously examined. In other words, it is necessary to search for the coincidence of national and corporate interests rather than to assume it. Furthermore, it must be recognized that there are instances where the clear perception of material advantages is hard to discern and which, even when it is realized, will not necessarily prevail over attitudes or emotions which have their roots in very different ideologies, cultures, or political and social imperatives.

This means that developing countries must be increasingly selective in their approach to transnational corporations, and the factor that has permeated the discussions in the UN on this topic is that decisions of the governments of developing countries should be based on a critical and sophisticated analysis carried out in terms of economic and other relevant criteria. There is clearly an urgent need for governments of new countries to improve their institutional mechanisms for dealing with transnational corporations. But it has also become evident that the UN must go further in this field. A central theme which has run through all the discussions and reports is the search for a reasonable "accountability" to the international community. This is not easy to define or to bring about.

As early as 1948, the UN played a pivotal role in the preparation of the Havana Charter which sought to institutionalize international monitoring and control of trade and production. While, in retrospect, the timing of such a role may have proved inopportune, coordinated international action in this matter was considered essential. The UN has been involved in this subject in various ways since that time and a number of UN organizations, such as UNCTAD and ILO, are presently active in specific areas. In 1974, however, the Economic and Social Council came to the unanimous conclusion that, given the growing importance of this subject, the necessary machinery should be established to deal with this matter in an overall manner and on a continuing basis.

It therefore established the Commission on Transnational Corporations—an intergovernmental body composed of 48 governments—as well as the Center on Transnational Corporations, within the UN Secretariat. The tasks of the Commission and the Center are geared to three objectives. First, to further the understanding of the nature and the political, legal, economic, and social effects of the activities of transnational corporations. Second, to secure effective international arrangements for the operations of transnational corporations. Third, to strengthen the negotiating capacity of most developing countries in their dealings with transnational corporations.

The Commission has already laid the foundation upon which the future work of the UN in this field will be built. The decisions which have been taken by the Commission and, equally important, the spirit in which they were taken, provide important indicators of the progress that can be expected during the next few years. Its meetings have so far been characterized by a determined effort on the part of all governments to avoid confrontation and to make progress through the achievement of consensus decisions. While many of the differences that have manifested themselves in the past still exist, all members of the Commission recognized the necessity not to be hamstrung by them. Full and unanimous agreement has been reached on initial areas to be given close attention and on the modalities to be followed. The significance of this approach should not be underestimated, for the objective has been to prepare the ground effectively so as to yield results within a reasonable period of time. The progress made so far has reflected a commitment by governments to take effective action on this subject through the UN.

From the dialog and debate, international rules of behavior, culminating in a comprehensive and equitable code of conduct, could emerge. This is very much needed, especially as international law in this field is sketchy and very controversial. It cannot be expected that this will be achieved rapidly. Nonetheless, the popular demand for such a set of rules and the ultimate advantage which they would offer to all parties are so great that the initiation of serious UN work in this field cannot be deferred. The Commission has already decided to assign the highest priority to the preparation of such a code. Toward this end, it has established a working group whose task is to prepare a full text of the code by the spring of 1978.

At the governmental level a more precise articulation of views and proposals on a code is necessary. Toward this goal two procedures are envisaged. First, individual governments will be invited to submit their views and proposals. Second, regional meetings will be organized to bring together representatives of developing countries in Africa, Asia, and Latin America, respectively, with a view to defining proposals for a code in the light of the particular conditions and needs in each of the regions. The Commission has also recognized the necessity of receiving inputs from nongovernmental interested parties, in particular from business, trade unions, and consumer groups. Their views and proposals on a code of conduct are being solicited and will be placed before the working group. Provision has also been made for the participation in the working group, in an advisory capacity, of individuals with profound experience in business, trade unions, and other interest groups.

This decision actually goes beyond the work on the code of conduct. When establishing the Commission, the Economic and Social Council called upon it to select persons with extensive practical experience in the areas mentioned above so that they can be associated with its work in an appropriate manner. The Commission has requested that, after consultations with all members of the Commission, the names of 12 to 15 persons with extensive practical experience in trade unions, business, consumer groups, and other public interest groups be proposed to it by the Secretary General. These persons will then be available to assist, not only the working group but also the Commission itself.

The Center has been requested to prepare two important documents. One will deal with the various substantive issues related to the scope and content of the code to help governments when defining their own views and proposals. The second document will focus on issues related to the actual formulation of the code, particularly the structural alternatives and their implications, including possible institutional arrangements. Of course, the working group has been requested also to take into account the relevant work done elsewhere, both within and outside the UN system, such as UNCTAD or the OECD.

While stressing that the formulation of a code of conduct receive the highest priority, the Commission recognized the importance of moving ahead concurrently in a number of other areas. In this connection, the Commission requested the Center to move ahead speedily with the collection of information of a general or specific nature, including the preparation of profiles on individual transnational corporations. The Commission also stressed the importance of moving ahead speedily with the development of international standards for corporate reporting. In this regard, a group of experts has been constituted for the purpose of identifying a minimun list of items for inclusion in corporate reports.

In the equally important area of research, the Commission has decided on a considerable amount of work to be carried out by the Center, ranging from a comprehensive integrated survey of the role of transnational corporations in world development to in-depth studies covering such vital issues as the impact of transnational corporations on the balance of payments (particularly of developing countries), the effects of investments by transnational corporations on investment, and production by domestic enterprises and the effects of transnational corporations on employment. In addition, the Center will examine the role and impact of transnational corporations in a number of sectors, notably in banking, insurance, shipping, tourism, and the extractive, food, and pharmaceutical industries.

The Commission has also attached great importance and urgency to the Center's technical cooperation program which is aimed at strengthening the negotiating capability of the developing countries. This assistance will take a variety of forms. Advisers will be made available to requesting governments to assist them on matters which could range from national investment policies and legislation to their application to specific investment proposals. Training workshops for government officials will also be organized and inquiries from governments for specific information will also be responded to. Effective and informed negotiators on both sides of the table can reduce significantly the areas of contention, which is clearly in the interest of all concerned.

The direct involvement of the UN in the subject of the transnational corporations is a very important innovation and the progress achieved so far substantiates that it is a very important one. The aim is to reach a better modus vivendi in which the positive effects of transnational corporations will be enhanced and their negative effects reduced, thereby achieving a better distribution of the benefits.

In conclusion, it should be stressed again that the present situation is one in which not only the collective political will of governments is essential to the solution of world problems, but in which other agencies, organizations, and machinery must be actively involved as well. What might be called the Second Tier—consisting of the business and academic communities, scientific and technical specialists, nongovernmental organizations, and concerned individuals—have a major part to play. Their role is twofold—produce ideas and facts for governments and international organizations, and assist in the implementation of specific policies for national and international action once they have been agreed upon by the governments concerned.

All this will require vision, imagination, hard work, and a commitment to the conviction that things cannot and must not continue as they are now. It is in the interest of all, whether they be in business or government, or any of the major professions, and whether they live in developed or developing countries, that these problems can be approached and resolved constructively and peacefully. Toward achieving that end, the UN serves increasingly as a catalyst for the management of global economic problems through international cooperation.

25

THE ENERGY CRISIS AND THE CAPITAL SHORTAGE

RICHARD R. WEEKS
Dean and Professor of Marketing Management,
College of Business Administration,
University of Rhode Island

There will be managers in the future. The future always moves toward us in a relentless, steady, and sometimes accelerated fashion. The pathologists can predict with certainty that bleeding will always stop. Managers can predict with certainity that the future will eventually involve them. Their concern is whether or not they are prepared for the changing social, economic, technological, and political environments that are emerging as the future approaches them.

John F. Mee

Of the many serious problems facing managers in the future, that of developing adequate energy sources and the technologies needed to utilize them ranks at the top of the list. There is far too little time remaining before world reserves of petroleum are exhausted; massive sums of capital must be made available during the next quarter century to develop new sources of energy and to increase efficient utilization of current supplies. Providing the needed capital will be exceedingly difficult, and incentives must be sufficient to encourage industry to devote maximum effort to solving the energy problem. Failure to find adequate solutions will not only seriously diminish the quality of life-style, but threaten our economic, social, and political institutions as well.

ENERGY PROBLEM IN PERSPECTIVE

While the energy problem has been broadly recognized, it is not well understood and far too little has been done about it. The public was quick to forget the energy problems of 1973 and early 1974 and conservation efforts instituted at that time were largely ignored. There was a rush back to intermediate and large automobiles, and purchases of small cars fell off. Yet, the long-term energy problem becomes more serious as every day passes and the time remaining to find solutions becomes shorter. The United States must begin to act now if timely solutions are to be found.

Shortage of Petroleum

Petroleum source fuels, which supply 76 percent of our current domestic energy, will be all but exhausted by the end of this century. Studies by the U.S. Geological Survey and the National Academy of Sciences show that petroleum production in the United States has already peaked and will be declining sharply by the mid-1980s. World production will probably peak soon and start to decline before the turn of the century.[1] New oil and gas deposits will be discovered, of course, but they will be insufficient for our dependence on petroleum to continue. For example, the Prudhoe Bay deposit, the largest discovery of oil and gas in North America in years, will yield by current estimates only a one-year supply of gas and a two-year supply of oil at present U.S. consumption rates.[2]

Project Independence was designed to make the United States self-sufficient from an energy standpoint, but a realistic assessment suggests that it will not only fail to achieve its goal, but will also fail to halt the erosion of our ability to supply our energy needs. Management faces both short-term and long-term problems: greater reliance during the next 25 years on imported oil, with its rapidly increasing price, and the need to develop alternative energy sources by the turn of the century.

Alternative Energy Sources

Alternative energy sources may not be able to fill the void before petroleum reserves are exhausted. Coal, oil shale, and nuclear, thermal, and other suggested forms of energy all suffer from serious technological, capital, or environmental problems.

COAL

Dependence on coal as an alternative energy source would require that we increase current production by approximately fivefold. Technology is available to accomplish both the mining of coal and its liquefaction or gasification, but the infrastructre is not. An enormous investment of capital and manpower would have to be made on the national level, and pollution and mining standards would have to be significantly reduced. The availability of such massive amounts of capital is highly questionable; but even if conversion to coal were accomplished, it has been estimated that total dependence on coal would exhaust our supply in 60 to 70 years, with current rates of increase in energy consumption.[3] At best, then, coal offers an extremely expensive alternative for a limited period of time.

OIL SHALE

Oil shale has most of the problems of coal as an alternative fuel source. An enormous commitment of capital and manpower would be required, serious environmental problems would be created, the supply is limited, and the oil produced would be very expensive. It has been estimated that "at least eight large coal mines would be needed to supply one modest refinery."[4] Oil shale, at best, would seem to be an extremely poor energy substitute for petroleum.

NUCLEAR ENERGY

While enormous amounts of research and development money have been channeled by the federal government into the development of nuclear energy, experts are now questioning whether there is sufficient nuclear fuel in the nation to supply projected needs beyond 1990.[5] Large deposits of uranium ore exist in other countries, but their growing nuclear power programs will create increasing competition for the ore and almost certainly cause its price to rise further. The price of uranium rose from $8 a pound to $35 a pound in two years, and every one-dollar increase in the price could cost American consumers over $200 million annually by the turn of the century.[6]

Early development of the breeder reactor would help alleviate the problem of spiraling cost of ore, as the breeder would "multiply the energy available from a pound of uranium by a factor or 60 or more."[7] The Clinch River demonstration project has been delayed by governmental red tape, however, and we almost certainly will be well into the next century before any appreciable amount of our total energy needs could be produced by breeder reactors.

Environmental hazards created by nuclear energy have been widely discussed and include such problems as radioactive waste storage. The capital needed to develop nuclear energy is enormous, and it has been estimated that nuclear plants begun during the coming year will cost $1 billion for a 1000 megawatt plant. One expert has estimated that it would take over 2500 of these plants by the year 2000 to keep us on our present energy growth curve.[8] Finally, a large growth in the trained manpower available would be needed to significantly increase the output of nuclear energy. Needless to say, the path to total nuclear energy will be extremely expensive and difficult, if not impossible, to accomplish, and it seems most unlikely that we will be able to maintain our present energy growth curve.

THERMAL AND OTHER ENERGY

Thermal energy has the potential of making a greater contribution to our energy pool, but little is being done to make this possible. Space heating and cooling and hot water make up approximately 25 percent of our energy consumption, but the high initial cost of installing thermal collectors and the absence of building codes designed to reduce energy consumption have kept thermal energy from making any meaningful contribution to date. Improved technology is needed, as is the case with other suggested energy sources such as tidal-flow and wind-driven generators. There is a growing need for research to aid in the development of new technology which will both stimulate new energy generation and help conserve energy utilization. Thermal and other energy supplies may help by making a contribution to energy sources, but they appear to offer little hope of providing any meaningful alternative to petroleum-based fuels by the turn of the century.

Overview of the Problem

In the short-term and intermediate-term problems management must contend with rapidly increasing energy costs, while in the long-term problems alternative sources of energy must be developed, as our supply of petroleum-based fuel will be substantially exhausted by the turn of the century. A commitment to research to develop new energy technology is essential, the necessary manpower must be trained, and massive amounts of capital must be provided. The task of providing alternative energy sources will be extremely expensive and difficult to accomplish; numerous reasons cast doubt on our ability to do so in time to avoid a major reduction in our quality of life. The particular concern is whether we can accumulate the capital needed to accomplish the task.

CAPITAL PROBLEM IN PERSPECTIVE

With out standard of living so closely pegged to the availability and cost of energy, we have been living on an energy consumption growth curve that has been doubling about every 10 years. Recognizing the heavy demand that this will create for new power plant capacity and that we have already experienced voltage reductions and brownouts because of difficulty in supplying peak-demand needs, it is useful to examine whether adequate capital will be available to finance construction of the new power plants which will be needed during the next quarter century. Unfortunately, analysis shows that prospects are not bright, and rapid action is needed if overwhelming problems are to be avoided.

Sources of Capital

Historically, the major proportion of our capital has been generated by business firms in the form of undistributed profits and accumulated depreciation reserves. Regrettably, this situation has changed in recent years as profits have dropped in real terms and inflation has eaten away at our investment in real assets. Arthur C. Nielson, Jr., highlighted this problem in a speech:

> **Business profits are inadequate to do the job required. Business savings, when you include depreciation, average from ten to twelve percent of our gross national product and have been declining. Furthermore, inflation has wiped out much of the investment in business assets.**

For example, in 1974 business lost $22 billion of assets through inflation. In fact, in that year U.S. corporations didn't even earn enough to meet their dividend requirements. In other words, many American corporations are slowly going broke. Their debt in relation to equity has been slowly rising for the last fifteen years. For example, in 1960 the debt to equity ratio was forty-five percent—today it is eighty-seven percent. This is a dangerous condition because many businesses are unable to finance their own growth, and some will be unable to ride through the inevitable next recession. . . .

True profits of U.S. companies are overstated due to inflation and some unfortunate shortcomings in our accounting systems. When you adjust for phantom profits created by inflation of inventories and eroded depreciation reserves, true U.S. profits declined sixty percent between 1965 and 1974. The real tax rate paid by corporations was close to eighty percent on the true earnings.[9]

When profits and depreciation reserves are inadequate to provide for sufficient investment in plant and equipment, business must turn to savings in the household sector to provide the additional capital needed. This means that households must be willing to save through reduced consumption to make this possible. The question, of course, is whether sufficient savings will take place to supply the demand for capital investment in the private sector. This is complicated even further by the huge federal deficit, which was increased by $85 billion in 1975. The federal government has to finance this deficit, so it becomes a competitor of the corporate sector in financial markets for these household savings. Thus, business firms have been under extreme pressure to generate capital funds in the debt and equity markets, and difficulties encountered in these markets, particularly in selected sectors, represent major obstacles to future capital formation.

Demand for Capital

Analysis of future requirements for capital during the next quarter century shows that there will be significant pressure for increased capital investment to: (1) satisfy the requirements of safety, health, and environmental legislation (for example, Data Resources, Incorporated, has estimated that as much as 4.5 to 5 percent of total investment in the economy might have to be devoted to pollution abatement over the next decade);[10] (2) provide for expansion of the labor force as our total population grows to 300 million by the turn of the century; (3) finance the inflated cost of inventory and provide the larger inventories needed to service the expanded population; (4) provide for the installation of newly developed capital—intensive technology; and (5) finance expanded sources of energy and the research needed to develop the technology necessary to conserve current sources of energy. Since the middle of the 1960s we have been investing 11 to 12 percent of gross national product annually.[11] It is certainly apparent that industry will need to greatly increase investment during the next 25 years if our standard of living is to remain at its current level. For it to advance, investment will have to increase still further, perhaps to a level as high as 15 percent of gross national product.

Building Power Plants

Since power plants are built by public utilities, it is necessary to consider the access of public utilities to capital markets as some sectors have much greater difficulty than others in borrowing funds. Unfortunately, this is becoming increasingly true of public utilities. Recent deterioration in the balance sheets of public utilities has been caused by low rates of return mandated by utility commissions under extreme pressure from consumer groups. Because of low rates of return and the negative effect of inflation on future earnings, it is no wonder that there has been great reluctance to invest in utilities where the net real expected rate of return is lower than available alternatives. As a consequence, public utilities frequently have difficulty gaining access to equity and long-term debt markets and have had to turn increasingly to short-term money and bank loans to finance their capital investment. Clearly, the amount of capital required to build new power plants during the next 25 years cannot be raised through short-term money and bank loans.

Overview of the Problem

The capital problem which we face has been created by sagging profits and inflation-reduced depreciation reserve on the supply side, and by multiple pressures for increased corporate investment on the demand side. Federal competition for savings has drained off monies which might otherwise have been available for corporate investment. Access to equity and debt markets has been particularly difficult for public utilities, where regulated rates of return have lagged and debt/equity ratios have deteriorated. Unfortunately, demand for new energy will cause public utilities to make massive new capital investments in power plants during the next quarter century, and their ability to finance this investment is questionable. Immediate action is needed on several fronts to keep the energy crisis from growing beyond manageable proportions and imposing drastic reductions on our standard of living.

RECOMMENDATION FOR ACTION

There is no simple solution to the energy crisis, but there are a number of things which can and should be done as rapidly as possible to provide relief. At the heart of the matter is our need to develop a long-run comprehensive energy policy for the nation. The Energy Policy and Conservation Act of 1975 has not accomplished this. In fact, legislation passed by Congress since 1973 seems to have weakened rather than strengthened energy producers, who have lost the percentage depletion allowance, have been subjected to price controls on oil and natural gas, are threatened by divestiture, and face increasing governmental regulations and controls which discourage exploration for and production of new energy sources. Congress seems unable to concern itself with any long-run project other than the next election, and our time horizons simply must be lengthened if solutions are to be found. Some of the needed changes worthy of management support and action at this time include greater participation by business leaders in government at all levels, greater investment in research aimed at the development of new energy technology, and greater attention to conservation measures.

Government

Since business functions in an environment dominated by the influence of government policies, management must assume a more active role and provide even greater leadership to bring about constructive change in legislation and policy. Business leaders should seek positions in Congress and state legislative bodies to influence the development of a comprehensive energy policy.

PROVIDE TAX INCENTIVES

Incentives must be provided to accelerate the development of new energy sources. New legislation is needed to:

1. Index depreciation to the rate of inflation.[12] This would halt the problem of inflation eroding investment in business assets and serve as a major stimulus to new investment.
2. Raise the investment tax credit. This would encourage business to increase investment in modern plant and equipment.
3. Eliminate double taxation of dividends. This tax both discourages savings and encourages debt financing.
4. Cut the corporate profits tax. By reducing the tax rate charged, additional profit will be available for capital investment.
5. Remove the capital gains tax. Many of our major competing countries do not have this tax, which applies to inflated gains as well as real gains and reduces the amount which would otherwise be available for capital investment.

These changes should go far to improve our competitive environment and provide incentives to stimulate the massive capital investment which will be required during the next quarter century.

REMOVE ARTIFICIAL CONTROLS

Energy producers have been limited in their efforts to earn larger profits to finance their rising capital investment needs. Removing artificial controls on oil and gas would let profits rise to levels sufficient to finance much of their investment needs and would also encourage greater efforts to reduce energy consumption. The prevailing attitude that we have a right to cheap energy must be altered, and controls must be removed if sufficient capital investment is to take place to meet our expanding energy needs.

REMOVE THREAT OF DIVESTITURE

The Senate Judiciary Committee's eight to seven vote approving a bill to break up the nation's 18 largest oil companies is indicative of the negative environment in Congress toward our energy producing companies. This bill must not pass and the threat of divestiture must be removed. Companies threatened with divestiture cannot be expected to make major commitments needed to provide new sources of energy. Reluctance to spend huge sums of money for oil exploration offshore Alaska and in the Georges Bank and Baltimore Canyon areas, for example, can only impede exploration for new energy sources and increase our dependence on foreign oil.

PROVIDE RATE RELIEF

State utility commissions must provide utilities with the rate relief needed to raise their return on investment so they can go to the equity and bond markets to raise the necessary massive amounts of capital. Decisions must be based on the financial realities of the marketplace, not on political considerations. Utilities must greatly improve their badly eroded financial positions if they are to supply our increasing energy needs.

Research

The development of approaches that are just beyond current technology would do much to conserve consumption of current energy sources, and research must concentrate on gaining these breakthroughs. The Energy Research and Development Administration (ERDA) represents the main source of funding for energy research. The ERDA budget is $2.4 billion, with $700 million going to nuclear research, $300 million to research on fusion, and $160 million earmarked for solar energy. While this is a large sum of money which should produce substantial results, bureaucratic red tape and political maneuvering have kept ERDA from having its expected impact. For example, the previously mentioned Clinch River demonstration project has been delayed, and initial funding for the proposed Solar Energy Research Institute has been reduced from the $50 million recommended by the National Academy of Sciences to about $5 million, midst intense political maneuvering over the location of the institute.

Management must focus its efforts on the development of new energy technology to supplement ERDA's efforts. A massive research and development effort is essential if we are to delay beyond the turn of the century the conversion from relatively cheaper petroleum-based fuels to other energy sources.

Conservation

We must develop new technology and apply existing technology to conserve current energy sources. Management must press conservation on all fronts by doing such things as insulating buildings, insulating heat pipes and ducts, installing storm windows, installing solar collectors, turing down thermostats, turning out unnecessary lights, and installing energy-efficient equipment and manufacturing processes. In addition, management should press for substantially higher taxes on large automobiles to discourage ownership of these heavy energy consumers, and should fight for new building codes which mandate the use of energy-efficient structures. While much has been written about the energy crisis, we continue to build inefficient cars and buildings without considering their impact on future energy consumption.

Much can be done that is not being done; management must move to apply strict conservation measures so we can get off the 10-year doubling curve in energy consumption. We have no choice; we must reduce energy consumption, for we live in a finite world with limited resources, many of which are being rapidly exhausted. Failure to act rapidly and aggressively almost certainly means an early end to the era of petroleum-based fuels, great reductions in our standard of living and quality of life, and changes in our economic, social, and political systems, which are terrifying to contemplate.

NOTES AND REFERENCES

1. Lewis D. Conta, "Our Nation's Energy Policies: Are We on the Right Track?" Essay invited by Beta Gamma Sigma, St. Louis, March 1976, p. 1.

2. Ibid.

3. Conta, op. cit., p. 2.

4. Ibid.

5. William M. Carley, "Fuel Shortage Forecast for U.S. Nuclear Plants within Decade or Two," *The Wall Street Journal*, June 7, 1976, p. 1.

6. Ibid.

7. Conta, op. cit. p. 2.

8. Ibid. pp. 2–3.

9. Arthur C. Nielson, Jr., "The American Business System: Its Present Strengths and Weaknesses and How It Might Be Improved," paper presented to the American Assembly of Collegiate Schools of Business Atlanta, Apr. 29, 1976, pp. 18–20.

10. Andrew F. Brimmer, "Capital Shortage: Real or Imagined," The Tenth Annual William K. McInally Memorial Lecture, Graduate School of Business Administration, the University of Michigan, Jan. 8, 1976, p. 14.

11. Ibid., p. 10.

12. Ibid. p. 20; Brimmer estimates that each dollar of revenue given up through this approach would produce 71 cents in the form of higher real capital expenditures.

26

THE ROAD AHEAD FOR MANAGEMENT: Evolution or Obsolescence

H. J. ZOFFER
Dean, Graduate School of Business,
University of Pittsburgh

Countless treatises have been written on the role of management in contemporary society, the process of management, the training of managers, and the managerial environment of the future. Inevitably the conclusions suggest that most of the problems faced by management today will become more severe, require additional competence on the part of the manager, and demand a need for continuing education of a quantity and quality not previously necessary. What management will look like some years ahead, be the prognostication for 5 or 50 years, depends almost entirely on what assumptions are made about a variety of questions such as the state of technology at that time, the level of acceleration of life-style changes, and the future role of the public sector.

One can come to any desired conclusion by varying the assumptions, changing the paradigm, and slightly amending the parameters of the matrix. By adopting the predictions of the *Limits to Growth,*[1] an environment can be structured which automatically sets the requirements for one kind of management posture needed in the years ahead. If one postulates the social order to be in chaos, the demands on managers become so onerous as to suggest that walking on water would be a proper skill to instill in tomorrow's managers. If one adopts a position of more equanimity, with more confidence in the ability of the system to solve its problems on an ongoing basis, the requirements of management and managers become less dramatic. In that case, one focuses on improved quality and the ability to deal with a complex environment. Such prognositications always end with confidence in mankind's ability to meet the task ahead.

The skepticism implied here suggests that any prediction of the management milieu of the future is tantamount to predicting the future of society. The societal fabric is composed of artifacts, currently known as institutions, which have been created to serve the needs of society. To the extent that these institutions continue, presumably they will need someone or some force to do something with regard to maintaining them. To the extent that institutions are no longer the device by which society operates, an entirely different set of considerations is brought into play. It is conceivable in the abstract, but almost impossible to formulate in the specific, that governments, hospitals, educational institutions, social agencies, and other institutions serving society will not continue to be a crucial part of our framework in the future. Perhaps the evolution of society may modify those institutions in 50 or 100 years, but to project such modifications in the next decade or two, given what we currently know about change in our society, would require the wildest kind of speculation, based almost solely on its titillation value rather than its expected probability of occurrence.

Thus, we are logically faced with an initial assumption that the institutions of society will continue to serve, albeit in a somewhat modified format, but most likely in roughly the same structure as they are found currently. Once such a relatively conservative position is espoused, projections for management needs in the future traditionally revolve around growth of current environments to a new plateau in somewhat of an evolutionary sense. Managerial requirements follow that projection on a one-to-one basis. Each change in the current institutional framework necessitates a modification in the requirements made upon managers. It is an almost sacrosanct piety that should there be institutions, there will need to be managers. And problems of institutions will require the highest skills of managers to solve. If one can document what the problems ahead will be, one automatically has access to the new set of skills required of managers.

The process is evolutionary and normative. It is comfortable and in line with the onward and upward philosophy that prevails in most evolutionary settings. In a sense it is an additive process. The manager of tomorrow will be like the manager of today, except that he or she will need more skills, better understanding, increased competence, and multifaceted personality characteristics. All that differentiates many of the predictions of managerial caricature is the set of assumptions as to what the society's problems will be in the projected period.

The great advantage of the evolutionary approach is its rationality. One can avoid problems of worrying about how one gets from the present to the future, because a great continuum is built. The past looms large in any approach to evolution. By carefully chronicling the past and comparing it to the present, one can develop a structured cause and effect model which suggests with comparative ease how the past led directly to the present.

What is so confusing about such an analysis is that it is hard to refute. In retrospect, it is possible to suggest a direct evolutionary process by which present environments relate directly, rationally, logically, and easily to those of the past. Based on similar thinking, a direct link to the future is possible.

Concern for the quality of life will require more sensitive managers. Expanding amounts of data and an increase in the velocity of the information flow will require greater analytical ability. The advent of a period of technological acceleration will demand more sophisticated understanding of the role of technology. Resource scarcity will limit productive capacity and thus engender more expeditious methods of resource allocation and research into alternative approaches. Change will run rampant and dynamism will feed on its own speed, implying vast gaps in the managerial knowledge base, a situation remedied by more and better executive development opportunities. And the list could be continued indefinitely.

There is a comfort to predicting on the basis of lines of development which build on an evolutionary concept. And yet, it is just possible that the function of management is tending toward obsolescence. Managers themselves are always moving in this direction. Life generally is a race between senescence and obsolescence. Recognition of this is found not only in the purpose statements for the multitudes of seminars, colloquiums, assemblies, and conventions which dot the atmosphere, but in the concerns about early retirement, mandatory ages for moving on, and midcareer changes. The latter is often a disguised method of inadequately solving a problem by moving someone "out" in a socially accepted context rather than "up" to perpetuate indequacy from a new vantage point. No one doubts that managers become obsolescent, but how about the function or practice of management. Could it suffer the same fate, and what might replace it?

IS THERE A NEED FOR LESS MANAGEMENT?

Most discussions of the future of management are built on the premise of the need for more. Management is not unique in this assumption. Be it energy, ecological improvement, technological research, or whatever, there is a tendency to see solutions in the light of increase. The increase may be in assets, resources, skills, or even in the amount of benign neglect. It is an understandable phenomenon. Units of input, if appropriately effective and intermixed with other inputs in certain strengths, sizes, and lengths, should yield more output. The solution is always an add-on. Nothing is ever given up or diminished.

The management function, as we know it in contemporary society, may be obsolescent and not subject to the wiles of evolution, primarily because there is no more space to add on, no more time to use, no more memory core to tap. In short, the system may short-circuit. The model is no longer able to absorb the load. This does not mean managers will not exist or management as a function will disappear. But the kind of management we know as practiced by the kind of manager we know, could cease to exist. In the case of some managers, it would be a blessing if it did not exist any further. For, in fact, that kind of management may be working itself into a state of obsolescence over a period of years.

There is too much material to read, too much information to absorb, too many data variables to feed into the decision process, too much legislation to digest, too many interpersonal relationships to structure. Short of a bionic miracle by which each executive could duplicate himself or herself and trot out an automated replacement for evening hours, there seems to be no open path left to add to the structure of the executive in an evolutionary manner to meet these cascading demands.

Certainly there is the possibility of having two managers where one formerly existed. But that begs the question, for it falls squarely into the evolutionary path as an additive solution. What may be needed is a subtractive solution, one that redefines the nature of management. Zero-sum budgeting has been highly touted as a healthy exercise to permit periodic review of approaches which tend to rigidify when current evaluative procedures are not applied. Perhaps what is needed is zero-sum managing by which we start at the beginning and build up the role of manager from its most essential elements. It is worth considering that rather than programming the manager to meet the increasing needs of the management profession and trying to figure out constantly how to make that executive more productive and responsive to those needs, it could be helpful to begin with the basic assumption that the current process of managing and management is becoming obsolescent. The task then becomes the restructuring and reformulating of the management process into a more workable format.

Occasionally, an organization is accused of being overmanaged, overadministered, or top-heavy, all of which suggest that there is too much managing going on or too many people doing the managing. This does not necessarily mean that what is being done is inappropriate, unproductive, or inefficient. What it means is that management is being used as a term to cover a variety of tasks which have in the aggregate become too cumbersome to be handled by a single function. If there is to be less management, it must follow that there will be a need for less of the function to be performed. This flies in the face of most conventional wisdom which decries the never-ending demands being placed in increasing fury on the manager and the managerial function.

If it is time to restructure what management means and what the manager does, future environments must reflect patterns differing markedly from current ones or the same old structure will be built. Institutions will always need administering, which must be differentiated from managing, though the two functions are frequently thought to be synonymous. This discussion postulates an increase in the amount of administration required in the future with a concomitant reduction in the amount of management. Administration is seen as more of an implementation and maintenance function without the decision-making element so crucial to management. The words can be equated to any concept. Administration is chosen for convenience, not because of an attempt to draw invidious comparisons between management and administration. Neither is administration necessarily a subset of management. In fact, one of the most serious problems for managers is their tendency to get involved in too much administration and too little management.

A number of factors suggest the feasibility of looking toward a future where less management is required, a situation which could be the salvation of today's overburdened managers. There may well be increasing tendencies toward decentralization, which will tend more readily to divorce the management function from the pure administrative function. Matters of policy and strategy will remain under the managerial umbrella, but matters of operation may well seek refuge elsewhere. Can a unit be adminstered without being managed? Obviously, the management function must exist, but if it can exist independently of the administrative function, managers may be relieved of vast numbers of tasks currently clogging their pipelines. What may be obsolescent is the way in which most managing is carried out and the series of tasks which creep into the job description. To keep society's managers sane, we might establish some priorities about what the manager of the future must do, using as a basic assumption that we begin from scratch.

AN INDUCTIVE APPROACH TO MANAGEMENT

One cannot deny that institutions need some available mechanism for establishing objectives; deciding what tasks must be done and assigning people to perform them; establishing communication with an ever-widening series of constituencies; and controlling, evaluating, and measuring performance. Somehow the questions of accountability, staff development, division of goals into pieces which can be handled expeditiously by selected individuals, and a multitude of others must be addressed. But do they necessarily have to be addressed by the manager?

Tomorrow's manager will have to consider focusing on other tasks without denying ultimate responsibility for those noted above. For example, someone has to have time to contemplate innovative directions. There must be thinking time if one is to cope with an escalating set of competitive and technological attacks on the system. In restructuring a potentially obsolescent set of tasks, it becomes important to recognize that the obsolescence is not because the tasks to be eliminated are unimportant, but that they are the responsibility of the wrong person.

A common complaint of managers is that they have no time to think, to plan in an unstructured and creative sense (though most are involved in a mechanized planning function that may be technically proficient but may lack the one crucial element of being based on creative assumptions), and to contemplate new directions. More attention is paid to the fact that increasing proportions of an organization's energies or profits are devoted to newly developed services, products, or markets. That trend will probably accelerate. Change has become almost institutionalized. While planning is a manager's acknowledged responsibility, too much planning proceeds without the precedent thinking about what one should plan for, where the planning should become operationalized, and how the planning is evaluated. Planning too often becomes a fancy name for setting quotas and goals. While that is important, the establishment of a high priority to a manager's responsibility for creative thinking, brainstorming, or whatever the activity should be called, will decrease the likelihood that tomorrow's manager will face a future of obsolescence. If the last shall be first, this is the proper place to begin the new job description for the manager of the future. It is the creative aspect of the job for which the typical manager finds no time, to the detriment of the manager and the institution.

Just how the discipline can be mustered to ensure that current crises will no longer drive out the reflective moments of creativity remains an evaluative factor in separating the excellent from the adequate manager. Even more critical than an evaluation of the availability and utilization of appropriate time for productive thinking is the evaluation of the effectiveness of the results. New criteria must be developed. Change for the sake of change has long been disparaged as an inefficient process. However, in an environment where change is almost a constant, the lack of change may signal a moribund organization and a moribund manager. Unless the situation in that particular organization specifically calls for adherence to the status quo, an important managerial criterion should be the amount of productive change or change plans generated in response to trends in society and industry, or to specific difficulties of the organization itself.

A second critical task for tomorrow's manager is the management of the change structured for the organization. If one assumes that management as a function is today heading toward obsolescence because it is burying its most creative aspects in an avalanche of operational detail, then one of the parameters of change in management is restructuring the operational detail so it does not have to be performed by the manager. Implicit in such thinking is the need to devote attention to getting from here to there. To the extent this means goals and objectives, that function may remain within the manager's purview, but even that set of tasks may well appear in a different context. If the manager begins with the identification of the kinds of change that should occur, the next step must relate directly to those changes. The questions to be asked include: (1) what has to happen before those changes can come about, (2) what stands in the way of emplacing the resources necessary to ensure those changes, (3) who can best wrestle with these problems and achieve the desired results, (4) what is the effect on the rest of the organization if these changes become reality, and (5) what is required to prepare for the impact these changes may have on a variety of constituencies with which the organization deals? In a very real sense these issues do not reflect the goal-setting procedure but an earlier step which leads to more appropriate goals being formulated.

At this point management begins to look elsewhere for specific talents. Whether such people are called administrators, operators, facilitators, or implementers is of little consequence. If our restructuring of functions is to have a chance of succeeding, it must break away significant portions of the current task base and place them in someone else's hands. Such people may or may not be on their way to becoming managers. They may have been managers who lacked some of the basic characteristics of the new-style manager. They will have high status, perform crucial tasks, and be well rewarded; but they will not be managers. If the manager has identified what has to happen, such staff members should be able to derive attainable goals and objectives. The manager should critically review such goals, approve their implementation, and maintain substantial accountability for what happens. But the process should be handled by a new level of people in the hierarchy. In one sense there is an analogy to be drawn with the executive officers found in the armed services. Such a person is not an assistant manager as we know the function today. The level of responsibility is higher; perhaps a comanager is closer to it. The function is decidedly staff rather than line, if one must use that dichotomy. There is just a bit of the extra pair of hands alluded to earlier in such a position. There is a partnership image to the relationship where managing and operating are separated in what is essentially a new definition for management.

A pedantic response to the approach is to piously suggest that managers should not be operating people, but have large staffs to ensure they will not "operate" but will "manage." In some cases, particularly at the chief executive level, that may be true. But in tremendous numbers of managerial situations, the manager does not have the luxury of such resources. It is not entirely clear that there is a requirement for a large amount of additional resources. There will obviously need to be some redeployment, but this may in itself be a beneficial result. Aspiring to management is a common phenomenon among the troops. But the generic term "manager" implies a multitude of skills, not all of which are equally discernible in each manager. This approach suggests a division of labor, one which might more adequately match up the round-hole tasks with the round-hole skills.

That a manager is a conglomerate of skills has been accepted for some time. And perhaps the fact that one image shines brighter than another or even several is also acknowledged. Some managers have their highest and best use in the political arena, some in the analysis and technical competence area, some in the broad human relations stadium, others in the systems administration area, and still others in the motivation–charisma–image-building mode. There are certainly more "types" of managers; these are representative. Those dividing the pie in this way suggest the need for different kinds of managers for different times and different requirements. If the slicing goes on to display the talents noted above, the current situation is perpetuated. To get all those qualities in one person would indeed be rare, and to be able to afford enough executives to meet the needs of each function seems unreasonable. The system is an obsolescent one. What may be needed is to slice the pie in a different way. Finding descriptive phrases to adequately represent a two-headed executive is not a trivial task. If one of them is manager, the other is automatically demeaned because of the status which the manager holds. This suggests that perhaps the word "manager" should be struck from the lexicon and two new phrases adopted. What those phrases should be will perhaps be a reflection of what the division of tasks begins to look like.

A third task of the new-type manager is the responsibility to be an impediment destroyer. Obviously, if people assigned to certain tasks do not perform, the changes developed by the manager will not take place. If equipment breaks down, people problems develop, or communication fails to inform, the system will not deliver on its programmed mission. But these are functions that might be lifted from the manager's shoulders to allow time to identify the impediments, locate appropriate depth charges or explosives, and selectively and skillfully blast a few holes without destroying the entire structure. Much of the other coordinating, problem-solving, communicating activity needs to be reassigned to someone else. This in no way suggests such tasks are less important or should be relegated to less capable people. It recognizes the newly developed sophistication in certain areas which makes them more amenable to orderly and rational approaches.

A fourth task of our "slimmed-down" manager is a thrust in the external direction. Relationships with society and its variety of institutions appear to be an area of unlimited growth for the future. Each institution has certain responsibilities to society, but just as importantly needs to have that role delimited. An organization cannot be a problem solver for the world. It can impact on areas because of its resources, personnel skills, or orientation. And these need to be identified, addressed, and evaluated. Many other needs of society are more appropriately the province of other institutions. Needing consideration are relationships with governments, legislators, customers, and society in general. These are not solely the responsibility of the chief manager of an organization but of its managerial cadre. We are today faced with a crisis in the credibility level of our institutions. Over a period of years they have lost the confidence of the public in large measure. To regain their standing as representing the best way for society to address crucial problems, institutions must engage the services of their members to communicate their confidence in how the institution serves society. No segment of the institutions' membership is more important to the success of the effort than the managers.

No attempt is being made to develop a fully formed model of the new-style manager. The duties listed above may be considered tentative and representative, though certainly not complete. Several principles are of interest. The selection of duties must be consonant with the special talents which managers of competence are expected to have. Many important tasks need to be reassigned, as the core of the approach is a reduction in traditional duties to permit the addition of some new ones and time to accomplish those that remain. We start with those duties which are evaluated as being crucial, knowing some cannot be fit into the current model because there is no more room. As a result, the process loses much of its add-on characteristic.

MANAGING RESIDUAL TASKS

The prior discussion did not consider many tasks generally regarded as an integral part of the managing game. For example, the questions of controlling and evaluating have been ignored. Admittedly, unless an organization is prepared to accord those considerations attention and concern, the problems ahead may be insurmountable. The parts of the earlier managerial mission marked for reallocation should have one characteristic in common. They should be amenable to an organized approach to the task, one based on relatively sophisticated tools of analysis and review.

The basic question which the manager must consider is what duties can be reassigned. That is a painful and perplexing issue. It is not so much a question of delegating authority or tasks, for that has always been the hallmark of an efficient manager. Such delegation does not generally mean that the responsibility disappears but that someone else pitches in to help. If the manager is to be relieved, or the managing function is to be made manageable, some modifications must be made. There are a number of candidates and perhaps some reasons why these particular functions could be considered for reassignment. Some extrapolation into the future will be required, admittedly on a sort of evolutionary basis. And some controversial results are bound to occur.

For example, over a period of years managers have been subject to increasing barrages of wisdom about the importance of human relations, the personal side of managing, and empathy considerations. And these have been crucial dimensions of understanding the environment in which one manages and positively affects the productivity and efficiency of the organization. As growth continues in all aspects of our culture, there appear to be more people to manage all the time. This could well lead to a less personal managerial style. In no way does this suggest a return to the autocratic bureaucratic approach of the past. But more of the human process of management is being spelled out in procedures, policy statements, letters of intent, employee manuals, government policy, and participative management sessions. It may be premature to suggest that less of the manager's time should be invested in this kind of activity or that others should assume the responsibility, but the opportunity is there.

If we attempt to structure two kinds of managers, whatever they may be called, perhaps Manager II should be concerned with these kinds of matters rather than Manager I, whose duties have been suggested earlier. To take an arbitrary stance, we might suggest that Manager II would be concerned with whatever aspects of the interpersonal relationships are called for within that managerial unit. A managerial unit would consist of two (perhaps more) manager types concerned with the scope of managing formerly associated with the single manager model. Obviously, it would be impossible to implement a clear dichotomy of tasks. Further, perhaps Manager II should be called something entirely different in an attempt to emphasize that we are restructuring the management process because it has become obsolescent due to systems overload.

Another managerial task that might be reassigned is the control and evaluation aspects. With data processing technology developed to the stage where the problem is not getting the information, but what to do with it, the control function will become more mechanized. There is little reason for most systems to be out of control very long before the green sheets herald the events. As time goes on, a manager's concern for control should be reduced, since the system should exert the control formerly required of the manager. There will always be the human element to be considered, and automation and mechanization will not be sufficient of themselves. For not only are data available, but systems technology is developed to the point where many out-of-control operations can be brought back into control without direct intervention of managers. The process by which this happens can be abetted by the development of artificial intelligence technology which attempts to simulate managerial judgment as well as retrieve information. While the process will always have to be monitored, relatively standardized procedures are being developed to respond to most situations. With the exception of the rare event, much of the controlling function should be the province of others. The system should operate to ring bells, blow whistles, or otherwise alert the appropriate administrator that the system is out of whack. The impersonality will rankle and a countersystem will appear to controvert the efficiency of the control system. The controls will need to have a people orientation, but it is not clear that the future will require a facsimile of today's manager to monitor the system. Not only must technology deliver appropriate data for control to operate, but its ultimate development must be to divorce the system of control and audit from the immediate responsibility of the manager.

Evaluation is another task that takes up an inordinate amount of the manager's time. It is almost blasphemy to suggest that managers should not evaluate, and yet the future may make possible evaluative systems which would operate without regard to the manager. Whether it be an assessment center or a computer-aided management by objectives review, the developing sophistication may relieve today's manager of much of that responsibility. Nothing takes the place of the one-on-one discussion. The open-door policy creates much to be condoned. But it also introduces a bias in evaluation and review, both on the positive and negative sides, that could be eliminated if more objective assessment were introduced. Someone must apply the evaluation and obviously the manager must be aware of it, should provide some input for it, and must use it in final selection procedures; but can we afford the luxury of the manager devoting substantial time to it?

While our education for managers stresses broad, general principles, we still impose on the typical manager a content-specific requirement that involves technical matters far more than the process of management. Many of today's managerial tasks could be performed more efficiently if specialized knowledge were applied to them. Evaluation, control, communication, and even interpersonal relations at certain levels may be more effectively handled by taking them out of the manager's bag and allowing groups of specialists to work on them, with some feedback loop provided so the manager can succinctly and expeditiously become aware of the process, the results, and the implications of these activities.

An important part of the process will be the development of ways of impacting on the manager with the kind of feedback which these activities and others may suggest. The manager cannot avoid ultimate responsibility for the removal of certain items to make room for other functions. If the feedback process takes up so much time as to eliminate any advantage in the reassignment of duties, no great advantage has accrued. The challenge will be to find ways to providing feedback that require a minimum amount of time. We must program the manager with data in much the same way as the computer is programmed, but with the major difference that there are severe limitations on memory core and on time available for programming. The manager must have confidence in the validity of the data, or the system will collapse. The format must be comprehensive enough to provide sufficient detail for decision making, but brief enough to meet the retrieval limitations.

MANAGEMENT AT THE CROSSROADS

Management can proceed in the years ahead to grow and develop as it has in the past. For some period the evolutionary approach may serve society's institutions reasonably well. But the trends now apparent, should they converge over a short period of time, could create a managerial crisis requiring a change in the structure of management and the role of the manager. Structural obsolescence rather than functional obsolescence could set in and worsen the credibility situation because of the inability of society's institutions to respond to the critical issues ahead.

The consumer movement and the broader social responsibility context are not likely to recede. While resource scarcities may be overcome through advancing technology, there will continue to be higher prices for and limited supplies of certain natural resources. Legislation will grow and extend its tentacles to cover more of the operations of society's institutions; some limitations to growth are likely to be maintained. Life-style changes will evolve as a more democratic social order tightens its grip on the fabric of society. Work may become a substantially less important part of the total satisfaction package of the individual, impacting on what can be accomplished by managers as they lead more and command less. The public sector is growing as a factor in managerial considerations and will inevitably continue to do so. Minority-majority issues will dominate management as gradual movement into upper levels of management occurs. Emphasis on productivity as a way of overcoming the problems of inflation and scarcity will pose new challenges. Conflicts will accelerate as unions extend their grip on new segments of the population and stress a societal view as opposed to the firm view. And these are but a few of the possibilities, perhaps even probabilities, ahead.

Management will respond in some way, either by shifting, modifying, adding, and merging, or by applying radical surgery. If a revolutionary approach is to be considered by redefining the expectations for management and managers, the results could be dramatic. Specialization could be less readily identified with the position of manager. Technical capability could be less important in the background of the manager, as a more generic and abstract form of management takes over, one that is relatively free of content. Loyalty to the profession rather than the institution may develop even further. If work becomes less central to an individual's existence, greater tolerance may exist for the less pleasant tasks of management. More willingness may be expressed to undertake the Manager II role in spite of the fact that much of the glamour of the profession is tied up in the Manager I role. Managers may rely more on computer simulation of judgment, as change accelerates. But unless that change can be effectively managed, it will be unproductive. As specialists focus on the communications area, vast improvements can be expected, particularly if the manager is not burdened with primary responsibility for that task also.

The future has always posed uncertainty for managers, but rarely have so many currents and crosscurrents made their appearance at the same time. Adaptation may no longer be a viable strategy. If management of change, planning for change, and creation of change turn out to be high priority items for the manager, he or she must have time and capacity to deal with these issues. If that takes restructuring, realignment, and reallocation of duties, that will be necessary. The alternative is obsolescence for management as well as the manager. The manager can become outdated without management suffering the same fate. But management obsolescence automatically makes the manager obsolete, so it is much more insidious.

Management has become a central core of civilization,with demonstrable impact on the speed and quality of our national progress. It represents a way of thinking and it is perhaps time to change that way of thinking. Some of the suggested solutions may appear to be harkening back to earlier concepts, but the swinging pendulum often requires some adustment if it begins to swing too wildly. In many contexts management has swung rather widely to embrace more than the manager can manage. Whether by evolution or revolution, by chance or design, in haste or in leisure, some change must be made if the future is to be met head-on and not proceed to take the initiative away from the managers.

If the essence of management is to deal with change, it is perhaps time to consider change in the process of management. All the seminars in the world to provide increased knowldege to managers will be severely limited if a systems overload occurs. Decision makers must have time to think, motivators must have time to motivate, challengers must have time to challenge, and managers must have time to manage. If a willingness to innovate is combined with a penchant for creativity, and a few drops of tradition are added, the resultant brew may be a new concept of management. If the process can resist obsolescence, the manager will be more likely to do so also. Be it evolution or revolution, currency or obsolescence, management is in for a run for its money.

REFERENCE

1. Dennis H. Meadows et al., *The Limits to Growth,* A Report from the Club of Rome's Project on the Predicament of Mankind (New York: Universe Books, 1972).

ABOUT THE CONTRIBUTORS

JAMES G. AFFLECK

Dr. Affleck is Chairman of the Board and Chief Executive Officer of American Cyanamid Company. He joined Cyanamid in 1949 as a research chemist and later served in a number of management posts for the company; in 1971 he became a Cyanamid vice president.

Dr. Affleck is on the executive committee and the Board of Directors of the Manufacturing Chemists Association and is Chairman of the Foundation of the College of Medicine and Dentistry of New Jersey. He is on the executive committee of the American Section, Society of Chemical Industry, and is a member of the Conference Board. He was formerly president of the Animal Health Institute and president of the Commercial Development Association. He served on the Board of Directors of the U.S. Chamber of Commerce.

Dr. Affleck was born on February 6, 1923, in Yonkers, New York. He received the B.A. and Ph.D. in chemistry from Princeton University.

LEWIS BENTON

Dr. Benton, the editor of this book, is Professor of Management at Hofstra University and is also on the faculties of the New School for Social Research and Adelphi University. His graduate work was done at Yale, the University of Michigan, and New York University. He was Chief of Personnel under the late General MacArthur, in Tokyo, and Director of Personnel for M. Lowenstein and Sons, one of the world's largest textile manufacturers. As a management consultant, he has served on four continents.

Dr. Benton's books include *A Guide to Creative Personnel Management, Supervision and Management, Supervision and Profitability,* and *The Management of Non-Profit Organizations.* He has written many articles on management. He is a member of the Board of Directors of the South Shore Child Guidance Association and the Committee on the Economy for Nassau County. He was a vice president of Phi Delta Kappa, the educational honor society, and a member of the Board of Trustees of the *Journal of Educational Sociology.*

KENNETH BLACK, JR.

Dr. Black is Dean of the School of Business Administration, Georgia State University, and Regents Professor of Insurance. He was born in Virginia, received the B.A. and M.A. from the University of North Carolina at Chapel Hill, and the Ph.D. at the University of Pennsylvania, studying under the S. S. Huebner Foundation for Insurance Education. He holds CLU and CPCU professional designations.

Dr. Black is coauthor, with the late Dr. Solomon S. Huebner, of two volumes: *Life Insurance* and *Property Insurance.* He also published, with Dr. G. Hugh Russell, three volumes on human behavior, the latest being *Human Behavior in Business.*

From 1953–69 he served as Chairman of the Department of Insurance at Georgia State University, becoming Dean of the School of Business Administration in 1969. Dr. Black is past president of the American Risk and Insurance Association, the Southern Risk and Insurance Association, the Southern Business Administration Association, and the Atlanta Chapter of the American Society of Insurance Management. He has also served as Regional Vice President of the Society of Chartered Property and Casualty Underwriters and is currently President/Director General and member of the Board of Directors of International Insurance Seminars, Inc. He is editor of *The JOURNAL of the American Society of Chartered Life Underwriters* and Insurance Editor for Prentice-Hall, Inc.

Dr. Black has served on the Board of Trustees of the Life Underwriter Training Council, as Vice Chairman of the President's Commission on Railroad Retirement, on the Board of Trustees of Educational Foundation, Inc. (Georgia State University), as a member of the Griffith Foundation for Insurance Education (Ohio State University), and on the board of directors of many U.S. business corporations.

CORNELIUS BREVOORD

Dr. Brevoord was born in 1925, in Amsterdam, the Netherlands. After World War II he was an officer in the Dutch Army for four years. He then spent five years in Indonesia, working in various commercial jobs. On his return to the

Netherlands, Dr. Brevoord earned a degree in economics at Rotterdam and became a certified accountant. From 1960–70 he was controller and chief accountant of Albert Heijn N.V., a large Dutch retailing organization. In 1969 he wrote *Distribution and Information,* a study of automation-information problems in the retailing industry.

In 1970 Dr. Brevoord joined the Interfaculteit Bedrijfskunde (Graduate School of Management) at Delft, the Netherlands, as professor in management accounting, and soon became the dean. He is active in research, has written several books about education in management and about productivity of clerical labor, has produced a number of publications about information problems, and is an active member of the Dutch organization of certified public accountants.

RALPH G. CASO

Mr. Caso, county executive of Nassau County, New York, is a leading spokesman for local government. Now serving his second term as county executive, Mr. Caso began his public service career in 1953 as a councilman in the Town of Hempstead. He became town supervisor in 1961, presiding supervisor in 1965, and county executive in 1970. In 1974 he was chosen as the candidate for lieutenant governor of New York State.

In 1971 Mr. Caso was the prime mover in the formation of the New York State County Executives Association; he is a director and past chairman of the Metropolitan Regional Council, and he helped to organize the National Council of Elected Officials for the National Association of Counties. He was chosen by the U.S. government in June 1976 to be one of five elected local government officials in this country's official delegation to the UN Conference on Human Settlements (Habitat) in Vancouver, Canada.

Mr. Caso was born in New York City. During World War II he served in the U.S. Army as a member of General Stillwell's renowned "Y" force in China. A graduate of Hofstra University and the New York University School of Law, he practiced law before entering public service.

KEITH DAVIS

Dr. Davis is Professor of Management at Arizona State University, author of books on management and social issues, and editor of the McGraw-Hill Book Company's Series in Management. He received the Ph.D. from Ohio State University and has taught at the University of Texas and Indiana University. He was an early contributor to the area of social issues as they affect management. He has been visiting professor at a number of universities, most recently at the University of Western Australia.

Two of Dr. Davis' recent books are: *Human Behavior at Work: Organizational Behavior.* and (with Robert L. Blomstrom) *Business and Society: Environment and Responsibility.* He has contributed chapters to over 50 other books and is the author of more than 125 articles on management published in such journals as *Harvard Business Review, Academy of Man-*

agement Journal, Management International, and *California Management Review.*

Dr. Davis, a former president of the Academy of Management, received the Human Relations Award from the Society for Advancement of Management. In 1975–76 he was nationally selected as a Beta Gamma Sigma Distinguished Scholar. He has taught in management development programs in business, universities, and government and has served as consultant to the Mobil Oil Company, Texaco, the U.S. Internal Revenue Service, and the state of Hawaii.

JOHN D. deBUTTS

Mr. deButts was born in Greensboro, North Carolina, in 1915. He was graduated from Virginia Military Institute in 1936 and shortly after began his Bell System career with the Chesapeake and Potomac Telephone Company in Richmond, Virginia. He served in various positions with that company before moving to New York City to work at AT&T headquarters and the New York Telephone Company. Then, after several years as a vice president of the C. & P. Company in Washington, D.C., he became president of Illinois Bell at the age of 46.

Mr. deButts was named AT&T executive vice president in 1966, board vice chairman in 1967, and chairman and chief executive officer in 1972. He is a director of Citicorp and its subsidiary, First National City Bank; Kraftco Corporation; United States Steel; and the United Fund of Greater New York. He is active in many business and community endeavors and has received many honorary degrees and awards.

HARRY E. EKBLOM

Mr. Ekblom is Chairman and Chief Executive Officer of European-American Banking Corporation and European-American Bank & Trust Company. He was born on April 24, 1928, in New York City. He received a B.A. from Columbia University in 1948, and an LL.B. from New York University School of Law in 1956. He was admitted to the New York Bar in 1957. In 1951–52 he served in the U.S. Army. In June 1970 Mr. Ekblom resigned his position as Senior Vice President with Chase Manhattan Bank and was appointed a director of European-American Banking Corporation and European-American Bank & Trust Company. In 1970, he was elected president and chief executive officer of these two companies and became chairman in 1973.

Mr. Ekblom is a director of the Hoover Company, North Canton, Ohio; Panhandle Eastern Pipe Line Company and the Trunkline Gas Company, Houston, Texas; and Thomas Cook, Inc., New York. He is a member of the Economic Club of New York, the Overseas Bankers Club in London, the Pilgrims, Reserve City Bankers, and is a director of the Downtown–Lower Manhattan Association, Inc. He is on the Board of Governors of the Human Resources Center of Albertson, Long Island; the Board of Governors of India

House; and the Board of Trustees of Hofstra University. He also serves on the Advisory Council of the Faculty of the School of International Affairs at Columbia University, the Advisory Council of Pace University, and is a trustee of the Research Foundation of the Long Island Association of Commerce and Industry.

HENRY FORD II

Mr. Ford, Chairman of the Board of Ford Motor Company, has been Chief Executive Officer of the company since 1945, when his grandfather, Henry Ford, retired. He has been a director of the company since 1938, and an employee since 1940, except for service as a naval officer in 1941–43. He is a trustee of the Ford Foundation and a member of the Business Council.

In January 1968 Mr. Ford was appointed by President Johnson as Chairman of the National Alliance of Businessmen, a group of U.S. business leaders seeking productive jobs for the hard-core unemployed and meaningful jobs for disadvantaged young people. He held the post until February 1969. He served as Chairman of the Board of the National Center for Voluntary Action in 1970–72. He is Cochairman of the Board of Detroit Renaissance and a member of New Detroit, Inc.

Mr. Ford was born in Detroit on September 4, 1917. He was a member of the class of 1940 at Yale University.

SIGMUND G. GINSBURG

Mr. Ginsburg is Vice President for Administration and Planning and Treasurer of Adelphi University. He served in the Office of the Mayor, City of New York, from 1966–72 and was Assistant City Administrator from 1967–72. He received the City of New York Merit Award for 1969. He has served in management positions with the Port Authority of New York and New Jersey, the Office of the Secretary of Defense, and Hudson Institute, and was an officer in the U.S. Army. He has taught graduate courses in management and public administration at City University of New York and is presently adjunct Associate Professor of Management at Adelphi University. He has lectured and delivered papers before many professional groups and societies and is the author of more than 25 published articles in the fields of management, personnel, public, and university administration. He was an Administration Fellow and received the M.P.A. from Harvard University, attended the London School of Economics and Political Science as a graduate research student, and was a Daniel Webster National Scholar at Dartmouth College, where he received the B.A. magna cum laude and was elected to Phi Beta Kappa.

ROSS LAWRENCE GOBLE

Dr. Goble is Dean of the School of Management and Professor of Marketing and Psychology at Clarkson College. Prior to joining Clarkson, he was

Associate Professor of Marketing and Psychology at the State University of New York at Albany, and during that time he was also President of University Research Associates—a multidiscipline group founded as a research, problem-solving team for all areas of management. In this capacity, Dr. Goble served as consultant to a number of leading corporations.

In addition, he has had over 10 years' business experience in the consumer goods and pharmaceutical industries and is a frequent lecturer for management seminars and executive development programs. At Clarkson, Dr. Goble recently established the Management Institute, as an integral part of the School of Management, to provide off-campus management education programs.

He received a B.A. from the College of William and Mary, an M.A. from the University of Richmond, and a Ph.D. from the University of Utah. Dr. Goble is a member of Sigma Xi, Beta Gamma Sigma, and Phi Kappa Phi. He has published a number of articles in professional journals and is the coauthor (with R. Shaw) of *Controversy and Dialogue in Marketing.*

ELLA GRASSO

Governor Grasso is Connecticut's 83d governor. She was born in Windsor Locks, Connecticut, on May 10, 1919. She attended Mt. Holyoke College, was elected to Phi Beta Kappa in her junior year, and received a B.A. with honors in 1940 and an M.A. in economics and sociology in 1942. During World War II, she served as Assistant Director of Research for the War Manpower Commission of Connecticut.

Mrs. Grasso was elected to the General Assembly in 1952 and 1954; she served as a floor leader in the State Legislature in 1955. In 1953–55 she was a member of the Long Lane Farm Study Commission and, at the same time, served on the Highway Financing Study Commission. She was Secretary of the State for 12 years (1959–70); vice chairman of the Executive Committee on Human Rights and Opportunities and chairman of the Planning Committee for the Governor's Commission on the Status of Women; chairman of the Bipartisan Commission to Prepare for the Connecticut Constitutional Convention and Democratic floor leader at the Convention in 1965. During two terms in Congress as U.S. Representative from the Sixth District, she served on the Veterans' Affairs Committee and the Education and Labor Committee. House Speaker Carl Albert appointed Mrs. Grasso as the first U.S. House of Representatives' member of the Federal Council on the Arts and Humanities.

Mrs. Grasso was chairman of the Democratic State Platform Committee from 1956–68, a member of the National Platform Committee in 1960, and cochairman of the Resolutions Committee of the Democratic National Convention in 1964 and 1968. President John F. Kennedy named her to the Board of Foreign Scholarships, and she was reappointed by President Lyndon B. Johnson, serving until 1966. She was appointed to the National

Commission for the Observance of International Women's Year 1975 by President Gerald Ford. She has received many other awards and honorary doctorates.

THOMAS R. HORTON

Dr. Horton is IBM Director of University Relations at the International Business Machines Corporation. Prior to joining IBM, he taught mathematics and received the Ph.D. in mathematics at the University of Florida. In the late 1950s he was responsible for IBM's early activities in artificial earth satellite orbital computations, first in connection with scientific satellites and later with manned flights. In the mid-1960s he was Vice President-Systems of the IBM division responsible for the development of the System/360. For the past several years he has been responsible for IBM's program of financial support to higher education. A member of the Mathematical Association of America, he serves on visiting committees and advisory councils to many colleges of engineering and graduate schools of business and is a member of the Visitation Panel of the American Assembly of Collegiate Schools of Business. Dr. Horton is active with several youth organizations, including A Presidential Classroom for Young Americans, in Washington, D.C.; and Learning about Learning, in San Antonio; and he is a trustee of Pace University and Bethune-Cookman College. His most recent book is *Traffic Control: Theory and Instrumentation.*

JACOB K. JAVITS

Senator Javits, senior U.S. Senator from New York, is now in his fourth Senate term. He was graduated from New York University Law School in 1926, and was admitted to the New York Bar in 1927. During World War II he served with the Chemical Warfare Service, U.S. Army, attaining the rank of Lieutenant Colonel.

The Senator's political career began in 1932, when he joined the Ivy Republican Club in Manhattan's 18th Congressional District. In 1937 and 1941 he was active in the reform movement of Mayor Fiorello LaGuardia. In 1946 he became the first Republican elected to the House of Representatives in New York's traditionally Democratic 21st District since 1923, and was reelected three times. In 1954, after eight years as a Congressman, he became Attorney General of New York State. In 1956 Javits was elected to the United States Senate and was reelected to his fourth term in 1974. He is senior Republican on the Committee on Labor and Public Welfare, the Joint Economic Committee, and the Select Committee on Small Business. He also serves on the Senate Foreign Relations Committee and the Committee on Government Operations. He is known for legislative accomplishments too numerous to mention in fields as diverse as health, education, housing, civil rights, small business, labor, fiscal policy, the arts and humanities, and foreign economic policy.

Senator Javits received the Congressional Distinguished Service Award of the American Political Science Association, and honorary degrees from 27 U.S. colleges and universities. He is the author of *Who Makes War* (with Don Kellerman); *Order of Battle: A Republican's Call to Reason;* and *Discrimination, U.S.A.* He is also a frequent contributor to leading newspapers, magazines, and periodicals.

JAMES M. JENKS

Mr. Jenks is the seventh president of Alexander Hamilton Institute, Inc., an organization founded in 1909. It is one of America's oldest centers for the collection, publication, and dissemination of management information. Mr. Jenks joined the institute in 1948 as a management trainee and held various management positions there until becoming president in 1964. He has contributed many articles to the business press on subjects ranging from advertising research to management development.

During the forties, Mr. Jenks's education was interrupted by World War II. He entered the army as a private in 1943 and was relieved from active duty as a captain in 1946. He received a B.A. in economics from Cornell University in 1948, and was elected to Phi Beta Kappa.

REGINALD H. JONES

Mr. Jones is Chairman of the Board and Chief Executive Officer of the General Electric Company. He became a vice president of the company in 1961, after a career in general management positions with the company which began in 1939. In 1972 he was elected President of the company, and became Chairman and Chief Executive Officer in the same year. He was born in England on July 11, 1917, and came to the United States as a boy. He is a graduate of the Wharton School of Finance and Commerce of the University of Pennsylvania. Mr. Jones is a member of the Executive Committee of the Business Council and co-chairman of President Carter's Labor-Management Group. He is also a trustee of the University of Pennsylvania.

HENRY A. KISSINGER

Dr. Kissinger was Secretary of State from 1973–77. He was born in Fuerth, Germany, on May 27, 1923, came to the United States in 1938, and was naturalized a United States citizen in 1943. During 1943–46 Dr. Kissinger served in the U.S. Army Counter-Intelligence Corps. He received the B.A. summa cum laude at Harvard College in 1950 and the M.A. and Ph.D. at Harvard University in 1952 and 1954, respectively.

From 1954–71 he taught at Harvard University, in the Department of Government and at the Center for International Affairs, where he was

Associate Director from 1957–60. He served as Study Director, Nuclear Weapons and Foreign Policy, for the Council on Foreign Relations in 1955–56; Director of the Special Studies Project for the Rockefeller Brothers Fund in 1956–58; Director of the Harvard International Seminar from 1951–71; and Director of the Harvard Defense Studies Program from 1958–71. (He was on leave of absence from Harvard during 1969–71.)

Dr. Kissinger has written 6 books and more than 40 articles on U.S. foreign policy, international affairs, and diplomatic history. He has received many awards including the Guggenheim Fellowship (1956–66); the Woodrow Wilson prize for the best book in the fields of government, politics, and international affairs (1958); the American Institute for Public Service Award (1973); the International Platform Association Theodore Roosevelt Award (1973); the Veterans of Foreign Wars Dwight D. Eisenhower Distinguished Service Medal (1973); the HOPE Award for International Understanding (1973); and the George Catlett Marshall Medal (1973). In October 1973 Secretary Kissinger and North Vietnamese Politburo member Le Duc Tho were awarded the Nobel Peace Prize for their efforts in bringing about a peace settlement in Vietnam.

He has served as consultant to the Department of State, U.S. Arms Control and Disarmament Agency, RAND Corporation, National Security Council, Weapons Systems Evaluation Group of the Joint Chiefs of Staff, Operations Coordinating Board, Director of the Psychological Strategy Board, Operations Research Office, and Assistant to the President for National Security Affairs.

HAROLD LAZARUS

Dr. Lazarus is Dean of the School of Business and Professor of Management at Hofstra University. He is also on the Board of Directors of Ideal Toy Corporation and of Superior Surgical Manufacturing Company, Inc. He has been a Professor of Management at New York University's Graduate School of Business Administration; visiting member of the faculty at Columbia University's Graduate School of Business Administration and Teachers College, and at New York University's Graduate School of Public Administration; and has taught at Harvard's Graduate School of Business Administration and Cornell's School of Industrial and Labor Relations.

Dr. Lazarus has served as management consultant to the U.S. Department of State, AT&T, New York City Personnel Department, Rockland Children's Psychiatric Hospital, the Boys' Club of America, State of New Jersey's Department of Higher Education, and New York State Department of Higher Education. He has published 6 books, 26 articles, and chapters, book reviews, and cases dealing with the management of human resources.

He received the Ph.D. in management from Columbia University and is a member of Phi Beta Kappa and Beta Gamma Sigma. He is president of the Middle Atlantic Association of Colleges of Business Administration; former president of the Hofstra Chapter of the American Association of University

Professors; and former president of the Eastern Academy of Management. Dean Lazarus was on the editorial board of the *Academy of Management Journal* and is now Director of the Hofstra University Management Series.

EDWARD M. MAZZE

Dr. Mazze received the Ph.D. in business administration from Pennsylvania State University. He is Dean of the W. Paul Stillman School of Business of Seton Hall University. Prior to assuming this position, he served as Professor of Business Administration and Coordinator of the Marketing Program at Virginia Polytechnic Institute and State University. He is author, coauthor, and editor of 9 books on management, marketing, and international business; 27 articles in major journals; and 50 other publications. He is on the editorial board of several journals and is contributing author to the *Encyclopaedia Britannica Book of the Year.* In 1975 Dr. Mazze was Project Director and Coordinator of Research Activities for the Governor's Electricity Cost Commission in the Commonwealth of Virginia. Previously, he was on the faculties of the graduate business schools of the University of Pittsburgh, West Virginia University, and the University of Detroit. He serves as consultant to a number of large corporations.

WILLIAM H. NEWMAN

Dr. Newman is Samuel Bronfman Professor of Democratic Business Enterprise at the Graduate School of Business of Columbia University in New York, a post he has held since 1951. He received a B.A. from Friends University in 1930 and the Ph.D. from the University of Chicago in 1934. From 1939–49 he was Professor of Industry at the Wharton School of the University of Pennsylvania. He was visiting Research Professor at the University of Hawaii in 1964 and Visiting Professor at the American University of Beirut and Robert College in Istanbul in 1964 and 1965, respectively. In 1969 he was Visiting Professor of Business Policy under a Fulbright grant at the London Graduate School of Business Studies. He has served on the board of directors of several firms and as consultant to large American corporations. During World War II, Dr. Newman was Executive Officer of the Petroleum Administration for War and Organization Consultant for the War Production Board. He has participated in executive development programs throughout the world and was a member of the Management Education Survey Team (USAID) in India in 1967.

Dr. Newman is a fellow and past president of the American Academy of Management; fellow of the International Academy of Management; and a member of the American Economic Association, American Management Associations, American Society for Public Administration, and the European Foundation for Management Development. His publications include *The Process of Management; Strategy, Policy, and Central Management; Constructive Control: Design and Use of Control Systems; Administrative*

Action; Cases for Administrative Action; Management of Expanding Enterprises; and *The Building Industry and Business Cycles.* He has also written articles for many professional journals.

DAVID P. REYNOLDS

Mr. Reynolds is Chairman of the Board and Chief Executive Officer of Reynolds Metals Company. He has been associated with the company for 40 years. He is a founder and a director of the National Center for Resource Recovery, Inc., and in 1973 directed construction of the first home built of recycled materials—to prove the market potential for such materials in residential building. For two years he was chairman of National Boy Scout Keep America Beautiful Day, and has served as chairman of the Aluminum Association's Clean Air, Water and Land Committee and its Board Resources Committee.

Mr. Reynolds has been a member of the Prime Aluminum Products Industry Advisory Committee of the federal government since 1951. He is also a member of the board of directors of various Reynolds subsidiaries; is on the board of United Virginia Bankshares, Richmond; is a vice president of the Muscular Dystrophy Association; and serves as a trustee of Lawrenceville School in New Jersey. A native of Bristol, Tennessee, Mr. Reynolds attended Princeton University.

WILLIAM J. RONAN

Dr. Ronan, former Chairman of the Port Authority of New York and New Jersey, received a B.A. magna cum laude from Syracuse University and a Ph.D. from New York University. He pursued graduate studies at Harvard University and the Geneva School of International Studies, and was a Penfield Fellow in International Law, Diplomacy, and Belles Lettres. He is a member of Phi Beta Kappa. He served as a lieutenant in the U.S. Naval Reserve in World War II.

Dr. Ronan has been Dean of the New York University Graduate School of Public Administration and Social Service; First Deputy City Administrator of the City of New York; and Executive Director of the Temporary Commission of the New York State Constitutional Convention. In 1959 he was named secretary to Governor Nelson A. Rockefeller; in 1965 he became Chairman of the Metropolitan Commuter Transportation Authority; in 1968 he was named chairman of its successor, the Metropolitan Transportation Authority. He resigned from that agency in 1974 to become Chairman of the Port Authority of New York and New Jersey.

Dr. Ronan is Chairman of the Board of the American Public Transit Association, and is on the Management Committee of the International Union of Public Transport. He has served as a vice president of that organization, the first American elected to that position, and as consultant to state and local governments, and to the federal government, both here and abroad. He is on the Board of Trustees of the New York State Power Authority; is Senior Advisor to the Rockefeller Family, Vice Chairman of the Continental Copper and Steel Industries, Inc.; and serves on the Board of Trustees of the Metropolitan Savings Bank.

ERIC SCHMERTZ

Dr. Schmertz is Professor of Law at the Hofstra University Law School. He is a professional labor-management arbitrator and has served as impartial chairman between the City of New York and the Uniformed Fire Fighters Association and the Uniformed Fire Officers Association; as arbitrator for the East Coast motion pictures laboratories; as referee of disciplinary cases in the New York City Transit Authority; as contract arbitrator between the General Electric Company and the International Union of Electrical Workers, AFL-CIO, in concluding their national agreement; as arbitrator for the New York and New Jersey brewery industries, the New York milk industries, the Off-Track Betting Commission, the aerospace industries, the New York City retail drugstore industries, major league baseball; and many other groups in government and industry. His professional activities and affiliations are too numerous to list here. His public service includes work as consultant to the government, unions, and industry of the Philippines for the establishment of an arbitration system under the Philippines labor code.

Professor Schmertz was born in New York City on December 24, 1925. He is a graduate of Union College, the Alliance Francaise in Paris, and the New York University School of Law, where he earned a doctorate in jurisprudence in 1954. He is a member of the New York Bar. His publications include *Personnel Administration and the Law* (with Russell L. Greenman) and numerous articles in professional magazines.

IRA O. SCOTT, Jr.

Dr. Scott has served as Executive Vice President of the Savings Banks Association of New York State since 1970. He has also been Vice Chairman and member of the board of the Dormitory Authority, State of New York, since 1973. He received the B.A. and M.A. in political science from the University of Kansas, and an M.A. and Ph.D. in economics from Harvard University.

He has taught economics and finance at Columbia and Harvard Universities, the University of Minnesota, and the University of Kansas. He was dean and professor of finance at Arthur T. Roth School of Business Administration, C. W. Post College.

He is a member of Phi Beta Kappa, American Economic Association, the National Association of Business Economists, and the American Association of University Professors. His best known books are *Government Securities Market* and *European Capital Markets*. In preparation is *Money and Credit*, a treatise on money and banking. He has written many articles for professional journals.

Dr. Scott has served as consultant to the Commission on Money and Credit, the House Banking and Currency Committee, the Comptroller of the Currency, the Joint Economic Committee, and the American Enterprise Institute. He received a grant from the Merrill Foundation for the Advancement of Financial Knowledge in 1956–57, a Fulbright to Sweden in 1960–61, a John Simon Guggenheim Foundation Fellowship in 1960–61, a Fulbright to Italy in 1964–65, and a National Science Foundation Grant in 1964–65.

JOHN E. ULLMANN

Dr. Ullmann has been Professor of Management and Marketing at Hofstra University since 1961. From that date to 1973 he was also Chairman of the Department of Management, Marketing, and Quantitative Methods. He is an industrial engineer, with his first training in civil and mechanical engineering. His undergraduate work was done at the University of London, where he took an honors degree in 1948. He received an M.S. in industrial engineering at Columbia University in 1951 and the Ph.D. in 1959. He is also a licensed professional engineer.

Dr. Ullmann was born in Vienna. After the German Anschluss in 1938, he settled in England with his surviving family. In 1948 he moved to New York, where he spent five years in engineering—plant design and project management in metal mining and processing, power plants, petroleum refining, and machinery manufacturing. He then started a consulting practice in product planning and market research. In 1957 he accepted an appointment as graduate assistant at Columbia University and in 1958 became Assistant Professor of Economics of Engineering at Stevens Institute of Technology.

Dr. Ullman has written many books, monographs, and articles on technical and economic planning, including statistics, operations research innovation, conversion of engineering skills, industrial planning, development and urban renewal, and industrial marketing. His most recent major work is *Quantitative Methods in Management.* He has been consultant and expert witness in his fields of interest; Chairman of the Section of Science and Public Policy of the New York Academy of Sciences; and a director and member of the executive committee of SANE.

KURT WALDHEIM

Dr. Waldheim was appointed Secretary General of the United Nations in 1972. The Secretary General was born at Sankt Andra-Wordern, near Vienna, Austria, on December 21, 1918. He was graduated from the University of Vienna as a doctor of jurisprudence in 1944. He is also a graduate of the Vienna Consular Academy. Dr. Waldheim joined the Austrian diplomatic service in 1945 and served in various capacities including important work with the United Nations until 1968, when he became Federal Minister for Foreign Affairs of Austria. After leaving the government, he was unanimously elected Chairman of the Safeguards Committee of the International

Atomic Energy Agency, and in October 1970 he became for the second time the Austrian Permanent Representative to the United Nations, a post he held until he was elected Secretary General of the organization. In April 1971, he was one of two candidates for the Federal Presidency of Austria. Dr. Waldheim is the author of a work on Austria's foreign policy, *The Austrian Example,* which has been published in German, English, and French.

RICHARD R. WEEKS

Dr. Weeks has been Dean and Professor of Marketing Management at the College of Business Administration, University of Rhode Island, since 1970. He received the B.S. from the University of Illinois, and the M.B.A. and D.B.A. from Washington University. He began his professional career in 1960 as Executive Secretary of the American Assembly of Collegiate Schools of Business. He has also served as Executive Secretary of Beta Gamma Sigma, Assistant Dean and Director of the M.B.A. Program at Oklahoma State University, and Dean of the Walter E. Heller College of Business Administration at Roosevelt University. He is on the Board of Governors of Beta Gamma Sigma; the Board of Directors of the American Assembly of Collegiate Schools of Business, the Council on Post-Secondary Accreditation, and the Eastern Finance Association. He is Secretary of the Commission on Education for the Business Professors of the National Association of State Universities and Land-Grant Colleges.

Dr. Weeks has served as consultant to many institutions of higher education and business firms; as editor of the *AACSB Bulletin,* the *Beta Gamma Sigma Exchange,* and *Faculty Personnel;* as contributing editor to the *Encyclopedia of Business Information Sources;* and on the Editorial Advisory Board of *Business and Society.* His writings have contributed extensively to management and marketing literature.

H. J. ZOFFER

Dr. Zoffer was appointed Dean of the Graduate School of Business of the University of Pittsburgh in 1968, following a career in teaching and university administration that began in 1956. He holds the B.B.A. and M.A., as well as the CPCU designation from the American Institute. He earned the Ph.D. at the University of Pittsburgh, where his major fields of interest were economics and corporation finance. He received a Ford Foundation Fellowship in Applied Mathematics and has taught courses in accounting, industrial organization and management, risk management, and corporation finance.

He is a member of Beta Gamma Sigma, the Institute of Management Sciences, the American Economic Association, the Society of Chartered Property and Casualty Underwriters, and the Society for the Psychological Study of Social Issues. He is past president of the Middle Atlantic Association of Colleges of Business Administration, a member of the executive committee and President of the American Association of University Administrators, a member of the Board of Directors of the Epilepsy Society of Pittsburgh, the Pittsburgh District Export Council, and the Student Consultant Project of the University of Pittsburgh, as well as many industrial concerns. He has written many articles and books on such subjects as individual and group decision making under risk, the social responsibility of business, continuing education for managers, and corporate risk analysis.

NAME INDEX

SUBJECT INDEX

Management for the future